The Rich World and the Impoverishment of Education

Diminishing Democracy, Equity and Workers' Rights

Edited by Dave Hill

Routledge
Taylor & Francis Group
New York   London

First published 2009
by Routledge
270 Madison Ave, New York, NY 10016

Simultaneously published in the UK
by Routledge
2 Park Square, Milton Park, Abingdon, Oxon OX14 4RN

Routledge is an imprint of the Taylor & Francis Group, an informa business

Typeset in Sabon by IBT Global.
Printed and bound in the United States of America on acid-free paper by IBT Global.

Library of Congress Cataloging in Publication Data
The rich world and the impoverishment of education : diminishing democracy, equity and workers' rights / edited by Dave Hill.
    p. cm. — (Routledge studies in education and neoliberalism ; 1)
Includes index.
"Simultaneously published in the UK."
ISBN 978-0-415-95775-5
    1. Education—Economic aspects—Developed countries—Case studes. 2. Neo-liberalism. 3. Education and state. 4. Democracy. I. Hill, Dave, 1945–
    LC65.R53 2008
    379.172'2 — dc22
    2008003879

ISBN10: 0-415-95775-3 (hbk)
ISBN10: 0-203-89466-9 (ebk)

ISBN13: 978-0-415-95775-5 (hbk)
ISBN13: 978-0-203-89466-8 (ebk)

Contents

Tables and Figures

TABLES

FIGURES

Foreword

The World Is Not Flat: Challenging Neoliberal Policies

David Hursh

> What Nandan is saying, I thought, is that the playing field is being flattened ... Flattened? Flattened? My God, he's telling me the world is flat!
>
> Thomas Friedman, *The World is Flat: A Brief History of the Twenty-first Century* (2005)

> The driving force behind globalization is free market capitalism—the more you let market forces rule and the more you open your economy to free trade and competition, the more efficient your economy will be. Globalization means the spread of free-market capitalism to virtually every country in the world. Therefore globalization also has its own set of economic rules—rules that revolve around opening, deregulating and privatizing your economy, in order to make it more competitive and attractive to foreign investment.
>
> Thomas Friedman, *The Lexus and the Olive Tree* (1999)

According to best selling author, Thomas Friedman, globalization, free markets, and privatization, or, more precisely neoliberal policies, are inherently beneficial and inevitable. The contributors to this volume challenge that assumption and point out how neoliberalism undermines equality, democracy, and education. What they have to say could not be more urgent or timely: How we respond to the rise and dominance of neoliberalism is *the* central question to our time. As Naomi Klein documents in *The Shock Doctrine: The Rise of Disaster Capitalism* (2007), neoliberal policies have contributed to the rise of authoritarianism, exploitation, inequality, and the destruction of the environment, and, if not reversed, will result in a distinctly unflat world of utopian "dreamlands" in which "the rich and near rich" retreat "into sumptuary compounds, leisure cities, and gated replicas of imaginary California suburbs" while "a demonized criminal underclass . . . everywhere stands outside the gate" (Davis & Monk, 2007, pp. xiii–xiv) in burgeoning urban slums (Davis, 2007). This volume focuses on the destructive consequences of neoliberalism in society and education, and what we can and must do to resist neoliberalism.

Neoliberals aim to "to repeal the twentieth century" (Frank, 2004, p. 8) by reversing the social democratic economic reforms instituted from the beginning of the century to the 1970s, including regulations on businesses and banks, the introduction of labor rights, social security and other social-welfare funding, and expanded access to education. Instead, neoliberals propose "that human well-being can best be advanced by liberating individual entrepreneurial freedoms and skills within an institutional framework characterized by strong private property rights, free markets and free trade" (Harvey, 2005, p. 2).

While neoliberals often claim that expanding free markets and free trade requires shrinking government, in reality they desire that governments reduce their corporate oversight while intervening, as necessary, to impose neoliberal policies and practices on society. For example, Robert Kuttner, in *The Squandering of America: How Our Politics Undermines Our Prosperity* (2007), describes how in the United States neoliberals pushed for deregulating the financial industry, including allowing bundling and re-selling of often high-risk mortgage debt as investment vehicles, which resulted in the current crisis in the housing industry and a likely economic recession. Kuttner argues that the government's blind embrace of laissez-faire principles and its corporate bail-out policies have made it the agent of financial elite.

While decreasing corporate regulation, neoliberalism requires that "the state create and preserve an institutional framework appropriate to such practices," (Harvey, 2005, p. 2) including international organizations, such as the World Bank and International Monetary Fund, that pressure national governments to eliminate trade barriers and reduce social spending. In the United States, state and federal governments have intervened to create testing and accountability requirements, including regulations privatizing public schools that serve the interests of private corporations. Neoliberals demand that governments reduce corporate regulations while intensifying their intervention into people's lives. Under neoliberalism, governments exist to promote corporate profit rather than public welfare.

Neoliberalism, therefore, radically transforms government and society by emphasizing competitiveness, decentralization, devolution, and attrition of political governance, deregulation and privatization of industry, land and public services [including schools]; and replacing welfare with "workfarist" social policies. (Leitner, Sheppard, Sziarto, & Maringanti, 2007, p. 1) Moreover, the nature of the individual is transformed as neoliberal subjectivity normalizes the logic of individualism and entrepreneurialism, equating individual freedom with self-interested choices, making individuals responsible for their own well-being, and redefining citizens as consumers and clients. (pp. 1–2)

Moreover, Thomas Friedman, like other neoliberals, asserts that globalization makes neoliberalism inevitable and, therefore, we have no choice but to adopt neoliberal polices. Such arguments, writes Norman Fairclough

(2006), hijack globalization "in the service of particular national and corporate interests (p. 8). In education, neoliberals argue that globalization requires creating education markets, competition, standardized testing, and accountability. President George W. Bush, for example, uses globalist discourses to promote education policies focusing on standardized testing, choice, and accountability:

> NCLB is an important way to make sure America remains competitive in the 21st century. We're living in a global world. See, the education system must compete with education systems in China and India. If we fail to give our students the skills necessary to compete in the world in the 21st century, the jobs will go elsewhere. (U.S. Department of Education, 2006, p. 2)

Other U.S. politicians and journalists endlessly echo the exaggerated fear (Bracey, 2007) of China and India to justify even more standardized testing, market competition, and privatization in the education. These warnings, which evoke parallels to the exaggerated fear used to stoke "the war on terror," come from both Republicans and Democrats alike. Hillary Clinton (2007), campaigning in Iowa for president, exclaimed: "We're not increasing the number of young people going into math and science. We're not turning out more engineers and researchers to compete with China and India."

However, neoliberalism has not resulted in increased national or individual wealth, nor better educational systems. Rather, neoliberalism, which is neither inevitable nor neutral, is "the restoration . . . of naked class power" through "a benevolent mask full of wonderful-sounding words like freedom, liberty, choice, and rights" (p. 119). Instead, as has been amply demonstrated, neoliberalism benefits the wealthy and impoverishes the rest (Davis, 2007; Faux, 2006; Harvey, 2005; Jomo & Baudot, 2007; Klein, 2007; Stiglitz, 2002). The income gap has grown within and between countries.

Moreover, not only has neoliberalism not achieved the promised economic gains, but prioritizing profits over non-monetary aspects of our lives has been disastrous for the environment, especially after the election of George W. Bush, who refused to endorse reductions in carbon emissions on the grounds that it might hinder economic growth (Bello, 2005, p. 183). In opting out of the Kyoto protocols, Bush claimed: "I will explain as clear as I can, today and every other chance I get, that we will not do anything that harms our economy. . . . That's my priority. I'm worried about the economy" (Bush, cited in McKibben, 2006, p. 18). Such policies have exacerbated global warming to such an extent that implementing carbon emission reductions now may be too late to halt continued melting of ice sheets in Greenland and Antarctica with the related rise in sea levels (Hansen, 2006).

The negative consequences of China's wholesale adoption of capitalist, neoliberal policies have become increasingly evident. Harvey (2005, p. 174) describes how neoliberal policies contributed to the degradation of China's environment. China now has sixteen of the twenty worst cities in the world with respect to air pollution (Bradsher, 2003) and has surpassed the United States as the top emitter of carbon dioxide (New York Times, 2007). Recent reports (Barboza, 2007) indicate that China's air and water pollution causes 750,000 premature deaths annually and costs $160 billion a year in damages. Furthermore, the drive for capitalist expansion at all costs has contributed to numerous ecological disasters (Yardley, 2004), including benzene and nitrozine spills in the Singhua River (Lague, 2005), which contaminated drinking water for millions of people, and exporting dangerous products, including toys with lead paint, defective auto tires, and poisoned toothpaste.

Moreover, in China "the gap between the rich and the poor, urban and rural is constantly widening" and "has now become one of the world's most unequal societies" (Broudehoux, 2007, p. 94). Under neoliberalism, people have lost health care, pensions, jobs, and homes previously provided by the government. Anne-Marie Broudehoux (2007) describes Beijing as a

> new metropolis [that] mirrors the society that builds and inhabits it: an increasingly individualist society that willfully sacrifices a more cohesive one, where a predatory elite of private entrepreneurs, technocrats, and party members prey on a disenfranchised and vulnerable populace. A city glittering on the surface but hollow at the core: a truly evil paradise. (p. 101)

We face, then, the descent into a neoliberal dystopian future, with the rich living in gated communities encircled by the poor who are unable to afford or access clean water, jobs, or health care, living in an environment that grows increasingly toxic and warmer. How to combat neoliberalism and create a world that focuses on developing educated and equitable communities in a sustainable world is the question we must address. It is a question this timely book, and the others in this series, powerfully addresses.

REFERENCES

Barboza, D. (2007, July 5). China reportedly urged omitting pollution-death estimates. *New York Times*, p. C1.

Bello. W. (2005). *Dilemmas of domination: The unmaking of the American empire*. New York: Metropolitan Books.

Bradsher, K. (2003, October 22). China's boom adds to global warming. *New York Times*, pp. A1, A8.

Broudehoux, A-M. (2007). Delirious Beijing: Euphoria and despair in the Olympic metropolis. In M. Davis & D. B. Monk (Eds.), *Evil paradises: Dreamworlds of neoliberalism* (pp. 87–101). New York: The New Press.

Bracey, G. (2007). *The rotten apple awards in education for 2006*. Retrieved from http://www.ameria-tomorrow.com/bracey/EDDRA/

Davis, M. (2006). *Planet of slums.* New York: Verso.

Davis, M., & Monk, D. B. (Eds.). (2007). Introduction. In M. Davis & D. B. Monk (Eds.), *Evil paradises: Dreamworlds of neoliberalism* (pp. ix–xvi). New York: The New Press.

Fairclough, N. (2006). *Language and globalization.* New York: Routledge.

Faux, J. (2006). *The global class war: How America's bipartisan elite lost our future—and what it will take to win it back.* New York: Wiley.

Frank, T. (2004). *What's the matter with Kansas? How conservatives won the hearth of America.* New York: A Metropolitan Book.

Friedman, T. (1999). *The Lexus and the olive tree.* New York: Farrar, Straus & Giroux.

Friedman, T. (2005). *The world is flat: A brief history of the twenty-first century.* New York: Farrar, Straus and Giroux.

Hansen, J. (2006, January 12). The tipping point (from a presentation to the American Geophysical Association, December 6, 2005). *New York Review of Books,* 53(1), 19.

Harvey, D. (2005). *A brief history of neoliberalism.* Oxford, United Kingdom: Oxford University.

Jomo. K. S., & Baudot, J. (2007). Preface. In K. S. Jomo & J. Baudot (Eds.), *Flat world, big gaps: Economic liberalization, globalization, poverty, and inequality* (pp. xvii–xxvii). New York: Zed Books.

Klein N. (2007). *The shock doctrine: The rise of disaster capitalism.* New York: Henry Holt and Company.

Kuttner, R. (2007). *The squandering of America: How our politics undermines our prosperity.* New York: Knopf.

Lague, D. (2005, November 24). Water crisis shows China's pollution risk. *The New York Times,* p. A4.

Leitner, H., Sheppard, E. S., Sziarto, K., & Maringanti, A. (2007). Contesting urban futures: Decentering neoliberalism. In H. Leitner, E. S. Sheppard, & J. Peck (Eds.), *Contesting neoliberalism: Urban frontiers* (pp. 1–25). New York: Guilford Press.

McKibben, B. (2006, January 12). The coming meltdown. *New York Review of Books* 53(1), 16–18.

Stiglitz, J. (2002). *Globalization and its discontents.* New York: W. W. Norton.

U.S. Department of Education (2006b, April 27). *Remarks by Secretary Spellings at No Child Left Behind Summit.* Retrieved from http://www.ed.gov.new.

Yardley, J. (2004, September 12). Rivers run black, and Chinese die of cancer. *New York Times,* pp. A1, A17.

Young, A. (2007, January 27). Transcript Hillary Clinton–Alan Young Conversation From Sen. Hillary Clinton's "Conversations With Iowans" Presidential Campaign Event. East High School, Des Moines, Iowa. Retrieved April 20, 2008, from http://64.253.100.148/Documents/RandD/Other/Hillary%20Clinton-Alan%20Young%20Transcript.doc

Acknowledgments

With thanks to my daughter Naomi Hill for her proofing and help and smiles and sunniness in Brighton, England, and to Eleanor Chan of IBT Global in Troy, New York for her proofing and efficiency and greatness to work with, and to Benjamin Holtzman at Routledge in New York for his support and encouragement and patience.

Thanks also to the radical academics, labour movement activists, and leftists and all those exposing and challenging the dominant neoliberal capitalist hegemony, and pointing the way to resistance to national and global economic, social and political injustices and oppression. Not all the writers by any means share my own democratic socialist/Marxist beliefs and activism—writers in this book come from a variety of left and radical political and ideological traditions and perspectives. But we, in this book, unite in our criticisms of neoliberal Capital, and in our belief at its replacement.

1 Introduction: Neoliberal Politics and Education in the Rich World

Inequality, Undemocracy, and the Resistant Possibilities and Roles of Critical Educators

Dave Hill

In this Introductory chapter, I look at what resistance teachers and education workers can and do make in the face of neoliberalizing (and sometimes nationalistic and neoconservative) capital and governments. Here, I argue that teachers and other education and cultural workers should act as critical, organic, public, transformative, egalitarian, socialist intellectuals. And that these workers should be active in resisting the depredations of neoliberal education in three arenas. These are the arenas of the classroom and school, more widely in local actions and communities—and more widely still—in the national and global struggle for dignity, equality, and a transformation to equality and to democratic Socialism.

This chapter is argued from a democratic socialist, or Marxist, perspective. Of course, the criticisms of the operations and effects of neoliberal capitalism in society and in education are shared generally by social democrats, "reformist socialists" and by various types of liberals. But the policy proposals and concern that teachers should act deliberately as critical pedagogues—and beyond that—as Marxist or Socialist or Revolutionary (in the sense of wanting major system change) Critical Pedagogues.

I then introduce each of the chapters in the book. This book examines neoliberal capitalist globalization in eleven different countries in the Rich World—from Europe, North America, West and East Asia, and Australasia. The countries are the United States, Canada, Australia, England and Wales, Finland, Greece, Taiwan, Israel, Singapore, and Japan. These present different models of neoliberal capitalist globalization and of education "reform" developments. There are differences, but there are important global similarities in education policy developments, and in the impacts of neoliberalism on education. These developments impoverish education and diminish democracy, equity, and education-workers' rights.

This book critically identifies and evaluates neoliberal policy and impacts on schooling and education in the Rich World—and it promotes resistance! Writers (Left academics and labor organizations and social-movement activists) interrogate developments.

Writers ask: "What neoliberal changes have taken place (e.g., privatization, vouchers, marketization, commercialization, school fees, new brutal-
ist public managerialism, and the assault on the comprehensive, common
school principles and on democratic control of schools)?" and they identify neoliberal "Drivers" or Levers—national/transnational corporations,
think tanks, pressure groups, state power, and ideologies/discourses.

The impacts of neoliberalism on equality, equal opportunities and access
to quality schooling and high quality education (social class, race ethnic/
linguistic groups, gender, rural/urban differentiation); democracy, democratic control, critical thinking, and the rights/pay and working conditions
of education workers are examined. Also examined, importantly, is what
local and national resistance is there, its bases, organizational forms, strategies, successes and failures, and prospects.

THE RESISTANT ROLE OF CRITICAL CULTURAL WORKERS

The Brazilian educator and political activist, Paulo Freire, argued that
although there are exceptional academics and a handful of organizations dedicated to conducting research that serves egalitarian ends, not
enough academics are working as critical "cultural workers" who orient
themselves toward concrete struggles in the public and political domains
in order to extend the equality, liberty, and justice they defend (Freire,
1998). He maintained that "[t]he movements outside are where more
people who dream of social change are gathering," but points out that
there exists a degree of reserve on the part of academics in particular, to
penetrate the media, participate in policy debates, or to permeate policy-
making bodies (Shor & Freire, 1987, p. 131).

Freire argued that if scholars, researchers, or educators want to transform education to serve democratic ends, they cannot simply limit their
struggles to institutional spaces. They must also develop a desire to increase
their political activity outside of the schools. To engage as critical cultural
workers would require academics to politicize their research by becoming
social actors who mobilize, develop political clarity, establish strategic alliances, and work closer to the nexus of power, or the "real levers of transformation" (Shor & Freire, 1987, p. 131).

Critical transformative intellectuals seek to enable student teachers and
teachers (and school students) to critically evaluate a range of salient perspectives and ideologies—including critical reflection itself—while showing
a commitment to egalitarianism. For McLaren, "critical pedagogy must...
remain critical of its own presumed role as the metatruth of educational
criticism" (2000, p. 184). This does not imply forced acceptance or silenc-
ing of contrary perspectives. But it *does* involve a privileging of egalitarian
and emancipatory perspectives.

It is necessary to be quite clear here. This *does* mean adhering to what Burbules and Berk (1999, p. 54) have defined as "critical pedagogy," as opposed

to "critical theory." The difference is this: The claim of *critical thinking* is the importance of thinking critically. Full stop! For many critical thinkers, critical thinking is not necessarily about thinking politically. In contrast, for critical pedagogy, and for revolutionary critical pedagogy in particular, this is a false distinction. That is, for critical pedagogues and revolutionary political pedagogues, disinterested critique/deconstruction, or indeed committed ethical moral critique and critical theory, need to be enacted politically. As Giroux and McLaren (1986) articulate, a transformative intellectual is someone "who is capable of articulating emancipatory possibilities and *working towards their realization*" (emphasis added). In more detail, Giroux and McLaren give their definition of a "transformative intellectual" as:

> one who exercises forms of intellectual and pedagogical practice which attempt to insert teaching and learning directly into the political sphere by arguing that schooling represents both a struggle for meaning and a struggle over power relations. We are also referring to one whose intellectual preferences are necessarily grounded in forms of moral and ethical discourse exhibiting a preferential concern for the suffering and the struggles of the disadvantaged and oppressed. Here we extend the traditional use of the intellectual as someone who is able to analyse various interests and contradictions within society to someone capable of articulating emancipatory possibilities and working towards their realization. Teachers who assume the role of transformative intellectuals treat students as critical agents, question how knowledge is produced and distributed, utilise dialogue, and make knowledge meaningful, critical, and ultimately emancipatory. (p. 215)

Giroux (1988) emphasized the interrelationship between the political and the pedagogical as follows:

> Central to the category of transformative intellectual is the necessity of making the pedagogical more political and the political more pedagogical . . . Within this perspective, critical reflection and action become part of a fundamental social project to help students develop a deep and abiding faith in the struggle to overcome economic, political and social injustices, and to further humanise themselves as part of this struggle. (pp. 127–128)

McLaren, in his work over the last decade, sometimes by himself, and sometimes with collaborators such as Ramin Farahmandpur, Nathalia Jaramillo, Noah de Lissavoy and Gregory Martin (former doctoral students of his) and with 'The British Marxists' such has Glenn Rikowski, Mike Cole and Dave Hill, (2000) has extended the "critical education" project into "revolutionary pedagogy," which is clearly based on a Marxist metanarrative. There have, of course, been hundreds of thousands of critical, socialist, communist,

Marxist, revolutionary egalitarian teachers and educators worldwide, most of them not calling their work critical pedagogy or revolutionary critical pedagogy at all. These are neologisms and are predominantly Northern and Latin American terms. Revolutionary pedagogy, which in other historical and geographical contexts might be termed socialist education,

> would place the liberation from race, class and gender oppression as the key goal for education for the new millennium. Education . . . so conceived would be dedicated to creating a citizenry dedicated to social justice and to the reinvention of social life based on democratic social-ist ideals. (p. 196; see also Hill and Boxley, 2007; McLaren, 2005; McLaren & Farahmandpur, 2005; McLaren and Jaramillo, 2007; Rikowski, 2007; Rikowski & McLaren, 2001, 2002, 2006).

Arenas of Resistance

What is to be done? In brief, there are at least *three arenas* of activity for critical transformative socialist intellectuals and egalitarian oppositional educators.

The first arena, as Peter McLaren analyzed powerfully (Aguirre, 2001; Hill 2007; McLaren, 2000; 2003b), is education, and, indeed, within other sites of cultural reproduction. Paula Allman (2001) put it this way:

> education has the potential to fuel the flames of resistance to global capitalism as well as the passion for socialist transformation—indeed, the potential to provide a spark that can ignite the desire for revolu-tionary democratic social transformation throughout the world.

However, the question of how far this transformative potential can be real-ized is the subject of considerable debate, for contemporary theory as well as practice. The autonomy and agency available to individual teachers, teacher educators, schools, and other educational institutions, is particularly chal-lenged when faced with the structures of capital and its current neoliberal project for education (as argued in Hill, 2001, 2005). It is necessary to high-light the phrase "potential to fuel the flames of resistance," in Allman's quote just discussed. Considerable caution is necessary when considering the degree of autonomy of educators (and, indeed, other cultural workers, such as jour-nalists and filmmakers) who attempt to fuel the flames of resistance.

I do not underestimate the limitations on the agency and autonomy of teachers, teacher educators, cultural workers, and their sites, and indeed (to use concepts derived from Louis Althusser, 1971), the very limited autonomy of the education policy/political region of the state from the economic region of the state. There are, in many states, increasing restrictions on the ability of teachers to use their pedagogical spaces for emancipatory purposes. The repressive cards within the ideological state apparatuses are stacked against the possibilities of transformative change through initial teacher education and through schooling. Within schools and universities in the United States, England, and other states, there have been the following changes:

- Increasing *concentration* both of and on pro-capitalist formal curricula (in England and Wales this includes rigorously monitored and assessed formal national curricula in schooling and in "teacher training"; in the United States, it includes what is, in effect, the national curricula of "high stakes testing" and the tyranny of the approved textbook; in India, a farcical rhetoric of joyful learning dominates in the aftermath of World Bank and neoliberal assault while the elements of criticality and dissent are being gradually done away with.
- Increased *marginalization* of resistant, anti-(capitalist) hegemonic alternative/oppositional curricula, texts, programs.
- Increasing *concentration* both of and on pro-capitalist hidden/informal curricula and pedagogy.
- Increased *marginalization* of resistant, anti-(capitalist) hegemonic alternative/oppositional education and educators—the compression and suppression of critical space.

Currently, and since the Thatcher-Reagan neoliberal/neoconservative assaults on the welfare state and on public/collective provision of services, the capitalist class has been ratcheting up the use of ideological state apparatuses in the media and education systems in particular to both "naturalize" and promote capitalist social, and economic relations on the one hand and to marginalize and demonize resistant/anti-(capitalist) hegemonic oppositional ideologies, actions, and activists. In the current period of capitalism, there is increasing and naked use of repressive economic, legal, military force globally to assert capital, ensure compliance and subordination to multinational capital, and its state agents. This includes repressive state apparatuses such as the police, prison, and legal systems, as well as surveillance procedures (Cole, Hill, McLaren, & Rikowski, 2001; Hill, 2004, 2005).

And for those who do protest, who do stick their heads above the parapet, sometimes get them blown off—in dramatic or in undramatic but effective ways. In the period prior to and since the US-led invasion of Iraq, oppositional school students, college students, and faculty, have suffered something of a witch-hunt in the United States (Fassbinder, 2006; Nocella, 2007). McLaren et al., detail what they term *witch-hunting* by teachers against students who participated in anti-war protests such as organizing teach-ins in both K through 12 (Kindergarten to Grade 12 schooling) and higher education, witch-hunts against students who express opinions critical of US policy. They give examples of disciplinary actions taken by school managements and by the police.

At a less dramatic, but more pervasive level, Gabbard describes the drip-drip, repression and sidelining of "those who have challenged the viability of the market as a mode of social organization." They receive no (positive) attention. "Neither does the school afford the vast majority of children the opportunity to study the lives of people like themselves, much less the opportunity to study their *own* lives" (Gabbard, 2003, p. 71).

Counter-Hegemonic Struggle

There is, however, space for counter-*hegemonic* struggle—sometimes narrower, sometimes broader (as in Western Europe and North America in the 1960s and 1970s). Having recognized the limitations, though, and having recognized that there is *some* potential for egalitarian transformative change, whatever space does exist should be exploited. Whatever we can do, we must do, however fertile or unfertile the soil at any given moment in any particular place. But schools, colleges, and newsrooms are not the only arenas of resistance.

The success of critical educators and cultural workers will be limited if their work is divorced from other arenas of progressive struggle. Successful resistance to neoliberalism necessitates the development of pro-active debate both by, and within, the Radical Left. But debate alone is not sufficient. Successful resistance demands direct engagement with ideologies and programs of both liberal pluralists (modernist or postmodernist) and with the Radical Right in all the areas of the state and of civil society, in and through all the ideological and repressive state apparatuses.

The ideological intervention of teachers and other educators, and cultural workers, is likely to have a different impact than that of sections of the workforce less saliently engaged in ideological production and reproduction. But, by itself, activity of transformative intellectual cultural/ideological workers, however skilful and committed, can have only a limited impact on an egalitarian transformation of capitalist society.

Working outside of the classroom on issues relating to education and its role in reproducing inequality and oppression is the second arena of resistance. Unless critical educators' actions within classrooms are linked to a grammar of resistance, their/our resistant and counter-hegemonic activity is likely to fall on relatively stony ground. Hence, using educational sites as arenas of cultural struggle, and education as a vehicle for social transformation is premised upon a clear commitment to work with communities, parents, and students, and with the trade unions and workers within those institutions.

When we say working "with," we do not mean simply "leading" or "talking at." Working with means "learning from" as well, learning from the daily, material existence of the exploited classes. Ideally, it means fulfilling the role of the organic intellectual, organically linked to, and part of, those groups. This means working with communities—and their own hope, despair, and anger. It means developing the perception that schools, education, and the media are sites of social, economic, and ideological contestation. These sites, or apparatuses are not "neutral" or "fair" or "inevitable," but are sites of economic, cultural, and ideological domination, of class domination. It is important to develop awareness of the role of education in the reproduction of capitalism and in the reproduction of class relations. Finally, working as an organic critical transformative intellectual, as a socialist activist, means illuminating and developing an understanding of whatever counter-hegemonic and resistant potential education-schools, colleges, universities has.

While we do not share Rikowski's view that educators are "*the* most dangerous of workers," they/we can certainly be dangerous to capital and have effect in the struggle for economic and social justice.

Globally and nationally, societies are developing, to a greater or lesser degree, critical educators, community activists, organic intellectuals, students, and teachers, whose feelings of outrage at economic and social class and racial and gender oppression fuel activism. Thus, the *third arena* for resistance is action across a broader spectrum, linking issues and experience within different economic and social sectors, linking different struggles.

Educators participating in mass (or mini) actions as part of a broader movement for economic and social justice is a key arena of resistance that must not be overlooked or underestimated. Ideological intervention in classrooms and in other cultural sites can have dramatic effect, not least on some individuals and groups who are "hailed" by resistant ideology. However, actualizing that ideology—that opposition to an oppressive law, state, or capitalist action, feeling the solidarity, feeling the blood stir, feeling the pride in action and joint learning that comes from that experience—can develop individual as well as collective confidence, understanding, commitment.

For example, the two-million-strong protest over the deregulation of labor laws by workers in Italy in March 2002 and the follow up strikes in October 2005—as well as similar actions in Spain, South Korea, France and the United Kingdom, over proposed labor deregulation and over low pay and pensions "reform" (making people work longer to get their pension—in Britain this resulted in the largest-scale official strike action since the 1926 general strike)—were massive learning experiences for the participants.

The mass protests against the WTO at Seattle, Genoa, London, and Barcelona, together with the various mass events associated with the ESF (European Social Movement) such as the 400,000 strong march in London against War on Iraq on November 8, 2002) and WSF (World Social Forum) in Porto Alegre (see Sader, 2002) and subsequent World Social Forums, serve as a key context for linking the work of critical educators to broader movements for economic and social justice. We, however, need to be cautious and critically analyze the direction of such movements because the danger of institutionalizing the social forums have also been expressed by many quarters—they are quite justified in the sense they have not been able to give lead movements against neoliberal capital but rather, have been reduced to periodic festivals and ultimately become instruments of co-opting resistances, especially seen in World Social Forum and Indian Social Forums in India (see R.U.P.E., 2003). In election after election in Latin America, peoples are voting out neoliberal Parties—in Brazil, Ecuador, Venezuela, Bolivia,

Chile, Peru, Nicaragua—and the economic melt-down of a former beacon of neoliberalism, Argentina, is helping create an anti-neoliberal bloc of governments (see Hearse, 2006; Saunois, 2002) albeit split between center-left governments in Chile, Brazil, Uruguay, Argentina, and more revolutionary, socialist governments in Venezuela and Bolivia (Katz, 2006). In the United Kingdom, the growing militancy of trade unions—not only over low pay but also against privatization and attacks on pension rights—has led to the re-emergence of the Socialist Campaign Group, the election of a new left-wing breed of trade union leaders in Britain, and levels of strike action in Britain unprecedented since 1979 (Bambery & Morgan, 2002). The militant struggle by the Radical Left in some Indian provinces, the resistances to Special Economic Zones (SEZs), or organized resistances to global corporations such as Honda, are some of the indicators of discontent and the popular will to resist. The need today is to treat these as sites of struggle by critical educators as well.

These events have been and continue to be a learning experience for those who thought such mass actions—whether internationally or nationally—were a product of a bygone age (Pilger, 2002). The pages of socialist newspapers (such as, in England and Wales, *The Socialist*, *Socialist Worker* and *The Morning Star*) regularly chronicle strike waves and growing industrial and workers' militancy around the globe.

Critical Action

Although critical political dispositions and analyses, such as those espoused by Marx and Freire, can provide political direction in the struggle for social change, they have been challenged on a number of points. Of course, conservatives permanently challenge such ideas, but they are also challenged from positions that *also* claim a radical mantle. For example, among feminist critiques, critical theory and some of the endeavors it supports have been accused (famously, for example, by Ellsworth, 1992) of "repressive myths." In this critique, a notion such as *empowerment*, for instance, can be imbued with paternalism and perpetuate relations of domination whether it be in the classroom, in academic discourse, or in everyday life.

This type of criticism is frequently made. Thus in their *Reflective Teaching: an Introduction*, Zeichner and Liston (1996) determinedly avoid taking a position on critical reflection (see Hill, 1997; 2008b; Zeichner & Liston, 1987), offering it as one of a range of types of reflection only. In their book there is absolutely no indication that critical reflection should be privileged or pursued. They claim that teacher education "needs to be fair and honest" and that "we have not written these texts to convince you to see schools and society as we do but rather to engage you in a consideration of crucial issues" (1996, p. x). They continued:

> When students and faculty engage in discussions of the social and political conditions of schooling and the effects of these conditions on

students and schools, it is likely that the talk will be lively and that controversies will emerge. In this area there are no absolutely "right" or "wrong" answers. (p. xi)

Certainly, none are given in their book. It is for that reason that in many respects, this tradition could be termed liberal-pluralist, albeit potentially of a progressive, egalitarian variety. It certainly debars them (and others) from advancing programs for transformation!

Aronowitz and Giroux (1991) associate some radical educators with critical pedagogy that

> at its worst . . . comes perilously close to emulating the liberal democratic tradition in which teaching is reduced to getting students merely to express or access their own experiences. Teaching collapses in this case into a banal, unproblematic notion of facilitation, self-affirmation and self-consciousness. (p. 117)

It is not enough for teachers merely to affirm uncritically their students' histories, experiences, and stories—this is to run the risk of idealizing and romanticizing them (Aronowitz & Giroux, 1991).

> Education workers must take seriously the articulation of a morality that posits a language of public life, of emancipatory community, and individual and social commitment . . . A discourse on morality is important . . . it points to the need to educate students to fight and struggle in order to advance the discourse and principles of a critical democracy. (p. 108)

In this enterprise,

> educators need to take up the task of redefining educational leadership through forms of social criticism, civic courage, and public engagement that allow them to expand oppositional space—both within and outside of school—which increasingly challenges the ideological representation and relations of power that undermine democratic public life. (Aronowitz & Giroux, 1991, p. 89)

Zeichner and Liston's "neutrality" stance within the classroom abdicates the responsibility and potential they otherwise display in various of their analyses as committed radicals. But their neutrality is, of course, a political position. The commitment we are defending here is clearly at odds with their *apparent* disinterest (as noted earlier).

In the teaching that I engage in, to undergraduates and to postgraduate students I make it quite clear that the lecturer is a Marxist with a class perspective. So, clearly, do many educators—but not enough.

When, occasionally (around once per year) a student suggests/asks me if I am brainwashing them, I ask the student group just how many Marxist teachers they have ever been taught by, just how many Marxist publications—newspapers, books, magazines—they have read, and, on the other hand, just how many teachers, books, and newspapers that they have come across that do *not* present Marxist/socialist analysis and arguments.

Numerous books, such as such as David Hursh and E. Wayne Ross's *Democratic Social Education: Social Studies for Social Change* (2000) and Peter McLaren's *Life in Schools* (now in its fifth edition, 2006) promote teachers and university educators to use Marxist analyses, and to call on teachers at all levels to themselves call upon their/our students to study, consider, and, if in agreement, adopt, and act upon those analyses. Thus, to take one example, Hursh and Ross (2000) attempt to guide social studies educators as to what they can do to help build a democratic society in the face of current antidemocratic impulses of greed, individualism, and intolerance. And in the writings of the Hillcole Group in England, aimed at school and university teachers, there are explicit delineations of a socialist education policy (Hillcole Group, 1991) and an explicit development of socialist principles for education (Hillcole Group, 1997).

The efforts to empower people in certain contexts can simultaneously strengthen the privileged position of those dispensing it. In the same sense, a Freirean approach to permeating policy-making contexts *may* involve a form of imposition by cultural workers, whereby representation, organization, and collective struggle may not necessarily build understanding or political efficacy among groups of people, but merely essentialize or exoticize the other.

Finally, the work of the Intellectual Left, and those who advance what in the USA are commonly called 'more radical forms of democracy,' is often criticized for being driven by a "politics of hope" that has lost its appeal. The desire for researchers and academics to become cultural workers and the struggle toward political mobilization of the Freirean nature is often nothing more than an unrealized ideal for those whose progressive ideas are continuously stifled in a political milieu overwhelmingly ruled by an egocentricity of elite culture and by an ideology of efficiency and control.

However, the concepts of critical cultural worker, of critical transformative intellectual, and of revolutionary pedagogy, extend the possibilities for dealing with policy conflicts (primarily but not irreducibly, class conflict) and are essential to building a generation of citizens who struggle to mitigate and *to transform* a society rife with economic and social injustice and oppression. Mike Cole, Glenn Rikowski, Peter McLaren, Dave Hill, Rich Gibson, Wayne Ross, Mas'ud Masazadarveh along with Marxist feminist writers such as Helen Colley, Teresa Ebert, Rachel Gorman, Jane Kelly, and Shahrzad Mojab, have challenged the claims of postmodernist and postmodernist feminist writers, such as Patti Lather in the United States and Elizabeth Atkinson in the United Kingdom, that postmodernism and poststructuralism can, overall, be forces for macro-social change and social justice. We argue that Marxism—

not postmodernism, fundamentalist religion, liberalism or neoliberalism, conservatism—or indeed, social democracy—remains the most viable option in the pursuit of economic justice and social change (Hill, McLaren, Cole, & Rikowski, 1999, 2002; Cole, 2007).

By engaging in critical transformative practice, we can work in solidarity with others as well as individually to mitigate and replace unjust policies and educational inequalities, and in doing so, build a fuller and richer democracy.

In keeping aloft ideals of plurality of thought, of economic and social justice, and of dissent, teachers, teacher educators, and the community must resist the ideological hijacking of our past, present, and future. Teachers and teacher educators are too strategically valuable in students' education to have slick media panaceas and slanted ministerial programs attempting to dragoon them into being uncritical functionaries of a conservative state and of the fundamentally and essentially anti-egalitarian and immoral society and education system reproduced by the capitalist state and its apparatuses.

Such radical cultural workers advocate education as an aspect of anti-capitalist social transformation where social justice and respect for difference is not enough—we can respect the beggar in the street as a human being. That does rather less for her or his future and the future of humanity in general than an economic system *not* based on the exploitation of labor power by ever-burgeoning capitalist expropriation of surplus value and ever increasing global immiseration and the imperialism of global capital and its governmental and super-governmental agencies.[1]

Well organized and focused nonsectarian campaigns organized around class and anti-capitalist issues, which are also committed to economic and social equality and justice and environmental sustainability, can help shape an understanding that we are part of a massive force—the force of the international working class—with a shared understanding that, at the current time, it is the global neoliberal form of capitalism that shatters the lives, bodies, and dreams of billions. And that it can be replaced. As Harman (2002) suggests

> what matters now is for this (new) generation (of activists) to connect with the great mass of ordinary workers who as well as suffering under the system have the collective strength to fight it. (p. 40)

The Chapters in the Book

In Chapter 2, *The American Privatization Campaign: Vouchers, Charters, Educational Management Organizations, and the Money Behind Them*, Karen Anijar and David Gabbard argue that privatization represents both a strategy and a destination for neoliberal/neoconservative reforms in the American system of compulsory schooling. The first two sections of their chapter discuss two major elements of the push toward privatization: school vouchers and charter schools. As framed by their neoliberal advocates, the arguments for vouchers and charter schools seek to manufacture public consent for privatization by convincing citizens that the problems with public education stem from the bureaucratic leviathan created by "big government's" monopoly over schools. This bureaucracy forestalls necessary changes and improvements in America's schools that will enable U.S. workers to become more competitive for the high-skill and high-wage jobs in the global economy. The logical solution, then—following this logic—is to break the government's monopoly by allowing parents greater "choice" in educational options for their children. Ironically, perhaps, the same neoliberal reformers who seek to promote greater choice in schools also promote other strategies (high-stakes testing and accountability) that have an inverse homogenizing effect on schools. As high-stakes testing schools are forced to compete for government funding on the basis of student test scores, those tests almost inevitably come to define the curriculum. Choice becomes an issue that schools can do the same thing (produce high test scores) more effectively than the other.

Anijar and Gabbard argue that none of this intends to actually improve the quality of education in American schools. As discussed in the latter third of the chapter, the neoliberal and neoconservative reforms in education represent one part of much larger social and political agenda designed to effect greater corporate control over the state apparatus. That agenda has deep historic roots, and has evolved over time alongside and within a vast international and national network of think tanks, foundations, and institutes created specifically to achieve the political aims of neoliberalism and neoconservatism.

In Chapter 3, *Neoliberalism and Education in Canada*, Adam Davidson-Harden, Larry Kuehn, Daniel Shugurensky, and Harry Smaller consider the impact of neoliberal trends in education and social policy on education at the K through 12 and postsecondary levels. With a preference for such policy paradigms well entrenched by successive federal governments as well as pliant provincial regimes, particularly from the 1990s to the present, fiscal pressures resulting from declining social transfers to the provinces have created a chronic funding crisis that has facilitated different forms of privatization, commodification, and marketization of education "on the ground." Such trends are evident in shifts toward increased private and teacher fundraising to cover basic school costs in the K through 12 area, or in the intensified move to reliance on tuition for financing university operations at the postsecondary level. Finally, this brief survey is balanced by a particular appreciation of the politics of teachers' work at the K through 12 level in this context.

In Chapter 4, *The New Built Environment of Education: Neo-liberalism on Trial in Australia*, Gregory Martin traces the rise of neoliberalism and its effects on education policy and practice in Australia. At the end of a prolonged period of economic upswing, Martin argues that reorganizers of the state have employed neoliberal policies and processes such as deregulation, decentralization, and de-zoning, to overcome any territorial barriers or blockages (psychological, social, and physical) to the accumulation process. Against the backdrop of uneven development and present discontent over the performance of state-owned enterprises such as education, the scalar restructuring of the state creates the political and pedagogical conditions for competing needs and priorities to be "reconciled" within a grounded imaginary of devolved decision-making, which operates to hold the interests of capital in place. Here, neoliberal educational "reforms" have expanded spheres of normalized life along narrowly individualistic, rationally self-calculating and highly competitive lines and re-inscribed the boundaries between the "haves" and "have-nots." Although neoliberalism is heralded as an innovative and flexible alternative to the failure of the Keynesian welfare state, Martin's analysis is that neoliberalism represents a defensive gesture to repoliticize the administrative ideological state apparatus as the state engages in a form of "crisis management" in order to shift the balance of forces back toward capital. While the overall balance of forces remains generally unfavorable to the labor movement inside Australia, it has recently moved onto the political offensive, and opportunities are opening up for critical educational work focused on civic engagement.

In Chapter 5, *England and Wales: Neoliberalized Education and Its Impacts*, Christine Lewis, Dave Hill, and Barry Fawcett recognize that education, along with other public and formerly publicly owned services, is being liberalized in many countries. They realize that the extent, mechanisms, and effects vary. Their chapter tests a series of hypotheses. These are, that

- Liberalization of schooling and education services has occurred in many countries around the world.
- Particular national and international levers are promoting the liberalization process.
- Educational services are becoming "Americanized" through policies and processes, such as privatization, decentralization, deregulation, "new public management" (business management methods), commercialization, and marketization.
- Liberalization is making provision of services more unequal and selective rather than universal. This is intensifying race-, gender, and class-based hierarchies, reflected in formally or informally tiered systems of schooling. In less developed countries, services are available mainly to middle-class or wealthier families. In developed countries, the quality and type of schooling is increasingly stratified.
- Liberalization is eroding workers' securities.
- Liberalization attempts to embed a shift away from universal citizenship rights and identities based on the provision of services toward a system of individual consumer rights and identities. In education, this involves treating young people as "human capital" and preparing them for "jobs" rather than providing broad-based learning and critical awareness.

These aspects and effects of the liberalization of schooling and other education services are part of a wider rejection of some of the social functions of the state by governments, international organizations and business groups. Public services such as education, health, and prisons are being, or have been, transformed into "tradable commodities."

Lewis, Hill and Fawcett produce evidence that the liberalization of education increases inequalities within and between countries, reduces the quality of education, is detrimental to democracy, and decreases workers' pay, rights, and conditions.

In Chapter 6, *Changing the Tide of Education Policy in Finland: From Nordic to EU Educational Policy Model*, Joel Kivirauma, Risto Rinne, & Piia Seppänen examine the changing position of education as a definer, producer, and result of social exclusion by analyzing and comparing Finnish educational policy changes with more general European trends. The effects and consequences of these changes are not yet very clear, but at least in Finland there seem to be astonishingly strong trends of diversification of the whole, old honorable Nordic social-democratic comprehensive school.

The last forty years of Finnish state education discourse can be divided into two narratives. Although Finland has experienced a forty-year-period of comprehensive schooling—and there were similar "comprehensive" features proceeding the whole period—there was quite a clear turning point in the late 1980s. The first narrative represents praise for abolishing inequality of educational opportunity and introducing the comprehensive school in order to strengthen the Finnish welfare state. The second represents the later, twenty-year-narrative of passing the peak of achievement of the welfare state, the narrative of decentralization, deregulation, marketization, and the rise of evaluation and choice.

The research also opens an interesting view of the change in the Nordic educational policy model. References in the new educational policy narrative to concrete problems in the Finnish educational system were very rare and they were ideological by nature in the fashion of "too little freedom, too much bureaucracy." The issue is clearly about a change of Finnish educational policy, not about correcting the existing and concretely evident problems. Abstract talk about improving the quality of education is enough in this narrative to legitimate the transition toward the neoliberal global and EU educational policy model. While in the earlier narrative the raising of the educational level of the entire nation was the key to success, the myth found in the new narrative is that better results are gained by investing in the highest achievers.

In Chapter 7, *The Neoliberal–Neoconservative Reform in Greek Education*, Georgios Grollios attempts to answer questions pertaining to the neoliberal–neoconservative reforms in Greek education: What are the main political forces that advanced these reforms? What are the most serious forms of resistance they encountered? He also discusses the implications and impacts of these reforms, taking into consideration the limited number of relevant studies in Greece, a fact that is not at all accidental because it reflects the ideological domination of the doctrines of neoliberalism–neoconservatism propelled by the prevailing bourgeois social and political authority.

Understanding the basic characteristics of the wider social, political, and ideological reforms that have taken place in Greece since 1974 are necessary in considering these issues. Specifically, Grollios' analysis is founded through approaching education as a mechanism that contributes to the wider reproduction of productive and social power relations. The forms of this educational mechanism and its special functions in the context of its reproductive role (distribution of human resources in the social division of labor and imposing the variations of bourgeois ideology), are put into shape on the basis of certain power correlations—formed by diverse confrontations, compromises, alliances, and struggles—between the social classes.

In Chapter 8, *The Third Way and Beyond: Global Neoliberalism, Education, and Resistance in Taiwan*, Hui-Lan Wang and Michael Loncar note that for much of the world, the 1980s marked the beginning of the era of neoliberalism, a period dominated by New Right ideology in which governments connect economic development with political liberty and focus on promoting efficiency in the public sphere. These developments globally have been associated with the introduction of "New Public Management" (NPM). NPM has been very influential in many countries, including the United States, United Kingdom, Canada, Australia, New Zealand, and Asian NICs (New Industrial Countries). It has also been used both as a legitimizing basis and instrumental means for reforming state educational bureaucracies, educational institutions, and the processes that shape public policy.

In discussing contemporary issues of public policy and educational change under the impact of global capitalism and particularly of neoliberal ideology, Wang and Loncur analyze social developments in Taiwan during the last three decades. The discussions in this chapter are divided into four sections. The first explores the shift of educational control in Taiwan since the 1980s, from an emphasis on political to economic ideology, one that parallels the transformation of the government itself. The second offers a brief review of the impact of neoliberalism and globalization on education in Taiwan. The third illustrates how education in Taiwan, particularly higher education, has been recognized by the government as an important mechanism for the development of human capital and international competition based on the idea of a knowledge-based economy and New-Managerialism. The final section explores the reaction to neoliberalism, including the antiglobalization movements and the development of the NPOs in Taiwan.

In Chapter 9, *Israel: Neoliberal and Nationalist Education: Towards a Political Pedagogy*, Aura Mor-Sommerfeld, Ehud Adiv, and Arnon Dunetz suggest that the neoliberal perspective regards politics mainly as a moment in the direction of an apolitical reality, a means to destroy altogether the universal perspective of politics. The economic agenda of Israeli governments is affected by and linked to political-economical-educational changes that occurred worldwide in the last few decades. This is reflected best by a fundamental change in policy from a situation in which the state defines itself as the sole provider of its children's education to one in which the state seeks to shift this responsibility to private agencies or local authorities. This is mainly related to promoting big businesses and privatization, while diminishing social responsibility and avoiding implementing programs to promote equality.

The writers present the Israeli education system as a case study for examining political perspectives of education in the age of neoliberalization and globalization. It shows how the educational system in Israel has adopted the ideologies and cultural subjectivism of national patriotism to establish an ideology of segregation and neoliberalism. Its sections examine the economic agenda of Israel's governments; refer to the economic procedures related to schools, and sketch out the educational system focusing on language and curricula. Relying on historiography, it analyzes the connection between language education and the national ideology that controls the Israeli educational system. The chapter considers the general implications of left-radical political approach, discussing how it can challenge mainstream educational systems today and suggests bilingual education as a possible alternative (i.e., a political pedagogy alternative to the current segregated system), as well as to American Globalization.

Thus, in opposition to the power of American globalization and the cultural particularism of postmodernism, Mor-Sommerfeld, Adiv, and Dunetz consider what can make people transcend their unmediated "self love" by "exciting their minds with more desire to know" and to act. Education, as they see it, can be the medium by which this can and should happen; and for Israel, this transformation is most urgent and crucial.

In Chapter 10, *Education in a One-Party "Democracy": Singapore*, Steve McKenna and Julia Richardson consider the impact of neoliberalism on educational policy and practice in Singapore. Singapore is ostensibly a multi-party democracy but over the years since independence the People's Action Party (PAP) have successfully managed to manipulate and suppress the opposition and gerrymander electoral boundaries to ensure that it maintains one-party rule in the city-state. The PAP has ruled Singapore as a multinational corporation and has used education as a mechanism to ensure that the country attracts foreign investment in appropriate emerging sectors of the global economy. As a consequence, educational policy has always been at the service of the economy and attempts to introduce neoliberal initiatives into education—these are merely extensions of previous policy developments. In the context of Singapore, neoliberal interventions in the educational system (i.e., choice, competition, etc.) are not a break with the past but a logical extension of educational policy since the 1960s. McKenna and Richardson conclude by suggesting that the Singapore government will always follow fads and fashions that enhance the capability of the educational system to support economic policy.

In Chapter 11, *Education Reforms in Japan: Neoliberal, Neoconservative, and "Progressive education" Direction*, Kaori H. Okano claims that despite the media hype, Japan's educational reforms in the last three decades have been moderate and incremental, in comparison with Anglophone countries, which witnessed more drastic changes underpinned by a globally dominant neoliberal agenda. He suggests that the changes have been slow and gradual, formulated and implemented cautiously by the Ministry of Education. They have been underpinned by the Ministry's deliberate reluctance to exercise the executive power that it possesses, and its willingness to leave substantial scope for contexualization (interpretation and implementation) to lower levels of the education system. The result is great divergence across localities.

Japan's reforms represent a pragmatic package to accommodate demands from three directions: neoliberals, who pursue deregulation of schooling, greater individual choice, and accountability; neoconservatives, seeking to reinstate what they regard as "traditions"; and progressive educationalists, who want what they regard as rigid structured teaching to be replaced with student-centered and problem-solving learning. Thinking that student-centered learning would produce innovative elites, neoliberals supported a flexible curriculum. The left have criticized emerging national reform policies, but their views have been largely ignored at the national level. However, local governments have, to varying degrees, utilized the scope of contexualization in incorporating the left's views; and this has resulted in diversity in the local implementation of the national reform policies.

The most significant impact of the reforms, in McKenna and Richardson's analysis, is a widening gap in children's engagement with learning, increasingly determined by family background. This has come mainly from "the slimming of schooling," whereby Saturday school attendance was phased out, and roles once performed by schools have been delegated to communities and families. The "slimming of schooling" was justified on the grounds that children needed more time to develop outside school; but outside activities (including home study and sport and cultural activities) are more dependent on family resources than are many school-based activities. How the left would challenge this widening gap remains to be seen.

ACKNOWLEDGMENTS

We would like to thank Chris Brown, of the National Union of Teachers (in England and Wales) for this contribution to this chapter.

NOTES

1. Social Justice by itself is not enough. There cannot be social justice in a capitalist society, in situations of gross economic inequality. Human degradation through poverty, the relative poverty/life style that results from the class nature of a capitalist society; the social class-based power relationships that result from capital—exhibiting themselves, for example, in the differential values placed upon different cultural capitals, flowing from current and historical patterns of class domination and different historical and current patterns of economic capital—mean that social justice can only ever be partial. It is contingent on economic justice and injustice. The creation of true social justice

within capitalism is not viable. Furthermore, no capitalist class is going to give up its economic and political power willingly. Improvements in the relative position of the working class are brought about by class struggle, not by appeals to social justice, however much such appeals might aid that struggle in particular circumstances.

REFERENCES

Aguirre, L. C. (2001). The role of critical pedagogy in the globalization era and the aftermath of September 11, 2001. Interview with Peter McLaren. *Revista Electronica de Investigacion Educativa* (Electronic Review of Education Research), 3(2). Retrieved from http://www.redie.ens.uabc.mx/vol3no2/contenido-coral.html

Allmann, P. (2001). Foreword. In M. Cole, D. Hill, P. McLaren and G. Rikowski, *Red chalk: On schooling, capitalism and politics* (pp. 10–14). Brighton, UK: Institute for Education Policy Studies.

Althusser, L. (1971). Ideology and ideological state apparatuses. In L. Althusser, *Lenin and philosophy and other essays* (pp. 85–126). London: New Left Books.

Aronowitz, S., & Giroux, H. A. (1991). *Postmodern education: Politics, culture and social criticism*. Minneapolis: University of Minnesota Press.

Bambery, C., & Morgan, P. (2002, November). Anger into action? *Socialist Review, 268*, 9–11.

Burbules, N., & Berk, R. (1999). Critical thinking and critical pedagogy. In T. Popkewitz & L. Fendler (Eds.), *Critical theories in education: Changing terrains of knowledge and politics* (pp. 45–65). London: Routledge.

Cole, M. (2007). *Marxism and education: Origins and issues*. London: Routledge.

Cole, M., Hill, D., McLaren, P., & Rikowski, G. (2001). *Red chalk: On schooling, capitalism and politics*. Brighton, UK: Institute for Education Policy Studies.

Ellsworth, L. (1992). Why doesn't this feel empowering? Working through the repressive myths of critical pedagogy. In C. Luke & J. Gore (Eds.), *Feminisms and critical pedagogy* (pp. 90–119). New York: Routledge.

Fassbinder, S. (2006). The "Dirty Thirty's" Peter McLaren Reflects on the Crisis of Academic Freedom. *MRZine*, 4 June. Retrieved 28 April, 2008 from http://mrzine.monthlyreview.org/fassbinder060406.html

Freire, P. (1998). *Teachers as cultural workers*. Boulder, CO: Westview Press.

Gabbard, D. A. (2003). Education *is* enforcement: The centrality of compulsory schooling in market societies. In K. Saltman & D. Gabbard (Eds.), *Education as enforcement: The militarization and corporatization of schools* (pp.61–78). New York: Routledge.

Giroux, H. A. (1988). *Teachers as intellectuals: Toward a critical pedagogy of learning*. Granby, MA: Bergin & Garvey.

Giroux, H. A., & McLaren, P. (1986). Teacher education and the politics of engagement: The case for democratic schooling. *Harvard Education Review, 56*(3), 213–238.

Harman, C. (2002). The Workers of the world. *International Socialism, 96*, 3–45

Hearse, P. (2006, June) Resistance and Revolution. *International Viewpoint, 379*, Retrieved 20 April, 2008 from http://www.internationalviewpoint.org/spip.php?article1072

Hill, D. (1997). Reflection in initial teacher education. In K. Watson, S. Modgil and C. Modgil (eds.) *Educational dilemmas: Debate and diversity, vol. 1: Teacher education and training*. London: Routledge.

Hill, D. (2001). State theory and the neoliberal reconstruction of teacher education: A structuralist neo-Marxist critique of postmodernist, quasi-postmodernist, and culturalist neo-Marxist theory. *British Journal of Sociology of Education,* 22(1), 137–157.

Hill, D. (2004). Books, banks and bullets: Controlling our minds—the global project of imperialistic and militaristic neoliberalism and its effect on education policy. *Policy Futures,* 2(3 & 4). Retrieved 20 April, 2008 from http:www. wwwords.co.uk/pfie/

Hill, D. (2005). State Theory and the Neoliberal Reconstruction of Schooling and Teacher Education. In G. Fischman, P. McLaren, H. Sünker, & C. Lankshear (Eds.), *Critical theories, radical pedagogies and global conflicts* (pp. 23–51). Boulder, CO: Rowman and Littlefield.

Hill, D. (Ed.). (2009a). *Contesting neoliberal education: Public resistance and collective advance.* New York: Routledge.

Hill, D. (2009b). Critical Information Education, the Global Project of Neoliberal Capital, and Contemporary Resistence through progressive and revolutionary education. In S. Macrine, P. McLaren and D. Hill (Eds.) *Organizing for social justice within global neoliberalism.* London: Routledge.

Hill, D. and Boxley S. (2007). Critical Teacher Education for Economic, Environmental and Social Justice: an EcoSocialist Manifesto. *Journal for Critical Education Policy Studies.* 5 (2), November. Retrieved 28 April 2008 from http://www.jceps.com/index.php?pageID=article&articleID=96

Hill, D., McLaren, P., Cole, M., & Rikowski, G. (Eds.). (1999). *Postmodernism in educational theory: Education and the politics of human resistance.* London: Tufnell Press.

Hill, D., McLaren, P., Cole, M., & Rikowski, G. (Eds.). (2002). *Marxism against postmodernism in educational theory.* Lanham, MD: Lexington Press.

Hillcole Group. (1991). *Changing the future: Redprint for education.* London: Tufnell Press.

Hillcole Group. (1997). *Rethinking education and democracy: A socialist alternative for the twenty-first century.* London: Tufnell Press.

Hursh, D., & Ross, E. W. (eds.) (2000). *Democratic social education: Social studies for social change.* New York: RoutledgeFalmer.

Katz, C. (2006, April). The centre-left, nationalism and socialism. *International Viewpoint,* 366. Retrieved 20 April, 2008 from http://www.internationalviewpoint.org/spip.php?article717

McLaren P. (2000). *Che Guevara, Paulo Freire and the pedagogy of revolution.* Lanham, MD: Rowman and Littlefield.

McLaren, P. (2003a). The Dialectics of Terrorism: A Marxist response to September 11 (Part 2: Unveiling the past, evading the present). *Cultural Studies/Critical Methodologies,* 3, 103–132

McLaren, P. (2003b). *Life in schools: An introduction to critical pedagogy in the foundations of education* (4th ed.). Arlington, MA: Allyin and Bacon.

McLaren, P. (2005). *Capitalists and Conquerors: A Critical Pedagogy Against Empire.* Lanham, MD.: Rowman and Littlefield.

McLaren, P., Martin, G., & Farahmandpur, R. (2005). *Teaching against global capitalism and the new imperialism.* Lanham, MD: Rowman and Littlefield.

McLaren, P., and Jaramillo, N. (2007). *Pedagogy and Praxis in the Age of Empire.* Rotterdam: Sense Publishers.

McLaren, P. and Rikowski, G. (2006). Critical Pedagogy Reloaded: An Interview with Peter McLaren (interviewed by Glenn Rikowski), *Information for Social Change,* 23. Retrieved 28 April 2008 from http://libr.org.isc/issues/ISC23/C3%20Peter%20McLaren.pdf

Nocella, A. (2007). Fighting against the conservative agenda in the academy: an examination of the four Ss of academic repression and repressive pedagogy post 9/11/01. *Journal for Critical Education Policy Studies*, May. Retrieved 28 April 2008 from http://www.jceps.com/index.php?pageID=article&articleID=73

Pilger, J. (2002). *The new rulers of the world*. New York: Verso

The Research Unit for Political Economy (R.U.P.E.), (2003, September). Economics and politics of the world social forum., *Aspects of India's Economy, No. 35*. Retrieved September 5, 2006, from http://www.rupe-india.org/35/globalisation.html

Rikowski, G. (2007). Critical Pedagogy and the Constitution of Capitalist Society. The Flow of Ideas, 9 Sept. Retrieved 28 April 2008 from http://www.flowideas.co.uk/?page=articles&sub=Critical%20Pedagogy%20Capitalism

Rikowski, G, McLaren, P. (2001). Pedagogy against capital today: An e-interview with Peter McLaren (Peter McLaren interviewed by Glenn Rikowski). *The Hobgoblin: Journal of Marxist-Humanism, 4*. Retrieved 20 April, 2008 from www.members.aol.com/thehobgoblin/index.html.

Rikowski, G., & McLaren, P. (2006). Critical pedagogy reloaded. In P. McLaren (Ed.), *Rage and Hope* (pp. *355–374)*. New York: Peter Lang.

Sader, E. (2002). Beyond civil society, the Left after Porto Alegre. *New Left Review, 17*, 87–99

Saunois, T. (2002). Radical Latin America. *Socialism Today, 70*, 6–7.

Shor, I., & Freire, P. (1987). *A pedagogy for liberation: Dialogues on transforming education*. South Hadley, MA: Bergin & Garvey.

Zeichner, K., & Liston, D. (1987). Teaching student teachers to reflect. *Harvard Educational Review, 57*(1), 23–48.

Zeichner, K., & Liston, D. (1996). *Reflective teaching: An introduction*. Mahwah, NJ: Lawrence Erlbaum Associates.

2 The American Privatization Campaign
Vouchers, Charters, Educational Management Organizations, and the Money Behind Them

Karen Anijar and David Gabbard

There is a campaign under way to essentially destroy the public education system along with every aspect of human life and attitudes and thought that involve social solidarity. It's being done in all sorts of ways. One is simply by underfunding. So, if you can make the public schools really rotten, people will look for an alternative. Any service that's going to be privatized, the first thing you do is make it malfunction so people can say, "We want to get rid of it. It's not running. Let's give it to Lockheed."

Noam Chomsky, *The Progressive Magazine*, September 1999, p. 37

"The NEA (National Education Association) is a terrorist organization."

Education Secretary Rod Paige National Governors Association, Feb 23 2004 (King, 2004)

INTRODUCTION

In the United States, private corporations have (historically) always transacted with, and profited from, selling supplies and equipment to the public schools. Likewise, those same private interests were always able to count on the security state to manage schools as instruments for disciplining members of the domestic population into the proper behaviors and attitudes that would increase their use value as human capital and their docility as "good citizens." Though countervailing ideas on the purposes of education have circulated since the time of Thomas Jefferson, they never threatened to seriously alter the traditional role of compulsory schooling in America's market society. That changed, however, in the 1960s, when multiple sectors of the general public (those associated with the civil rights movement, the women's movement, the environmental movement, the labor movement, the peace movement, and others) recognized and acted to realize the democratizing potentials of education. As a result of the efforts of these various groups, schools and universities, from the perspective of entrenched business interests, began "allowing too much freedom and independence of thought, and that cannot be tolerated in a 'democracy,' because it might lead to consequences" (Chomsky, 2004). Beginning in the early 1970s, multiple sectors of that same business community began taking steps to overcome these deficiencies in the educational system, restoring the state-sponsored system of compulsory schooling to its traditional role. Those steps have entailed a variety of tactics (e.g., vouchers, tax tuition credits, charter schools) for "liberalizing" education for promoting a broader strategy ultimately designed to bring the management of schools (decision-making power over curriculum and modes of instruction) under the control of private corporations (Hursh, 2008a; Ross and Gibson, 2007; Saltman, 2001, 2007, 2008; Saltman & Goodman, 2002; Saltman & Gabbard, 2003). Privatizing the management of schools, of course, will also provide the added advantage, following the dominant pattern that we see in the defense, biotechnology, medical, and insurance industries, of socializing the costs of schooling while privatizing the profits.

Our analysis goes beyond disseminating statistics surrounding the progress of the neoliberal/neoconservative agenda in the United States' public schools, colleges, and universities. While we cover the primary elements of that agenda (e.g., school vouchers, charter schools, Educational Management Organizations [EMOs], along with the concurrent proletarianization of the educational labor force, a focus on essentialist curricula and high stakes testing) we also describe these neoliberal structural adjustment policies and initiatives as part of a broader project designed to strip public institutions of their democratizing power and potential. We "follow the dollar," tracing funding sources, while highlighting interconnections between various foundations and corporations who support a wide array of political, religious, and ideological strategies targeted directly at eliminating any remaining hopes in the United States for democratization. It is (in our estimation) crucial to understand the common source(s) attempting to privatize public schooling while imposing an ideological hegemony that parallels the dystopian nightmare in George Orwell's 1984.

VOUCHERS

Joel Belz, publisher of World—a Religious Right magazine—wrote a column several years ago sympathizing with those who oppose vouchers because they don't want government to play any role in education. He wrote: "If [supporting vouchers] helps bring down the statist system, which it will, it will be worth the temporary compromise." Supporting vouchers now, Belz argued, would help pro-privatization groups in the long run "gain a larger strategic advantage." (People for the American Way, 2003, p. 1)

Vouchers are publicly funded through taxpayer dollars and are used to pay the tuition at private schools. Advocates for vouchers represent a peculiar alliance forged at the juncture between the religious right and hyper-intensified capitalism. In modernism, the mode of production may well have been related to the mode of reproduction. In the United States at this particular moment in time, the mode of production and the ideological intent are increasingly obscured under rubrics (ruses) of sensible (seemingly objective) policy.

Vouchers for public education can be traced to economist Milton Friedman, who theorized that the that private sector delivers goods and services more efficiently than public institutions. "Ironically," as People for the American Way argue in their 2003 report *Voucher Veneer,*

> some of the conditions in public schools identified by critics as problems are rooted in the dynamics of the free market system they praise. Large schools were inspired largely by private enterprise, which has long encouraged "economies of scale." Boston University professor Philip Tate has observed that rigid class schedules, reliance on test scores and other traits of public schools "were instituted in the name of efficiency" and created a "factory model" of schooling. (People for the American Way, 2003, p. 2)

Contrary to popular mythology, vouchers did not emerge as a grassroots movement. Rather, in a carefully calculated and constructed campaign, voucher advocates developed public policy background materials prior to disseminating them to sympathetic lobbyists and state legislators. Voucher activists also provided legal assistance in order to insure the passage of legislation through respective state courts (should the constitutionality of voucher amendments and legislation be challenged). In the efforts to privatize schools, voucher advocates have also been elected and appointed to office. For example, United States Representative Tom Tancredo, R-Colorado, after his appointment to the House education committee said, "I think it's a lot easier to kill the beast when you get in the cave" (People for the American Way, 2003, pp. 11–12). Recently, the Bush Administration appointed Nina Shokraii Rees, a staunch voucher advocate, to head Department of Education's Office of Innovation and Improvement. (Kohn, 2004). The Heartland Institute (a right-wing think tank devoted to the privatization of American education) has declared public schools "islands of socialism in a sea of competition and choice." And, it has openly stated that "soon, most government schools will be converted into private schools or simply close their doors." The Heartland Institute has succeeded in forming a "board of legislative advisors" that includes more than 240 elected officials from nearly all 50 states. (People for the American Way, 2003, p.4).

Such candid and revealing comments contrast sharply with the public message of many pro-voucher groups. They publicly state: vouchers will actually help strengthen public schools by forcing them to improve through the magic of competition and market forces.

Suffice to say, language was deployed as a strategy in a form of ideological warfare. Comments (that reveal far more than they can conceal) made on the part of pro-voucher groups, more often than not, stand in direct contrast with the public messages. Among themselves, voucher advocates acknowledge that "the complete privatization of schooling might be desirable, but this objective is politically impossible for the time being. Vouchers are a type of reform that is possible now, and would put us on the path to further privatization" (People for the American Way, 2003, p. 7). When communicating with a broader public, however, they assert that "the answer lies in working to replace public (education) with private, consumer-responsive, unregulated, independent education" (Mercer, 2002).

Targeted "media" campaigns (sponsored by interested "parties") attempted to popularize vouchers as a "democratic" move transforming the national, state, and local conversations surrounding schooling. In the transpositioning of language, public schools became known as *government schools*. And those schools were *failing* miserably, because they were part of big government, bureaucratic state monopolies, contributing to the erosion of family values, teaching secular humanism, and promoting perverse sexuality, while American children were unable to read, write, and do arithmetic. These campaigns frame the language of vouchers in seemingly benign, benevolent, and often idealistic terms such as *individualism, parental rights and freedom, political and economic freedom, limited government, individual liberties, free markets*, and *strengthening democratic capitalism* (Spring, 2008). For example,

> The Future of Freedom Foundation contended that the "free market" would enable parents to "select the best educational vehicle for each of their children." Earlier this year, a like-minded columnist asserted, "The answer lies in working to replace public (education) with private, consumer-responsive, unregulated, independent education." . . . the Florida-based James Madison Institute has stated that it "believes that parents should have the freedom to make decisions in the best interests of their children." Most Americans, including those who strongly support public education, would likely agree with this vague statement. These words, of course, leave unmentioned the fact that the James Madison Institute's education policy director has signed a proclamation that calls for scrapping the public education system (People for the American Way, 2003, p. 6).

Vouchers seemed to provide a pragmatic utilitarian solution emanating from the "manufactured crisis" (see Berliner & Biddle 1995) of failing schools. Nevertheless,

Chester E. Finn, Jr., who heads the Fordham Foundation, notes that it is generally hard to find private school leaders "who want their schools to grow, to open additional campuses, to recruit more clients." Finn also recently admitted that "there aren't enough private schools to go around" for would-be voucher students. Indeed, a massive number of schools would have to be built to replace all or most of the 92,000 public schools operating across America. . . . Concerns about quality are magnified by the fact that private and religious schools are not held accountable in the same manner as public schools. In fact, the CATO Institute's David Salisbury recently argued that private schools' ability to disregard state standards is "the very basis for school choice." (People for the American Way, 2003, p. 15)

The use of language in the push for vouchers has enabled private corporations to reduce regulation on what has traditionally been seen in the United States as part of the public interest, obscuring the argument of the differences between democracy and capitalism, creating a sense of looming crisis and an effective epidemic, while further eroding the separation of church and state in the United States. A majority of the schools participating in voucher programs are religious schools. Though voters in various states have defeated eight referenda that would either have created or permitted private-school voucher programs, such programs have taken root in Wisconsin (1990), Ohio (1995), Florida (1999), Colorado (2003), and Washington, D.C. (2004).

In Wisconsin, the Milwaukee Parental Choice Program, the nation's longest-running and largest publicly funded voucher program, serves Milwaukee students in Grades K through 12 whose family incomes are at or below 175% of the poverty level. During the 2002–2003 school year, 13,231 students and 106 private and parochial schools participated in the program, costing Wisconsin taxpayers well over $60 million. Because voucher schools do not have to administer or report test results, as noted in a Wisconsin state audit released in February 2000, it is impossible to assess academic achievement in these schools. No system currently exists that would hold private schools accountable for how funds are spent, nor for measuring their impact on student achievement, as pro-voucher legislators have consistently rejected proposed accountability measures (General Accounting Office, 2003).

In Ohio, the Cleveland Scholarship and Tutoring Program serves Cleveland students in Grades K through 8. For students whose family income is less than 200% of the federal poverty level, the scholarship covers up to 90% of a private school's tuition, or up to a maximum of $2,250 (whichever is less). For eligible families earning more than 200% of the federal poverty level, the state pays 75% of a participating school's tuition or a maximum of $1,875. As of December 2002, there were 5,147 students enrolled in the program. Including administrative costs, the program cost approximately $33 million for the 2001–2002 school year. According to research conducted during the previous year (2000–2001), nearly 33% of the students receiving aid through the Cleveland voucher program previously had been attending private schools, whereas only 21% had gone to public schools in Cleveland. The remaining 46% enrolled as kindergarteners or came from elsewhere. (Metcalf, 2003a). Furthermore, Policy Matters Ohio has revealed that less than one half of 1% of students in the Cleveland program use their vouchers to attend secular schools. Nearly all of them attend private, religious schools. Because many of these schools operate on different schedules than public schools, regular public school bus services can only serve the transportation needs of voucher students by paying more overtime pay for drivers on days when the private schools operate but public schools do not, such as public school holidays and teacher planning days. Some voucher students' homes are so far from their schools that they cannot even be served by public school busses. Instead, the Cleveland Municipal School District has had to pay an estimated $1,200 to $1,800 per pupil, per year, to transport them by taxi. In all, $12 million is spent annually to transport non-public school students around Cleveland. (Schiller, 2001; Hanauer, 2002).

Given the conclusions reached by Kim Metcalf's *Evaluation of the Cleveland Scholarship and Tutoring Program* (2003a, 2003b), it would appear that school vouchers do little to improve the academic performance of students participating in the voucher program. According to her report,

> After adjusting for students' minority status and family income, there is no consistent pattern either of enhanced or diminished academic achievement for students who have used a scholarship to attend public schools from kindergarten through fourth grade. Further, students who exit the program to return to public schools often experience a comparative drop in achievement during their first or second year after leaving the program, but return over time to levels of adjusted achievement that is comparable to other students. (Metcalf, 2003b)

These conclusions are supported by the findings of Helen Ladd, professor of public policy studies and economics at Duke University. Citing studies conducted by Paul Peterson, Ladd contends that

> Based on three years of data from New York and Washington, D.C., and two years from Dayton, the authors find no evidence of an overall achievement difference between the public and the private schools either in the aggregate or for any of the individual cities. This finding that the private schools are no better at raising the performance of low-income students than are the public schools flies in the face of well-known claims made by pro-voucher researchers such as John Chubb and Terry Moe that the autonomy of private schools will make

them more productive than the more bureaucratic public schools. (Ladd, 2002)

The state of Florida passed two pieces of voucher legislation in 1999. One of the legislative acts established the Opportunity Scholarship Program that provides vouchers to students enrolled in public schools that received an "F" grade on the state report card for two out of four consecutive years. Vouchers can be used in any participating private school or a higher-performing public school. The voucher amount is equal to the state's share of an eligible student's per pupil expenditure (an amount averaging from $3,500 to $3,900 during the 2001–2002 school year). Participating private schools have to accept the voucher amount as full tuition. Though approximately 8,800 students at ten public schools were eligible to receive "opportunity" vouchers in the summer of 2002, only about 600 students used these vouchers to attend private schools in the fall. Though the state of Florida did not release a figure on the program's cost, it is estimated to have cost taxpayers $2.1 million for the 2002–2003 school year.

The second piece of voucher legislation passed in Florida was the McKay Scholarship for Students With Disabilities. Although it was originally enacted as a pilot program, the Florida Legislature expanded it to become a statewide program in 2000–2001. The McKay Scholarship offered vouchers to students with disabilities who had attended a public school in the previous year and whose parent reported dissatisfaction with the student's progress. In order to be eligible for the scholarship, however, the student must have also been accepted into a participating public or private school. As People for the American Way reports, however,

> the vast majority of Florida's private schools have declined to participate in the McKay program, reflecting the views expressed earlier this year by the National Association of Independent Schools (NAIS), a private schools group. NAIS President Pat Bassett told private school operators that he opposed voucher plans that would curb private schools' "freedom to accept students who are mission-appropriate . . . our mission is to educate whatever population you define as your population. . . ." In other words, private schools do the choosing, not parents. (2003)

In August of 2004, the Florida Courts of Appeals upheld the ruling of a Leon County Circuit judge in 2002, declaring that this program violated the state constitution by using tax dollars to aid private and religious schools. This decision, along with a similar decision that struck down the voucher law in Colorado, seemingly contradicted the decision handed down by the United States Supreme Court in Zelman v. Simmons-Harris that defended the voucher program in Cleveland.

CHARTER SCHOOLS AND EDUCATIONAL
MANAGEMENT ORGANIZATIONS

The second element of the far-right's efforts to dismantle public schools involves the establishment of charter schools. The first charter school opened in Minnesota in 1991. Today, there are more than 2,695 charter schools in 41 states and the District of Columbia. Nearly 685,000 students attend these schools. Arizona has the highest number of charter schools, with 464 schools serving more than 60,000 students. California runs a close second with 428 charter schools, followed by Florida (227), Texas (221), and Michigan (196). Unlike the private schools who serve voucher students, charter schools are predominantly funded with public money. Nevertheless, they are not regulated by the same structures as other more "traditional" public schools. They enjoy far more autonomy concerning hiring and firing practices, curricula, and budget spending. These factors make them very attractive to educational management organizations (EMOs), such as Edison Schools, Inc., which attempt to run these schools "for-profit." When Arizona State University's Education Policy Studies Laboratory (EPSL) began issuing its annual Profiles of for-profit education management companies in 1999, 13 EMOs managed 135 for-profit schools in 15 states. Today, 51 companies manage 463 schools in 28 states and the District of Columbia, 81% of which are charter schools. As EPSL reports,

> The for-profit management of public schools generally takes two major forms: local school districts contracting with an EMO for the management of existing traditional K-12 public schools (termed "contract schools") or EMOs managing public charter schools either as the charter holder or under the terms of a contract with the charter holder. In the early 1990s, EMOs tended to pursue the contract school approach. In the latter half of the 1990s, EMOs have taken the opportunity afforded by permissive charter school legislation and focused on the management of publicly funded charter schools. (Molnar *et al*, 2004, p. 2)

While advocates assert that operating without the bureaucratic constraints of regular public schools will enable charter schools to help students to experience higher rates of educational achievement, the first national comparison of test scores among children in charter schools and traditional public schools shows charter school students demonstrated unequivocally (by the very measures chosen as the rationale for charter schools) that they perform worse than comparable students in traditional public schools.

> The findings, buried in mountains of data the Education Department released without public announcement, deal a blow to supporters of

the charter school movement, including the Bush administration. The data show fourth graders attending charter schools performing about half a year behind students in other public schools in both reading and math. Put another way, only 25 percent of the fourth graders attending charters were proficient in reading and math, against 30 percent who were proficient in reading, and 32 percent in math, at traditional public schools. Because charter schools are concentrated in cities, often in poor neighborhoods, the researchers also compared urban charters to traditional schools in cities. They looked at low-income children in both settings and broke down the results by race and ethnicity as well. In virtually all instances, the charter students did worse than their counterparts in regular public schools. Charters are expected to grow exponentially under the new federal education law, No Child Left Behind, which holds out conversion to charter schools as one solution for chronically failing traditional schools. (Schemo, 2004).

Chester E. Finn Jr., once the Assistant Secretary of Education under Ronald Reagan and an early supporter of charter schools, asked the Bush administration to do the comparison. "Finn and other backers of charter schools contended, however, that the findings should be considered as 'baseline data'" (Schemo, 2004).

Federal officials said they did not intend to hide the performance of charter schools and denied any political motivation for failing to publicly disclose that the data were available. "I guess that was poor publicity on our part," said Robert Lerner, commissioner of the federal Education Department's National Center for Education Statistics. Lerner said further analysis was needed to put the data in its proper context (Schemo, 2004).

Other comparisons reveal the same trend. According to the American Federation of Teachers' 2004 report, *Charter School Achievement on the 2003 National Assessment of Educational Progress,* charter school students demonstrated lower rates of achievement than students in regular public schools. In Grade 4, they scored six scale points lower in math and seven scale points lower in reading. In Grade 8, charter school students scored five points lower in math and two points lower in reading. Along these same measures of achievement (NAEP scores in math and reading in Grades 4 & 8) "the percentages of charter school students performing at or above *Basic* and at or above *Proficient* were lower than the corresponding percentages for regular public school students." Finally, the AFT reports,

the achievement gap between students who were and were not eligible for free or reduced-price lunch was similarly substantial in both subjects and both grades, but the gap was slightly larger in charter schools than in regular public schools in grade 4 reading and grade 8 math. (Nelson et al, 2004)

Robert Bifulco and Helen Ladd arrive at the same conclusions when examining the impact of charter schools on student learning in North Carolina. "We find that students make considerably smaller achievement gains in charter schools than they would have in public schools" (Bifulco & Ladd, 2004, p. 3). We see the same patterns reflected in the following tables reporting the ratings of charter schools versus public schools in the state of Ohio for the 2002–2003 and 2003–2004 school years.

Charter schools under-perform relative to public schools in other important ways. While a recent study (Allegretto et al, 2004, p. 2) reveals that since 1993, teacher wages have fallen 11.5% relative to workers with similar education and skills (with no improvement in benefits that offset this increased wage disadvantage), and the salaries of teachers in charter schools lag even further behind. According to the 1999–2000 SASS, 41% of charter school teachers had total yearly earnings under $30,000 (compared to 20% in regular public schools). Research suggests that teachers choose charter

Table 2.1   The ratings of charter schools versus public schools in the state of Ohio for the 2004 school year

Charter Schools	ODE Report Card Ratings	Public Schools
19.8%	Not Rated	0%
41.7%	Academic Emergency	6.5%
15.6%	Academic Watch	3.7%
18.8%	Continuous Improvement	35.7%
5.2%	Effective	26.8%
0.0%	Excellent	27.1%

Table 2.2   The ratings of charter schools versus public schools in the state of Ohio for the 2003 school year.

Charter Schools	ODE Report Card Ratings	Public Schools
34%	Not Rated	0%
39.7%	Academic Emergency	11.1%
9%	Academic Watch	7%
10.2%	Continuous Improvement	39.1%
3.4%	Effective	24.1%
3.4%	Excellent	20%

(Ohio Federation of Teachers, 2004)

schools for reasons such as working with like-minded colleagues in innovative educational settings, but it is difficult to create this environment when, according to SASS, teacher turnover exceeds 35% (compared to about 15% in regular public schools; Nelson et al, 2003, p. 9).

THE IDEOLOGY AND ORGANIZATIONS BEHIND THE MOVEMENT

In the most general of terms, the various manifestations of liberal thought emerged from a complex confluence of forces at work in Europe across many centuries. The scientific revolution of the early 17th century gave birth not only to a concomitant technological and industrial revolution that fueled the growth of capitalism and the rise of a nascent merchant class, but also an Age of Reason and a period of Enlightenment that provided this same merchant class with much of the philosophical scaffolding to support their political struggles against the traditional authority of the monarchy and church. In combination, these various material and ideological movements produced what we know as Modernity or *Liberal* Modernity. In epistemological terms, Modernity privileged the authority of the individual and her or his powers of reason and rationality over the power of established institutional authorities of crown and church to determine Truth. This epistemological liberty helped lay the basis for the *political liberalism* that, as David Hursh (2008b) explains,

> reconceptualized the relationship between the individual and the secular and sacred state, aiming to free individuals from state interference and portraying individuals as rational choosers pursuing their self-interest, which served societal interests and promoted social progress.

Hursh adds that

> Such political views soon influenced economic theories, and the idea that society could best be served by individuals pursuing their self-interest was reflected in Adam Smith's notion of the "invisible hand." Smith argued that the individual "intends only his own gains, as he is in this, as in many others, led by an invisible hand to promote an end which was no part of his intentions" (Smith 1776/1952). For Smith, the individual pursuing their own interests in a "market system was the best mechanism of the allocation of resources in a society" and "brought economic gains to each party, and ultimately to the nation as a whole." (Olssen et al., 2004, p. 88)

This, then, accounts for some of the intellectual history behind the economic brand of liberalism embraced under the ideology of neoliberalism. Philosophically speaking, we find it tempting to deny that there is anything *neo* or new about neoliberalism. The proponents of neoliberal policies embrace the same brand of economic liberalism as their 18th and 19th century forbearers. Neoliberalism is "new" only in the sense that, as a political movement, it signals a resurgence of economic liberalism. The economic liberals behind this movement seek to affect a reclamation of the dominance they enjoyed prior to the global crisis of capitalism in the first half the 20th century. In the United States, that crisis took the form of the Great Depression and ushered in a period of state intervention and regulation of the economy that leading industrialists and financiers—those who benefited most from the shocking inequalities of income, wealth, and political power during America's Gilded Age—opposed widely and bitterly. Though there were previous interventions, such as the passage of the 16th Amendment authorizing the taxation of the primary source of the robber barons' massive profits and incomes—capital gains, the various components of Franklin D. Roosevelt's New Deal incited their ire the most.

The New Deal, we must remember, did not come about strictly as an exercise in government beneficence. Massive populist pressures stemming from the growing labor movement demanded some form of protection from the ravages of the market system. Similar and stronger movements toward state planning and intervention took hold in Europe, leading the "captains of industry" there, particularly in Germany and Italy, to fund and otherwise support the creation of fascist states to protect and enhance corporate interests. Both Hitler and Mussolini, readers should recall, smashed the trade unions and imprisoned or assassinated many of their leaders. As Jules Archer describes in *The Plot to Seize the White House* (1973), similar plans were set in motion in the United States, with leading industrialists sending agents to Europe to study and bring back lessons from the ascent of fascist corporatism in Italy and Germany. General Smedley Butler, an extremely popular and populist Marine Corps officer who'd been awarded two Congressional Medals of Honor, foiled the plot when he reported having been recruited in 1933 by Gerald C. MacGuire on behalf on Grayson Mallot-Prevost Murphy to lead the American Legion in staging a coup against Roosevelt. Murphy, Archer reveals,

> not only operated one of Wall Street's leading brokerage houses but was also a director of Guaranty Trust, a Morgan bank, and had extensive industrial and financial interests as a director of Anaconda Copper, Goodyear Tire, and Bethlehem Steel. A West Point graduate, Murphy was a veteran of the Spanish-American War and World War I with the rank of colonel. (p. 12)

Even more disturbingly, General Butler discovered that Murphy "had been decorated by Benito Mussolini, who had made him a Command of the Crown of Italy" (ibid).

While the story of what John L. Spivak (see Archer, 1973) described in 1935 as "Wall Street's Fascist Conspiracy" to overthrow Roosevelt never fully entered America's collective memory, readers should know that much of the information presented in Archer's book comes directly from the recorded testimony of Butler and other witnesses called before McCormick-Dickstein House Committee on un-American Activities. This same Committee would later come to be associated with the anti-communist crusades of Senator Joseph McCarthy. Its origins, however, remain crucial for our understanding of neoliberalism as a reaction against the New Deal. For while Butler may have foiled the fascist plot against Roosevelt, the fascist tendencies of its perpetrators remain characteristic of the neoliberal/neo-conservative agenda under consideration here. Those tendencies, in fact, help us introduce a further question in our analysis of that agenda. Namely, what makes the economic liberalism of neoliberal ideology conservative?

Although neoliberals love to invoke the name of Adam Smith in support of their project, which David Harvey (2005) so aptly characterizes as a project aimed at "the restoration of class power," we should consider their reading of Smith's *The Wealth of Nation* as selective at best. They demonstrate a special reluctance to discuss those aspects of Smith's book that offer us crucial insights into why the doctrine of economic liberalism would eventuate in a "new conservatism" marked by a strong authoritarian/anti-democratic temperament. "It cannot be very difficult," Smith wrote, "to determine who have been the contrivers of this whole mercantile system; not the consumers, we may believe, whose interest has been entirely neglected; but the producers, whose interest has been so carefully tended to; and among this latter class our merchants and manufacturers have been by far the principal architects" (1776, p. 288). And these "principal architects," Smith noted, though "incapable of considering themselves as sovereigns, even after they have become such . . . , by a strange absurdity regard the character of the sovereign [the state] as but an appendix to that of the merchant, as something which ought to be made subservient to it" (ibid, p. 277). Part of the dominance that economic liberalism enjoyed in America throughout the 19th and early 20th centuries was its dominance over state power.

We would do well to recall that America's "founding fathers" were among the richest men in the former colonies, and that the Revolution itself was motivated by their desire to liberate their economic activities from the arbitrary power of the British crown. Furthermore, in establishing the new republic, they took special pains to limit democratic governance to their own class. At the Constitutional Convention, for example, James Madison argued that "our government ought to secure the permanent interests of the country against innovation, putting in place checks and balances in order to protect *the minority of the opulent* against the majority" (Madison, 1787, cited in Gonsolves, 2001). Alternatively, in the words of John Jay, "the people who own the country ought to govern it" (Monaghan, 1935, p. 323). Consequently, the "founding fathers" limited voting rights to white males of sufficient property. Later, as private power evolved into its modern corporate form, the Supreme Court ruled in *Santa Clara County v.*

Southern Pacific Railroad in 1886 that private corporations possessed the same rights of "personhood" as individual citizens.

As Howard Zinn has written, Smith

> understood very well how capitalism could not survive a truly free market, if government was not big enough to protect it. He wrote in the middle of the eighteenth century: "Laws and governments may be considered in this and indeed in every case, a combination of the rich to oppress the poor, and preserve to themselves the inequality of the goods, which would otherwise be soon destroyed by the attacks of the poor, who if not hindered by the government would soon reduce the others to an equality with themselves by open violence." (Zinn, 1999)

"Big government" only became a threat to economic liberalism when it succumbed to popular pressures from the masses to redress their grievances or expand their own political liberties. Economic liberals, then, have always regarded democracy as a threat to their exclusive control of state power. It is this control, along with the wealth that affords them their privilege, which they seek to conserve.

Prior to the New Deal, economic liberals succeeded mightily in conserving their hegemony over state power. Owing to this hegemony, the captains of industry were left free to deal with popular unrest as they saw fit. The struggle for an eight-hour workday, for example, met tremendous resistance from the ownership class, and that resistance sometimes took violent forms. There was also strong elite resistance to popular suffrage, and the recent records of voter suppression in Florida in 2000 and Ohio in 2004 reveals that elites continue to oppose widespread participation in the electoral process. Writing in 1909, Graham Wallace and A. L. Lowell warned that popular elections "'may work fairly well as long as those questions are not raised which cause the holders of wealth and power' to make full use of their resources. However, should they do so, "'there is so much skill to be bought, and the art of using skill for production of emotion and opinion has so advanced that the whole condition of political contests would be changed for the future'" (cited in Carey, 1996, p. 21). That same year, a vice-president of AT&T described what he termed *the public mind* as "the only serious danger confronting the company" (cited in Chomsky, 1989, p. 30). To control the danger posed by the public mind, those "holders of wealth and power" dedicated considerable resources to buy the "skills" needed for the "production of emotion and opinion" favorable to their interests. The early 20th century, then, marked the origins of the science of propaganda.

One of propaganda's pioneering theoreticians was Walter Lippmann. In his view, "the common interests very largely elude public opinion entirely, and can be managed only by a specialized class whose personal interests reach beyond the locality." Lippmann characterized common people as "the bewildered herd." Any members of this herd that might think to press her or his demands on the state he characterized as "ignorant and meddlesome outsiders." Citizenship, under Lippmann's model, did not entail an active civic role for average citizens (see Chomsky, 1991, p. 367). It is not for the public, Lippmann held, to "pass judgment on the intrinsic merits" of an issue or to offer analysis or solutions, but merely, on occasion, to place "its force at the disposal" of one or another group of "responsible men." The public "does not reason, investigate, invent, persuade, bargain, or settle." Rather, the public acts only by aligning itself as the partisan of someone in a position to act executively, once he has given the matter at hand sober and disinterested thought. It is for this reason that "the public must be put in its place." The bewildered herd, trampling and roaring, "has its function": to be "the interested spectators of action," not participants. Participation is the duty of "the responsible man" (ibid, pp. 367–368).

Lippmann's name holds significance for the evolution of neoliberalism in the wake of the New Deal for one primary reason. His ideas inspired the convening of the Colloque Walter Lippmann in Paris in August of 1938. Two of the founders of neoliberal ideology from the original Austrian School of Economics, Ludwig von Mises and Friedrich von Hayek attended this colloquium and based many of their ideas for neoliberal tactics on Lippmann's ideas on propaganda and the role of the "responsible men." Immediately afterward, Hayek would attempt to assemble a group of responsible men, noted for their commitment to the principles of economic liberalism under the banner of the Society for the Renovation of Liberalism. Though World War II would stymie their efforts, Hayek would renew them in 1947 when he convened the first meeting of the Mont Pelerin Society. Lippmann also attended that meeting.

We should not underestimate the significance of Lippmann's associations with Hayek and the Mont Pelerin Society. In 1944, Hayek published *The Road to Serfdom*, in which he appropriated and applied a pseudo-Darwinian argument to explain that social history reveals a pattern of "natural selection" very similar to that revealed in natural history. Hayek used this argument to contend that only the "fittest" institutions survived. Older and more primitive institutions, he argued, suffered from a "collectivist" or "communal" orientation that inhibited individual liberty. Ignoring the corporate power behind Italian and German fascism, Hayek equated this "collectivist" principle with both fascism and socialism. He used this rhetoric to attack the anti-liberal policies of John Maynard Keynes and Roosevelt's New Deal, arguing that any form of state intervention or planning would lead society toward fascism. Returning to his theory of social evolution, Hayek contended that history had proven three institutions to be of greatest value to humanity: the family, the church, and the free market.

Hayek, of course, recognized that economic liberalism had fallen into disrepute after the Great Depression. To facilitate its restoration and, thereby, to liberate the market from state control, Hayek advocated waging a war of ideas through the carefully planned and calculated use of think tanks such as the Foundation for Economic Education in the United States that provided a model for Hayek's own Mont Pelerin Society. As Philip Kovacs and Deron Boyles explain, "think tanks are non-profit organizations that both produce and rely on research and expertise to aggressively influence the public, political leaders, and policy" (2005, p. 2. Also see Kovacs, 2008a). Hayek advanced the idea of think tanks as institutions that would assemble and hire scholars dedicated to the resurgence of economic liberalism through a slow but steady effort to establish hegemony for neoliberal ideology over the whole of society. In many regards, Hayek's proposals appear strikingly similar to Lippmann's advocacy for the cultivation of a "specialized class" of "responsible men" to manage people's ideas and perceptions on the world. Chief among those influenced by Hayek's ideas was British millionaire Antony Fisher, who would go on to create the Institute for Economic Affairs in 1955. According to the National Center for Policy Analysis,

> No single person was more important in encouraging the spread of think tanks than Sir Antony Fisher. An RAF pilot in World War II who went on to become successful in business, Fisher sought advice from Nobel Laureate Fredrich Hayek on how to stop the spread of collectivism and encourage a resurgence of 19th century classical liberal ideas. Don't go into politics, Hayek advised. Focus instead on the world of ideas. (Goodman, 2005)

Hayek's ideas also had a lasting influence on Milton Friedman, perhaps the leading American figure in the history of neoliberal economic theory. Students of education, of course, will recognize Friedman as the originator of the idea for school vouchers. Friedman worked closely with Hayek when the latter moved from the London School of Economics to the University of Chicago. With this move, what had once been known as the Austrian School of Economics became the Chicago School, and Hayek, Friedman, and others came to be known as the "Chicago Boys."

ENTER NEOCONSERVATISM

By the time Hayek came to the University of Chicago in 1950, Leo Strauss already occupied a position in its philosophy department. Though we have thus far discovered no evidence to suggest even a meeting, much less an exchange of ideas, between the two men, Strauss' ideas have proven central to the neoliberal movement. In her two books (1999/2005) on his philosophy, Shadia Drury presents Strauss as the intellectual godfather of the neoconservatives that ran the administration of President George W. Bush.

Strauss' neoconservatism begins to align with neoliberalism at the point where he would agree with Hayek and Lippmann that a society's population must be controlled through the careful management of ideas and beliefs by a specialized class. Holding great antipathy toward Modernity, Strauss claimed to have derived his own wisdom from the Ancients, especially Plato. For Strauss, the class of men best suited to serve as the specialized class were philosophers or, in Plato's terms, *philosopher kings*. Not only are the philosophers the only ones capable of discerning the truth about the world, they are also the only ones who can bear the truth. And they, if they are to observe their self-understood role in society, must keep that truth secret from the rest of the population. Ironically, that sacred truth is that there is no truth, only socially constructed representations of reality. This nihilism, for Strauss, represents the root of the human condition, and only through their wisdom can the philosophers bear that condition. Through the "gentlemen" whom the philosophers must advise in governing the republic, for the philosophers must always and only govern from behind the curtain, they dispense noble lies to the rest of the population in order to maintain their allegiance to the state and those institutions that provide society its structure and order. Strauss regarded patriotic nationalism and religion, along with the inculcation of irrational fear and hatred of enemies, both foreign and domestic, as crucial to this task. Just as he denied the existence of truth, Strauss himself also viewed morality as nothing more than a human construct, though requisite for building the sort of emotional attachments to family, church, and other institutions that would ensure the preservation of social order.

Perhaps the most appealing aspect of Strauss' thought for neoliberalism, however, lies in the philosophical justification that he provides for economic elites ruling society. He claims to find this justification in Plato's *Republic* in the dialogue between Socrates and Thrasymachus on the nature of justice. Conventional readings of Plato would lead us to believe that we should listen to the advice given by Socrates, but Strauss views it the other way. For Strauss, Thrasymachus provides the guidance on justice that Plato wanted the philosopher kings to receive. Justice, Thrasymachus tells them, arrives through whatever actions serve the interests of the powerful.

To repeat an earlier passage from *The Wealth of Nations*, Adam Smith once observed that the chief beneficiaries of economic liberalism, "by a strange absurdity regard the character of the sovereign [the state] as but an appendix to that of the merchant, as something which ought to be made subservient to it" (Smith, 1776, p. 277). For Strauss, this is no "strange absurdity" but only the outcome of *natural right*, wherein the superior few rule over the inferior many. Elite rule by the most successful merchants is not only *just*, but it is *just* because the elite possess a natural right to rule by virtue of having demonstrated, through their accumulation of wealth and power, their natural superiority. Justice serves them in *conserving* their power to rule. Likewise, even the noble lies serve them, for those lies aid in *conserving* their rule and the stability of social order. The think tanks advocated by Hayek have played a vital role in fabricating and distributing noble lies on behalf of economic elites and the advancement of the neo-liberal agenda to restore their class power over the state and society. We also suggest that those same elites perceive the proper role of schools and universities as functioning toward those same ends.

THE RISE OF THE THINK TANKS

We must acknowledge that institutions such as the National Association of Manufacturers, the Hoover Institution, and the Foundation for Economic Education predated and certainly provided prototypes for Hayek's ideas on how to best restore economic liberalism's dominance over the state and society. We must also point out that the formation of the Mont Pelerin Society and Fisher's Institute for Economic Affairs did not generate an overnight proliferation of think tanks. That proliferation did not begin until the early 1970s, when leaders in business and government confronted the massive populist movements of the 1960s. The title of Samuel L. Huntington's entry in the 1973 report of the Trilateral Commission, "The Threat of Democracy," perhaps best characterizes their perceptions of the high levels of popular activism demonstrated by the Civil Rights Movement, the anti-war movement, the environmental movement, the consumer protection movement, and the feminist movement among others (see Sklar, 1980). Each of these movements symbolized, of course, an expression of the same *political liberalism* that gave rise to Roosevelt's new deal—the idea that government should respond to needs and concerns of the general population, not just the "minority of the opulent" as dictated by economic liberalism.

At the behest of Eugene B. Sydnor, former National Director and, then, Chair of the Education Committee of the U.S. Chamber of Commerce, Lewis F. Powell wrote a secret memorandum (1971) for the Chamber, which many regard as a catalyst for the proliferation of right-wing, neoliberal/neoconservative think tanks since the 1970s. As a corporate attorney for the tobacco industry, Powell had worked diligently to protect tobacco firms from government regulation. We take no surprise, then, in discovering that his memorandum, "The Attack on American Free Enterprise System," reflects the strong influence of Hayek's ideas. The principles of economic liberalism deem any form of regulation as an abridgement of the individual's/corporation's economic "liberty," even when that regulation occurs on behalf of the public interest.

Powell began his memo by expressing alarm over the "dimensions of the attack" against the "American economic system." On the one hand, and reflective of his reputation as political moderate, he acknowledged an established American tradition of dissent against that system, even admitting that some criticisms of the system were "wholesome and constructive so long as the objective was to improve rather than to subvert or destroy." Powell regarded even more severe dissent as safely benign when confined to "a relatively few extremists or even from the minority socialist cadre." By 1971, however, the problem of dissent had grown more malignant. No longer confined to a small number of individuals, "the assault on the enterprise system" had, in Powell's view, become "broadly based and consistently pursued, . . . gaining momentum and converts" (1971).

The breadth of the mounting dissent led Powell to address his concern over the "sources of the attack." The malignancy of the problem for Powell rested not in the mere fact that an increasing number of individuals had begun criticizing the "American economic system." The problem was that it had spread to "perfectly respectable elements of society," including the "college campus, the pulpit, the media, the intellectual and literary journals, the arts and sciences, and . . . politicians." He claimed that this trend was also "increasingly evidenced in the high schools" (ibid).

Powell was particularly concerned over the role of the media and the college campus in providing a platform for anti-corporate dissent, for these institutions play a "predominant role in shaping the thinking, attitudes and emotions of our people" (ibid). He also expressed bewilderment over the paradox that these particular institutions, insofar as they are effectively owned and controlled by corporations, would "tolerate, if not participate in" the destruction of capitalist system. "The campuses," he wrote,

> from which much of the criticism emanates are supported by (i) tax funds generated largely from American business, and (ii) contributions from capital funds controlled or generated by American business. The boards of trustees of our universities overwhelmingly are composed of men and women who are leaders in the system.

> Most of the media, including the national TV systems, are owned and theoretically controlled by corporations which depend upon profits, and the enterprise system to survive. (ibid)

Most revealing of his familiarity with the ideas of Hayek and his associates, in Powell's discussion of the tone of the attack, he cites two of the leading figures within the neoliberal movement. He first cites Arthur Shenfield's lectures at Rockford College to support his argument that "members of the intellectual community are waging ideological warfare against the enterprise system and the values of western society" (ibid). Shenfield worked closely with Hayek as a visiting professor at the University of Chicago, chairing the Mont Pelerin Society's Conference in 1962. He would go on to become the Director of Antony Fisher's International Institute for Economic Research and the President of Hayek's Mont Pelerin Society. Immediately after citing Shenfield, Powell cites Milton Friedman's assertion that

> It (is) crystal clear that the foundations of our free society are under wide-ranging and powerful attack—not by Communist or any other

conspiracy but by misguided individuals parroting one another and un-
wittingly serving ends they would never intentionally promote. (ibid)

To counter these attacks, Powell, in broadest terms, contended that

> A significant first step by individual corporations could well be the desig-
> nation of an executive vice president (ranking with other executive VP's)
> whose responsibility is to counter—on the broadest front—the attack on
> the enterprise system. The public relations department could be one of
> the foundations assigned to this executive, but his responsibilities should
> encompass some of the types of activities referred to subsequently in this
> memorandum. His budget and staff should be adequate to the task. (ibid)

Demonstrating how neoliberal ideology opposes "collectivism" for the
larger society while holding it as central to corporate domination of that
society, Powell went on to add that

> independent and uncoordinated (sic) activity by individual corporations,
> as important as this is, will not be sufficient. Strength lies in organiza-
> tion, in careful long-range planning and implementation, in consistency
> of action over an indefinite period of years, in the scale of financing
> available only through joint effort, and in the political power available
> only through united action and national organizations. (ibid)

Through this joint action, Powell argued, corporations should use think
tanks to monitor schools and universities, the media, the courts, and politics for anti-business ideas, and aggressively target them for the distribution of pro-business and neoliberal ideas.

Distributed only to members of the Chamber of Commerce, the Powell Memo remained secret for two years. A leaked copy sent to colum-
nist Jack Anderson would later provide this neoliberal manifesto with
abundant publicity and widespread interest from various corporations
and business groups. Shortly afterward, former Secretary of the Trea-
sury William Simon openly championed the creation of the necessary
counter-intelligentsia for waging the war of ideas. In a report highlighted
by Media Transparency, the National Committee on Responsive Philanthropy (NCRP) observed that

> waging the war of ideas has required the development of a vast and
> interconnected institutional apparatus. . . . This apparatus was appro-
> priately described by moderate Republican and author John Saloma as
> the "new conservative labyrinth." (1997)

According to NCRP, that labyrinth today has grown so large and sophisticated that it is

increasingly able to influence what gets on—and what stays off—the public policy agenda. From the decision to abandon the federal guarantee of cash assistance to the poor to on-going debates about the federal tax structure to growing discussion of medical savings accounts and the privatization of social security, conservative policy ideas and political rhetoric continue to dominate the nation's political conversation, reflecting what political scientist Walter Dean Burnham has called the "hegemony of market theology." (1997)

That hegemony quickly extended to educational policy as well (see Gabbard, 2000; Siebold, 2004; Saltman, 2001; Kovacs & Boyles, 2005; Johnson & Salle, 2004). Reflecting the same nervousness over the "threat of democracy" posed by the populist activism of the 1960s and early 1970s, Jimmy Carter's President's Commission for an Agenda for the Eighties concluded that America's public schools suffered from a "temporary confusion of purpose" (cited in Gabbard & Ross, 2005, pp. xxvi). "Continued failure by the schools to perform their traditional role adequately," the commission stated, "together with a failure to respond to the emerging needs of the 1980s, may have disastrous consequences for this nation" (ibid, pp. xxvi-xxvii). Only months later, after the neoliberals and neoconservatives helped win election for Ronald Reagan, who entered office promising to eliminate the Department of Education, neoliberal ideologues began a propaganda campaign to prepare the public mind to receive the essential messages of "A Nation At Risk" (1983).

While the "temporary confusion of purpose" that had led many Americans to look to schools as a means of strengthening the foundation of democracy, the National Commission for Excellence in Education's (NCEE) "A Nation At Risk" report represented the first stage in restoring schools to their traditional role of servicing the demands of economic elites. In addition to unfairly blaming schools for the economic recession that would only worsen under neoliberal economic policies, "A Nation At Risk" also blamed liberal reforms of the 1960s and 1970s for school failure. Shortly after stepping down from his position as Executive Director of the NCEE, Milton Goldberg went to work for the National Association of Manufacturers (NAM), one of the earliest propaganda machines for the corporate elite, and now operates as a member of the Business Roundtable (see Gabbard, 2003; Haas, 2008; Kovacs, 2008b). Together, NAM and the Business Roundtable have been two of the most powerful proponents of privatizing Social Security and other planks of the neoliberal agenda.

For the staunchest of neoliberals, however, the propaganda campaign initiated by "A Nation At Risk" to condition the public into viewing education solely as a vehicle for increasing their economic-use value was not enough. As suggested by the ominous title of the neoliberal education magazine, *EducationNext,* operated out of the Hoover Institute, also home to the notorious neoconservative David Horowitz commissioned to lead the assault against liberalism in higher education (see Johnson, 2003), they seek nothing short of school privatization. Through the "high stakes testing" and "accountability" imposed under No Child Left Behind, neoliberals have adopted an effective strategy for eliminating the democratic threat posed by liberal education policies. Anthony Carnevale, a Senior fellow at the National Center on Education and the Economy, sheds much on this strategy now being enforced when he stated: "You tie their teaching methods to standards so that in a very aggressive way they learn to teach to the results of those tests, like a soldier. . . . The voluntary military," he added, "didn't always get the best of human capital. But what you did was make the training so rigorous it didn't matter" (cited in Hartocollis, 2005). Secretary of Education Margaret Spellings could not agree more: "Good education has always been about good testing. . . . Teaching to the test is fine and dandy, keep on." (Lucadamo, 2006) And if schools and teachers don't teach to the test well enough, if their students don't meet standards, they expose their schools to the risk of being placed under the management of a private corporation

THE ASSAULT ON EDUCATORS

A survey of 500 school districts found that the average teacher salary had declined by nearly 2% over the past ten years. ("Schools Chiefs Lead The Way in Pay Trends," Gewertz, 2004.). Nevertheless, teachers comprise approximately 4% of the entire work force in the United States; "there are, for example, more than twice as many K-12 teachers as registered nurses and five times as many teachers as either lawyers or professors (U.S. Bureau of the Census, 1998)" (Ingersoll, 2001). The profession has a very high attrition rate, but that seems to be growing. For example, the National Commission on Teaching and America's Future (NCTAF) found "a national attrition rate of about 75% from the beginning of an undergraduate teacher education program through about the 3rd year of teaching" (Zeichner, 2003).

NCTAF estimates that 40% to 60% of those who earn teaching credentials in the state do not seek employment as teachers. Working conditions and salaries continue to deteriorate as both teachers and the unions to which they belong have been under tremendous pressure as a result of a concerted public political pedagogy directed against them. Proponents and the financial backers of privatization, euphemistically called *school choice*, view teachers and teacher unions as major impediments to privatization. Indeed, one of the advantages that proponents of *school choice* see is that they will seriously undermine the collective power of teachers, and teacher unions. Media is inundated with pseudo-"research" that is anti-school, to the extent that privatizers (both corporate, neoconservative, and the religious right) control the text and context of issues. Subsequently, they define the terms of any national dialogue surrounding education, and increasingly create one sided debates. For example,

- Teachers' unions are positioned as an impediment to progress. In 2000, Republican Oklahoma Governor, Frank Keating was asked what was "the best way to deal with the (teachers') union." Keating smiled and said, "Homicide." Keating (aligned with the Edison Corporation) pushed for merit pay (without teacher tenure), and spearheaded charter and voucher legislation in his state. During the same year in New York City, "America's mayor" Rudolph Giuliani said "The whole [school] system should be blown up . . . I feel like a prophet today" (Blood, 1999). Not to be outdone, former Senator Robert Dole (who was the Republican Nominee for President in 1996) lashed out at teachers' unions in his acceptance speech at the Republican convention, blaming them for the failure of American education: "If education were a war, you [the teacher unions] would be losing it. If it were a business, you would be driving it into bankruptcy. If it were a patient, it would be dying." Unions were right up there, in Dole's speech, with notorious public enemies like Saddam Hussein, "Libyan terrorists," "voracious criminals," and the United State's old adversary, the Soviet Union. It is not surprising that President Bush proclaimed with typical hyperbole "We must," he said, "end the teachers' unions' stranglehold if we are going to have successful schools."

And,

- Privateers promote and publicize non-unionized teachers as being far more capable (working for merit) than "government teachers" or "unionized teachers." Newspaper, and magazine articles abound surrounding teachers who challenge their respective unions with such stories as "younger teachers are more entrepreneurial, and they see the unions as impediments to their individually negotiating with a school . . . Individual teachers may support things like school choice, merit pay, the changing of the single-salary scale. Unions always oppose those," since they protect incompetent teachers. And, hiring more teachers might be good for teachers unions, which would love to see their membership rolls expand at taxpayer expense. Further, the current administration and the right wing think-tanks does not see the need for certified teachers.

Add to that the increased focus on imposed high stakes testing and performance criteria that are based on rote measures (in many classrooms teachers are forced to teach from scripted curriculums) while the National Board for Professional Teaching Standards (NBPTS) is defunded in favor of the newly invented, pro-voucher, misnamed American Board for Certification of Teacher Excellence (ABCTE). ABCTE emerged out of Education Leaders Council (ELC) and the National Council on Teacher Quality (NCTQ), both funded by the Wal-Mart family and Milwaukee's Bradley Foundation.

The contempt for public school educators is demoralizing for teachers who have been forced to endure all sorts of measures (including the reinstatement of dress codes as a measure of professionalization) but no measure has been more reprehensible than that which took place in the state of Florida when Governor Jeb Bush voted to spend $174 billion to buy debt-ridden Edison Schools, Inc., investing public school teachers' pensions in a company trying to destroy public schools (Hurst, 2003).

In conclusion, this brief survey of various elements of the assault against education and democracy leads us to question whether or not progressive citizens should use the term *liberalization* to describe this pattern. Perhaps *fascification* comes closer to the mark. On the other hand, even fascism may not be the most appropriate term. After all, Mussolini himself claimed that "Fascism should more appropriately be called Corporatism because it is a merger of State and corporate power."

In *Knowledge and Propaganda,* Joseph Goebbels wrote that

> politics is governed not by moral principles, but by power. If a movement conquers the state, it has the right to form the state. You can see how these three elements combine ideals and personalities. The idea leads to a worldview, the worldview to the state, the individual becomes a party, the party becomes the nation. (Goebbels, 1928)

The assault on public institutions currently undertaken by extremist ring-wing groups within the traditional business elite and their allies in fundamentalist Christianity represents nothing short of an effort to conquer the state. Eerily similar to Goebbels' position on politics and the aims of power, Randall Terry, the fundamentalist leader of Operation Rescue (an anti-abortion group suspected of being involved in the bombing of several abortion clinics in the United States) described his organization's agenda in the following terms:

> I want you to just let a wave of intolerance wash over you . . . I want you to let a wave of hatred wash over you. Yes, hate is good . . . Our goal is a Christian nation. We have a biblical duty, we are called by God, to conquer this country. We don't want equal time. We don't want pluralism. (Terry, 1993)

Once public schools fall into corporate hands under the neoliberal/neoconservative privatization agenda, this alliance between corporate oligarchs and Christian theocrats will expand their means for imposing such a unified worldview on the population as part of the larger campaign against democracy.

Recent pressures from inside the labyrinth led the National Council for the Accreditation of Teacher Education (NCATE) to remove any mention of "social justice" from its standards (see Powers, 2006). Those pressures came from the National Association of Scholars, which is home to some of the major figures in the neoliberal/neoconservative movement, including Jeanne Kirkpatrick, Irving Kristol, and Chester Finn. Those pressures also came from the Foundation for Individual Rights in Education, "a major proponent of the 'intellectual diversity' movement which aims to dismantle the so-called liberal bias in higher academia." David Horowitz, of course, serves as the leading figure of this movement from his Center for the Study of Popular Culture at the Hoover Institution. He regularly appears on Fox News, which functions as the primary propaganda arm for the neoliberal/neoconservative agenda.

The pressure on NCATE to drop its commitment to social justice also stemmed from the American Council of Trustees and Alumni (ACTA), an institution founded by Lynne V. Cheney, wife of Vice-President Dick Cheney. In November of 2001, ACTA issued a report titled *Defending Civilization: How Our Universities Are Failing America and What Can Be Done About It* that launched what Joel Beinin describes as "The first post-September 11 expression of the link between the neo-conservative political agenda and the attack on critical thinking about the Middle East" (Beinin, n.d.) In Beinin's words,

> As the title suggests, ACTA maintained that criticism of the Bush administration's war on Afghanistan on campuses across the country was tantamount to negligence in "defending civilization" and proof that "our universities are failing America." ACTA alleged that American universities were brought to this sorry state by inadequate teaching of western culture and American history. Consequently, students and faculty did not understand what was at stake in the fight against terrorism and were undermining the defense of civilization by asking too many questions.

> The original version of "Defending civilization" named and quoted comments by 117 university faculty members, staff and students in reaction to the September 11 attacks. ACTA's ire was aroused by my statement that, "If Usama bin Laden is confirmed to be behind the attacks, the United States should bring him before an international tribunal on charges of crimes against humanity." Other remarks in the report's list of unacceptable speech included "Ignorance breeds hate" and "[T]here needs to be an understanding of why this kind of suicidal violence could be undertaken against our country." (ibid)

CONCLUSION

Our point in this chapter has been to demonstrate how the attack on public schools represents a small part of a much larger attack on the public and its role in a liberal, constitutional democracy. David Harvey (2005) has characterized neoliberalism as a project aimed at the restoration of class power (See Ross and Gibson, 2007; also Cavanagh and Collins, 2008). When we take the neoconservative elements of that project into account, we might more accurately describe it as being aimed at the restoration of total class domination.

We would hope that teachers and teacher educators everywhere can now understand that the neoliberal/neoconservative agenda places more than the future of public schools at risk (See for example Hill, 2006; Hill and Kumar, 2007; Klein, 2008). As Michael Parenti (1995) has written,

> When the power of capital is increasingly untrammeled, all of us are put at risk: the environment, the sacred forests, the beautiful and mysterious creatures of the sea, the ordinary people who, with their strength and brains and inventiveness create community and give to life so much that's worthy of our respect. The real burden to society is not the poor, but the corporate rich. We simply can no longer afford them.

> Conservatives complain whenever we fight back; they say we're engaging in "class war." Well, I believe it is class war, but I also have another name for it. When people unite against the abuses of wealth and privilege, when they activate themselves and militantly attack the hypocrisies and lies of the powers that be, when they fight back and become the active agents of their own destiny, when they withdraw their empowering responses and refuse to toe that line, I call that "democracy." (1995, p. 6)

We agree with Parenti that, in light of all we see happening around us and to us, we must all

> get a lot angrier and a lot more determined. They want everything, and everything is at stake. Many people are getting angry; our job is to see that they direct their anger at the real perpetrators of their misery, and not against the very people who want to make common cause with them. (ibid)

In order to do this, those of us in teacher education and in education more widely, need to "call them out" and reveal the anti-school movement for what it is. The question is: Will we find the courage to do so?

REFERENCES

Allegretto, S. A., Corcoran, S. P. & Mishel, L. (2004). *How does teacher pay compare? Methodological challenges and answers.* Retrieved October 15, 2004, from http://www.epinet.org/content.cfm/books_teacher_pay

American Federation of Teachers. (2004). *Charter school achievement on the 2003 National Assessment of Educational Progress.* Retrieved 10 October 2004, from www.aft.org/pubs-reports/downloads/ teachers/NAEPCharterSchoolReport.pdf.

Archer, J. (1973). *The plot to seize the White House.* Retrieved July 6, 2007, from http://www.clubhousewreckards.com/plot/plottoseizethewhitehouse.htm.

Beinin, J. (n.d.). *The new American McCarthyism: Policing thought about the Middle East.* Retrieved July 6, 2007, from http://www.stanford.edu/~beinin/New_McCarthyism.html

Berliner, D. C., & Biddle, B. J. (1995). *The manufactured crisis: Myths, fraud, and the attack on America's public schools.* Reading, MA: Addison-Wesley.

Bifulco, R., & Ladd, H. (2004). *The impacts of charter schools on student achievement: Evidence from North Carolina.* Retrieved October 15, 2004, from www.pubpol.duke.edu/people/faculty/ladd/SAN04–01.pdf.

Blood, M. (1999). Rudy unviels 35B budget plans school vouchers, tax cuts, and more cops, *New York Daily News,* April 23, 1999. Retrieved March 16, 2007 from http://www.nydailynews.com/archives/news/1999/04/23/1999–04–23_rudy_unviels_35b_budget_pla.html

Carey, A. (1996). *Taking the risk out of democracy: Corporate propaganda versus freedom and liberty.* Urbana-Champaign: University of Illinois Press.

Cavanagh, J. and C. Collins. (2008). The Rich and the Rest of Us. *The Nation,* 11 June. Retrieved June 20, 2008 from http://www.thenation.com/doc/20080630/cavanagh_collins

Chomsky, N. (1989). *Necessary illusions: Thought control in democratic societies.* Boston: South End Press. Retrieved July 6, 2007, from http://www.zmag.org/chomsky/ni/ni-c01-s05.html.

Chomsky, N. (1991). *Deterring democracy.* Boston: Hill and Wang.

Chomsky, N. (1999). An Interview with David Barsamian *The Progressive.* Retrieved October 15, 2004, from http://www.progressive.org/chom999.htm

Chomsky, N. (2004). *Noam Chomsky speaks out: Education and power.* Retrieved October 15, 2004, from http://www.indymedia.ie/newswire.php?story_id=66441&condense_comments=false#comment88500

Drury, S. (1999/2005). *The political ideas of Leo Strauss* (updated ed.). New York: Palgrave Macmillan.

Drury, S. (1999). *Leo Strauss and the American right.* New York: St. Martin's Press.

Gabbard, D. (2000). *Knowledge and power in the global economy: Politics and rhetoric of school reform.* Mahwah, NJ: Lawrence Erlbaum Associates.

Gabbard, D. (2003, September/October). A nation At risk—RELOADED, part I. *The Journal of Critical Educational Policy Studies,* (1)2. Retrieved April 20, 2008, from http://www.jceps.com/index.php?pageID=article&articleID=15.

Gabbard, D., & Ross, W. (2005). *Defending public schools: Education under the security state.* Westport, CT: Greenwood/Praeger.

Gewertz, C. (2004, June). Schools chiefs lead the way in pay trends. *Education Week,* 23(41), 1, 16–21.

Goebbels, J. (1928). *Knowledge and propaganda.* Retrieved October 27, 2004, from The German Propaganda Archive Web site: http://www.calvin.edu/academic/cas/gpa/goeb54.htm

Goodman, J. (2005, December 20). What is a think tank? Retrieved July 6, 2007, from http://www.ncpa.org/pub/special/20051220-sp.html

General Accounting Office. (2003, October). Public schools: Comparison of achievement results for students attending privately managed and traditional Schools in six cities (GAO-04–62), *Report to the Chairman, Committee on Education and the Workforce, House of Representatives.* Retrieved April 20, 2008, from http://www.gao.gov/new.items/d0462.pdf.

Haas, E. (2008). Propaganda. in D. Gabbard (Ed.), *Knowledge and power in the global economy: The effects of school reform in a neoliberal/neoconservative age.* (pp. 141–150). Mahwah, NJ: Lawrence Erlbaum Associates.

Hanauer, A. (2002). *Cleveland school vouchers: Where the students go.* Retrieved October 15, 2004, from http://www.policymattersohio.org/voucherintro.html.

Hartocollis, A. (2005, July 31). Who needs education schools? *New York Times.* Retrieved July 6, 2007, from http://www.nytimes.com/2005/07/31/education/edlife/hartocollis31.html?ei=5090&en=1dd897f32b3d8f4b&ex=1280462400&partner=rssuserland&emc=rss&pagewanted=all.

Harvey, D. (2005). *A brief history of neoliberalism.* Oxford: Oxford University Press.

Hayek, F. (1944). *The road to serfdom.* Chicago: University of Chicago Press.

Hill, D. (2006). Education Services Liberalization. In E. Rosskam (Ed.) *Winners or Losers? Liberalizing public services,* ed. E. Rosskam, 3–54. Geneva: ILO.

Hill, D., and R. Kumar. eds. (2009). *Global neoliberalism and education and its consequences.* New York: Routledge.

Hursh, D. (2008a). *High-stakes testing and the decline of teaching and learning: The real crisis in education.* Lanham, MD: Rowman and Littlefield.

Hursh, D. (2008b). Neoliberalism. In D. Gabbard (Ed.), *Knowledge and power in the global economy: The effects of school reform in a neoliberal/neoconservative age* (pp. 35–41). Mahwah, NJ: Lawrence Erlbaum Associates.

Hurst, M. (2003, October 8). Teachers riled by Edison deal. *Education Week,* 1.

Ingersoll, R. M. (2001, Autumn). Teacher turnover and teacher shortages: An organizational analysis. *American Educational Research Journal,* 38(3) 499–534.

Johnson, D. C., & Salle, L. M. (2004). *Responding to the attack on public education and teacher unions.* Retrieved July 6, 2007, from www.commonwealinstitute.org

Johnson, D. (2003,October 2). Who's behind the attack on liberal professors? *History News Network.* Retrievd April 20, 2008, from http://hnn.us/articles/1244.html

King, J. (2004). Paige Calls NEA "Terrorist Organization." *CNN News.* Retrieved October 15, 2004, from http://www.cnn.com/2004/EDUCATION/02/23/paige.terrorist.nea/

Klein, N. (2008). *The Shock Doctrine: The rise of disaster capitalism.* New York: Picador.

Kohn, A. (2004, April). Test today, privatize tomorrow: Using accountability to "reform" public schools to death, *Phi Delta Kappa,* 85(8), 568–577. Retrieved April 20, 2008, from http://www.alfi ekohn.org/teaching/testtoday.htm

Kovacs, P. (2008a). Think tanks, foundations, and institutes. In D. Gabbard (Ed.), *Knowledge and power in the global economy: The effects of school reform in a neoliberal/neoconservative age.* (pp. 229–238). Mahwah, NJ: Lawrence Erlbaum Associates.

Kovacs, P. (2008b). Think tanks, foundations, and institutes. In D. Gabbard (Ed.), *Knowledge and power in the global economy: The effects of school reform in a neoliberal/neoconservative age.* (pp. 239–250). Mahwah, NJ: Lawrence Erlbaum Associates.

Kovacs, P., & Boyles, D. (2005, May). Institutes, foundations, & think tanks: Neoconservative influence on public schools. *Public Resistance 1, no. 1.* Retrieved July 6, 2007, from http://www.publicresistance.org/journals/1.1–3Institutes.htm.

Ladd, H. (2002). *School vouchers don't make the grade.* Retrieved October 15, 2004, from http://www.epinet.org/content.cfm/webfeatures_viewpoints_hl_testimony_20030509

Lucadamo, K. (2006, March 15). Ed sec'y sez test focus "fine, dandy." *New York Daily News.* Retrieved July 6, 2007, from http://www.nydailynews.com/news/local/story/399731p-338704c.html

Madison, J. (1787/2001, June 19). quoted by Sean Gonsolves, "The Crisis in Democracy." *Cape Cod Times*. Retrieved July 6, 2007, from http://www.commondreams.org/views01/0619–01.htm.

Mercer, I. (2002). *Eliminate Government-Funded Education!* Retrieved October 15, 2004, from www.wnd.com.

Metcalf, K. (2003a). *Evaluation of the Cleveland scholarship and tutoring program:Exploring families' educational choices 1998–2002, (Technical Report)*. Retrieved April 20, 2008, from the University of Indiana's Center for Evaluation and Educational Policy Web site: http://www.indiana.edu/~ceep/projects/project.php4?id=37

Metcalf, K. (2003b). *Evaluation of the Cleveland scholarship and tutoring program 1998–2002, executive summary*. Retrieved April 20, 2008, from the University of Indiana's Center for Evaluation and Educational Policy Web site: http://www.indiana.edu/~ceep/projects/project.php4?id=37

Molnar, A. (2005). *School commercialism: from Democratic ideal to market commodity*. New York: Routledge.

Molnar, A., Wilson, G., & Allen, D. (2004*). Profiles of for-profit education management companies, sixth annual report, 2003–2004*. Retrieved October 15, 2004, from Arizona State University's Education Policy Studies Laboratory Web site: http://www.asu.edu/educ/epsl/CERU/Documents/EPSL-0402-101-CERU.pdf or at: ttp://www.asu.edu/educ/epsl/EPRU/documents/EPSL-0402-101-CERU.pdf

Monaghan, F. (1935). *John Jay: Defender of liberty*. New York: Bobbs-Merrill.

Naes, R. G. (2003). *Funding a movement: U.S. department of education pours millions into groups advocating school vouchers and education privatization*. Retrieved October 15, 2004, from http://www.pfaw.org/pfaw/general/default.aspx?oid=12856

National Commission on Excellence in Education. (1983). *A nation at risk*. Retrieved April 20, 2008, from www.ed.gov/pubs/NatAtRisk/index.html

National Committee on Responsive Philanthropy. (1997). *Moving a public policy agenda: The strategic philanthropy of conservative foundations*. Retrieved July 6, 2007, from http://www.mediatransparency.org/conservativephilanthropy.php

Nelson, F. H., Rosenberg, Muir, E., Drown, R. (2003). *Paying for the vision: Charter school revenue and expenditures*. Retrieved October 15, 2004, from http://www.aft.org/topics/charters/

Nelson, F. H., Rosenberg, B., & Van Meter, N. (2004). *Charter school achievement on the 2003 national assessment of educational progress*. Retrieved October 15, 2004, from www.aft.org/pubs-reports/downloads/ teachers/NAEPCharterSchoolReport.pdf

Ohio Federation of Teachers, Distribution of Schools Across ODE Ratings Categories. (n.d). Retrieved October 15, 2004, from www.oft-aft.org/issues/CPE_charter_moratorium_campaign/Charter_vs_public_ratings_corrected_9.8.04.pdf

Olssen, M., Codd, J., & O'Neill, A. M. (2004). *Education policy: Globalization, citizenship and democracy*. Thousand Oaks, CA: Sage Press.

Parenti, M. (1995). *Fascism: The false revolution*. Retrieved April 20, 2008, from http://64.233.161.104/search?q=cache:7NzasHYWcp8J:www.suddenlysenior.com/PDf_fi les/Fascisim%2520in%2520US.pdf+parenti+%22fascism

People for the American Way. (2003). *Voucher veneer: The deeper agenda to privatize public education*. Retrieved October 15, 2004, from http://www.pfaw.org/pfaw/general/default.aspx?oid=11371

Powell, L. F. (1971). *The Powell memorandum*. Retrieved July 6, 2007 from http://reclaimdemocracy.org/corporate_accountability/powell_memo_lewis.html

Powers, A. (2006). A spirited disposition debate. *Inside Higher Ed*. Retrieved June 6, 2006, from http://www.insidehighered.com/news/2006/06/06/disposition

Ross, E.W. & Gibson, R. (2007). *Neoliberalism and education reform*. Cresskill, NJ: Hampton Press.

Rosskam, E. (ed.) (2006) *Winners or Losers? Liberalizing public services.* Geneva: ILO.

Saltman, K. (2001). *Collateral damage: Corporatizing Public schools, a threat to democracy.* Lanham, MD: Rowman and Littlefield.

Saltman, K., & Goodman, R.T. (2002). *Strange love: Or how we learned to stop worrying and love the market.* Lanham, MD: Rowman and Littlefield.

Saltman, K., & Gabbard, D. (2003). *Education as enforcement: The militarization and corporatization of schools.* NY: Routledge.

Saltman, K. (2007). *Capitalizing on disaster: Taking and breaking public schools.* Boulder, CO: Paradigm Press.

Saltman, K. (2008). Privatization. in D. Gabard (Ed.), *Knowledge and power in the global economy: The effects of school reform in a neoliberal/neoconservative age.* (pp. 269–282). Mahwah, NJ: Lawrence Erlbaum Associates.

Santa Clara County v. Southern Pacific Railroad. (1886). Supreme Court of the United States. 118 U.S. 394

Schemo, D. J. (2004). Education study finds weakened charter results Public school students often do better–data bode ill for Bush's philosophy. *The San Francisco Chronicle (SFGate),* August 17. Retrieved October 15, 2004, from at http://www.sfgate.com/cgi-bin/article.cgi?fi le=/c/a/2004/08/17/MNGCT89CA51.DTL

Schiller, Z. (2001). *Cleveland school vouchers: Where the students come from.* Retrieved October 15, 2004, from http://www.policymattersohio.org/voucher-intro.html.

Siebold, T. (2004). *A brief framework for understanding the anti-public school movement.* Retrieved October 15, 2004, from http://www.teacherprofessional-ism.com/UnderstandingtheOpposition.html.

Sklar, H. (1980). Trilateralism: *The trilateral commission and elite planning for world management.* Boston: South End Press.

Smith, A. (1776/1952). *An inquiry into the nature and causes of the wealth of nations.* Chicago: Encyclopedia Britannica.

Spring, J. (2008). Choice. in D. Gabbard (Ed.), *Knowledge and power in the global economy: The effects of school reform in a neoliberal/neoconservative age.* (pp. 251–258). Mahwah, NJ: Lawrence Erlbaum Associates.

Terry, R. (1993, August 16). *The News-Sentinel, Fort Wayne, Ind.* Retrieved April 20, 2008, from holysmoke.org at http://www.holysmoke.org/hs00/hatred.htm

Zeichner, K. (2003, April). The Adequacies and inadequacies of three current strategies to recruit, prepare, and retain the best teachers for all students. *Teachers College Record, 105*(3) 490–519.

Zelman v. Simmons-Harris. (2002). Supreme Court of the United States. 536 U.S. 639

Zinn, H. (1999, April). Big business for whom? *The Progressive Magazine.* Retrieved July 6, 2007, from http://www.thirdworldtraveler.com/Zinn/BigGovernWhom_Zinn.html

3 Neoliberalism and Education in Canada

Adam Davidson-Harden, Larry Kuehn, Daniel Schugurensky, and Harry Smaller

INTRODUCTION

Canada makes for an interesting case study in appreciating the impact of recent trends in the restructuring of education in the world's wealthier countries. Neoliberal education policy imperatives, while impacting severely on less economically powerful and developed parts of the hemisphere, have already substantially negatively impacted Canada's developed social programs and provincial education systems. Trends in the 1990s in particular, toward aggregate social funding cutbacks, have coincided with what may be described as a "creeping privatization" in many sectors of public services including, notably, health and education. These shifts show a disturbing trend in terms of the goal of public education in engendering equity through public education. This neoliberal "Washington consensus" in policy toward trade liberalization and social funding cutbacks continues to affect social systems and equity in Canada and, more broadly, in the Pan-American setting, albeit unequally, as is reflected in the asymmetries in development and relations between countries in this context along "north and south" lines. Seen in wide perspective, neoliberal policy trends in education—buttressed by interested private "edupreneurs" as well as by aggressive international trade regimes—have the potential to further the dominance of the "Washington Consensus" through increased reliance on marketizing and privatizing trends in educational restructuring in Canada, resulting in the inevitable danger of further social polarization and inequity. The critical perspective adopted here reflects an effort to critically analyze these policy trends, taking into account as well the impact of these trends on teachers in Canada.

As compared with, England and the United States, for example, the onset of neoliberal social policy in Canada may have come slightly later, but with no less force. Under the tenure of the Liberal governments in the 1990s, overall funding for social programs was reduced substantially (CMEC, 2001), with approximately a $5 billion cut from federal transfers to the provinces (who have jurisdiction over educational matters) over the years 1995 through 1998 alone. Education indicators for the country as a whole show—particularly during the nineties—an overall decrease in basic secondary and postsecondary education funding per capita (Statistics Canada and CMEC 1999: 20ff; see Appendix 1 for a related table). The study from which these data have been cited look to develop a set of pan-Canadian education indicators whereby researchers may be able to track trends in changes to Canada's education systems. As stated reasons for appreciating these per capita decreases in education funding across Canada, the study mentions changing fiscal policy, including a focus on federal and provincial government deficit reductions (Statistics Canada and CMEC 1999). These types of social spending cuts, roundly criticized and challenged in various quarters as excuses for the "trimming of the welfare state" as per neoliberal social policy aims, have indeed figured prominently in the dynamics of reduced funding for both schools and universities in Canada in recent years. For example, federal transfer grants to the provinces for both health and education were drastically cut back during an initiative to change the format of federal transfer funds to the provinces for these sectors during the 1990s. As separate transfer grants were merged into one source of "block funding" (the "Canada Health and Social Transfer" or CHST) in 1995, aggregate funding for the transfer was cut in constant 1998 dollars relative to the amounts of the previous two grants in 1994–1995, amounting to the cut of approximately $5 billion alluded to earlier (Mendelson 1998). This policy move to block funding had been advocated for Canada by teams from the International Monetary Fund (IMF; Halifax Initiative, 2003), notorious internationally for the imposition of conditions on loans, debt relief, and aid in the world's poorest countries through the rubrics of "structural adjustment" and now "poverty reduction" programs that have enforced the curtailing of social spending in whichever states they are operating (cf. Chossudovsky, 1998). In both Canada and the international context, as will be further argued later, this kind of systematic abdication of central government responsibility for adequate funding of education has resulted in the *de facto* privatization and "neoliberalization" of education at the ground level through the devolution of more financial risks and responsibilities to students, parents, and teachers.

Issues in Basic and Secondary-Level Education

Bearing this context of decreasing funding in mind, neoliberal dynamics in Canadian basic and secondary-level education reflect an interesting trend toward government funding decreases on the one hand, and legislative encouragement and facilitation of private provision and participation in education systems on the other, with significant movement coming from certain provinces. All provincial education ministries in Canada are bound by commitments articulated through the country's constitution, including commitments made in the Charter of Rights and Freedoms. These make specific reference to minority language educational rights in French and English, as well as stipulating education to be provided through public funding. In addition, currently three provinces at the basic and secondary education levels fund both "secular" public school boards and "separate" Roman Catholic school boards, as per a requirement in section 93 of the Constitution Act, 1982, to respect and keep in place minority educational systems already in place at the time of confederation (these three are Ontario, Alberta, and Saskatchewan). Two provinces (Quebec and Newfoundland) successfully reversed this obligation to publicly fund Catholic education by securing a constitutional amendment of their "terms of union" in the confederation that Canada represents (Quebec accomplished this in 1997, Newfoundland in 1998). Currently, five provinces in Canada maintain arrangements whereby different forms of private schooling may be approved to receive public funding; in 2003, Ontario's current government quashed an earlier legislative attempt to provide funding via a substantial tax credit to families with children in private schools.

In terms of the general state of public education funding (meaning public education systems supported by provincial expenditure and tax revenues), it is interesting to note that some of the most noted shortfalls in funding have been reported from provinces with the most "busy" recent history of developing tax credit programs for various forms of private education in recent times. These provinces include Ontario (whose tax credit scheme was cancelled, as mentioned earlier), Alberta, and British Columbia. Ontario and Alberta make interesting examples of these trends. Mackenzie (2002) has shown how, accounting for changes in enrolment and inflation factors, a shift in provincial education funding mechanisms in Ontario in 1997 led to the cutting of nearly $1.2 billion from Ontario's basic- and secondary-level education systems. This shift represents perhaps the most dramatic example of cuts to education across Canada during the 1990s. At the same time, the same provincial government in Ontario introduced a legislative framework in 2001 enabling the aforementioned private schools tax credit scheme that has now been cancelled. Ontario had earlier been embarrassed by a United Nations Human Rights Commission ruling that—as a result of a complaint lodged by an Ontario citizen—deemed the province's system of denominational school funding inequitable and discriminatory in 1996 (Johnston & Swift, 2000).

This shift has led to the emasculation of social programs across Canada's provinces as these jurisdictions deal with—and in some cases pass on to citizens through cutbacks—aggregate transfer cuts from the federal government (Fisher & Rubenson, 2000, p. 81). These dynamics have progressed at the same time as privatization initiatives have been underway across Canada, particularly with respect to postsecondary education. This trend is evidenced by movements like Ontario's legislation to approve the development of new private universities (Post-secondary Education Student Opportunity Act, 2002), as well as through the increasing links and pressure for linkages between industry and academia in a context of developing "academic capitalism" and "private public partnerships"[1] across the hemisphere. These trends in turn have been researched by Canadian and other scholars in an attempt to trace the increasing behavior of university sectors across the hemisphere along more market and corporate lines (Torres & Schugurensky, 2002; Slaughter & Leslie, 1997; Newson, 1998; Fisher & Atkinson-Grosjean, 2002).

The province of Alberta provides an analogous example. Also in a context of decreased funding (particularly during the 1990s) and under the Conservative Klein government (Neu, 2000; Peters, 2000), Alberta has led the way so far in substantive legislatively driven change providing for public funding of independent "charter" schools, which, in effect, have been placed in a position of competition with public schools (Flower, 2004). Kachur (2000) has argued that this type of development reflects neoliberal thinking inasmuch as "alternatives" to public education are touted while public systems themselves are left increasingly under funded. This type of development concomitantly reflects a shift toward the figuring of the parent and student as education "consumers" who ought to be offered a choice between public and private avenues for education, with both receiving public support. Because charter schools are not prevented from charging tuition, whereas public education systems are premised on the idea of universal and free access, this development reflects a move toward social stratification in access to education, as it does in other countries. Statistics Canada has documented the trend of declining numbers of students from wealthy families (with an income of over $100,000) attending public schools, with a simultaneous rise in attendance by such students in private institutions at the K through 12 level (Statistics Canada, 2001; follow the weblink in our list of references for the full statistical profile of this trend done by StatsCan). Total enrolment in private schools at the basic and secondary levels have increased since the 1970s, with 6% current enrolment in private schools as a percentage of total basic- and secondary-level enrolment (Canadian Council for Social Development, 1999). The process of funding private education with public dollars has been questioned along similar lines for contributing to the erosion of public education in terms of goals of accessibility and social cohesion (Paquette, 2002). Data from the 1990s show that concurrently, average family income in Canada has declined, and poverty levels—even particularly child poverty levels—have increased (CCSD, 1999). The aforementioned private schools tax credit debate and initiative in Ontario is another example of the introduction of a "marketized" vision of education provision and consumption in the province with similar attendant controversies and implications. Complementing this sketch of the growing role of private education in Canada currently, many elite and other types of basic- and secondary-level private schools exist in the country today. For instance, Ontario's Conference of Independent Schools (Conference of Independent Schools of Ontario,

2004) represents several of the oldest elite schools in the country, whose high tuition charges reflect the focus on limitations on access based on social class.

Two additional sets of interrelated neoliberal dynamics that also deserve mention additionally impact on matters of social equity as well as "marketization" of the public sphere in the context of basic- and secondary-level education across Canada. These also relate to decreases in public education funding. First, private fundraising in different arenas at the local level has evolved—particularly since the mid 1990s—to the extent that existing inequalities of resources between school districts populated by different families with different socioeconomic status have been further exacerbated. Pressure on governments to rely less on property tax revenues and a move to centralize and cut back provincial funding has built alongside disturbing trends in "private" funding for public education at the operational level. Secondly, the development of "public–private partnerships" (P3s) as a current modality of neoliberal social policy (discussed below) has also been shown to have an impact—albeit problematic and challenged—on public school systems and public/government involvement in education. Pressure on governments to rely less on property tax revenues and a move to centralize and cut back provincial funding has built alongside disturbing trends in "private" funding for public education at the operational level.

Weiner (2003) of the Canadian Teachers' Federation (CTF) cites some disturbing examples of these trends, which represent a growing reliance of communities and teachers on commercial interests for funding of basic educational supplies in the basic- and secondary-level systems. As one example, Weiner cites a study of teachers that found their average personal expenditure toward purchasing needed for classroom materials was $593 per year (Weiner, 2003). In another example concerning parent-led fundraising cited in the same presentation, it was found that fundraising activities centered in the Vancouver (British Columbia) Parent Advisory Council generated from $500 to $35,000, depending on the location of the school and the socioeconomic composition of its community and families. Weiner also mentions the Toronto-based public education advocacy group, People for Education's report that approximately $20 million is raised annually in schools through vending machine sales and corporate donations (Weiner, 2003). These types of dynamics attest to the fact that in many jurisdictions in many provinces, parts of public schooling are already "privatized" per se. Through the contracting out of ancillary services—from cleaning to transportation and food—a trend emerges that blurs the divide between public and private, and further introduces the private sector into more expansive roles in schools and education systems. These trends, coupled with the patterns of increased reliance on private fundraising by teachers, parents, and communities, have increased in a context where essential school services such as libraries, counseling and social work have been cut back in the context of chronic underfunding.

Finally, a further example of fundraising in schools is the growing phenomenon of school boards attempting to attract international students to pay for Canadian secondary school programs to be taken here in Canada or abroad. An OECD study on the issue reported that, worldwide, this "industry" generated $30 billion annually, as well as millions in Canada alone (Weiner, 2003). Because programs for school boards in Canada charge tuition (sometimes over $10,000 per year), such a service is increasingly a lucrative one for participating boards and schools. A Canadian association—the "Canadian Education Centre Networks"[2] (CECN)—charges fees to school boards in turn for the boards' representation in the CECN's marketing efforts at various international fairs (cf. Grieshaber-Otto & Sanger, 2002). These types of dynamics could have serious ongoing consequences for Canadian education and privatization by their relation to international trade regimes involving Canada. This matter will be discussed in a distinct section below.

In British Columbia, revenue raised by fees charged to international students brought more than $75 million to school districts in the 2003–2004 school year. The ability of school districts to supplement government grants with this and other sources of revenue is very unequal. The school district with the highest socioeconomic status in the province earned $1,131 per student to add to grants from government. Many districts in rural areas and the far north of the province earned less than $100 per student. Existing inequities between communities are being increased by depending on commercial activity to supplement public funding (Lowry, 2004). This phenomenon of attracting foreign private tuition dollars into Canadian public school boards raises significant dilemmas for Canadian education, resulting in a de facto "two-tiered" education system dichotomized between tuition-based and free universal education models. In addition, the ramifications for the public system as a whole are implicated through this type of dynamic, throwing into question the very foundation and rationale behind a "public" education system.

The boundaries between public and private have been further blurred in British Columbia with an act of the legislature to allow public school districts to create wholly-owned "School District Business Companies." These companies act as private, profit-making companies, but with public ownership and profits to go to subsidize public education. The government is encouraging these companies to create private, for-profit schools in Asia, with accreditation to issue British Columbia high school graduation certificates and access to British Columbia universities for students in China, Japan, and Korea.

Unfortunately, as in the postsecondary sector, this paucity of examples reflects just the "tip of the iceberg" in terms of growing commercialism and private fundraising in schools in a context of dwindling public education funding. Many such related studies documenting similar trends have been conducted by prominent Canadian educational researchers affiliated with, or based in the Canadian Centre for Policy Alternatives (CCPA)[3]. For those encouraged by such trends, so-called P3 initiatives represent another possible significant avenue in terms of privatization dynamics in Canadian education. One of the most prominent examples of P3 initiatives in education can be found in Nova Scotia, whose Liberal government in the late 1990s pledged to construct 55 schools that were to be privately financed, owned, and run, and subsequently leased back to the public for school use (Meek, 2001). These experiments with the private financing and ownership of school buildings arguably resulted in the defeat of the government that initiated the plan because of skyrocketing costs to the public. However, despite much negative press for P3 initiatives resulting from this debacle in Nova Scotia, interest and discussion remains high in the area of possible P3s in education as well as other sectors (Mehra, 2003; Canadian Union of Public Employees (CUPE), 2003; Robertson, 2002; Grieshaber-Otto & Sanger, 2002).

Issues in Postsecondary Education

As a matter of consequence, universities have also suffered the results of the aggregate cuts through transition to the CHST in federal social transfer payments to the provinces. As one pronounced example of this trend, a report commissioned by the Council of Ontario Universities (COU, 2000) shows that over the period from 1995–2000, Ontario ranked 58th out of 60 jurisdictions in North America (this particular study looked at both American States and Canadian Provinces) in terms of percentage change in support for university operating expenses. The study examined areas with comparable institutions across the United States and the rest of Canada. Related and connected dynamics of declining provincial share of university operating funding (Melchers, 2001) have seen universities turn increasingly to students to shoulder increasing costs. In a related and signal development, these realities were documented in a paper by an Ontario Legislative Library Research Officer in 2000 as the provincial government of the time was gearing up for further legislative change to enable introduction of different types of private universities (Johnston, 2000).

Across Canada today, university tuition fees have more than doubled on average since 1990 (Statistics Canada, 2003; Doherty-Delorme & Shaker, 2000), and consequent student debt upon graduation from a first undergraduate degree has risen from approximately $8700 in 1990 to $28,000 in the year 2000. "Deregulation" or the relaxation of provincial regulations on tuition levels in certain programs, both in colleges and universities, has contributed to this massive increase both in tuition and student debt (as two sides of the same coin). Consequently, Canadian researchers have pointed out some of the critical negative consequences in terms of social inequity and access to postsecondary education as a result of these developments (e.g., Quirke, 2001), just as researchers have analyzed these effects in the basic and secondary levels as different sorts of costs of education have increased. Many of the same neoliberal dynamics at work in the basic and secondary levels are reflected in the postsecondary sector, although most commentators acknowledge—including globally and comparatively—that postsecondary education is far more advanced in terms of the impact of privatization processes, including increasing commercialism of both research and university operations, as well as corporate presence on university boards.

In the area of research and development in education, somewhat disconcerting is the recent announcement about the "transformation" of the Social Sciences and Humanities Research Council of Canada (SSHRC) from primarily a *granting* to a *knowledge* council. Presumably, the subtle change in mission statement is to encourage more research collaboration and to focus on the impact and utilization of the knowledge produced. Although this may be an innocuous evolution, it does evoke ominous echoes of the "bizspeak" agendas of neoliberalism and implies that research projects without potential practical utilitarian payoffs may no longer be eligible.

Canada has its own body of researchers and business-friendly civil society groups who trumpet the idea of substantial introduction of further private universities, including not-for-profit, incorporated institutions reliant on endowments and tuition (such as the American "ivy league" schools), as well as for-profit ventures of various kinds. The Fraser Institute as well as the C.D. Howe Institute have agitated for further privatized education and postsecondary education particularly. Following this tide, and in search of a new frontier for educational "business," several for-profit postsecondary education institutions, as well as other for-profit tutorial services groups, have set up operations in Canada, with three of the most prominent being well-established previously as "edupreneurial" money-makers in the United States. Sylvan Learning Systems operates offices throughout Canada providing tutorial and private education programs. The Apollo Group, under its "University of Phoenix" brand, has established a campus in Vancouver offering both bachelors' and Masters' degrees in Business as well as two Master of Arts in Education programs (University of Phoenix Vancouver campus, 2007). Additionally, DeVry has set up campuses in Toronto and Calgary under the name of "DeVry Institute of Technology." Several Canadian for-profit and not-for-profit universities have also come on the scene in recent years, due to enabling legislation. Unexus (now known as Lansbridge), a Toronto-owned and Fredericton, New Brunswick-based Canadian private online university initiative specializing in business MBA degrees, is one such example of a profit-motivated institution with exporting ambitions, with operations and partnerships with Indian training companies focusing on computers (Dopp, 2001). The CCPA has led the way in documenting these types of privatization trends in postsecondary education in Canada. Shaker, for example, cites the introduction of for-profit PSE institutions into Canada in recent times, such as the DeVry institute,

ITI Education Corporation and International Business Schools (Shaker, 1999). Recently, endeavors to further privatize delivery of postsecondary education have taken the form of the P3 initiatives and directions mentioned previously. Another example of public–private collusion in relation to privatizing education is the Ontario Ministry of Education's approval of hundreds of private vocational schools listed through the province's "Private Career Colleges Act" (Ontario Ministry of Education, 2002). Though such institutions receive no operating or capital funds from the government, their students are often eligible for provincially and federally subsidized student loan schemes and thus, are privy to one form of public subsidy in this sense.

International Trade Regimes and Issues for Canada

In addition, different types of neoliberal policy dynamics and restructuring processes at work in the various levels and jurisdictions of Canadian basic, secondary and postsecondary education have been shown to be implicated in a variety of trade regimes involving Canada. Such regimes, from the North American Free Trade Agreement (NAFTA) to the proposed Free Trade Area of the Americas (FTAA), as well as the proposed General Agreement on Trade in Services (GATS) of the World Trade Organization (WTO), seek to transform "services" economics such that different spheres of educational provision will be encompassed and governed by international trade rules. As such regimes seek to 'liberalize' trade in education, commercial practices conducted under the auspices of public governance— such as those discussed earlier with respect to school boards—could be found susceptible to trade challenges and sanctions through the dispute settlement mechanisms of the various regimes.

In the case of the proposed GATS, for example, this could result because of the so-called "governmental authority" exclusion and rules regarding modes 1 and 2 of the agreement ("cross-border supply" and "consumption abroad," respectively; cf. Robertson, 2003; Schugurensky & Davidson-Harden, 2003). Specifically at issue within this area of concern is both the GATS preamble's statement of governments' "right to regulate," as well as the "governmental authority" exclusion, article 1.3. Proponents of the GATS argue that the preamble's recognition of governments' "right to regulate" tempers aspects of GATS articles that represent encroachment on publicly funded and provided services of all kinds, including education. In addition, it is claimed by GATS supporters that the "governmental authority" exclusion, contained in article 1.3, prevents specifically this type of encroachment, making an exception for services "provided in the exercise of governmental authority," with the limitation on this exception being that such a service must not be applied on a "commercial basis," or "supplied . . . in competition with one or more service suppliers" (Sinclair & Grieshaber-Otto, 2002, p. 18). The authors go on to note that under this "limitation to the exception," one would be hard pressed to find a "pure" example in any country of a "public service" that was not—at least in some facet or aspect—provided on a "commercial basis" (whether in the form of fees, insurance, and so on) or in "competition" with a similar "service provider." Any level of education, if financed and delivered (to whatever degree) publicly, or subsidized by any level of government, could be susceptible to a GATS challenge in the WTO if either of these limitations to the "governmental authority" exception applied.

The GATS has been characterized as a "bottom-up" agreement, due to the fact that beyond universal commitment to clauses such as the Most-Favored-Nation (MFN) rule, countries must specifically commit to liberalization measures in various sectors on a case-by-case basis. A different set of problems comes to the fore when dealing with the "top-down" trade agreements, such as the NAFTA and the proposed FTAA. Under NAFTA and similar articles and measures included in the FTAA, protection for investors is taken to the extent that any efforts on the part of governments to amend or change existing privatization measures could be fraught with difficulty. The much-criticized chapter 11 of NAFTA—that concerning investment—stipulates that "expropriation" of private investments in any sector, including different types of social services, could result in forced payments of compensation to the affected investors. Perhaps the most powerful aspect of NAFTA and the proposed FTAA is also part of its dispute settlement process. In these agreements/regimes, as opposed to the GATS, complaints may be brought directly from affected investors against the countries in question (the so-called "investor-to-state" dispute settlement mechanism). Such grievances are decided through secretive and super-national dispute settlement tribunals, which are not accountable to citizens. Mechanisms of trade regimes such as these and in the GATS (as well as other WTO constituent agreements, and various bilateral trade agreements) have been roundly criticized as a means to attack various government policies and legislation as "barriers to trade" in various respects. With respect to education, the field remains wide open for investors to attempt to leverage further commodification and privatization of education through trade regimes. While Annex II of the NAFTA includes reservations from Canada regarding the protection of social services, critics agree that NAFTA, and the proposed FTAA, could continue to pose a threat of entrenching privatization measures in public sectors that currently exist, as well as facilitate private investment in increasing layers of what is currently the sphere of public services (CCPA & HSA, 2001; Sinclair, 2003). To date, no dispute has been brought under either the NAFTA or the GATS affecting trade in education services[17]; however, although this is encouraging, we would argue that citizens valuing publicly funded education must be vigilant to call the significant powers of such trade regimes in facilitating neoliberal aims for education into question. The fact that private (i.e., commercial/for-profit) educational companies operating in Canada have not

attempted to use GATS or NAFTA rules to leverage funds or compensation from government authorities as of yet, does not rule out the possibility that such rules could be used for this purpose. Similarly, the fact that
federal government authorities in Canada have asserted that education is
"off the table" at the present time in trade negotiations, at least in terms of
the GATS (Government of Canada, 2002), should not in the least mollify
critics of these processes. As Weiner (Weiner, 2002) and others have noted,
privatization trends in Canadian education have continued apace despite
lack of significant progress in officially "liberalizing" trade in education
services as per the aims of the GATS or the proposed services chapter of the
FTAA. Different Canadian players—from "edupreneurs" seeking to tap
interprovincial as well as international export markets, to citizens valuing
equitably accessible public education—stand to either win or lose from the
continuing march toward increasing privatization of education. This process continues to gain steam, despite ambiguity over whether or not these
trends will be amplified and strengthened through super-national legal
mechanisms such as those embodied in international trade regimes. As a
final thought, though international trade regimes have been first to take
the spotlight of civil society's attention for their potential effects, where
such regimes have not achieved what proponents hoped for, actors driving neoliberal models of trade liberalization continue to seek alternatives.
Through carefully worded bilateral trade agreements or "preferential trade
agreements" as they have become known in the jargon, states and the edupreneurs that stand to benefit will doubtless continue to seek leverage to
open new markets in education.

Neoliberalism and Teachers in Canada

In the context of attempting to unpack the ways in which neoliberalism
has been influencing policies and practices in the sphere of public education in Canada, it is perhaps useful to look briefly at the results of a specific research project that has been ongoing over the past seven years. This
project, consisting of a series of studies undertaken in association with
the Canadian Teacher's Federation and its provincial affiliates, has been
conducted by a group of scholars based at York University, the Ontario
Institute for Studies in Education at the University of Toronto (OISE/UT),
and the Ontario Secondary School Teachers' Federation. Overall, the purpose of the project is to examine the relationships between the material
conditions of teachers' work, and ways in which teachers engage in their
own informal and formal learning and professional development. In addition, the study seeks to explore the intersections between these factors,
and changes over time brought on by government reforms affecting both
teachers' workplace conditions, and formal, government-initiated, professional development programs. This project evolved from the confluence
of three distinct, but related, themes. The principal theme underlying the

research centers around discourses and realities of schooling reform and "restructuring." Critiques of state schooling systems and demands for their reform (whether popular, political, or academic) have been in place almost from the inception of state schooling itself (Katz, 1971; Curtis, 1988). However, one could argue that recent demands for change can be differentiated from earlier injunctions in at least two ways. On the one hand, to a much greater extent than ever before, schooling reform is now more closely linked to transformations in the larger political economy of provinces and nations—a move to more globalizing, neoliberal economies, including tighter control over, but less funding for, public sector social institutions (Althouse, 1929; Royal Commission on Education, 1950; Goodman, 1995; Smyth, Dow, Hattam, Reid, & Shacklock et al., 2000). In this regard, teachers' work in many provincial and state jurisdictions is also rapidly being restructured as well (Hargreaves, 1992; LeBlanc, 1994).

In addition, while the recent reforms in education continue to range across the many aspects of schooling—funding, governance, curriculum, resources, facilities, etc.—a strong argument can be made that the ways in which teachers have been singled out for special attention are quite unlike anything that has occurred before. Formerly, teachers were often addressed as a collective entity, and improvements to education were often associated with the need to improve conditions for teachers—class sizes, resources, salaries, benefits, pensions, and job security. Even where and when teachers were seen to be in need of further education themselves, governments at various levels often moved to expand and improve teacher education programs, and/or to offer incentives for teachers to engage in further study, whether pre-service or in-service (Hopkins, 1969; Robinson, 1971; Fleming, 1972).

Today however, teachers seem bathed in a different light. From the media, from school and government officials, and from community and corporate leaders, teachers are increasingly being subjected to a critique of the individual. Individual teachers themselves, it is widely claimed, constitute the main "problem" in education. While the prescriptions for improvement vary widely across the schooling domains of Canada and the United States in many cases the underlying intentions are abundantly clear. Individual teachers themselves, need to be more carefully selected, trained, directed, evaluated, tested, and controlled (Holmes Group, 1990; Labaree, 1992; Darling-Hammond, 1998; Darling-Hammond & Ball, 1998; OECD, 1998; Ontario Government, 2000). Often, these initiatives are being promoted through the rhetoric of a "need" for increased professionalism, and in at least two jurisdictions (British Columbia and Ontario), government-initiated and controlled "colleges of teachers" have been established, with a mandate to control the training, certification, and practice of teachers (Popkewitz, 1994; Ontario Government, 1995). In many areas of the United States, salaries, promotion, and even basic job tenure for individual teachers are increasingly being determined by teacher testing regimes, increased external evaluation of teacher practice, and/or by the "success rate" of students on standardized examinations (OSSTF, 1999). Although these measures have yet to gain a foothold in Canada, in Ontario at least, student results from external examinations now appear in the public press, displayed on a school-by-school basis. The implications for individual teachers in these schools are certainly clear.

Methodologically, the project also stems from, and remains a part of, a much larger national project—New Approaches to Lifelong Learning (NALL)—that studies formal and informal learning among the general population, directed by David Livingstone at OISE/UofT, and funded by Canada's Social Sciences and Humanities Research Council (NALL, 2007).

Brief Summary of the Research

Briefly described, the overall project has involved a series of studies, utilizing a range of methodologies. First, in November of 1998, and again in November of 2003, an eight-page survey questionnaire was mailed out to approximately 2000 randomly selected elementary and secondary school teachers across Canada (response rates were approximately 40% and 50% respectively—considered quite acceptable given the mode of inquiry). Second, in the fall–winter of 1999–2000, 13 secondary school teachers in Ontario, who had completed the 1998 survey, participated in a diary-study for one week in November and another week in February. On each occasion, they were asked, using a standard diary template, to keep track of every activity they engaged in over the week, for all 24 hours of each day. In addition, they were asked, for each activity, to note whether any learning (informal or formal) had taken place as a result. Third, in-depth interviews were undertaken in September of 2000 with four of the teachers who had participated in the diary study. Finally, in June and July of 2004, a total of eight focus groups, each consisting of five to seven teachers, and lasting from two to three hours, were held in various parts of three provinces—Alberta, Ontario, and Nova Scotia. Although it is impossible to document all of the results and analysis here (see Smaller, Hart, Clark, Livingstone, & Noormohammed, 2000, & Smaller, Hart, Clark, & Livingstone, 2001 for further details), it is certainly worth-while commenting on some of the findings, particularly those relating to discussions about the possible effects of neoliberal reforms in Canadian education on teachers and their work.

Teacher Workload

First, on the original 1998 survey, the full-time respondents reported an overall average workload of 47 hours per week, comprised of assigned and voluntary labors. On average, teachers were assigned 28 hours per week for working directly with students, and such additional tasks as school administration, library coordination, administration, hall supervision, preparation and marking, and so on. In addition to these formally assigned hours, teachers reported that, on average, they spent a further 19 hours per week on school related tasks—approximately 10 hours at school, and 9 hours at home and elsewhere. Such tasks ranged from preparing and marking student work and supervising extracurricular activities, to communicating with students and parents, and participating in subject, school, board, and teacher federation meetings. This overall workload of 47 hours per week was consistent between those who indicated they spent most or all of their time directly in the classroom (teachers and department heads), and those respondents who held other educational positions (such as principals, consultants, program coordinators). Five years later, in the 2003 national survey, results indicated that there was a moderate increase in teachers' workload, averaging at least an extra hour per week overall.

These teacher workload findings are similar to studies that have asked teachers in other jurisdictions the same kinds of questions. Recent studies of teachers in Nova Scotia and secondary teachers in Alberta found them working 52.5 and 53.3 hours per week, respectively (Harvey & Spinney, 2000; Alberta Teachers' Association, 2000). Earlier studies of teachers in Ontario and Saskatchewan reported weekly working hours of 52.3 and 47.4 respectively (Saskatchewan Teachers' Federation, 1995; Ontario English Catholic Teachers' Association, 1996). Similarly, a 1994 national study of U.S. full-time elementary and secondary public school teachers found that they were required to be at school 33 hours per week, and that they worked an additional 12 hours per week, before and after school and weekends, for a total of 45 hours per week (National Centre for Education Statistics, 1997).

However, when respondents on the 2003 survey were asked more specific questions about their workload, and the ways it had changed over the previous five years, the responses suggested a qualitatively different set of perceptions than the quantitative data might have signaled. Over three-quarters (77%) of respondents reported that their overall workload had "significantly increased" (43%) or "increased" (34%) in the past five years (or less, if relatively new to teaching), while 19% stated it had remained about the same, and only 4% stated it had "decreased" or "significantly decreased." Among the changes in this overall workload, those aspects for which highest increases were reported were: "Dealing with administrative requests for information, forms, data, student attendance, etc"—81%; "Time/effort required for assessing and reporting on student progress"—78%; "Size of classes"—62%; "Number of hours of other [than teaching] timetabled duties"—46%. As the results of the subsequent focus groups confirmed, having to devote more hours attending to increased bureaucratic requirements, and away from attention to students themselves, understandably lead teachers to conclude that the overall workload had increased considerably.

Perhaps not unrelated, over 80% of all respondents reported that the "overall level of stress" in their work had "significantly increased" (43%)

or "increased" (38%). When asked "how often do your find your job stressful?" over 40% responded "most" (34%) or "all" (7%) the time, while a further 46% believed that their job was stressful at least "half the time." In spite of these pressures, however, 32% reported that they were "very satisfied" with their jobs, while a further 55% were at least "somewhat satisfied." By comparison, only 8% were "dissatisfied" and 2% "very dissatisfied" with their job.

Methodologically, it is interesting to note some clear anomalies found from the workload data obtained from the set of 24 weekly diaries completed by 13 teachers who had previously submitted survey questionnaires. In total, the diaries of these 13 respondents reported an average of 48.4 hours per week on duties directly related to their paid employment (with a range from 36.6 to 61.1 hours for those weeks reported). Although this average work load of 48.4 hours per week, based on their daily log sheets, compares closely with the overall national average obtained in the survey questionnaires, in fact, these particular teachers reported an average of only 41.5 hours on their survey forms! Virtually every one of these teachers had significantly underestimated the amount of work they actually did each week—in two cases, both women with children at home, by 75% and 35% respectively! On this basis, it is interesting to reflect on the results of a number of studies that have recently been undertaken in a number of jurisdictions to assess teacher workload on the basis of similar generalized estimations self-reported by teachers. Although they consistently report average work-weeks of 45 to 53 hours, one is left wondering if these are also under-representations of actual work loads for teachers (see, e.g., Harvey & Spinney, 2000; Alberta Teachers' Association, 2000; Statistics Canada, 1997; National Centre for Education Statistics [USA], 1997). For example, recent analyses undertaken by Milosh Raykov of data from Statistics Canada's General Social Survey suggest that Canadian teachers have the highest weekly workloads, and highest unpaid overtime work, of any professional employee group in Canada (Raykov, 2001).

These diaries were also very useful in unpacking the overall structures and contexts of a teacher's work life. Among many other findings, the diaries indicated clearly that a "normal" 8- to-5 work day, with time off for lunch, was certainly the exception rather than the rule. Lunches, if they happened at all, were often punctuated with ad hoc calls on their time. (One example: "12:10–12:30—Eating lunch—dealing with students re. co-op application sheets—and with staff—seldom do you ever get to sit down for a sandwich"). These diaries also indicated clearly that much of the course preparation, and student-marking, and evaluation work was undertaken by these teachers on their "own" time in their own homes—over five days of each week/weekend. In total, a weekly average of 10.7 hours of work was undertaken outside of the regular 9-to-5 work day, with a range of 5 to 21 hours. In addition to working at home, during the two reporting weeks several teachers had noted that they had stayed at, or returned to, their schools for evening events, including parents' nights and supervising at student dances and sport events.

TEACHERS' FORMAL AND INFORMAL LEARNING PRACTICES

Related to the changing nature of teachers' work, both the 1998 and 2003 surveys also included a number of questions asking about teachers' engagement in formal and informal learning practices, and in professional development activities. Overall, teachers were much more likely than the general labor force to take further education courses and workshops, devoting an average of 8 hours a week to such organized studies. In 1998, 86% of all respondents stated they had been involved in at least one formal learning activity—defined as a course, conference, or workshop—during the previous twelve months, and most had engaged in several such programs. Work-related matters, computers, and academic courses rated as the top three themes of interest. By 2003, this number had increased to over 90% of all teachers.

The national teacher surveys were undertaken alongside of similar surveys taken of the general Canadian population. By comparison, teachers' engagement in upgrading courses and workshops clearly stand out as being significantly higher than most, if not all, other occupational groups. For example, as compared to the 90% engagement rate posted by teachers, even occupational groups requiring a university degree averaged only 53.5% engagement in one or more courses or workshops in the previous twelve months (see Table 3.2).

Interestingly, as Table 3.2 suggests, all teachers reported overwhelming engagement in further formal education, regardless of their age or years of teaching experience. Although there is a slight reduction in educational pursuits among those with more than twenty years of teaching seniority, 87% of these senior teachers are still participating in formal courses and workshops to enhance their own learning (and more frequently than their counterparts five years earlier). Again, follow-up interviews and focus groups made it perfectly clear that this increase over the past five years in participation in formal

Table 3.1 Taken one or more courses or workshops in the previous 12 months

2003	1998	2003 NALL study		
All teachers	All teachers	Adult population not in school	Labor force	Labor force, degree required
90.2%	86%	31.8%	40.5%	53.5%
n = 1024	752	2771	2221	535

Table 3.2 Length of teaching experience and involvement in courses 2003 and 1998 Survey Taken course in past 12 months by teaching experience*

Years of experience	2003		1998	
	%	N	%	N
All respondents				
1–10	94	219	89	
11–20	93	300	89	
21+	87	330	82	
Total	91	849	86	
Full-time teachers				
1–10	94	176	87	
11–20	94	205	89	
21+	86	242	83	
Total	91	623	86	

*Excludes those with less than one year of experience.

education among teachers of all ages is highly related to the restructuring activities of school boards and provincial ministries of education, and the need for teachers to engage in more courses and workshops related to these changes.

Conclusion: Canadian Education in the Ongoing Neoliberal Context

Although it is true that Canada does not show the drastic effects of neoliberal policy imperatives evidenced in developing countries—one need look no further in the pan-American context than Latin America for proof of this—teachers as well as the various levels of education systems in this more prosperous nation have shown evidence of strain under neoliberal policy trends. The nuanced studies drawn upon here (Smaller et al., 2000, 2001) elaborate upon the dynamics of intensification of teacher workload at the basic and secondary levels, a trend that, with its "flip side" of persistent underfunding, has led to considerable strain on teaching and learning at these levels across the country. Intensification of workload has been accompanied by the disturbing pattern of increased outlay of funding for education on the part of both teachers and parents, symptoms of communities dealing with the encroachment of neoliberal policy on a welfare state under siege. Although the phenomenon of underfunding has its root ultimately in insufficient federal transfers to the provinces for social programs, individual provincial governments preferring neoliberal policy prescriptions have too often facilitated this agenda, actively cutting back funding education in particular. Concomitantly, an atmosphere of mistrust of teachers, shown through policy discourses of increased accountability and surveillance, has contributed to a prevailing context of confrontation with public education workers, who continue to stand as the first line of defense against finance-driven restructuring initiatives. The accompanying neoliberal policy initiatives of encouragement of, and experimentation with, private-sector roles in education has also continued, facilitated by interested provincial government regimes across the country[4]. These trends as well have been called into critical question, led by teacher, student, and Faculty federations who question both the underfunding and privatizing components of these policies. The resulting conditions in Canadian education have seen a continuing struggle between governments eager to facilitate a neoliberal policy agenda, and private investors seeking to "break in" to the education market, and on the other side, federations and research coalitions who question the effect of these trends on besieged welfare state social programs, and by extension, social rights. In general, the neoliberal context shows no signs of

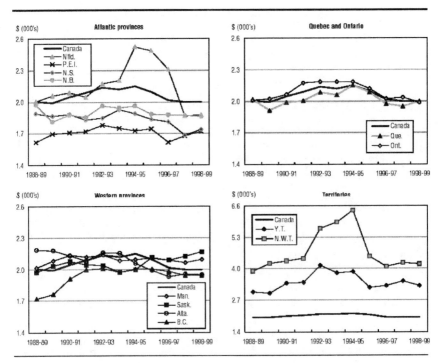

Figure 2.1   Figures on per capita education funding in Canada. (Statistics Canada, CMEC, 1999)

abating, and both global and regional/local initiatives to deepen these types of shifts in education policy continue apace.

However, just as global forces and mechanisms reinforce a neoliberal agenda in education policy emphasizing entrenched commodification, marketization, and privatization, an international movement continues to come together to question these trends. Embodied not only in critical Canadian groupings of educators and researchers such as the CCPA and educator union affiliates nationwide, this movement spans the hemisphere, and indeed the planet, through alliances to promote values and goals distinct from those reflected in policy discourses of neoliberalism. Organizations such as the Hemispheric Secretariat on Education (HSE, 2001; associated with the World Social Forum [WSF] and alternative World Education Forum [WEF][5]) and the Civil Society Network for Public Education in the Americas[6] represent examples of such dynamic, transnational alliances to agitate for the defense and expansion of adequately funded, and equitably accessible public education both within the Canadian and pan-American context, as well as beyond.

NOTES

1. The "Corporate-Higher Education Forum" in Canada is one example of such a trend.
2. http://www.cecnetwork.org
3. http://www.policyalternatives.ca
4. While one of the most aggressively neoliberal provincial governments—that of Ontario's Progressive Conservative party—was replaced by the currently governing Liberals in October 2003, the effects in this province of substantial restructuring, including of teacher governance and teachers' work, continue to be felt despite small gains. For instance, the governing Liberals in Ontario have cancelled both the programs of mandatory recertification and the required Ontario Teacher Qualifying Test instituted by the previous Conservative regime, although teacher representation and control of their own "self-regulating" professional body, the Ontario College of Teachers, remains an issue to be addressed substantially, though British Columbia's College of Teachers has been restructured to reflect actual teacher self-governance.
5. http://www.forumsocialmundial.org.br/home.asp; http://www.portoalegre.rs.gov.br/fme/default.asp?mst=5
6. http://www.vcn.bc.ca/idea/intro_eng.htm

REFERENCES

Alberta Teachers' Association. (2000). *Teacher workload study.* Edmonton: Alberta Teachers Association.
Althouse, J. G. (1929). *The Ontario teacher: A historical account of progress, 1800–1910.* Ph.D. Diss. University of Toronto; reprinted, Ontario Teachers' Federation, 1972.
CCPA (Canadian Centre for Policy Alternatives) & HSA (Hemispheric Social Alliance). (2001). NAFTA investor rights plus: An analysis of the draft investment chapter of the FTAA. *Trade and Investment Briefing Paper Series, 2*(5).

Retrieved June 2007, from http://policyalternatives.ca/index.cfm?act=news&call=360&do=article&pA=BB736455.

CCSD (Canadian Council for Social Development). (1999). *Thinking ahead: Trends affecting public education in the future. Ottawa: Canadian council for social development.* Retrieved June 2007, from http://www.ccsd.ca/pubs/gordon/part2.htm.

CUPE (Canadian Union of Public Employees). (2003). *Workshop 1: New forms of privatization.* Workshop at the CUPE National Privatization Conference, *"New ways of winning: Fighting privatization and contracting Out,"* March 27–30, Toronto, Ontario, Canada.

Curtis, B. (1988). *Building the educational state: Canada West, 1836–1871.* London: The Althouse Press.

Chossudovsky, M. (1998). *The Globalisation of Poverty: Impacts of IMF and World Bank Reforms.* Halifax: Fernwood.

Conference of Independent Schools of Ontario. (2004). *CIS schools directory.* Retrieved June 2007, from http://www.cisontario.ca/main_school_directory.asp

Constitution Act, 1982, being Schedule B to the Canada Act 1982 (U.K.), 1982, c. 11

CMEC (Council of Ministers of Education, Canada). (2001). *The development of education in Canada.* Report of Canada, in response to the International Survey in Preparation for the Forty-sixth Session of the International Conference on Education, Geneva, September 5–8.

COU (Council of Ontario Universities). (2000). *Comparing Ontario and American public universities.* Retrieved June 2007, from http://www.cou.on.ca/content/objects/Ontario%20vs%20US%20peers.pdf

Darling-Hammond, L. (1998). Teachers and teaching: Testing policy hypothesis from a national commission report. *Educational Researcher 27*(1) pp. 5–15.

Darling-Hammond, L., & Ball, D. (1998). Teaching for high standards: What policymakers need to know and be able to do. CPRE Publications, University of Pennsylvania, Graduate School of Education.

Davidson-Harden, A., & Majhanovich, S. (2004). Privatization in Canadian education: A survey of trends. *International Review of Education, 50*(3/4) pp. 264–287.

Doherty-Delorme, D., & Shaker, E. (2000). What Should We Spend on Education? Highlights from the Year 2000 Alternative Federal Budget and the Ontario Alternative Budget. Retrieved June, 2007 from http://policyalternatives.ca/index.cfm?act=news&do=Article&call=795&pA=A2286B2A&type=6

Dopp, S. (2001). Unexus university at-a-glance. In D. Doherty-Delorme & E. Shaker (Eds.), *Missing pieces II: An alternative guide to Canadian post-secondary education* (p. 140). Ottawa: Canadian Centre for Policy Alternatives.

Fisher, D., & Rubenson, K. (2000). The changing political economy: The private and public lives of Canadian universities. In J. Currie & J. Newson (Eds.), *Universities and globalization: Critical perspectives* (pp. 77–98). London: Sage.

Fisher, D., & Atkinson-Grosjean, J. (2002). Brokers on the boundary: Academy–industry liaison in Canadian universities. *Higher Education, 44,* 449–467.

Fleming, W.G. (1972). *Ontario's educative society.* Toronto: University of Toronto Press.

Flower, D. (2004). *Public education as the Trojan Horse: The Alberta case.* Retrieved June 2007, from http://www.teachers.ab.ca/Quick+Links/Publications/Magazine/Volume+85/Number+1/Articles/Public+Education+as+the+Trojan+Horse+The+Alberta+Case.htm

Goodman, J. (1995). Change without difference: School restructuring in historical perspective. *Harvard Educational Review, 65*(1) pp. 1–29.

Government of Canada. (2002). *The GATS and health, public education and social services*. Retrieved June 2007, from http://www.dfait-maeci.gc.ca/tna-nac/TS/gats-ps-h-edu-en.asp

Grieshaber-Otto, J., & Sanger, M. (2002). *Perilous lessons: The impact of the WTO services agreement GATS on Canada's public education system*. Ottawa: Canadian Centre for Policy Alternatives.

Halifax Initiative. (2003). *The IMF's structural adjustment program for Canada*. Retrieved June 2007, from http://www.halifaxinitiative.org/index.php/Issues_Cond_SAPs/765

Hargreaves, A. (1992). Time and teachers' work: An analysis of the intensification thesis. *Teachers College Record, 94*(1) pp. 87–108.

HSE (Hemispheric Secretariat on Education). (2001). *Final declaration of the Hemispheric Forum on Education, Second People's Summit of the Americas, Québec City*, April 17–18. Retrieved June 2007, from http://www.secretaria.ca/eng/declaration.htm

Holmes Group. (1990). *Tomorrow's schools: Principles for the design of professional development schools*. East Lansing, MI: Author.

Harvey, A., & Spinney, J. (2000). *Life on and off the job: A time-use study of Nova Scotia teachers*. Halifax: St. Mary's University.

Hopkins, R.A. (1969). *The long march: A history of the Ontario public school men teachers' federation*. Toronto: Baxter Press.

Johnston, L. (2000). Private universities in Ontario. *Ontario Legislative Library, Current Issue Paper 203*. Retrieved June 2007, from http://www.ontla.on.ca/library/repository/mon/2000/10285780.htm

Johnston, L., & Swift, S. (2000). Public funding of private and denominational schools in Canada. *Ontario Legislative Library, Backgrounder 39*. Retrieved June 2007, from http://www.ontla.on.ca/library/repository/mon/1000/10286133.htm

Kachur, J. (2000). Privatizing public choice: The rise of charter schooling in Alberta. In T. Harrison & J. Kachur (Eds.), *Contested classrooms: Education, globalization and democracy in Alberta* (pp. 107–122). Edmonton: University of Alberta Press.

Katz, M. (1971). *Class, bureaucracy and schools*. New York: Praeger Press.

Labaree, D. (1992). Power, knowledge, and the rationalization of teaching: A genealogy of the movement to professionalize teaching. *Harvard Educational Review 62*(2), 123–54.

LeBlanc, C. (1994). Teacher time: Education's critical resource. *Education Canada, 34*(2) pp. 12–15.

Lowry, M. (2004). *Fee-generation as an indicator of developing funding inequalities in the B.C. school system*. Vancouver,: B.C. Teachers' Federation.

Mackenzie, H. (2002). *Cutting classes: Elementary and secondary education funding in Ontario 2002–3*. Ottawa: Canadian Centre for Policy Alternatives.

Meek, J. (2001). School's out: The jury is out on who benefited from Nova Scotia's public–private partnership for the building of schools and from the decision to cancel it. *Summit Magazine*. Retrieved June 2007, from http://www.summitconnects.com/Articles_Columns/Summit_Articles/2001/0301/0301_Schools_out.htm

Mehra, N. (2003). First hospitals . . . next schools: Why education workers should look more closely at P3s. Ontario *Health Coalition*. Retrieved June 2007, from http://www.web.net/ohc/docs/first.htm

Melchers, R. (2001). University finance in Canada: 1972–the present. In D. Doherty-Delorme & E. Shaker (Eds.), *Missing pieces II: An alternative guide to Canadian post-secondary education* (pp. 109–117). Ottawa: Canadian Centre for Policy Alternatives.

Mendelson, M. (1998). No treasure CHST for health services. Website retrieved June 2007, from http://www.caledoninst.org/Publications/PDF/chstreasure.pdf.

New Approaches to Lifelong Learning. (2007). Retrieved June 2007, from http://www.oise.utoronto.ca/depts/sese/csew/nall/sur_res.htm

National Centre for Education Statistics. (1997). *Time spent teaching core academic subjects in elementary schools.* Washington: U.S. Department of Education.

Neu, D. (2000). Re-investment fables: Educational finances in Alberta. In T. Harrison & J. Kachur (Eds.), *Contested classrooms: Education, globalization and democracy in Alberta* (pp. 75–83). Edmonton: University of Alberta Press.

Newson, J. (1998). The corporate-linked university: From social project to market force. *Canadian Journal of Communication, 23*(1), 107–124.

OECD. (1998). *Teachers for tomorrow's schools.* Paris: Centre for Educational Research and Innovation.

Ontario English Catholic Teachers' Association. (1996). *Workload and worklife study: A membership survey.* Toronto: OECTA.

Ontario Government. (1995). *Province to proceed with Ontario college of teachers.* Ministry of Education News Release Communique, November 21.

Ontario Government. (2000). *Ontario teacher testing program.* Toronto: Ontario Ministry of Education.

Ontario Ministry of Education. (2002*). Registered private career colleges* Retrieved November 2004, from http://www.edu.gov.on.ca/eng/general/list/pvs02.html

Ontario Secondary School Teachers' Federation. (1999). *A report on teacher testing.* Toronto: OSSTF.

Paquette, J. (2002). Public funding for "private" education: Enhanced choice at what price in equity? *Education & Law Journal—Revue de droit de l'education, 12*(2), 133–195.

Peters, F. (2000). Deep and brutal: Funding cuts to education in Alberta. In T. Harrison & J. Kachur (Eds.), *Contested classrooms: Education, globalization and democracy in Alberta* (pp. 85–97). Edmonton: University of Alberta Press.

Popkewitz, T. (1994). Professionalization in teaching and teacher education: Some notes on its history, ideology, and potential. *Teaching and Teacher Education, 10*(1).

Post-secondary Education Choice and Excellence Act. (2000). S.O. (Statute of Ontario) 2000, c. 36. Sch., pp. 1–14.

Quirke, L. (2001). Access in jeopardy? Social class, Finances and university attendance. In D. Doherty-Delorme & E. Shaker (Eds.), *Missing pieces II: An alternative guide to Canadian post-secondary education* (pp. 63–74). Ottawa: Canadian Centre for Policy Alternatives.

Raykov, M. (2001). *Teachers hours of work and working conditions.* Unpublished paper; OISE/UofT NALL Project.

Robertson, H. J. (2002). *Why P3 schools are D4 schools, or how private–public-partnerships lead to disillusionment, Dirty dealings and debt.* Retrieved June 2007, from http://bctf.ca/IssuesInEducation.aspx?id=5960

Robertson, S. (2003). Introduction. *Globalisation, Societies and Education 1* (3), special issue on WTO/GATS and the Global Education Services Industry.

Robinson, S. G. B. (1971). *Do not erase.* Toronto: Ontario Secondary School Teachers' Federation.

Royal Commission on Education in Ontario. (1950). *Report 1950.* Toronto: Ontario Government.

Saskatchewan Teachers' Federation. (1995). *Teacher Workload Study.* Regina: STF.

Schugurensky, D., & Davidson-Harden, A. (2003). From Cordoba to Washington: WTO/GATS and Latin American education. *Globalisation, Societies and Education 1* (3), pp. 321–357.

Schugurensky, D., & Davidson-Harden, A.. (2004). The GATS and 'trade in educational services': Issues for Canada in the panamerican context. In J. Zajda (Ed.), *International Handbook of Globalisation, Education and Policy Research*: Kluwer, pp. 457–480.

Shaker, E. (1999). Privatizing schools: Democratic choice or market demand? *Education Monitor 3*(1). Ottawa: Canadian Centre for Policy Alternatives, pp. 1–25.

Sinclair, S. (2003). FTAA: A dangerous NAFTA-GATS hybrid Canada's initial offer threatens vital interests. *Trade and Investment Briefing Papers Series,* 4(2). Retrieved June 2007, from http://policyalternatives.ca/index.cfm?act=new s&do=Article&call=352&pA=F4FB3E9D&type=5

Sinclair, S., & Grieshaber-Otto, J. (2002). *Facing the facts: A guide to the GATS debate.* Ottawa: Canadian Centre for Policy Alternatives.

Slaughter, S., & Leslie, L. (1997). *Academic capitalism: Politics, policies and the entrepreneurial university.* Baltimore: John Hopkins University Press.

Smaller, H., Hart, D., Clark, R., & Livingstone, D. (2001). *Informal/formal learning and workload among Ontario secondary school teachers.* Retrieved June 2007, from http://www.oise.utoronto.ca/depts/sese/csew/nall/res/39learning&workoad.htm

Smaller, H., Hart, D., Clark, R., Livingstone, D., & Noormohammed, Z. (2000). *Teacher learning, informal and formal: Results of a Canadian teachers' Federation survey.* Retrieved June 2007, from http://www.oise.utoronto.ca/depts/sese/csew/nall/res/14teacherlearning.htm

Smyth, J., Dow, A., Hattam, R., Reid, A. & Shacklock, G. (2000). The critical case study method. In the Author's, *Teachers' work in a globalizing economy.* London: Falmer Press.

Statistics Canada, CMEC (Council of Ministers of Education, Canada). (1999). *Education indicators in Canada: Report of the Pan-Canadian education indicators program.* Ottawa: Canadian Education Statistics Council and Council of Ministers of Education, Canada.

Statistics Canada. (2003). University tuition fees. *The Daily,* August 12. Retrieved September 2007 from http://www.statcan.ca/Daily/English/030812/d030812a.htm

Statistics Canada. (2001). Trends in the use of private education. *The Daily,* July 4. Retrieved June 2007, from http://www.statcan.ca/Daily/English/010704/d010704b.htm

Statistics Canada. (1998). *Education in Canada.* Catalogue number 0009781-229-x1B. Ottawa: Statistics Canada.

Torres, C., & Schugurensky, D. (2002). The political economy of higher education in the era of neoliberal globalization: Latin America in comparative perspective. *Higher Education, 4,* 429–455.

University of Phoenix, Vancouver campus. (2007). *Programs.* Retrieved June 2007, from http://phoenix.19gi.com/campus/Vancouver/programs.php

Weiner, H. (2002). Trade, privatization, and public education: Issues and concerns. Retrieved March 6, 2003, from http://www.ctf-fce.ca/E/WHAT/Global/trade_private_pulic_education.htm

Weiner, H. (2003). *The funding of public education in Canada—Privatization by stealth?* Presentation to the 14th annual CAPSLE conference, Jasper, Alberta, Canada, April 27–30. Retrieved June 2007, from http://www.ctf-fce.ca/en/issues/ni/charter/capsle.pdf

4 The New Built Environment of Education
Neoliberalism on Trial in Australia

Gregory Martin

INTRODUCTION

Neoliberal restructuring is driving a dramatic rescaling of Australian political economy that has transformed it into a rapidly growing "success story" ("Australia's Economic Performance," 2006). In 2006, the Executive Board of the International Monetary Fund (IMF) "commended the authorities on their sound macroeconomic management and continuing structural reform efforts that have underpinned the sustained strong economic performance." Adding to this, the IMF ranked the Australian economy as one of the most resilient in the world, with economic growth surpassing most industrialised nations. Closer inspection reveals, however, that the prospects are not so "bright" for an increasing number of mostly poor, working class Australians who are having trouble putting food on the table or filling up their cars with fuel to get to school, work, or town (Bramble, 2004; Wynhausen, 2005). Having been seduced by the illusions of self-propelled neoliberalism, this daily battle for survival in the everyday world openly contradicts the claim that the "free market" is a classless meritocracy. Capitalism relies upon ideologies of meritocracy, which conceal the changing nature of exploitation (the origins of profits) and the enduring relevance of class. Emblematic of how class boundaries are blurred and concealed in Australia, the supposedly "outdated" concept of class is increasingly replaced with such generic terms as Aussie *Battler* and *aspirational* families (Scanlon, 2004). Within the realm of collective memory, this ideological trend creates a challenge for a political system that organizes or mobilizes that historical consciousness for the purpose of radical social change, as these terms actually glide over the real, material effects of class.

As a mechanism that plays a central role in the ideological production and reproduction of capitalist relations, Althusser (1971) points out that the educational system actively solicits and recruits individuals into restricted forms of identity and subjectivity through the everyday "lived" experience of schooling. Although these social identities and contradictory subjectivities do not always necessarily fit well or comfortably within the dominant narrative of meritocracy or any facile celebrations of the Australian Dream, they are accepted by those who progressively internalize the values, beliefs, and norms embedded within the rituals and social practices of schooling, such as individualized and competitive high-stakes testing. In the selective process of meritocracy, education produces and legitimates the class system by preparing students for, and stratifying them into, the hierarchy of labor: workers, the petty bourgeoisie, and capitalists.

Today, capitalism is in a permanent state of crisis, which is not a beautiful sight to behold. Ultimately, capitalist decline is, as Lenin (1916) fatefully described, "horror without end." Without forgetting its historical accomplishments, it is impossible to deny that capitalism is now threatening to destroy life in every possible way through environmental damage, the destruction of irreplaceable natural resources, endless war and repression, famine, and genocide. To illustrate the failed neoliberal strategy, we can talk about the real, material, everyday effects of corporate downsizing, and the degradation of social infrastructure, as well as the non-human environment. These calamities are contributing to new crises, which are potentially unsolvable. This is not the place to stop and discuss this in empirical detail. However, we might ask, what is the significance of these changes for public education?

From an ethnographic point of view, the public school system is a showcase of capitalism in decay. Once acknowledged and upheld as a basic social right, Australian education has endured significant and successive funding cuts and the working class faces escalating costs under a "user pays" system, including "voluntary" fees or contributions at public schools (Luke, 2004, 2007; Byrne, 2004; "When the Levies Break," 2003). Under the guise of "raising standards" and redressing social inequality and exclusions constituted in and through education, the Howard conservative government is following and intensifying the Hawke/Keating Labor neoliberal "reform" agenda, in the name of "globalization." At the end of a period of prolonged economic growth, this is not simply a schoolyard fight between capital and labor. Shifting the gears of free-market capitalism, the ruling class must accelerate the pace of reforms in order to guarantee the general conditions of surplus accumulation, which includes management of the economy through budgetary expenditures, as well as the provision of welfare and education.

Adopting an interdisciplinary approach, this chapter argues for a more spatialized and scalar understanding of globalization and its relationship to education. I argue that the development of a critical perspective of space and geographical scale helps to map and analyze the multiple and contradictory processes and practices the neoliberal state has engaged in to develop a "spatial fix" (Harvey, 1982) or "scalar fix" (Smith, 1995) as a concrete means of resolving its inherent crises. Indebted to the work of critical geographers such as David Harvey (2000) and Henri Lefebrve (1991), this chapter argues that space/scale is not a neutral or static backdrop against which the state has intervened in the production and distribution of knowledge. Within this neoliberal moment, the rescaling of state power via strategies of privatization, deregulation, and decentralization has enabled the bourgeoisie to reorganize the geography of capitalist education in order to "promote the health of the accumulation process" (Frankel, 1978, p. 38). Driven by the slow and steady tendency of the rate of profit to decline and a corresponding need for capital investment in an era of competitive "globalization," the ever-changing place-making practices of neoliberalism have enabled the capitalist state to overcome certain ideological, social, and physical barriers to surplus accumulation through new spatial and scalar configurations.

In a groundbreaking article about the transformation of social practices and processes in the education sector of the economy, Robertson (2002) examines "the scale question" (Lefebrve, 1991) and "the difference that scale makes" (Cox, 1996, p. xviii). In this deregulated and degraded environment, the strategic territory of education has been rescaled to articulate a new vision of the world through the intrusive force of neoliberal policies and ideas. Harvey defines spatial scale as "nested hierarchical structures of organization" that are articulated at a variety of local, regional, national and global levels (cited in Robertson, 2002, p. xviii). Scale, in this sense, is more than a unit of spatial measurement used to define smaller or larger areas, but rather is a process through which social and economic relations are configured spatially. Summarizing the work of geographer Sally Marston, Conway (2005) argues that it is important to understand "scalar narratives" as a "way of framing reality and [which] have material consequences." Scale, therefore, is useful for mapping the configuration of a new political cartography of education. In particular, Robertson (2002) focuses on Neil Brenner's overview of developments in the field (at present a lively debate in Marxist human geography, see Marston 2000; Brenner, 2001; Purcell, 2003), noting that scale:

> (i) is methodologically important as a spatio-temporary unit of analysis, (ii) it involves a critical dimension in the unfolding wave of global capitalist restructuring-referred to as re-scaling, (iii) is a key strategy of social and political transformation, (iv) it is a metaphorical weapon in the struggle for hegemony over social and political space, and (v) a space fought over by social actors in the process of territorialization. (pp. xviii–xix)

The upshot of all this is that reorganizers of the state have scaled all sorts of ideological, social, and physical barriers to create a newly built environment in education. Of course, this multilayered process of territorialization has not just profitably transformed the realm of physical space (e.g., the privatization of state assets). It has also led to the expansion of flexible labor, surplus accumulation and social regulation. In the context of class struggle and the struggle for power, Robertson (2002) notes that the contemporary processes of de- and re-territorialization has involved "strategic

relational moves by actors to work beyond the boundaries of existing institutionalized relations that represented various interests in various ways to
'fix' a new hierarchical pattern and set of boundaries" (p. xix).

Within the current wave of social, spatial, and scalar restructuring, the
capitalist state has in fact engaged in a defensive strategy of preventing
(or at least delaying) legitimization crises from disrupting social relations
(Frankel, 1978). Against the backdrop of the class struggle between capital
and labor for state power, the labor intensive and highly unionized state sector has effectively been re-politicized in Australia through "market replacing" and "boundary blurring" activities that have disciplined various state
enterprises such as education to market forces. Pointing to the dynamic
character of the emerging political geography of spatial scales under neoliberalism, Swyngedouw (1992) contends that "geographical scale is both
the realm and outcome of the struggle for control over social space" (p. 60).
As part of the struggle over space, neoliberal rescaling has changed the balance of class forces in society, enabling capital to engage in a form of "crisis management" through a re-politicized ideological and administrative
state sector that has expanded spheres of normalized social life, including
the gendering and racialization of labor and reproduction (Frankel, 1978).
Here, the ideology of neoliberalism is being interwoven through institutions
such as schools into the broader moral fabric of everyday life. Within these
highly complex forms of human labor power production, the emphasis is
on the production of ideal citizen-subjects who are self-regulating, self-
interested, and self-calculating for the purposes of capital accumulation
in increasingly competitive global markets. At the same time, given that
attempts by the capitalist class to improve efficiency and raise productivity
have caused a high degree of subaltern discontent at the base of Australian
society, this is a "precarious process because of the danger of class conflict"
(Frankel, 1978, p. 36). Indeed, the last section of this chapter looks at one
source of a possible solution to the contractions of neoliberalism in the
form of the workers' movement. To reinforce the fighting capacities of the
working class, as well as to build the "common ground" on which the class
struggle can be dialectically played out at multiple geographic scales in the
face of "globalization," this chapter argues that it is important to learn
from the rich experience of emergent and militant social forces on the left
(Bailey & Iveson, 2000; Houston, 2008).

PRIVATE IS THE "NEW" PUBLIC: GLOBAL RESTRUCTURING

At this historical juncture, the prevailing wisdom is that, in terms of the
total horizon of economic and social possibilities, it is imperative that we
accept capitalist institutions and methods (Gamble, 1999). In the name of
economics and efficiency, the Australian Federal Treasurer Peter Costello
(2001) is on record as saying that "Globalisation is not a value, it is a

process. Globalisation describes what is happening. And ranting against globalisation is like ranting against the telephone." In *Capitalism and its Economics,* Douglas Dowd (2000) reveals that classical political economists such as Adam Smith and David Ricardo were long interested in efficiency of production and the accumulation of surplus value. Classical economics tends to privilege private property, self-interest, and efficiency of production. Beyond the abstract principles of classical economics, Dowd argues that, in flesh-and-blood terms, efficiency is a myth as demonstrated by the obscene and absurd destruction of food to keep prices high when millions are starving (a capitalist solution to the crisis of "overproduction" that allows wealth to "grow" through the imposition of scarcity).

However, perhaps more interesting is that a long list of classical economists such as John Stuart Mill, Paul Samuelsson, and Kenneth Arrow recognized the limits of the market to provide for the public good, with the use of the lighthouse as a classic schoolbook example. According to Mill (1965) and his fellow travelers, it would be impossible to charge single boats according to their use or benefit from a well-placed lighthouse, which casts a warning signal regardless of who has paid. With regards to this classic free-rider problem, it is therefore appropriate for the government to construct and fund the lighthouse from taxpayer dollars.

In 1974, a famous revisionist paper by Ronald Coase attacked in detail this orthodox theory of public goods.[1] A 1991 Nobel Prize winner in Economic Science, Coase examined the actual history of lighthouse finance and found that in Britain numerous lighthouses were constructed by private individuals and financed through user fees right up to 1836, when the government-chartered monopoly, Trinity House, began to buy out owners, which it did by 1842 (Foldvary, 2003). Recent research demonstrates that the British government was more involved in the lighthouse industry than Coase suggested (Fischel, 2000; Van Zandt, 1993). Regardless, his argument has been used to justify neoliberal economics that favor "small government" and market discipline to promote competition and economic growth.

Amidst all the huffing and puffing, it is clear that a good deal of controversy exists about what constitutes a collective or "public good." Powell and Clemens (1998) argue that the public good will always be "unsettled and contested and is part of the unsettled and contested nature of politics itself" (cited in Kezar, 2003). However, in Australia the social and economic policy debate over the future of public services, or rather between the public good and private interests, was settled under the Hawke/Keating Labor governments of the 1980s and 1990s. With the collapse of the former Soviet Union, the earlier postwar social democratic consensus on the Keynesian welfare state was replaced with the neoliberal option, which came into vogue throughout the advanced capitalist world.

Since the mid 1990s, the economic theory promoted within the Washington Consensus, or neoliberalism, has ushered in a new era of "reforms" and "structural adjustment" programs. Within Australia, the Howard conservative government has attempted to build consensus around an extreme form of neoliberalism with the stage-managed policy shift from the provision of public goods and services to market-led solutions, which has led to an emphasis on self-sufficiency and individual responsibility. Here, as a vital safeguard against the captious exercise of tyranny "from above" or the anarchy of popular revolt "from below," self-responsibility is valorized in the current social environment as a virtue or public good in itself. Armed with this belief in self-reliance and moral individualism, and under the sign of human progress and freedom, the neoliberal state has sought to "commodify" social life through the imposition of policies that have led directly to the enclosure and destruction of the global commons and collective good.

The basic tenet of government policy in Australia is that public goods and services ought to be provided by the private sector through superior "free market" mechanisms, no matter how much pain or damage this causes. With the ideological tide running in the favor of market forces since the late 1980s, the privatization of state owned assets has offered the possibility of "raising revenue for the state" and "raising investment capital for the industry or company being privatized" (ACTRAV, 1997). Furthermore, privatization is perceived as introducing greater efficiency by reducing the role of government in the economy and disciplining state-owned enterprises to the "normal measures" of market forces. Within this context, the underlying economic rationale for restructuring the scalar configurations and institutional fabric of the state has been similar throughout the world (Starr, 1990).

The blind acceptance of market discipline that has radically transformed existing scalar configurations of the state is fuelled in part by a noxious discourse of "globalization." Since the mid 1990s, the term *globalization* has been used among certain intellectuals on both the digitally empowered Right and Left to describe certain "quantitative" changes in the world economy, which are understood to herald a post-historical period. Even though such diverse writers as Friedman (1999) and Giddens (2000) differ on the finer details, they tend to agree in broad and general terms that a new technological–economic system has emerged to remedy the failure of nation states, which have prevented the market from delivering its eternal promise of greater wealth and equality for all.

Linked to processes of global modernization (Giddens, 1998), the arrival of new information and communication technologies (ICTs) are understood to have contributed to the development of a "global networked society," which has created the material conditions, not only for vast new technological and production possibilities, but also for a greater level of individual/group interaction through the proliferation of on-line chat rooms, protest sites and other social networks. Even more bewildering, although advocates of globalization, armed with their own Palm Pilots and terminology, recognize that its effects are uneven, they steadfastly argue that as a total process it has contributed, through the "Information Revolution," to the collapse of "authoritarian regimes" and to the reform and reinforcement of existing democratic institutions and structures (Giddens, 2000).

Although it may have a distinctly hollow ring in the wake of recent events such as the terrorist attacks in New York and the U.S. led invasion of Iraq, it is important to recognize that the globalization thesis is not simply "descriptive" of objective conditions but rather constitutes a new form of bourgeois ideology (Hanson, 2000). Bolstered by the "collapse of communism," what it announces is a world in which "there is no alternative." Turning a blind eye to the abuses of capitalism, it holds that bourgeois property rights are no longer threatened by socialism or other liberation struggles. As an ideology, therefore, globalization is a form of market "triumphalism" used to paper over the material reality in which capitalist exploitation manifests itself. As a phenomenon, it is also clearly linked to neoliberalism, especially in that its political and economic practices are systematically geared toward enabling the bourgeois state to dismantle barriers to the international free-flow of goods and services (Hill, 2006). To help kick start the so-called "free" market, the objective, of course, is to produce the necessary ideological and material conditions favorable for international capital. Here, serving as a gendarme for the ruling class, the neoliberal state has minimized the rights and conditions of workers in order to weaken the labor movement, achieve flexibility and, in doing so, reap greater surplus profits (Hanson, 2000).

Turning to the current situation in Australia, the cumulative effect of more intensive management regimes is a corresponding increase in labor intensity as workers are pushed to work longer hours, to speed up the pace of work, and to cope with poor working conditions. Although stonemasons and building workers in Melbourne first won the 8-hour day from their employer in 1856, recent workplace reforms designed to "raise productivity" mean that Australians work some of the longest hours in the developed world (Denniss, 2004; Mascarenhas, 2004). Research conducted by the International Labour Organization (2004) found that the Australian workforce is increasingly working in excess of 50 hours a week, with an overall trend in that direction in defiance of a general slide downwards in OECD countries (Lee, 2004; Messenger, 2004). According to Hearn and Lansbury (2005), "The increase 'seems to be almost entirely composed of increases in unpaid overtime,' contributing to poor occupational health and safety and placing stress on family and community relationships." Putting a human face to neoliberalism, Currie (2005) cites several case studies (Campbell, 2002a, 2000b; Allan, O'Donnell, & Peetz, 1999; Peetz et al., 2003; Probert, Whiting, & Ewer, 1999, 2000), which highlight the adverse effects of extended working hours and intense work demands.

With respect to higher education, Marginson (2003) states that neoliberal reforms "bit deeper in Australia than in most other OECD countries" (cited in Currie, 2005). Huge cuts to university funding combined with diminished income support (e.g., tightening of eligibility criteria for Aus-tudy/Abstudy, which is a living allowance designed to address particular educational disadvantages) and increased upfront and Higher Education Contribution Scheme (HECS) fees under a "user pays" system mean that the worst affected include the working class, women, Aboriginals, and Torres Strait Islanders. And despite resistance from student organizations such as the National Union of Students (NUS), the government was able to impose Voluntary Student Unionism through its control of the Federal Senate in December 2005.[2] A recent study undertaken by the National Tertiary Education Union (NTEU, 2007) highlights some disturbing statistics and trends. For example:

- Australia's financial contribution to the cost of a university education has declined relative to other OCED counties since the election of the Howard conservative government in 1996.
- At an average fee of AUD $5,033[3] per year at a public university, Australian students are required to pay some of the highest tuition costs in the world (only less than students attending public universities in the United States and the same as their public counterparts in Japan and Korea; p. 5).[4]

Without admitting it, the Howard government has attempted to privatize the higher education sector in terms of contributions to costs. A case in point is the erosion of government funding and support. According to Gunstone (2007), "In 2006, the Australian public university system received just over 40 per cent of its recurrent funds from government. This is the lowest figure for any public university system in the world."[5]

While market-based reforms have led to a gradual disengagement from public education, tax dollars are being handed over to private universities for profit, such as the University of Notre Dame, which expects to gain 28% of its total income from public funds for its private war chest by 2008 (Illing, 2004; cited in Currie, 2005).[6] Extending public subsidies to private providers, the Howard government has promoted the growth of private institutions to encourage "increased productivity and a culture of continuous improvement and innovation" (Department of Education, Science and Training, 2001). Such neoliberal methods are the hallmarks of an agenda to "Americanize" Australia's higher education system (Moodie, 2004, cited in Currie, 2005), where public universities are increasingly dependent on fees for sources of revenue and are forced to devote more time and limited resources to the development, promotion, and selling of their "brand," or risk loosing valuable market share.

Despite an increased emphasis on privatisation and marketization, Corden (2005) writes that commercialization of research and consultancy activities "accounted on average for only about 5 per cent of a university's revenue" in 2002. Clearly, as the plug is pulled on federal funding, short-term windfalls from commercialization are not a panacea that will provide an automatic financial fix. Despite a number of stumbling blocks, overseas fee income from foreign students is the most significant growth in revenues for cash strapped universities. The NTEU (2007) reports that overseas fee income "in 2005 dollar values rose from $658m in 1996 to $2,135m in 2005, an increase of 224.7%. By 2005 overseas student income accounted for just over 15% of total university income" (p. 8). In 2004, education was Australia's fourth largest export industry and the Howard government sees liberalization of market access as a means of further extending international markets for Australian educational services (Minister for Foreign Affairs and Education, Science and Training, 2005).

Indeed, as universities are forced to battle for free market dollars, academics are being turned into slaves to the bottom line. Against a shortage of charitable and philanthropic capital to compensate for lost revenue (Marginson, 1997), academics are confronted with fewer resources, increased teaching loads, worsening staff–student ratios, and the unremitting pressure to become more "entrepreneurial" and assert the short-term commercial value of their work (Martin, 2005; NTEU, 2007; Slaughter, 1985, 1998). Although universities may appear, from the outside, to be safe havens from the ugliness of the "real world," an Australian national study into occupational stress reported that job stress for academics put them at 50% risk of psychological illness compared with only 19% for the Australian population (Winefield, Gillespie, Stough, Dua, & Hapuararchchi, 2002, cited in Currie, 2005). What's more, as universities attempt to establish areas of strength and comparative advantage, Slaughter (1993, 1998) observes that the growth in disciplines and fields of academic study that take up new directions aligned with market realities is occurring at the expense of the social sciences and humanities. For example, the Queensland University of Technology recently announced that it was dropping its "old" humanities program in favor of its Creative Industries faculty, which focuses on specific training in the creative arts field to meet the needs of industry (Livingstone, 2007).

In this atmosphere, workers in all industries really do have a lot to be afraid of right now as countries such as Australia strive to compete with economic powerhouses in the region such as China and India in a "race to the bottom" to attract capital investment for their respective home-based industries. It is absolutely obvious that Howard's preposterously named WorkChoices legislation (passed March 27, 2006), is tied up with this neoliberal agenda of flexible labor law changes, calculated to "strip away" the basic rights and conditions of workers established over a hundred years of class struggle ("Government's extreme," 2005). WorkChoices, or the Workplace Relations Act 1996 as amended by the Workplace Relations Amendment (Workchoices) Act 2005, is one of the most comprehensive changes to industrial relations in Australian history, with direct impacts on the working class. Abandoning a central pillar of the Keynesian welfare state that shaped industrial relations in Australia, the Howard government replaced the regulatory space of the Arbitration Commission with a politically appointed Australian Fair Pay Commission (AFPC) charged with setting "fair" minimum wages (Cook, 2006b). The ideological rationale for this move can be located with the neoliberal belief that wages must be kept low so that the unemployed are not priced out of low-waged labor markets. According to Waring, Ruyter, and Burgess (2006), the Australian Chamber of Commerce and Industry (ACCI) claims that Australia has the highest minimum wage rate in the world relative to the overall labor market. Wrapped up in a cocoon of material comfort, the former Minister for Employment and Workplace Relations, Kevin Andrews (2005), endorsed this view saying that the adult minimum wage was too high and it is hardly surprising that it is now defined as a wage that does not hamper employment and productivity benefits for Australian companies. Under these conditions, surplus value is the accumulated product of the unpaid labor expropriated from the working class as a whole (Marx, 1967). At a time when Australian chief executive officers (CEOs) are commanding breathtaking salaries and obscene bonuses (see Cook, 2006a),[7] the depths of government and ruling class hypocrisy is that the cost of daily living "is no longer a criterion in wage setting" for Australia's lowest paid workers (Weller, 2007). To make matters worse, Greg Combet, Australian Council of Trade Unions (ACTU) Secretary, recently pointed out that, "Under these laws, unions and workers can be fined $66,000 for even *asking* for workers to be protected from unfair dismissal or individual contracts, or for clauses that protect job security."

Throwing a two-punch combination at the trade union movement, the Conservative Coalition Howard government is forcing the implementation of its WorkChoices legislation through punitive funding arrangements at all levels of the educational system. For example, the Federal Education Minister made a pool of $260 million contingent on universities implementing the Commonwealth Government's Higher Education Workplace Requirements (HEWRRs), which allow for greater casualization of employment and the use of fixed term contracts. Tied to a valuable source of Commonwealth government funding, this dictatorial action threatens to undermine existing entitlements, such as long service leave and severance benefits, and "simplifies" dispute and termination procedures, with no direct role for unions. Using the political rhetoric of individual choice that sounds so appealing but requires a massive taxpayer funded advertising campaign run by the Department of Employment and Workplace Relations (Hall, 2006), HEWRRs require universities to offer university staff the "choice" of individual Australian Workplace Agreements (AWAs) at any stage of the performance management process.

Under the Howard government's Workplace Relations Act (1996), AWAs introduced individual agreements to allow workers the choice to negotiate directly with an employer over wages and conditions rather than to have a union negotiated agreement. At a time when productivity is at an all-time high, much of the rhetoric surrounding AWAs is that they enable "managerial prerogative" in relation to "underperforming" or "disruptive" workers. On that score, Prime Minister John Howard has sent a clear message that the government intends to weed out undesirable and underperforming teachers and researchers, who have been put on notice. From bonus packages to merit pay, AWAs are seen to reward individual effort by providing flexibility for performance-based incentives. For example, under the pretence of helping students in "underperforming" state schools, Julie Bishop, the Federal Minister for Education, Science and Training, recently attempted to link cash bonuses for individual teachers who turn out "high-achieving" students to AWAs (Topsfield, 2006). Expressing bullheadedness on the subject, she told *The Age* "There are a range of options, from a bonus paid to salary packages, to teachers being employed under AWAs, which provide flexibility for performance-based incentives" (Topsfield, 2006). Looking to undercut and emasculate the high membership and density of the Australian Education Union (AEU), AWAs will enable the Federal government to have greater control over teachers who are currently under state awards and agreements negotiated by unions. It seems worth noting that the International Labour Organization (ILO) has previously criticized certain provisions, including AWAs, of the Workplace Relations Act for breeching Conventions 87 and 98 that protect the right to collectively bargain and to strike (Isaac, 2006). With commendable courage and passion, teachers have joined thousands of other workers to attend union-organized rallies that protested the Howard government's WorkChoices legislation.

Denying workers a traditional means of emotional and political catharsis, the WorkChoices legislation reduced AWAs to five minimum standards (as contained in the Australian Fair Pay and Conditions Standard), curtailed trade union access to worksites and gave the Workplace Relations Minister the authority to declare strikes illegal. Providing an avuncular voice of reason on behalf of all Australians, the Prime Minister took a swipe at teachers who participated in rallies in support of the Your Rights at Work campaign, "Let me say that I worry about this kind of behaviour undermining the quality of government education in Victoria and around Australia" (Madigan, 2006). Blinded by dogmatism, he has flagrantly ignored the AEU's call for 2.9 million (AUD) in funding and played down its assessment that the overall decline in Federal funding spent on public education has impacted negatively on equity and fairness, with the significant increase in public funding to private schools fortifying their inherent privilege and influence in the marketplace (Byrne, 2007; Martin, in press).

CLASSICAL LIBERALISM TO NEOLIBERALISM

We can trace the origins of the apparent 180 degree U-turn in attitude toward the role of the state in the late 1980s and early 1990s to "the condition of

neoliberalism" (Harvey, 2005). In the historiography of classical economics, neoliberalism is the metaphorical brick thrown through the window of
Keynesian economics, which challenged the orthodoxy of the "laissez faire"
model of economics associated with Adam Smith, David Ricardo, Thomas
Malthus, and John Stuart Mill. Based upon the ideas of a centrally planned
or mixed economy developed by the British economist John Maynard Keynes
(1883–1946), Keynesian economics evolved out of the hardship, suffering,
and depths of despair caused by the Great Depression. With seemingly no
end in sight to this economic and social crisis, this domesticated brand of
collective economics influenced President Roosevelt's New Deal administration in the United States and Britain's post-war Labour government. Taking
on the final comforting cadence of a religious hymn, Keynesian economics
were institutionalized in the Bretton Woods system of international monetary management (1944–1971/73), which gave birth to the IMF and World
Bank (Brenner, R., 1999; Foster, 2003). However, Keynesian economics were
stomped out by the revisionist neoclassical economists who fetishized speculation and, in particular, the speculation of financial capital as a functional
"organizing" element of capitalism. With its origins in the political thinking
of the 1970s, the ascendency of neoliberalism in the 1980s and 1990s inau-
gurated a transition to the current era of liberalized capital movements.

Expanding the franchise of imperialism through a revival of classical
liberal economics in the 1970s, many of the current ideas surrounding the
notion that market forces must be unrestricted and that economic freedom
is at the essence of democracy, can be attributed to the recently deceased
University of Chicago economist, Milton Friedman, who wrote popular
polemics such as *Capitalism and Freedom* (1982) and *Free to Choose*
(1980). In 1970, he wrote in an article for *The New York Times Magazine*,
"The only responsibility of companies is to make a profit." Sharing this
sentiment, in the 1980s, his neoclassical economics inspired Prime Minister Thatcher, President Reagan, and Chilean dictator Augusto Pinochet.
This shift to neoliberal thinking has orientated the state away from its commitment to public goods such as education.

Catapulting us into the new millennium, Friedman's influence remains
a driving force behind many of the market-friendly proposals for "choice,"
which is seen as a popular interventionist policy prescription for optimal
resource allocation. Choice is the new mantra that holds that the "over-
heads" of the public sector must be annually downsized because competition is required to promote quality, diversity, and innovation in the face
of "globalization." With regards to the advantages of a free market in the
public education realm, Friedman (1955) wrote, "The interjection of competition would do much to promote a healthy variety of schools. It would
do much, also, to introduce flexibility into school systems. Not least of its
benefits would be to make the salaries of school teachers responsive to market forces." Clearly, Friedman has left an indelible mark on contemporary
economic thinking that has changed the built landscape of public education.

Here, behind the façade, the theoretical foundations of laissez-faire economics are repudiated by forms of state intervention (often defined as neoliberalism, e.g., the introduction of user fees, the distribution of school vouchers, and the contracting out of services to public and private providers) that have taken a huge toll on the lives of millions of working-class children.

Indeed, the enduring relevance of class in the historiography of Australia puts a spike in the myth of meritocracy, demonstrating its robust value as a sociological concept as well as an axis of potential political organization. A fact sheet put out by Education Foundation Australia (2006) states, "There is strong evidence that educational achievement in Australia is significantly determined by individual socio-economic status or social background as measured by parents' occupation. Australia shows a stronger relationship between social background and educational achievement than most Organisation for Economic Co-operation and Development (OECD) countries." Contrary to the mind-shredding propaganda put out by the proponents of the "free market," Argy (2006) points out:

> Already, the interaction of market forces and policy developments in Australia is creating a two-tier society in employment, health, education, housing and public transport, as well as wide regional disparities in opportunities and growing poverty traps. And the outlook is more of the same. For people with individual market power, the recent spate of workplace and welfare reforms will offer wider choice and greater scope for income and occupational mobility. But for the more disadvantaged in our community, the new policy environment will mean *less* choice and *less* scope for upward income mobility.

Notorious for ratcheting up social division through the so-called Australian values debate, the sharp turn to the right by the Howard government is part of an obsession against alleged political bias in schools that is seen to threaten equity, standards, and the national interest. In 2004, the Prime Minister blamed the fall in public school enrolments on state schools being "too politically correct and too values-neutral," with particular attention paid to the effects of a warped/left-wing bias in the curriculum (Crabb & Guerrera, 2004). Missing from this narrative, of course, is the fact that the movement toward "choice" and "competition" in education has required the injection of massive amounts of public money into the private school system. In effect, this funding arrangement constitutes "a de-facto voucher system" whereby the costs of parents sending their children to a "better quality" private school of their choice is subsidized (Donnelly, 2007a). With regards to the Howard government's 2005–2008 education funding package, Zimmer (2004) wrote,

> For the first time, more federal money will be allocated to private, non-Catholic schools than to government schools. Independent schools, which currently have 13 percent of student enrolments, will receive

$7.6 billion; Catholic schools, with approximately 18 percent of total students, have been allocated $12.6 billion. Government schools, attended by 68 percent of students, will get $7.2 billion or only 26 percent of federal funding. This subsidization has contributed to the exodus from the state system to private schools and spawned a mushrooming number of religious schools.

But this is only the first step. Hardly content to stop there, the Howard government is experimenting with vouchers and the idea of charter schools as a possible way forward. Searching for an appropriate entry point to help facilitate change or "choice," the Minister for Education, Science and Training, Julie Bishop (2006), announced the Reading Assistance Voucher program. Under the program, parents and caregivers of eligible children receive up to $700 worth of reading tuition for their child. Despite a low take up for the literacy voucher (Leung, 2005), rightist "culture warriors" such as Kevin Donnelly (2007b)[8], who are linked to the state, continue to push their privatization agenda with the backing of Murdoch's press empire. Attempting to ground neoliberalism in a rescaled ideology of citizenship from the state level to the individual level (based in a romanticized or idealized form of liberal democracy—that is also cheap), Donnelly (2007b) recently wrote:

> On the grounds of equity and social justice, it makes sense if more parents, especially those from disadvantaged backgrounds, are able to choose between government and non-government schools. Ideally, such a voucher would be set at $10,000 and the money would follow the child. Vouchers and charter schools, reflecting a commitment to choice, competition and accountability, present new territory in the education debate. (p. 28)

Providing a concise and unsettling glance into the state of liberalized schooling in four continents, Hill (2006) connects the seductive language of "standards" and "choice" to a narrow form of neoliberal ideology that is being used to stigmatise and suppress oppositional activity and critical thought. Noting that the demands, benchmarks, and standards of capital are inherently antagonistic to the interests of labour, Hill (2004) states:

> On the one hand, capital requires educated and flexible workers, but on the other hand it cannot countenance workers thinking fundamental critique for themselves—or coming across it in schools, vocational education or universities. So free thinking, and oppositional thinking has been chopped, curtailed, circumscribed.

With a view to reasserting "traditional" Australian values and "moral discipline" amongst the next generation of workers, the Howard government is pushing a sugar-coated curriculum[9] that places renewed emphasis on patriotism. It has also allocated $90 million over three years to fund the appointment of religious counsellors or chaplains to provide "spiritual and pastoral" guidance to primary and secondary school students in both the secular public and private school systems (Zimmer, 2007; "God in the Machine," 2006; Wiltshire, 2006). But it's a veneer for creating a new Frankenstein monster. The objective, of course, is to regulate social norms, values, and ethical frameworks in order to fashion a new vision of the ideal state citizen (Martin, in press).

Against much of the manufactured crisis talk surrounding education in Australia, the federal government is justifying the proposed takeover of the public school system by cloaking it in the neoliberal ideology of standards, performance, and accountability (Luke & Woods, in press). At its most ambitious, the neoliberal state is trying to effect a change from the public to the private provision of public goods and services, such as education. In Australia, constitutional responsibility for the establishment and oversight of K through 12 education resides with the six states and two territories, including the formation of policy, statutory reporting to State and Federal Ministers, and financial management, with the federal government the main provider of funding (Miner, 2006). All of which means that Howard has an ace up his sleeve as the federal government controls the purse strings and allocates funds on basis of state and territory governments meeting certain conditions in relation to primary and secondary education. Hence, the attempt of the Howard government to sneak in through the backdoor in order to change the landscape of education provision through its emphasis on standards, choice, and efficiency, which are all tied to funding arrangements designed to ensure "accountability." To thwart that threat, the AEU has recently undertaken an aggressive advertising campaign in marginal seats across Australia to make public education a priority in the lead up to the next Federal election due to be held in 2007 or as late as 19 January 2008.[10]

NEOLIBERALISM: RESCALING STATE
POWER AND FUNCTIONS

Devolution, decentralization, and de-zoning (open enrolment) are all "boundary-blurring" activities that are expected to lay the groundwork for future privatization (Starr, 1990). With a keen eye to the policy future, Starr (1990) defines "boundary-blurring" policies and proposals such as providing parents with "choice" through the provision of school vouchers "as a second-best alternative to eliminating public spending for many services altogether." In developing and implementing a class-based policy, the state provides a space at multiple scales (e.g., national, regional, local) through which diverse interests can be "reconciled" with its neoliberal agenda setting and resource allocations. In Australia, Cahill (2007) argues that neoliberalism is part and parcel of a broader hegemonic project that is reorganising the relational space of everyday life through "a unique combination of material inducements and economic and extraeconomic coercion" (p. 221). Lefebrve (1991) makes clear that the regulatory state is not neutral in furthering the interests of the ruling class through the "production of space." Without a doubt, the hierarchical ordering and production of space secures the scalar fixes required for capital accumulation. Here, market orientated restructuring projects that invite greater private sector involvement "in the performance of functions that government cannot entirely surrender" are designed to subject state enterprises such as education to the sharper discipline of market forces (Starr, 1990). Under these circumstances, the state is being radically restructured along neoliberal lines, with Kryptonic effect. Neil Brenner (1999) points out:

> On the one hand, state re-scaling can be viewed as a neoliberal strategy of "deregulation" to dismantle the nationally configured redistributive operations of the Fordist-Keynesian order, frequently by undermining the social-welfare functions of municipal institutions. On the other hand, just as crucially, state re-scaling has served as a strategy of "reregulation" to construct new institutional capacities for promoting capital investment. (p. 440)

With regards to shifting scales of state regulation in Australia and the allocation of resources, it is not Adam Smith's "invisible hand of the market" that is driving the market model for the funding of social infrastructure. Against the backdrop of reckless disinvestment in the public sector, the Howard government's home-grown recipe for neoliberalism leaves nothing to chance.

Reorganizing the social and economic landscape of Australia, the state is rescaling its functions and power in a desperate bid to secure the general conditions for capital accumulation. Focusing on the complexities of this process, Starr (1990) argues, "Privatisation ought to be understood not merely as reducing the state but as restructuring it." In Australia, the fly in Howard's ointment is that the six states and two territories are constitutionally required to provide free public education, which acts as a break on privatization, unlike other sectors of public infrastructure, such as electricity, water, and telecommunications. Amidst a sea of subaltern discontent over the performance of state-owned enterprises at the local scale of community, which is fostered by a heightened level of neoliberal crisis talk, "boundary-blurring" activities, such as devolution and decentralization, are a necessary consequence of the class struggle (Zimmer, 2003). In essence, the scalar shift of state territorial power, grounded in an imaginary geography of devolved decision-making, operates to hold the interests of capital in place.

In the United States, educational vouchers provide an example of "boundary challenging" and "boundary blurring" as reorganizers of the state seek to build their interests into the institutional fabric of state-owned enterprises (Starr, 1990). Representing a political gift for true believers, such a move actually represents a defensive gesture to repoliticize the administrative ideological state apparatus as the state engages in a form of "crisis management" to shift the balance of forces back toward capital. At a time when Australia's public institutions have fallen into a shameful state of decay, a meritocratic education system is understood to be a great equalizer of opportunity. Whatever one might think of this belief, nothing is more of a threat to working-class aspirations in "egalitarian" Australia than mediocre schools.

Having repeatedly terrorized the working class through savage cuts to public services, the state is attempting to cut itself free from any ethical relation to community. Following the neoliberal template, the Howard government is appealing aggressively to community expectations through the rhetoric of freedom and choice. Due to historical processes of uneven development that segmented the metropolitan regions of Australia into a patchwork of disparate communities, this discourse is very appealing to working-class parents who, forced to live in isolated and outer urban areas, are structurally separated from the protected islands of affluence in certain suburbs. Take, for example, the working-class neighborhoods located in the far western suburbs of Sydney, which are characterized by hard-to-staff schools, entrenched unemployment, and poor social and welfare services (Vinson, 2002; Zimmer, 1999). Making a pitch to those "battlers" living in concentrated poverty, as well as to the "election deciders" residing in the relatively affluent suburban mortgage belt of the capital cities, the cultural politics and appeals that mobilize support for choice are seductive in an era of uncertainly, particularly as it applies to the bare necessities of life.

With the pressure to introduce "quasi-market" forces into the public school sector, what is most interesting is how "democracy" has been articulated to organize and regulate social and spatial practices of schooling (Kamat, 2000). Privatization of the state sector, even in formerly strong social democratic countries such as Australia, has been met with scarcely a murmur of protest or resistance. On the face of it, reorganizers of state enterprises have engaged in a strategic politics of revitalization, which has removed pressures from the central state to increase spending and shifted responsibility for any failure onto local government and specific service providers. Under the rhetoric of "empowerment," reorganizers of the state have willingly devolved some traditional functions and operational authority to lower level agencies and localities, which must then manage and prioritize limited resources within globally imposed budgetary constraints (Kamat, 2000).

It is clear, however, that real power will be exported to a higher administrative political scale of the state bureaucracy if the Australian Federal government takes control of schooling through the establishment of "national curricula, statewide testing, national standards and competencies, teacher appraisal and curriculum audits" (Smyth, cited in McInerney, 2001). It's a pretty safe bet that national standards of assessment will be introduced in Australia, regardless of which government is in power after the next Federal election. Under current arrangements, newly empowered public school principals in states such as New South Wales can now employ teachers through "partial local selection" (Zimmer, 2005). Despite the inherent dangers of favoritism and victimization, principals also have "the 'choice' of employing casual staff to replace absent teachers or allocating the money to other areas of need: books, photocopying, paying the power or water bill" (Zimmer, 1999).

Clearly, devolution is a highly political, complex, and fragile process of engagement and adherence fraught with pitfalls, tensions, and challenges, particularly in a dynamic and insecure global economy (McInerney, 2001). Like a recipe that has gone terribly wrong, Rizvi has described a shift in Australia "from a social democratic view of devolution to approaches incorporating managerialist and market-driven responses" (McInerney, 2001). It is hard not to feel nostalgic when research conducted into the version of devolution adopted in Australia over the past ten to fifteen years under titles such as "school-based management," "site-based decision-making," and "school-centred forms of education," has found that local authorities may exercise greater participation in decision making and "choice" but only within certain pre-defined parameters, particularly in the curriculum (Smyth, cited in McInerney, 2001). And herein is the rub, as recentralization will inevitably enable the Federal government to regulate educational standards, content, and behavior at the national level through the threat of punitive funding arrangements. Conveniently enough, it will also enable the Federal government to recycle blame for poor performance back down to the local level if the desired outcomes are not delivered.

As capital rescales the state to overcome any territorial barriers or blockages to the accumulation process, a growing number of scholars are interested in studies that examine the "allocation of powers to different tiers of the education system from the state bureaucracy to the school" (Kamat, 2000). "Steering at a distance" (Ball, 1994, p. 54) is an especially apt concept for describing this process and explains how the moral and coercive authority of the state is exerted in a seemingly "invisible" manner (Kamat, 2000). Despite the jumbled claims of globalization theorists who argue that the nation state is "withering away," it is still a key actor in regulating these integrative relationships at multiple geographical scales. Upon closer scrutiny, it is clear that reorganizers of the state have embarked on a "new 'built' environment of decentralisation" (Kamat, 2000). Trapped in a horror of its own making, capital must restrict and deny working people access to space (mental and physical), if it is to maintain the social division of labor, which is necessary to the production of value. Within this violent field of value, the newly built environment in education is purposefully designed to predispose individuals and groups toward more individualized thinking and self-interested behavior in competitive settings. The illusion of transparency, which surrounds neoliberal "common-sense" notions of space, explains why so many parents and caregivers embrace market-based reforms in education, including the freedom of school choice, even though the results are far from satisfactory and deteriorating (Walford, 1996).

TO THE LIGHTHOUSE

Despite all the hoopla surrounding the term *globalization,* Lenin's (1916) original insights into the economic dynamics of combined and uneven development demonstrates that it is just a fancy new name for an old and cruel phase of capitalism. The plain fact is that the huge changes in the spatial/scalar organization of production, as well as the superstructure of capitalism, are actually a sign of the weakness and desperation of imperialism. The emphasis on "leaner and meaner" social policy is part of imperialism's arsenal for gaining competitive advantage. By awful necessity, the imperialist nation state must search for new spatial/scalar "fixes" to absorb excess capital and idle labor in a world of deregulated markets. Within the education sector of the economy, neoliberal policies and processes such as deregulation, decentralization, and de-zoning are all "boundary-blurring" processes that pave the way for future privatization. Heralding a new topography of education in the 21st century, this move is part of the capitalist class struggle to prevent the state sector from operating potentially profitable units of commodity production (particularly as it relates to the production of labor power) by subjecting state-owned enterprises such as schools to the discipline of market forces (Frankel, 1978). The capitalization and commodification of education is an extension of a pernicious form of internal colonization, which secures, partially or provisionally, the conditions for capital accumulation.

In this sense, the production of state space in the education sector of the economy must be understood as part of the wider struggle over social priorities, between capital and labor. With the decay of capitalism increasingly visible in everyday life, the rescaling of the nation state is connected to regulating ways of thinking and knowing that legitimate and reproduce social-cultural spaces of capitalist value. Within this material and imaginary landscape, the production of identity is grounded in the elaboration of what Raymond Williams (1977/1988) called a distinctive "structure of feeling" and "knowable community." What this means is that at the level of everyday life or "community" (e.g., school, family, workplace, leisure), neoliberalism generates social values and practices that cause individuals to feel as though they belong to a place. Within the current neoliberal regime, the political discourses and habitual practices of community have been "reduced to a pedagogical tool that reduces us to the status of alienated and atomized individuals, who compete with other equally alienated and atomized individuals for the means of subsistence" (Martin, 2005). Through this cultural script or ideology of "free" market/globalization, our "mental" space (consciousness) is subjugated through its daily interaction with these socially produced spaces, which has the desired effect of naturalizing the existing social world as the only possible and "reasonable" one. Moreover, the hegemonic force of this spatiality is maintained through the systematic denigration and annihilation of spaces that materialize values that are antagonistic to the social universe of capital (e.g., the Keynesian cradle-to grave-welfare state; Mitchell, 2003). All in all, neoliberalism is designed to help capital to escape control of value systems that threaten the basis of exchange relations (e.g., education as a use-value based in human and non-human needs rather than as an exchange value for private profit needs).

But it is also undeniable that the effects of neoliberalism are not evenly distributed and that the repeated attacks on living standards, particularly the anti-union WorkChoices legislation, have sparked widespread anger and militancy. Workers are beginning to say enough is enough and to learn and relearn the lessons of militancy and direct action. A good instance of this is at the University of Ballarat, where workers experienced firsthand Howard's industrial relations "reform" agenda, when told they had to accept an AWA to get a job or receive a pay rise. Making a mockery out of Howard's claim that changes to the Industrial Relations system are all about "expanding individual choice, freedom and opportunity," it was clear that workers had no choice but to obey the contract under WorkChoices (Byrne, 2005; Fletcher, 2005). Ballarat University NTEU branch president Jeremy Smith (Ball, 2005) told *Green Left Weekly:*

> We are possibly the only group of NTEU members being threatened with stand-downs. Many of our members felt really nervous about the future going into today's meeting. Yet despite all the threats and intimidation, our members are prepared to fight on. It's a gutsy effort. General staff members are not threatened with stand-downs,[11] but they showed that they will stand by their union comrades against the despicable threats of the vice-chancellor.

After standing their ground, the union scored a victory in the form of a collective agreement (NTEU, 2006). It is a testimony to the more militant and confrontational tendencies of the trade union moment that the government has been forced onto the back foot on industrial relations.

Indeed, the news is not all bleak. The results of the Australian National University's Australian Survey of Social Attitudes revealed a progressive shift in attitudes in 2003, as compared to 1987 (Macdonald, 2005). Using data from the survey, Meagher (2004) states

> responses show limited and selective support for private sector delivery of social services. Most Australians believe that governments are best suited to delivering child, aged, and health care than *any other form of organisation,* including families and relatives. (italics in the original).

Contrary to what one might suppose, Australians placed a high value on state-run education, with "over two-thirds" prepared to pay more tax to improve it (Wilson & Meager, 2004). Despite neoliberalism's promise of increased individual opportunity, Connell (2003) argues that the "ethic of a fair go" is still strong in Australian working-class life, which has mitigated the drift toward "market-type behaviour" (p. 248). Finding a range of attitudes and concerns, he argues that working-class families still rely heavily "on the bureaucratic machinery of state education to deliver a reasonable education for their children" (p. 249). On the ground, he notes that, "There is still a great deal of good will and respect for schooling, and some schools make very good use of it" (p. 249).

It is easy to lose sight of hope in the face of widespread indifference to the suffering and pain inflicted by global capitalism. However, rather than adopt a fatalistic and pessimistic outlook, it is also possible to see every outbreak of protest and rebellion as a tactical training ground in preparation for substantial social change in the future (Martin, 2006). Challenging the speculation theory of armchair activists on the postmodern left, McLaren (2003, 2005) discusses the rise of grassroots political and labor organizations that are looking to build a "world outside of capitalism's value form of labor." Focusing on such real life processes and struggles, the premise of this chapter is that we are living in a period of opportunity when the movement of the working class can learn from the rich experience of other countries and forces, particularly in oppressed capitalist countries in Asia, Latin America, and Africa (Percy & Lorimer, 2001, p. 11). More work needs to be done to understand this, but the conditions leading up to a deepening crisis in advanced capitalist countries are also being prepared for by the thousands of minor skirmishes and struggles engaged in today (Martin, 2006; Percy & Lorimer, 2001). For example, over a period of ten weeks in early 2006, youth and workers across France transformed mass mobilizations against the introduction of the "first job contract," known as the CPE—a youth employment law that makes it legal for employers to sack workers under the age of 26 without notice or compensation—into a general strike (Clancy, 2006; Smith, 2006). This mass pressure from the streets was instrumental in defeating the law and demonstrates the real and potential power of the working class when it goes on the political offensive. But to take this offensive a step further and build a movement for radical change will require more than anger and lobbying for concessions. It will require a militant politics that can be the basis for united action. On this point, it is important to clarify that, in the class struggle for a more humane, caring, and ecologically sustainable society, Marxists are opposed to both state terrorism and individual acts of terrorism (Trotsky, 1909, 1911). Reaching out to the future, they are absolutely opposed to terrorist methods, which negate the formation of "a positive vision of a new society, what Karl Marx called 'positive humanism'" (Hudis, 2001).

These are fighting words. At the same time, a strategic problem is that the ruling class in Australia has popular support having sidetracked the class struggle into "aspirational families" during a period of "social peace" (Lenin, 1913). On the economic front, however, neoliberalism is failing to deliver the goods and resistance is starting to grow. Although the antagonism between capital and labor never really went away, at a time when many Australians were beginning to wonder whether the trade union movement (under right-wing influence) had a political pulse, this emerging crisis of reproduction threatens to undermine new strategies developed by the state to legitimate a neoliberal agenda. According to Marois and Irias (2006), the fight for a credible and viable alternative to neoliberalism will require the development of "critical consciousness" as well as "real-life working practices" that are capable of "capturing and creating local spaces as a foundation for a conscious and critically-minded solidarity that can feed national and international movements of resistance" (p. 51). Living under the glare of constant surveillance, this will require fighting the standardization, deskilling, and isolation that teachers experience in the corporate classroom through the development of innovative, participatory, and transgressive forms of teaching and research (Luke, 2004; Kincheloe, 1991; Kincheloe & Steinberg, 1998; Kincheloe, 2004). With a focus on recovering a space for critique and human agency, radical/socialist/Marxist educators such as Allman (1999, 2001), McLaren (2005, 2006), Hill (2003, 2004, 2007a, b, c) Hill and Boxley (2007), Kelsh (1998), Mallot (2006), Scatamburlo-D'Annibale (2006) and Rikowski (2001, 2006) argue that education can play a role in this effort by serving all of society rather than the private profit interests of a few. Regrettably, the real and imagined geography of neoliberalism has increased the individual worker's psychic vulnerability to ideological manipulation. In doing so, it has reduced the scale of class struggle. It is against this period of ideological reaction that we find ourselves fighting for a pedagogical project, which is capable of producing the "common ground" for an actively engaged, politically informed, and critically reflective citizenry.

NOTES

1. Economists such as Paul Samuelson, John Stuart Mill, Henry Sidgwick, and Arthur Pigou used the lighthouse as a classic example of a public good. Samuelson (1964), who is credited with first developing the theory of public goods, wrote: "Its beam helps everyone in sight. A businessman could not build it for a profit, since he cannot claim a price for each user" (p. 159). In demonstrating that privately maintained lighthouses actually existed in Britain, Coase's revisionist historical analysis challenged the prevailing rationale for government intervention in the provision of certain public goods and infrastructure.
2. Voluntary Student Unionism (VSU) legislation, introduced across Australia from July 1, 2006, requires membership and payment of membership fees

to university student organizations to be voluntary. Prior to VSU, students were required to become a member of their student campus organization and pay compulsory fees. Student groups and organizations including the National Union of Students (NUS) actively opposed the introduction of the legislation, with grave concerns about their financial ability to continue to provide social, academic, and political services (e.g., childcare, taxation and legal advice, education advocacy, women support services, and sporting/recreation programs).

3. All dollar amounts are Australian unless otherwise indicated.

4. Australian citizens and (with some limitations) Australian permanent residents do not have to pay up-front fees at a public university if enrolled in a Commonwealth Supported Place (CSP). A CSP is a higher education place for which the Commonwealth makes a financial contribution toward the cost of a student's education. The contribution a student makes to the cost of his or her education varies significantly depending upon which course they are enrolled in and the corresponding level of government support that is provided. Eligible students in CSP places can pay the entire Student Contribution Charge upfront and receive a 20% discount or opt to defer all or part of their contribution (previously known as a HECS liability) via a loan made available through the HECS-HELP scheme. Domestic students may also enroll in a non-Commonwealth Supported Place, known as a FULL-FEE place, and must pay all upfront fees for courses, which are typically greater than a standard HECS-HELP debt. Within the overall pattern of decline in funding, public universities have relaxed the normal academic entrance requirements for these students with the provision of "alternative entry pathways," further entrenching middle-class advantage in higher education. Overseas students are required to pay full sticker price for their education and are ineligible for any loans from the Australian government (Going to Uni, n.d.). According to Kostas (2006), a Senate committee investigated the financial strains placed on university students and expressed concern

> that students are being forced to work longer hours, often in low-paid or cash-in-hand jobs, as a direct result of inadequate income support. Reports of students resorting to product testing and even turning to prostitution as a source of income raise serious moral, health and safety concerns.

5. On Tuesday, May 8, 2007, the Federal Treasurer, Peter Costello, delivered his 12th Budget. Over the period 2007–2008 to 2010–2011, the Commonwealth Government will use budget surpluses to invest an additional $3.514 billion in education, of which half, or 1.7 billion, will be spent on higher education (NTEU, 2007). Against the backdrop of a decline in investment over the past decade, an initial $5 billion will be placed in the "U.S. style" Higher Education Endowment Fund (HEEF), a perpetual investment fund designed to generate surplus profits to fund infrastructure (Higher Education Endowment Fund, n.d.; Lewis, 2007). Despite the fact that the Treasurer boasted higher education was a budget winner, the NTEU warned, "only dividends from the $5b, not the substantive amount itself is to be invested into universities" (NTEU, 2007).

6. In 2008, there are 37 public universities in Australia and only two private institutions, Bond University and the University of Notre Dame Australia (Higher Education Summary, n.d.). The Group of Eight is a coalition of the oldest and most prestigious institutions, which are all public universities.

7. Cook (2006a) cites research conducted by John Shields at the University of Sydney that indicates

the average annual CEO pay climbed by 564 percent over 15 years, rising from $514,433 in 1989–90 to $3.42 million in 2004–05. The average compounded yearly rise was 13.5 percent, or five times the inflation rate of 2.8 percent. Over the same period, the average wage of full-time adult workers rose just 85 percent, or by 4.2 percent a year, from $29,198 to $54,080. In 1989–90 the total salary of a CEO, including base pay and bonuses, was 18 times that of an average worker; today it is 63 times higher. Translated into weekly earnings, an average CEO is paid $65,000 a week, or around $11,000 more than the annual wage of an average worker or nearly $40,000 more than the annual earnings of the 1.6 million basic wage workers who make up 20 percent of the Australian workforce. These workers struggle to make ends meet on just $25,188 a year, or $484 a week.

8. Kevin Donnelly is a policy insider who is a former chief of staff to Federal Employment Minister Kevin Andrews and author of books such as, *Why Our Schools Are Failing* (2004), and *Dumbing Down: Outcomes-Based and Politically Correct—The Impact of the Culture Wars on Our Schools* (2007).

9. Mining racist sentiment, the Howard government is pushing a restrictive national curriculum that is easier to swallow than the so-called "Black Armband" view of Australian history. The phrase "black armband" view of history was coined by Australian historian Professor, Geoffrey Blainey, in his 1993 *Sir John Latham Memorial Lecture*. It gained popular currency in Australia after it was picked up and used by right wing think tanks and conservative politicians, historians, and commentators to denote an overly critical view of Australian history, which did not focus enough on European successes and achievements (what Henry Reynolds described as the "white blindfold approach"; Nettleheim, 2001). In his 1996 *Sir Robert Menzies Lecture*, Howard argued: "This 'black armband' view of our history reflects a belief that most Australian history since 1788 has been little more than a disgraceful story of imperialism, exploitation, racism, sexism and other forms of discrimination."

10. On November 24, 2007, the Howard Coalition government was defeated in the federal election by the Kevin Rudd Labor Government. However, during the election campaign, Kevin Rudd dampened expectations of "change" if elected. Claiming "it's a badge I wear with pride," Rudd (2007) stressed that he was an "economic conservative" and pledged that Labor would impose fiscal discipline. Within the first hundred days of government this has meant that the self-identified Rudd "razor gang" has focused on cutting government spending (except Defence) and running a strong surplus budget, taking a hard line on unions in order to keep wages and inflation in check and supporting the US alliance. Indeed, symbolic changes such as signing Kyoto, offering a formal national apology to Aboriginals in Parliament, and appointing the first female Governor-General have all masked a deep "continuity." Indeed, Rudd has put a premium on upholding his promise of "continuity". rather than announcing major policy reversals. Thus, transitional legislation introduced in Parliament to "dismantle" the draconian Workchoices has fallen short of abolishing it. And with its emphasis on productivity growth. the labor governments's so-called Education Revolution is clearly freighted toward meeting the knowledge and human capital needs of corporate Australia (Michaels, 2007; Symonds, 2007). This flagship election policy is part of the Federal government's public investment in a "human capital revolution" and includes providing affordable childcare to encourage women into the workforce, ensuring every secondary student has access to

reliable high-speed broadband as well as their own computer, raising the status of vocational and technical training in schools, and ensuring education standards through a uniform national curriculum. Meanwhile, the stage is set for major industrial confrontations between public sector workers including teachers and state Labor governments as part of campaigns in Victoria, New South Wales and Western Australia over fair pay and working conditions including statewide staffing and security of tenure.

11. In Australia, the phrase "stand down" refers to suspension of employment. Under the Workplace Relations Act 1996, an employer can stand down an employee without pay in one or more of the following circumstances, "a strike, a break down in machinery; or a work stoppage for which the employer cannot reasonably be held responsible; eg, a natural disaster" (WorkChoices and the right, 2006).

REFERENCES

ACTRAV. (1997). *National framework for globalization [Project INT/97/M01/ ITA]. Geneva: Bureau for Workers' Activities, International Labour Office.* Retrieved May 13, 2007, from http://www.itcilo.it/english/actrav/telearn/ global/ilo/seura/mains.htm

Allman, P. (1999). *Revolutionary social transformation: Democratic hopes, political possibilities and critical education.* Westport, CT: Bergin & Garvey.

Allman, P. (2001). *Critical education against global capitalism: Karl Marx and revolutionary critical education.* Westport, CT: Bergin & Garvey.

Althusser, L. (1971). *Lenin and philosophy and other essays by Louis Althusser.* New York: Monthly Review Press.

Argy, F. (2006, May 24). Equality of opportunity: Levelling the playing field. *New Matilda.* Retrieved April 28, 2007, from http://www.newmatilda.com/policy-toolkit/policydetail.asp?PolicyID=397&CategoryID=16

Australian Council of Trade Unions (ACTU) (2005). *Government's extreme and radical IR legislation confirms union campaign–Australian workers' rights and conditions to be stripped away.* (2005, November 2). ACTU Media Release. Retrieved December 18, 2006, from http://www.nuw.org.au/articles/nat/campaigns/wr2005/articles/newlegis

AXISS Australia: A Division of Invest Australia. (2006, June 8). Australia's Economic Performance. Retrieved April 30, 2007, from http://www.axiss.gov.au/ assets/documents/axissinternet/06%20Data%20Alert%20Australia%27s%20E conomic%20Performance%208%20June%20200606008162007%2Epdf

Bailey, J., & Iveson, K. (2000, December). 'The Parliaments call them thugs': Public space, identity and union protest. *The Journal of Industrial Relations,* 42(4), 517–534.

Ball, S. (1994). *Education reform: A Critical and post-structural approach.* Buckingham, UK: Open University Press.

Ball, S. (2005, August 10). University to fight stand-downs. *Union Fightback.* Retrieved April 30, 2007, from http://www.unionfightback.org/modules.php? name=News&file=article&sid=3

Bishop, J. (2006, May 9). *Help for children struggling with reading skills.* Retrieved April 29, 2007, from http://www.dest.gov.au/ministers/bishop/budget06/bud0606.htm

Blainey, G. (1993, July/August). Drawing up a balance sheet of our history. *Quadrant,* 37(7–8), 10–15.

Bramble, T. (2004). *Contradictions in Australia's 'Miracle Economy.'* Retrieved December 17, 2006, from http://www.anu.edu.au/polsci/marx/interventions/ contradictions.htm

Brenner, N. (1999). *Globalization as reterritorialization: The re-scaling of urban governance in the European Union.* Retrieved May 18, 2007, from http://sociology.fas.nyu.edu/docs/IO/222/1999.Brenner.Urb.St.pdf

Brenner, N. (2001). The limits to scale? Methodological reflections on scalar structuration. *Progress in Human Geography, 25*(4), 591–614.

Brenner, R. (1999). Competition and class: A reply to Foster and Brenner. *Monthly Review.* Retrieved April 30, 2007, from http://www.monthlyreview.org/1299bren.htm

Byrne, P. (2004, Autumn). Yes, let's talk about values! *Australian Educator, 9.*

Byrne, P. (2005, Winter). Howard's July 1 grab for power. *Australian Educator, 7.*

Byrne, P. (2007, May 8). *Public school students lose out again.* Retrieved July 8, 2007, from http://www.aeufederal.org.au/Media/MediaReleases/2007/0805(2).pdf

Cahill, D. (April, 2007). The contours of neoliberal hegemony in Australia. *Rethinking Marxism, 19*(2), 221–233.

Clancy, E. (2006, April 26). France shows the way: We can stop Howard's anti-worker laws. *Green Left Weekly, 665,* p. 13.

Coase, R. (1974, October). The Lighthouse in Economics. *Journal of Law and Economics, 17*(2), 357–376.

Connell, R. (2003). Working-class families and the new secondary education. *Australian Journal of Education, 47*(3), 235–250.

Conway, J. (2005). *The empire, the movement, and the politics of scale: Considering the WSF.* Retrieved May 7, 2007, from http://www.openspaceforum.net/twiki/tiki-read_article.php?articleId=159

Cook, T. (2005, April 30). Australian government poised to make sweeping industrial relations "reform". *World Socialist Web Site.* Retrieved April, 15, 2008 from http://www.wsws.org/articles/2005/apr2005/indu-a30.shtml

Cook, T. (2006a, February 13). *Australia: A widening gap between CEO salaries and average wages.* Retrieved June 17, 2007, from http://www.wsws.org/articles/2006/feb2006/ceos-f13.shtml

Cook, T. (2006b, September 12). *Australian Fair Pay Commission lays the groundwork for wage cuts.* Retrieved June 17, 2007, from http://www.wsws.org/articles/2006/sep2006/fpco-s12.shtml

Corden, W. (2005). Australian universities: Moscow on the Molongo. *Quadrant.* Retrieved July 9, 2007, from http://quadrant.org.au/php/article_view.php?article_id=1232

Costello, P. (2001). *Address to the Sydney Institute "Challenges and Benefits of Globalisation."* Retrieved December 17, 2006, from http://www.treasurer.gov.au/tsr/content/speeches/2001/003.asp

Cox, K. (Ed.). (1996). *Spaces of globalization: Reasserting the power of the local.* Surrey, UK: Guildford Press.

Crabb, A., & Guerrera, O. (2004, January 20). PM queries values of state schools. *The Age.* Retrieved February 3, 2007, from http://www.theage.com.au/articles/2004/01/19/1074360697635.html

Currie, J. (2005). *Organisational culture of Australian universities: Community or corporate?* Retrieved April 25, 2007, from http://conference.herdsa.org.au/2005/pdf/refereed/paper_currie.pdf

Denniss, R. (2004, December). *Take the rest of the year off. No 41. The Australia Institute.* Retrieved April 25, 2007, from http://www.tai.org.au/documents/downloads/NL41.pdf

Department of Education, Science and Training. (2001). *Backing Australia's Ability: An Innovation Action Plan for the Future.* Retrieved July 18, 2007, from http://www.austms.org.au/Jobs/Library9.html

Department of Education, Science and Training (2007) *Higher Education Endowment Fund.* (n.d.). Retrieved August 2, 2007, from http://www.dest.gov.

346

8101234

au/sectors/higher_education/programmes_funding/programme_categories/higher_ed_endowment_fund/

Department of Education, Science and Training (n.d.). *Higher Education Summary*. (2007). Retrieved August 2, 2007, from http://www.dest.gov.au/sectors/higher_education/higher_education_summary.htm

Department of Education Science and Training (n.d.) *Going to Uni higher education for students in Australia.* (n.d.). Department of Education, Science and Training. Retrieved August 2, 2007, from http://www.goingtouni.gov.au/Main/Quickfind/PayingForYourStudiesHELPLoans/Default.htm

Donnelly, K. (2004). *Why our schools are failing.* Potts Point, NSW: Duffy & Snellgrove.

Donnelly, K. (2007a, April 28). *Brave words, but Labor's policy offers more of the same. The Australian.* Retrieved April 29, 2007, from http://www.theaustralian.news.com.au/story/0,20867,21632875–12332,00.html

Donnelly, K. (2007b, June 9–10). Vouchers are the way to go. *The Weekend Australian*, p. 28.

Dowd, D. (2000). *Capitalism and its economics: A critical history.* London: Pluto Press.

Education Foundation Australia. (2006). *How equitable are our schools? An Education Foundation Australia fact sheet.* Retrieved April 28, 2007, from http://www.educationfoundation.org.au/downloads/How%20Equitable%20Are%20Our%20Schools.pdf

Fischel, W. (2000). *Public goods and property rights: Of Coase, Tiebout, and just compensation.* Retrieved April 11, 2007, from http://www.dartmouth.edu/~wfischel/Papers/00–19.pdf

Fletcher, K. (2005). White collar blue: Resisting attacks on universities. *Green Left Weekly.* Retrieved December 18, 2006, from http://www.greenleft.org.au/2005/628/34609

Foldvary, F. (2003). *The lighthouse as a private-sector collective good. Working Paper #46.* Retrieved April 15, 2007, from http://www.independent.org/publications/working_papers/article.asp?id=757

Foster, J. (2003). The new age of imperialism. *Monthly Review, 55*(3). Retrieved February 12, 2007, from http://www.monthlyreview.org/0703jbf.htm

Frankel, B. (1978). Marxist theories of the state: A critique of orthodoxy. *Arena Monograph, 3.* Melbourne: Arena Publications Association.

Friedman, M. (1955). *The Role of Government in Education.* Retrieved May 2, 2007, from http://www.friedmanfoundation.org/friedman/friedmans/writings/1955.jsp

Friedman, M. (1970, September 13). The social responsibility of business is to increase its profits. *The New York Times.* Retrieved May 13, 2007, from http://www.colorado.edu/studentgroups/libertarians/issues/friedman-soc-resp-business.html

Friedman, M. (1980). *Free to Choose.* New York: Harcourt Brace Jovanovich.

Friedman, M. (1982). *Capitalism and Freedom.* Chicago: University of Chicago Press.

Friedman, T. (1999). *The Lexus and the olive tree: Understanding globalisation.* New York: Anchor Books.

Gamble, A. (1999). Why bother with Marxism? In A. Gamble, D. Marsh, & T. Tant (Eds.), *Marxism and social science* (pp. 1–8). London: Macmillan Press.

Giddens, A. (1998). *The third way: The renewal of social democracy.* Cambridge, UK: Polity Press.

Giddens, A. (2000). *Runaway world: How globalization is shaping our lives.* New York: Routledge.

Gunstone, D. (2007, March 12). The awful truth about HECS. *The Age*. Retrieved July 9, 2007, from http://www.theage.com.au/news/education-news/the-awful-truth-about-hecs/2007/03/09/1173166992128.html.

Hall, R. (2006). Australian Industrial Relations 2005—The Work Choices Revolution. *Journal of Industrial Relations, 48*(3), 291–303.

Hanson, R. (2000). *Of neoliberalism and socialist organization*. Retrieved March 3, 2001, from http://democratic-socialists.uchicago.edu/activist/current/neoliberal-socialist.html.

Harvey, D. (1982). *The limits to capital*. Oxford, Blackwell.

Harvey, D. (2000). *Spaces of hope*. Berkeley, CA: University of California Press.

Harvey, D. (2005). *A brief history of neoliberalism*. Oxford: Oxford University Press.

Hearn, M., & Lansbury, R. (2005). *Reworking citizenship: Reworking workplace rights and social citizenship in Australia*. Retrieved April 27, 2007, from http://www.econ.usyd.edu.au/wos/worksite/citizenship.html.

Hill, D. (2003). Global neo-liberalism, the deformation of education and resistance. *Journal for Critical Education Policy Studies, 1*(1). Retrieved February 11, 2007, from http://www.jceps.com/index.php?pageID=article&articleID=7

Hill, D. (2004). Educational perversion and global neo-liberalism: A Marxist critique. *Cultural Logic*. Retrieved February 12, 2007, from http://clogic.eserver.org/2004/hill.html.

Hill, D. (2006). Education services liberalization. In E. Rosskam, (Ed.), *Winners or Losers? Liberalizing Public Services* (pp. 3–54). Geneva: International Labour Office.

Hill, D. (2007a) Education: Their agenda and ours. *Socialist Resistance*, 49. Sept. http://www.socialistresistance.net/49resistance.pdf.

Hill, D. (2007b) Socialist Educators and Capitalist Education. *Socialist Outlook*, 13. http://www.isg-fi.org.uk/spip.php?article576. Also at http://www.gseis.ucla.edu/~mclaren/blog/?p=152.

Hill, D. (2007c) Critical teacher education, New Labour in Britain, and the Global project of neoliberal capital. *Policy Futures*, 5(2) pp. 204–225. http://www.wwwords.co.uk/pfie/content/pdfs/5/issues5_2.asp.

Hill, D. and Boxley, S. (2007) Critical teacher and education for economic environmental and social justice: an Ecosocialist Manifesto. *Journal for Critical Educational Policy Studies*, 5(2). http://www.jceps.com/index/php?pageID=article&articleID=96.

Houston, D. (2008). Upon which to act: Pedagogy, place-making and collective histories of praxis. In S. Macrine, K. Saltman & D. Hill (Eds.), *Critical Pedagogy: In Search of Democracy, Liberation and Transformation*. London: Palgrave.

Howard, J. (1996). The liberal tradition: The beliefs and values which guide the Federal Government, 1996 Sir Robert Menzies Lecture. *National Library of Australia*. Retrieved June 12, 2007, from http://web.archive.org/web/19970212063226/http://www.nla.gov.au/pmc/pressrel/menzies.

Hudis, P. (2001, October). Editorial—To the barbarism of terrorism and war, we pose the new society: Terrorism, Bush's retaliation show inhumanity of class society. *News & Letters*. Retrieved April 30, 2007, from http://www.newsandletters.org/Issues/2001/Oct/lead_10–01.htm.

International Monetary Fund (2006). IMF Executive Board Concludes 2006 Article IV Consultation with Australia. (2006, October 23). *Public Information Notice (PIN) No. 06/123*. Retrieved April 30, 2007, from http://www.imf.org/external/np/sec/pn/2006/pn06123.htm.

Isaac, J. (2006, 29 September). Reforming Australian Industrial Relations? *New Matilda*. Retrieved February 7, 2007, from http://www.newmatilda.com/policytoolkit/policydetail.asp?PolicyID=513&CategoryID=13.

Kamat, S. (2000). Deconstructing the rhetoric of decentralization: The state in education reform. *Current Issues in Comparative Education.* Retrieved May 17, 2007, from http://www.tc.columbia.edu/cice/Archives/2.2/22kamat.pdf.

Kezar, A. (2003). *Obtaining Integrity? Reviewing and examining the charter between Higher Education and Society.* Retrieved May 12, 2007, from www.thenationalforum.org/Docs/Word/obtaining_integrity.doc.

Kelsh, D. (1998). Desire and class: The knowledge industry in the wake of post-structuralism. *Cultural Logic.* Retrieved January 9, 2001, from http://www.eserver.org/clogic/1–2/kelsh.html.

Kincheloe, J. (1991). *Teachers as researchers: Qualitative inquiry as a path to empowerment.* London: Falmer.

Kincheloe, J. (2004). *Critical pedagogy primer.* New York: Peter Lang Publishing.

Kincheloe, J., & Steinberg, S. (1998). *Unauthorized methods: Strategies for critical teaching.* New York: Routledge.

Kostas, J. (2006, November 10). International students turning to sex work to pay fees. *ABC News.* Retrieved July 9, 2007, from http://abc.net.au/news/stories/2006/11/10/1785381.htm.

Lee, S. (2004). Working hour gaps: Trends and issues. In J. Messenger (Ed.), *Working time and workers' preferences in industrialized countries* (pp. 29–60). London: Routledge.

Lefebrve, H. (1991). *The production of space.* Cambridge, MA: Blackwell.

Lenin, V. I. (1913). *The historical destiny of the doctrine of Karl Marx.* Retrieved May 7, 2007, from http://www.marxists.org/archive/lenin/works/1913/mar/01.htm.

Lenin, V. I. (1916). *The "Disarmament Slogan."* Retrieved December 18, 2006, from http://www.marx.org/archive/lenin/works/1916/oct/01.htm.

Leung, C. (2005). Parents urged to act quickly on literacy offer. *The Age.* Retrieved April 29, 2007, from http://www.theage.com.au/news/national/parents-urged-to-act-quickly-on-literacy-offer/2005/09/25/1127586746532.html.

Lewis, S. (2007, May 9). Prime Minister hints at more endowment funds. *The Australian.* Retrieved August 2, 2007, from http://www.theaustralian.news.com.au/story/0,20867,21697988–601,00.html?from=public_rss.

Livingstone, T. (2007, April 21). QUT drops humanities. *Courier Mail.* Retrieved May 14, 2007, from http://www.news.com.au/couriermail/story/0,23739,21594681–3102,00.html.

Luke, A. (2004). Teaching after the market: From commodity to cosmopolitan. *Teachers College Record, 108*(7), 1422–1443.

Luke, A. (2007). Using Bourdieu to make educational policy. In J. Albright & A. Luke (Eds.), *Bourdieu and Literacy Education.* Mawah, NJ: Lawrence Erlbaum.

Luke, A., & Woods, A. (in press). Policy and adolescent literacy. In L. Christenbury, R., Bomer, & P. Smagorinsky (Eds.). *Handbook of adolescent literacy research.* New York: Guilford Press.

Macdonald, L. (2005). Are Australians moving rightwards? *Green Left Weekly.* Retrieved February 10, 2007, from http://www.greenleft.org.au/back/2005/611/611p9.htm.

Madigan, M. (2006, November 29). Protest triggers teacher tirade. *The Australian.* Retrieved April 15, 2008 from http://www.news.com.au/couriermail/story/0,23739,20839344-953,00.html.

Mallot, C. (2006). Schooling in an era of corporate dominance: Marxism against burning tires. *Journal for Critical Education Policy Studies, 4*(1). Retrieved June 17, 2007, from http://www.jceps.com/index.php?pageID=article&articleID=58.

Marginson, S. (1997, November). Imagining Ivy: Pitfalls in the privatization of higher education in Australia. *Comparative Education Review, 41*(4), 460–480.

Marois, T., & Irias, S. (2006, January–February). Modelling institutionalised dissent: NAFTA's environmental commission. *Socialist Register, 9,* 50–51.

Martin, G. (2005). You can't be neutral on a moving bus: Critical pedagogy as community praxis. *Journal for Critical Education Policy Studies, 3*(2). Retrieved August 12, 2006, from http://www.jceps.com/index.php?pageID=article&articleID=47.

Martin, G. (2006). Remaking critical pedagogy: Peter McLaren's contribution to a collective work, *International Journal of Progressive Education, 2*(3). Retrieved August 2, 2007, from http://www.inased.org/v2n3/martin.htm.

Martin, G. (in press). Neoliberalism, education and cost-effectiveness state terror in Australia. In C. Malott & B. Porfilio (Eds.), *An international perspective of urban education: The destructive path of neoliberalism* (pp.). Rotterdam, Netherlands: Sense.

Marston, S. (2000) The social construction of scale. *Progress in Human Geography, 24*(2), 219–242.

Marx, K. (1967). *Capital.* New York: International Publishers.

Mascarenhas, A. (2004). The 70-hour week. *Sydney Morning Herald.* Retrieved April 25, 2007, from http://blogs.smh.com.au/radar/archives/2004/12/the_70hour_week.html.

McInerney, P. (2001). *Moving into dangerous territory? Educational leadership in devolving education systems.* Paper presented at the Australian Association for Research in Education (AARE) Annual Conference. Retrieved May 17, 2007, from http://www.aare.edu.au/01pap/mci01414.htm.

McLaren, P. (2003, June). Traveling the Path of Most Resistance: Peter McLaren's pedagogy of dissent: Interview with Peter McLaren. *Professing Education.* Retrieved April 30, 2007, from http://profed.brocku.ca/docs/vol2/num1/anum1.htm.

McLaren, P. (2005). *Capitalists & conquerors: A critical pedagogy against empire.* Boulder, Co: Rowman & Littlefield.

McLaren, P. (2006). *Rage and hope: Interviews with Peter McLaren on war, imperialism, and critical pedagogy.* New York: Peter Lang.

Meagher, G. (2004, May 3). Do Australians want a private welfare state? Are they getting one anyway? *Australian Review of Public Affairs.* Retrieved February 10, 2007, from http://www.australianreview.net/digest/2004/05/meagher.html.

Messenger, J. (Ed.). (2004). *Working time and workers' preferences in industrialized countries: Finding the balance.* London: Routledge.

Michaels, F. (2007, December 14). Australia: Labor's "education revolution" to deliver for business. *World Socialist Web Site.* Retrieved April 16, 2008, from http://www.wsws.org/articles/2007/dec2007/educ-d14 prn.shtml.

Mill, J. (1965). *Principles of political economy: With some of their applications to social philosophy.* New York: A.M. Kelley.

Miner, B. (2006, Winter). Australia battles privatization. *Rethinking Schools Online.* Retrieved February 2, 2007, from http://www.rethinkingschools.org/archive/21_02/aust212.shtml.

Minister for Foreign Affairs and Education, Science and Training. (2005, September 7). *Australia's Export Success in Education. Joint Media Release.* Retrieved July 21, 2007, from http://www.foreignminister.gov.au/releases/2005/joint_nelson_070905.html.

Mitchell, D. (2003). *The right to the city: Social justice and the fight for public space.* New York: Guilford Press.

National Tertiary Education Union. (2006). *Kerry Cox: The last desperate act of a desperate man.* Retrieved April 30, 2007, from http://www.nteu.org.au/news/2006/2006/13440.

National Tertiary Education Union. (2007). *The funding of Australian universities 1996–2005: An examination of the facts and figures.* Retrieved April 30, 2007, from http://vic.nteu.org.au/bd/vic/nexus/11945?file=Nexus_Autumn_2007_web.pdf&friendly=.

Nettleheim, G. (2001). Reconciliation: Challenges for Australian law. Retrieved June 2, 2007, from http://www.austlii.edu.au/au/journals/AJHR/2001/3.html.

Percy, J., & Lorimer, D. (2001). *The democratic socialist party and the Fourth International*. Chippendale, NSW: Resistance Books.

Purcell, M. (2003). Islands of practice and the Marston/Brenner debate: Toward a more synthetic critical human geography. *Progress in Human Geography, 27*(3), 317–332.

Rikowski, G. (2001). *The battle in Seattle: Its significance for education*. London: Tufnell Press.

Rikowski, G. (2006, Summer). Education and the politics of human resistance. *Information for Social Change, 23*. Retrieved August 2, 2007, from http://libr.org/isc/issues/ISC23/B3%20Glenn%20Rikowski.pdf.

Robertson, S. (2002). The politics of re-territorialisation: Space, scale and teachers as a professional class. *Curriculo sem Fronterias*. Retrieved May 2, 2007, from http://www.curriculosemfronteiras.org/vol2iss2articles/robertsonen.pdf.

Rudd, K. (2007). LaborTV - Kevin Rudd: economic conservative. Retrieved April 16, 2008, from http://www.alp.org.au/labortv/TFmNiVCncl.

Samuelson, P. (1964). *Economics* (6th ed.). New York: McGraw Hill.

Scanlon, C. (2004, April 17). A touch of class. *The Age*. Retrieved September 24, 2007, from http://www.theage.com.au/articles/2004/04/16/1082055641506.html.

Scatamburlo-D'Annibale, V. (2006). Imagining the impossible: Revolutionary critical pedagogy against the 21st Century American imperium. *International Journal of Progressive Education, 2*(3), 21–46.

Slaughter, S. (1985). From serving students to serving the economy: Changing expectations of faculty role and performance. *Higher Education, 14*, 41–56.

Slaughter, S. (1993). Retrenchment in the 1980s: The politics of prestige and gender. *Journal of Higher Education, 64*(3), 250–282.

Slaughter, S. (1998). Federal policy and supply-side institutional resource allocation at public research universities. *Review of Higher Education, 21*, 209–244.

Smith, M. (2006, April 26). Mass movement defeats anti-worker law. *Green Left Weekly, 655*, p. 22.

Smith, N. (1995). Remaking scale: Competition and cooperation in prenational and postnational Europe. In H. Eskelinen & F. Snickars (Eds.), *Competitive European Peripheries* (pp. 59–74). Berlin: Springer.

Starr, P. (1990). The new life of the liberal state: Privatization and the restructuring of state-society relations. Retrieved February 12, 2007, from http://www.princeton.edu/~starr/newstate.html.

Swyngedouw, E. (1992). The Mammon quest: "Glocalisation," interspatial competition and the monetary order: The construction of new scales. In M. Dunford & G. Kafkalas (Eds.), *Cities and regions in the new Europe* (pp. 39–68). London: Belhaven Press.

Symonds, P. (2007, December 4). Rudd Labor government commits to "economic conservativism". *World Socialist Web Site*. Retrieved April 16, 2008, from http://www.wsws.org/articles/2007/dec2007/labor-d04.shtml.

The Australian. (2006). God in the Machine: John Howard's chaplaincy program is smart politics. (October 31). *The Australian*. Retrieved February 11, 2007, from http://www.theaustralian.news.com.au/story/0,20867,20672292-7583,00.html.

Topsfield, J. (2006, September 21). State schools should "pay more to good teachers." *The Age*. Retrieved May 2, 2007, from http://www.theage.com.au/news/national/state-schools-should-pay-more-to-good-teachers/2006/09/20/1158431783213.html.

Trotsky, L. (1909). *The bankruptcy of individual terrorism*. Retrieved February 10, 2007, from http://marxists.org/archive/trotsky/1909/xx/tia09.htm.

Trotsky, L. (1911). *Why Marxists oppose individual terrorism.* Retrieved February 10, 2007, from http://www.marxists.org/archive/trotsky/1911/11/tia09.htm.

Van Zandt, D. (1993, January). The lessons of the lighthouse: "Government or 'private' Provision of Goods." *Journal of Legal Studies, 22,* 47–72.

Vinson, T. (2002, September 27). *The Sir Harold Wyndham Memorial Lecture. Schools in a just society: The renewal of public education in NSW.* Retrieved February 4, 2007, from http://www.pub-ed-inquiry.org/events/upload/Wyndham_Address.doc.

Walford, G. (Ed.). (1996). *School choice and the quasi-market.* Oxford: Triangle.

Waring, P., De Ruyter, A., & Burgess, J. (2006) The Australian Fair Pay Commission: Rationale, operation, antecedents and implications. *Economic and Labour Relations Review,* 16(2), 127–146.

Weller, J. (2007, June). *Power and scale: The shifting geography of industrial relations law in Australia* . . . Retrieved June 17, 2007, from Melbourne University, Centre for Employment and Labour Relations Law Web site: http://celrl.law.unimelb.edu.au/download.cfm?DownloadFile=04AB6678-1422-207C-BAE52B2DC980583C.

When the Levies Break. (2003). Retrieved December 18, 2006, from http://www.aeufederal.org.au/Publications/AE/Spr03pp04–05.html.

Williams, R. (1977/1988). *Marxism and literature.* Oxford: Oxford University Press.

Wilson, S., & Meagher, G. (2004). *Where to for the welfare state? Attitudes to spending, welfare and social services.* Retrieved February 10, 2007, from, http://www.assa.edu.au/policy/papers/2004/welfare.pdf.

Wiltshire, K. (2006, September 23). In defence of the true values of learning. *The Australian.* Retrieved February 3, 2007, from http://www.theaustralian.news.com.au/story/0,20867,20459395–12332,00.html.

WorkChoices and the right to stand down employees: Fact Sheet 37. (2006, December 12). Retrieved July 10, 2007, from https://www.workchoices.gov.au/NR/rdonlyres/EDC3C10F-CE43–43EC-8898–66178C496443/0/termination_right_to_stand_down.pdf

Wynhausen, E. (2005). *Dirt cheap: Life at the wrong end of the job market.* Sydney: Macmillan.

Zimmer, E. (1999, July 27). Shortages of casual teachers highlight education inequality. *World Socialist Web Site.* Retrieved February 3, 2007, from http://www.wsws.org/articles/1999/jul1999/edu-j27.shtml.

Zimmer, E. (2003, September 11). Australia: Teachers union calls strike in bid to regain credibility. *World Socialist Web Site.* Retrieved February 4, 2007, from http://www.wsws.org/articles/2003/sep2003/teac-s11.shtml

Zimmer, E. (2004, April 15). Australia: Public schools to be reduced to a residual safety net. *World Socialist Web Site.* Retrieved February 3, 2007, from http://www.wsws.org/articles/2004/apr2004/edu-a15.shtml.

Zimmer, E. (2005, May 28). Australia: school principals given right to select teachers. *World Socialist Web Site.* Retrieved April 12, 2008, from http://www.wsws.org/articles/2005/may2005/teac-m28.shtml.

Zimmer, E. (2007, January 11). Australian government to fund chaplains in public and private schools. *World Socialist Web Site.* Retrieved February 12, 2007 from, http://wsws.org/articles/2007/jan2007/educ-j11.shtml.

5 England and Wales
Neoliberalized Education and Its Impacts

Christine Lewis, Dave Hill, and Barry Fawcett

INTRODUCTION

Education, along with other public and formerly publicly owned services, is being neoliberalized in many countries. The extent, mechanisms, and effects vary. However, this chapter suggests and tests a series of hypotheses.

- Neoliberalization of schooling and education services has occurred in many countries around the world.
- Particular national and international levers are promoting the Neo-liberalization process.
- Educational services are becoming "Americanized" through policies and processes such as privatization, decentralization, deregulation, "new public management" (business management methods), commercialization, and marketization.
- Neoliberalization is making provision of services more unequal and selective rather than universal. This is intensifying race-, gender, and class-based hierarchies, reflected in formally or informally tiered systems of schooling. In less developed countries, services are available mainly to middle-class or wealthier families. In developed countries, the quality and type of schooling is increasingly stratified.
- Neoliberalization is eroding workers' securities, pay and conditions of work.
- Neoliberalization attempts to embed a shift away from universal citizenship rights and identities based on the provision of services toward a system of individual consumer rights and identities. In education, this involves treating young people as "human capital" and preparing them for "jobs" rather than providing broad-based learning and critical awareness.

These aspects and effects of the neoliberalization of schooling and other education services are part of a wider rejection of some of the social functions of the state by governments, international organizations, and business groups. Public services, such as education, health, and prisons, are being, or have been, transformed into "tradable commodities."

This chapter produces evidence that the neoliberalization of education increases inequalities within and between countries, reduces the quality of education, is detrimental to democracy, and decreases workers' pay, rights, and quality of work conditions. Despite these effects, neoliberalization has proceeded apace around the globe.

LIBERALIZING POLICIES

Deregulation and decentralization of educational services have opened the way to privatization, commercialization (marketing of products within schools), marketization (marketization of schools within a competitive market or quasi-market), and have also introduced "new public management" (business management methods) into schools, colleges, universities and education services. These policies were initially accompanied by cuts in spending on publicly funded schools and further education services, and by a discourse of antagonism to public services, workers, and unions. Since 1997, under the New Labour administrations of Tony Blair and Gordon Brown, investment in education has risen significantly, but much of the additional resource is directed into quangos, consultancies, and the more expensive decentralized, mixed economy of provision.

Privatization

The private sector is involved in education services almost everywhere, with activities ranging from selling services to educational institutions to managing and owning schools and other facilities. "Peripheral" services, such as cleaning, catering, security, and reprographics, have been privatized within institutions. Nationally, services such as inspection, student fees and loans, and record keeping, are increasingly run by private corporations rather than by local or national governments.

In the United Kingdom, "peripheral" services such as catering and cleaning were subjected to competitive tendering in the 1980s and many were privatized (contracted out). Since then, school inspection has been externalized/privatized as has the ownership of some state schools, the management of some or all functions of local education authorities (school districts), and control of the new Academies—privately run but publicly funded secondary schools. These Academies require a private sponsor to contribute up to £2 million (most have donated far less), in return for which the Government contributes over £20 million in capital costs plus the school's annual operating costs. Yet the sponsor appoints a majority of the school governors and has the power to vary nationally agreed staff pay and conditions, alter the skill mix of staff, and modify the school curriculum. Trade unions fought to achieve a Best Value Code of Practice (Office of the Deputy Prime Minister, 2003), which requires contractors to match the protected rates of transferring staff for newly recruited staff. This code does not however apply to academies, colleges, or universities as they do not have public sector status, but rather are deemed to be publicly funded private bodies.

Commercialisation

Direct commercial penetration is evident in the increasing use of commercially sponsored materials in the classroom and around the school. Whitty (2000) suggests that some aspects of marketization contribute to privatization in an ideological if not a strictly economic sense, by fostering the belief that the private sector approach is superior to that traditionally adopted in the public sector, requiring public sector institutions to operate more like those in the private sector, and encouraging private (individual/family) decision-making in place of political and professional judgments. The increasing emphasis on competition and choice has also brought with it what Whitty calls a "hidden curriculum" of marketization.

Possibly the most consistent and thorough analysis of "schoolhouse commercialism" (Molnar, 2001, 2003, 2005; Molnar et al., 2004) identifies the following eight types in the United States, most of which are on the increase:

- corporate sponsorship of school programs and activities;
- agreements giving marketers exclusive rights to sell a product or service on school or district grounds;
- incentive programs for commercial products or services as rewards for achieving an academic goal;
- appropriation of space to sell naming rights[1] or advertising on school premises or property;
- corporate-sponsored educational materials;
- electronic marketing for media, such as radio, television, and internet companies to target students through schools;
- private management of public schools, public charter schools, and the involvement of private for-profit schools in voucher programs;
- fundraising.

Decentralization and Deregulation

Liberalized education policies promote decentralization. In Latin America, decentralization efforts have been aimed at scaling down the direct responsibility of central governments for different aspects of education and bolstering increased provincial/regional, municipal, and private involvement in education (Borón & Torres, 1996; Munín, 1998; Carnoy, 2002; Hill and Rosskam, 2009).

In England and Wales, decentralization of further education colleges (for the 16–19 age group) has eroded worker securities, and there are fears that the Academies program will have a similar effect in the secondary school system.

The Discourse of Derision and Hate against Public Service Workers: "Are teachers what is wrong with education?"

Teachers are being singled out for special attention in a manner unlike anything that has occurred before. Formerly, improvements to education were often associated with the need to improve conditions for teachers— class sizes, resources, salaries, benefits, pensions, and job security. Even when teachers were seen to be in need of further education themselves, governments moved to expand and improve teacher education programs and/or offered incentives for teachers to engage in further study, whether pre-service or in-service. Today, however, teachers are increasingly being criticized. Teachers themselves, it is widely claimed, constitute the main "problem" in education.

EDUCATION WORKERS' SOCIAL AND ECONOMIC SECURITY

Impact of Neoliberalization on Teachers and Other Education Workers

Neoliberalization in education affects a number of aspects of workers' securities. It commonly results in increased casualization of labor, the replacement of national pay agreements by local or institution-based bargaining, greater difficulties in securing recognition for trade unions and their right to represent workers, lower pay, increased differentials in pay and conditions through individual performance-related pay, increased intensification of work and, for school teachers and college lecturers in further education (predominantly teaching 16–19-year-olds), decreased autonomy over curriculum, pedagogy, and assessment. These developments have been accompanied by increases in levels of report writing, testing, accountability, monitoring, and surveillance, both by in-house local management and by government external agencies. Where full-time permanent contracts with publicly managed employers have been replaced by casualized work, and where that work or educational service has been contracted out or otherwise privatized, there has often been a decline in public service morale and standards of provision.

In England and Wales, the experiences of workers in further education colleges since decentralization (known as "incorporation") in 1993 show clear negative effects on a number of workers' securities in most of the areas just discussed, including pay, conditions, casualization, intensification of work, facilities for professional development and further training, and working under "new public management." The experience for students has been larger classes and a lowering of standards, such as less contact time with staff (Lewis, 2004b).

The seven forms of socio-economic security identified by the ILO's Socio-Economic Security Programme (ILO, 2002) are:

- labor market security;
- employment security;
- work security;
- job security;
- skill reproduction security;
- income security; and
- representation security.

There is overlap between these types of security; they are analytical categories and affect each other. For example, casualized workers (reduced employment security) are usually paid less and have fewer rights to sick pay, holiday pay, pension, and other benefits (reduced income security), and fewer rights to in-service training and career progression (reduced skill reproduction security).

Labor Market Security

Labor market security refers to the provision of adequate employment and work opportunities, through high levels of employment ensured by macroeconomic policy. Although globally there does not appear to have been a reduction in the full-time equivalent teaching workforce, there has been an identifiable trend in many countries to reduce the number and ratio of full-time jobs in both teaching and ancillary educational services. This is developed under "employment security" in the next subsection. However, it affects labor market security, insofar as there is decreasing opportunity for full-time and permanent contracted work.

Employment Security

Employment security refers to the terms and conditions of employment, including protection against arbitrary dismissal and employment stability compatible with economic dynamism. This concerns contractual issues in particular, such as full-time or part-time contracts, permanent or short-term contracts, flexi-time, levels of staffing, turnover rates, and issues of employment protection.

Employment security has been weakened by Neoliberalization, in particular by casualization. Staff on fixed-term contracts have the least employment security in the sector, and often have inferior terms and conditions to their permanent colleagues. Fixed-term (temporary) contracts, as opposed to permanent contracts:

- leave many staff feeling exposed and undervalued;
- lead to difficulty in obtaining loans, mortgages, and other financial benefits;
- lead to significant recruitment and retention problems;

- are discriminatory, as their use disproportionately affects women and minority groups;
- destroy or damage career progression, as individuals find themselves stuck on the lowest pay grades on a succession of short-term contracts that offer little or no room for staff development;
- mean staff coming to the end of contracts must inevitably spend time applying for funding or other posts.

Part-time staff may well not be invited to staff meetings, and in various countries are not entitled to institutional benefits such as holiday pay, paid sick leave, or maternity/paternity leave. Finally, most part-time workers are paid hourly rather than on permanent fractional or full-time contracts and hence, have no job security other than that commonly agreed for the year (or other short-term period) ahead. They are second-class citizens in the workplace.

Neoliberalization of further education (for the 16–19 age group) in England and Wales has taken the form of decentralization of power from democratically elected local authority control to individual boards of governors, very much led by the principal, running further education colleges. They now have the status of corporations; publicly funded privately run bodies. At the same time there has been a crisis in funding. Ten years after incorporation, The National Association of Teachers in Further and Higher Education (NATFHE) noted that core funding had declined by 10%, a 12% gap in pay had opened up between colleges and schools, 30% of full-time lecturers had been made redundant, and casualization had increased (NATFHE, 2003). In the last 10 years funding has been increased but the funding regime, administered by the Learning and Skills Council (LSC) breeds instability with its target drivers and superficial measurements. There is also a tendency in locally managed institutions with delegated budgets to try and maintain a surplus, which is dead, hoarded public money.

This has resulted in increasing casualization, a growing part-time workforce, more use of temporary contracts and an increase in the use of (private) agency staff, who are not eligible for the same employment benefits as staff directly employed (Lewis, 2004b).

In 1995–1996, the Further Education Funding Council estimated that 55% of all college staff and 39% of teaching staff worked part-time. This compares to an estimate by the National Association of Teachers in Further and Higher Education (NATFHE; the college lecturers' union) of 15% part-time working prior to incorporation in 1993.

As well as more part-time employment, the post-incorporation further education sector has made greater use of temporary staff. Using the census returns to the funding council in 1994–1995, NATFHE estimated that 42% of staff employed for more than 15 hours per week had temporary contracts. This compared to a national average across all sectors of 9%.

NATFHE also suggested that the use of agency staff avoided contractual obligations, citing examples where colleges had dismissed their part-time lecturers and re-employed them through a third-party provider. Many were on lower pay, self-employed, and responsible for their own professional indemnity (House of Commons, 1997, col. 1133).

Work Security

Work security refers to occupational health and safety (protection against accidents and illness at work) through safety and health regulations, including limits on working time and unsocial hours. Deteriorating working conditions, greater stress, and intensification of work are likely to be reflected in high rates of labor turnover.

The main effects of Neoliberalization on work security have been the intensification of work and more accountability. Many countries have required teaching staff to meet externally imposed standards, accompanied by increased levels of monitoring and surveillance.

For example, since 1979 the real autonomy of state education structures in England and Wales has diminished substantially as a result of increased surveillance and control mechanisms (Hill, 2001, 2003, 2004a, 2004b, 2005a, 2005b, 2006a, 2006b, 2007). These include: compulsory and nationally monitored externally set assessments for pupils/students and trainee teachers; publication of performance league tables; a policy emphasis on "naming and shaming," closing or privatizing "failing" schools and local education authorities (school districts); and merit pay and performance-related pay systems for teachers, usually dependent on student performance in tests (Jeffrey & Woods, 1998).

The drive toward performance improvement places enormous pressures on teachers and students. Teacher disaffection, stress-related illness, and early retirement have led to a recruitment crisis. Teachers face increasing surveillance while their workload increases.

The consequences in terms of lowered morale of schoolteachers and lecturers between 1992 and today are clearly measurable. In 1992, only 10% of teachers and lecturers thought that they had to "work at high speed all or most of the time," compared to 18% for other occupations. By the end of the decade, this position was reversed (33% vs. 25%), with teachers and lecturers experiencing a hefty rise in stress. Over the same period, the proportion of teachers who were "dissatisfied with their job" more than doubled, from 6% to 13% (Beckman & Cooper, 2004).

The increase in the proportion of part-time and hourly paid staff means that more of the administrative workload is falling on the shoulders of fewer full-time workers. There has been increased "managerialization" of schooling and intensification of teachers' work, with "teachers . . . driven to burnout." (Whitty, 1997, p. 305)

Job Security

Job security is defined as "a niche designated as an occupation or 'career,' the opportunity to develop a sense of occupation" (ILO, 2002). This refers to the existence of a career progression structure and opportunity for promotion, as well as the sense of being a part of a profession, with a shared professionalism.

Teachers and other educational workers on short-term and temporary contracts do not have much job security. However, for all workers there is, in many countries, a declining level of job security and status for teachers and other education workers.

Many governments are centralizing certain educational services, setting national goals, agendas, curricula, standards, and evaluations. Examples include the 1988 Education Reform Act in England and Wales, and the No Child Left Behind legislation of 2001 in the United States. A centralized curriculum leads to a loss of professional autonomy, and reflects in part the deprofessionalization of a vocation that has lost both autonomy and collegiality (Beckmann & Cooper, 2004).

The culture of "New Public Management" entails complementary and increasing control by management bodies. Intensified formal assessments require teachers to produce detailed and prescriptive "learning aims and outcomes." This managerial approach has direct implications for the work of educators. There is no attempt here to balance issues of professional autonomy with issues of control. "Trust" in a teacher's professionalism is displaced by a requirement to meet specified performance standards (Alexiadou, 2001, p. 429).

Another aspect of deprofessionalization is the loss of critical thought within a performance culture (Ball, 1999; Mahoney & Hextall, 2000; Boxley, 2003). School principals have become "distracted from the core purposes of improving the quality of learning and the lives of the pupils because of the unfamiliar and overwhelming demands placed on them" (Walker & Stott, 2000, p. 67). They have become focused on short-term economic objectives, failing to acknowledge the role of education in promoting a caring, cohesive, democratic society, built on notions of "citizenship" where "critical participation and dissent" are viewed as desirable (Bottery, 2000, p.79).

Skill Reproduction Security

Skill reproduction security refers to the existence of opportunities to gain and retain skills through innovative means as well as apprenticeships and training courses.

As noted earlier in connection with the decline in employment security, workers on fixed-term temporary contracts, and those on hourly paid contracts, have little opportunity for career progression. Managements, whether public or private, are less willing to pay for in-service training for staff they may not re-employ.

> It is obvious that casualization will lead to a training deficit. From the support staff point of view, and looking at, say, the school meals service, contracting out has led to demanning and deskilling . . . Most catering assistants work 10–15 hours a week and employers will not invest in them. They are just units of labour. (Lewis, 2004a)

In England and Wales, the increased use of casual staff in further education colleges affects the quality of the service as "casual staff are disconnected from wider college matters, curriculum issues, student welfare and extra-curricula activities" (Lewis, 2004b). The Further Education Development Agency (FEDA) also expressed concern that not all colleges are applying the full range of development opportunities to part-time staff (House of Commons, 1998, para 179).

Income Security

Income security refers to the provision of adequate and reliable incomes. This relates not only to wages and salaries, but to other benefits and rewards with a cash value including pension rights, health insurance, statutory sick pay, and all-year contracts, as opposed to "term-time" contracts and pay.

Teachers and school support services are expensive. The climate of fiscal restraint in recent years has threatened income security as well as employment security in many countries

Localized/decentralized pay bargaining can lead to lower local pay deals. This power over workers' pay and conditions is given to the managements of Academies in England like the privately managed public sector charter schools in the United States.

In England the widespread contracting out of school meals, school cleaning and other services to schools and colleges since the 1980s led to severe deterioration of pay and conditions for thousands of low-paid, mainly women, workers. Although the Best Value Code of Practice requires contract documentation to require equal terms and conditions for staff, it cannot control the proliferation of short hour contracts or casualisation.

Representation Security

Representation security refers to the protection of workers in the labor market through independent trade unions and other bodies able to represent the interests of workers and working communities. This means the right of workers to organize in trade unions, and the recognition by managements of the right of bona fide unions to represent their members. By contrast, the "company unions" or "professional associations" often preferred by management may be "tame" associations, for example, committed to no-strike action and/or less effective in negotiating on behalf of members.

Representation security is under attack through a number of liberalizing policies, especially decentralization, privatization, and individualized pay bargaining (for instance, through performance-related pay). A fourth policy is the deliberate weakening of trade unions, for example, by removing their national bargaining rights (England and Wales) or vilifying them in the public debate (the United States).

The transfer of negotiations from the national to the provincial or local (school and college) level leads to different pay scales for workers in comparable institutions. This strikes at the heart of the concept of professional equity, under which teachers or staff engaged in similar jobs with similar qualifications can expect the same pay and conditions at any education institution of the same level across the country. It also weakens trade union bargaining power. Without strong unions, the pay and working conditions of education workers will further deteriorate, except for the few who receive performance-related pay enhancements or other "merit rewards."

Prior to "incorporation" in 1993, the pay and conditions of lecturers in further education colleges in England and Wales were bargained nationally. However, the Further and Higher Education Act 1992, which established colleges as publicly funded independent bodies,

> . . . was to open the door to pay bargaining chaos, significant attacks on working conditions, increased casualization and instability for the sector. Staff were to suffer from the impact of working for "little businesses," funded precariously by a giant quango (the Further Education Funding Council) and bedevilled by targets and a bureaucratic inspection regime. Trade unions struggled to protect their members in this corporate environment. (Lewis, 2004b)

Although national bargaining for colleges exists in both England and Wales, the ensuing agreements have the status of recommendations and many colleges ignore them.

Neoliberalization entails not only variations in pay and conditions between workers in different institutions, but also between workers of similar status within the same institution, through individualized performance-related pay schemes that have been introduced in a number of countries.

Power within Schools

Finally, and as an aggregate consequence of all the aforementioned trends, it is clear that the locus of power in U.K. education has become centralized within nations and much less democratic.

School head teachers, for example, have unprecedented levels of authority handed down to them by a government that has weakened almost every other vestige of local democratic choice that parents or elected politicians once enjoyed. Even though there is a consensus from all mainstream political groups that head teachers need to enjoy greater freedoms to manage, it is difficult to imagine what those might be or precisely which freedoms they are lacking. The most pernicious powers in the eyes of many rank-and-file teachers are those whereby the head teacher has simultaneous control over statutory performance management systems as well as an increasingly variegated pay structure. It has become more than it could possibly be worth for an employee to challenge the status quo inside a modern school for fear of being overlooked for annual or additional pay progression. Thus, complicity in many school regimes is often bought rather than earned. Indeed debate and discussion under certain regimes can be deemed insubordination worthy of disciplinary action.

Local authorities have long since lost their general powers to raise their own revenue, apart from the prescribed rates of Community Charge that cover services often uncontrolled by the recipients, like levels of policing, but the 2006 Education Act finally confirmed their specific role as mere *commissioners* of education, not *providers*. The new key role of the School Improvement Professional may well be filled by someone with little educational management or practitioner history. There are fewer prescribed places for school parents under the new guidelines for the Trust schools that the government wishes to replace community comprehensives with.

Though Wales and Scotland enjoy devolved autonomy and veto on educational matters, which their Assemblies have been at pains to exercise in such matters as testing and class sizes, the ironies of increased central control being excused in England via a rhetoric of localism and choice is seldom criticized. Quite specifically, the government's preferred structural option to address what it deems to be endemic secondary stage educational failure in certain communities, is the Academy, a privately managed entity funded from public funds. The legal institution of an Academy is enshrined in its funding agreement, written as an accord between any particular successful bidder and the government. Effectively the government nationalizes the school, whether it exists already or is created anew, while privatizing its administration. Thus, we have the bizarre situation that, should the government reach its initial target of 200 such Academies by 2010—though Prime Minister Blair doubled the figure in a number of latter-day speeches—it would become by far the single largest provider of secondary education in the United Kingdom. Any parent wishing to challenge matters at any one of those schools would have to travel to Whitehall Westminster, not their local Town Hall, for redress. Although academies have governing bodies, the power of the sponsor is unassailable.

FORMS AND LEVERS OF NEOLIBERALIZATION

Free Trade, the WTO, and the GATS

The move toward global Neoliberalization implies freer trade in services such as education, health, social service provision, as goods. The main global mechanism for Neoliberalization of services trade is the General Agreement on Trade in Services (GATS) of the World Trade Organization (WTO), though there are many other global, regional, and bilateral/multilateral levers.

The GATS covers four modes of supply of services, including education services:

- *Mode 1:* provision of services from abroad, for example, through distance education or the internet (cross-border supply);
- *Mode 2:* provision of services to foreign students (consumption abroad);
- *Mode 3:* establishment in a country of foreign education service providers, for example, to set up schools and other institutions (commercial presence);
- *Mode 4:* movement of workers between countries to provide educational services (movement of natural persons).

Under GATS rules, WTO members decide which services they will open to foreign competition, under which modes of supply, and subject to which limitations if any. There is also an exclusion clause for "services supplied in the exercise of governmental authority," which are outside the scope of the GATS. However, the GATS goes on to define such a service as one "supplied neither on a commercial basis nor in competition with one or more service suppliers." This could imply that where public and private sectors co-exist, as they do in most countries, public services are covered by the agreement. Some argue that public institutions requiring the payment of fees could be deemed to be engaging in "commercial activity" and would thus fall outside the GATS exception. Though the WTO and member governments say there is no intention to apply GATS to public education and health services (WTO, 2003), the distinction between public and private services is becoming increasingly blurred (see, e.g., the case study on England and Wales below). In strict legal terms, only when a service is provided entirely by the government does it unambiguously fall outside the GATS rules. This could make countries vulnerable to pressure in current and future GATS negotiations to open up areas of the public education

The Irreversibility of GATS

Once a country commits itself to opening a service to foreign competition, it cannot escape. The WTO is "the only global institution that even the

United States and the European Union are supposed to obey," whereas the World Bank and the IMF have influence only over "weak developing countries" (Wolf, 1999; see also Devidal, 2008).

In the WTO dispute settlement process, tribunals operate in secret to settle disputes between member states. Only national governments are allowed to participate. In the case of an adverse ruling, countries must either comply (which may require legislation) or pay compensation (in the form of trade benefits). Refusal or inability to do either can result in trade sanctions imposed by the winning side.

The WTO argues that this claim of irreversibility is another "scare story" (WTO, 2003) and lists a number of circumstances under which a country can permanently or temporarily suspend or cancel specific GATS obligations. However, it does admit, "on request, 'compensation' may need to be negotiated with Members whose trade is affected." Where a municipality, or a local or national government, wants to take back into public ownership a service that has been privatized and opened to competition under the GATS or a similar free trade agreement, it may be almost impossible to do so.

Other Levers for Neoliberalization

It is not only the WTO and GATS that are levers for "Neoliberalization" of trade in services. Regional and bilateral trade agreements, such as the North American Free Trade Agreement (NAFTA), the Common Market of the South (MERCOSUR), and the European Union (E.U.) play an important role. The World Bank and the OECD are also significant bodies in promoting the liberalized education agenda (see, e.g., Rikowski, 2002; Puiggrós, 2002; Leher 2004, 2008; Delgado-Ramos, & Saxe-Fernández, 2005, 2008; Halimi, 2004; Hirtt, 2004, 2008; Hill and Kumar, 2009; Hill and Rosskam, 2009). They are supported by national and international business organizations such as the International Chamber of Commerce, the Confederation of British Industry, and the Institute of Directors in the United Kingdom, the European Round Table of leading multinational companies, and the Partnership for Educational Revitalization in the Americas (PREAL), which comprises public and private organizations.

At the same time, there is opposition to free trade in services from trade unions, political parties, civil society groups, and some governments. These recently combined to force the withdrawal, at least temporarily, of the so-called Bolkestein Directive, the E.U.'s draft Services Directive seeking to open up trade in services. The draft Directive sought to expose almost all services to market-based competition. Though public education services were specifically excluded, the draft Directive would have applied to "peripheral" services supplied to schools and, like the GATS, was unclear where the line between public and private services would be drawn.

Under the "country of origin" principle, a company providing services would follow the rules and laws of the country in which it was based or "established," rather than the country in which the service was provided. A U.S. education multinational, for example, could "establish" itself in Latvia, simply by registering its presence there. It would then be able to trade in the rest of the E.U., while conforming only to Latvian law on matters such as health and safety, employees' rights, or environmental protection. Latvia, not the country where the service was provided, would be expected to send inspectors to ensure compliance with its laws.

Critics say the draft Directive would encourage "social dumping" since companies would have an incentive to opt for establishment in the least regulated E.U. member requiring the lowest standards. The Directive "would have been quite a blow to national level regulation, as it would tend to make services available in the least regulated way, rather than bringing all services operators up to best standards" (Malins, 2005). However, the current E.U. Internal Market Commissioner, Charlie McCreevy, says he is committed to re-introducing the Directive in some form during his five-year term, which ends in 2009. With 70% of economic activity in Europe being in services, "you don't have to have a degree in economics to know that if you can open up the services market you're going to have an impact on economic activity and we need increased economic activity in the E.U." (McCreevy, cited in McLauchlin, 2005).

SCHOOLING ACCESS, EQUITY, AND QUALITY

Increased and Increasing Inequalities

The Neoliberalization of schooling and further education is playing a significant part in widening inequalities within countries, intensifying differences in access and attainment between different groups (for instance, between races, between girls and boys, between social classes and, in developing nations, between rural and urban areas).

Increasing Inequalities: Polarized Schooling

One common criticism of the Neoliberalization of schooling, training, and university education revolves around loss of equity, economic and social justice, and the polarization of the labor force. There has been an increase in (gender-, race-, language-based) social class inequalities in educational provision, attainment, and subsequent position in the labor market. For example, the movement to voucher and charter schools, as well as other forms of privatized education, such as chains of schools in the United States (Molnar, 2001; Molnar et al., 2004), has proved disproportionately beneficial to those groups who can afford to pay for better educational opportunities and experiences, leading to further social exclusion and polarization (Whitty et al., 1998; Gillborn & Youdell, 2000). Reimers notes that

> . . . the poor have less access to preschool, secondary, and tertiary education; they also attend schools of lower quality where they are socially segregated. Poor parents have fewer resources to support the education of their children, and they have less financial, cultural, and social capital to transmit. Only policies that explicitly address inequality, with a major redistributive purpose, therefore, could make education an equalizing force in social opportunity. (Reimers, 2000, p. 55)

Hirtt suggests that the apparently contradictory elements driving Neo-liberalization of education, "to adapt education to the needs of business and at the same time reduce state expenditure on education," are resolved by the polarization of the labor market. Thus, from an economic point of view, it is not necessary to provide high-level education and general knowledge to all future workers.

It is now possible and even highly recommendable to have a more polarized education system. . . . education should not try to transmit a broad common culture to the majority of future workers, but instead it should teach them some basic, general skills. (Hirtt, 2004, p. 446)

In other words, manual and service workers receive cheaper, inferior, transferable-skills education and knowledge, in contrast to the elite workers, who receive more expensive, superior education. Thus, the outcome of Neoliberalization is a more hierarchical school system that militates against the principle of equal access to education for all.

Cherry-picking and Undermining Public Schooling

One of the greatest sources of weakness for public services is "cherry-picking," "where the affluent are able to purchase better quality services for themselves alone and avoid contributing to the public service" (Hall, 2003, p.28). This undermines the financial solidarity on which public services are based, and the political consensus needed to sustain them. It draws resources away from those services into a consumer-oriented market. The impact on public services may be exacerbated by cuts in public sector resources, which reduces the quality of the public service and encourages those who can pay to buy more resources for themselves from the private sector.

More recently, this has been subsumed under the government's doctrine of "choice and diversity" for parents. They, as the prime consumers, are deemed worthy of a set of competing local institutions from which to choose the best for the needs of their child. Schools themselves are expected to specialize in certain curriculum areas to ensure a diversity of provision, and, with the 2006 Education Act, provide more Vocational Diplomas in Key Stage 4 (14–16-year-olds).

Yet, such a free market in school admissions has many losers, with class, ethnic, and religious segregation often increasing. The international evidence cited by Peter Mortimore for the National Union of Teachers suggests that there is little to support such a competitive ethos. "Indeed, in Finland—the country which performs best in PISA—competition plays no part in the education system." (2006, p. 22)

CURRICULUM, CRITICAL THOUGHT, AND DEMOCRATIC CONTROL

Effects of Neoliberalization on Curriculum and Pedagogy

One set of effects of Neoliberalization concerns the loss of democracy and democratic accountability. Ownership and control are transferred to unelected and democratically unaccountable private companies and corporations. Private business and shareholders own and/or manage schools and educational institutions instead of locally or nationally elected representative bodies.

A second set of effects is the loss of democracy and collegiality among teachers and other education workers as a result of "New Public Management" (NPM). This replaces collective collegiality and decision-making (or decision-influencing) with individualistic, competitive, and hierarchical work relationships. There is the siphoning upwards of power to senior management teams—or the senior manager, head teacher, or principal—who may have no educational experience or background at all (as in the United States, and as envisaged in England and Wales). And, with a non-collegial hierarchal 'chain of command,' management, middle managers can bully 'shop floor' teachers and lecturers/professors with far greater impunity. In such management systems, senior managers rarely meet their shop-floor workforce.

As noted in the discussion on work security, stress and deprofessionalization arises from increased control and monitoring of the curriculum. Teachers have little time to devote to alternative visions and versions of the curriculum, when intensification of school and college work is so tightly tied to testing of prespecified learning.

Standardization of the School Curriculum and Pedagogy

In some countries, such as the United States and the United Kingdom, pedagogy and the curriculum are being standardized. In McNeill's view, "standardization reduces the quality and quantity of what is taught and learned in schools . . . Over the long term, standardization creates inequities, widening the gap between the quality of education for poor and minority youth and that of more privileged students." (McNeil, 2000, p. 3; See also Hursh, 2008.)

In England, increased standardization of pedagogy—with teachers teaching to the test—is taking place across the curriculum. It is a teacher-centred pedagogy, giving little space for pupil/student "talk" and feedback, and thereby giving less space for validation and recognition of different social-class, ethnic, and religious subcultures.

Within schools as well as universities and vocational further education, the language of education has been widely replaced by the language of the market. The concept of education is being redefined and standardized in economic rather than educational terms. Teachers and lecturers "deliver the lesson" or "deliver the product," "operationalize delivery," and "facilitate clients' learning," within a regime of management by tightly predefined objectives, subject to "quality management and enhancement," where students have become "customers." In vocational and higher education, "customers" select "modules" on a pick'n'mix basis. "Skill development" at universities has surged in importance, to the detriment of development of critical thought.

Effects on Critical Thinking Skills and Opportunities

Some analysts argue that liberalizing education is suppressing oppositional, critical, and autonomous thought (e.g., Hill, 2003, 2004a, 2004b, 2005b, 2006a, 2007). As McMurtry (1991) noted, this leads to "opposite standards of freedom."

> Freedom in the market is the enjoyment of whatever one is able to buy from others with no questions asked, and profit from whatever one is able to sell to others with no requirement to answer to anyone else. Freedom in the place of education, on the other hand, is precisely the freedom to question, and to seek answers, whether it offends people's self-gratification or not. (McMurtry, 1991, p. 213)

The emphasis on education for marketable skills, uncritically embraced, can only promote a consumerist, individualistic approach in which "human capital" becomes another tradable commodity. The ILO has argued that it would be "a deplorable outcome if the commercial and labour market aspects of schooling and training crowded out other aspects of education" (ILO, 2004).

From Social and Political Democracy to "Economic Consumer Democracy"

In liberalized school systems throughout the globe, the economic goals of education are sidelining social and collective goals, and have also replaced education and learning for its own sake. What matters now is how many years and credits we have accumulated, in order to get a better job.

In the 1960s and early 1970s, there was a real, if limited, commitment to greater equality in many governments and state educational institutions in Western Europe, North America, and elsewhere. In the United Kingdom, the avowed aims of education policy were "education for a fairer society" and "education for education's sake." In the United States, education was seen as a democratizing force by an increasingly activist civil society, associated, for example, with the civil rights movement, women's groups, environmental groups, and labor unions. As a result, schools and universities began "allowing too much freedom and independence of thought, and that cannot be tolerated in a 'democracy,' because it might lead to consequences" (Chomsky, 2004). Starting in the 1970s in the United States, policy began to shift toward Neoliberalization strategies such as voucher schemes, tax tuition credits, and charter schools.

In the United Kingdom, government policies on education and training have increasingly focused on education's role in human capital development. The former U.K. Education Secretary, David Blunkett, said the work of his Department "fits with a new economic imperative of supply-side investment for national prosperity" (cited in Jones, 2003, p.144). Educational priorities are now tied to market-driven growth and the more active involvement of private interests in education provision. The cultural meaning of schooling is being changed; it is now explicitly geared to performance, results, and efficiency. Schools have become "places where management authority, rather than collegial culture, establishes the ethos and purpose of the school" (Jones, 2003, p.161).

England and Wales: Pay and Conditions, Privatization and the GATS

Impact of Neoliberalization on Teachers' Pay and Service Conditions[2]

Prior to the 1988 Education Reform Act, local education authorities (LEAs) in England and Wales had financial and managerial responsibility for schools, and national collective bargaining machinery determined teachers' pay and conditions of employment. Since then, the national framework has been broken up in various ways with a considerable impact on teachers' pay and conditions of service. The most recent, perhaps greatest, threat is the establishment of the Government's Academies program.

The Abolition of National Collective Bargaining

A key step in the program of "Neoliberalization" in the schools sector pursued by the current New Labour and previous Conservative Governments was taken in 1987, with the abolition of the national collective bargaining machinery covering pay and other conditions of employment relating to working time and duties. Subsequently replaced by the present Review Body system, this has allowed the Government to impose other changes to teachers' pay and conditions that it could never have secured through collective bargaining.

Since 1987, the main developments in the teachers' pay structure have been the expansion of "flexibility" and discretion over teachers' pay, and the promotion of performance-related pay and payment by results.

The National Union of Teachers has consistently expressed concern about the loss of its national collective bargaining rights. The ILO found in 1990 that the U.K. Government was in breach of the relevant ILO Convention by continuing to deny negotiating rights to teachers.

The Delegation of Staffing Powers to Schools and the Impact of Pay Flexibility

Soon after the abolition of the national negotiating machinery, the Education Reform Act 1988 introduced local management of schools. Under the Act, many financial and managerial responsibilities previously under the LEAs' control were delegated to the governing bodies of schools. These included the ability to determine the school's staffing structure, to make appointments, and to take discretionary decisions with regard to teachers' pay.

There is now more scope in the salary structure for pay differentiation. The level of discretion available in schools means that placement and progress in the pay structure can depend on factors unrelated to the merits of the teacher, such as the school's financial position. Teachers doing effectively the same job can receive very different salaries in different schools.

The impact of these discretionary elements has been compounded by the introduction of performance-related pay. Access to a new higher pay scale beyond the main scale has been made subject to an application-based "performance threshold" assessment, and progression on the higher scale is also performance-related.

Delegated powers of management, combined with budgetary constraints in schools, have led to an increase in "casualization" by way of short-term contracts and agency-supplied temporary teachers. The use of short-term contracts deprives teachers of job security and, in the case of agency teachers, also deprives them of other entitlements because few agencies apply the national pay and conditions.

Workload

In 1994, the School Teachers' Review Body commissioned the first in a series of surveys on teacher workload in response to lobbying from teacher unions. They highlighted the "deep and continuing concern about teachers' workloads and the effect that heavy workloads were having on morale" (School Teachers' Review Body, 2002, p. 11). Although teachers have annual contractual limits on working hours, these do not cover marking and lesson preparation, which are subject to an additional working-time obligation. Between 1994 and 2000, primary school teachers' hours increased by 8% and secondary teachers' hours by 5%. For both groups, time spent on planning, preparation, and marking increased by 17% and teachers were working on average about 52 hours a week (UNESCO, 2004, pp.12–15). Workload has been a leading factor in making teaching an increasingly stressful occupation. Stress is now the main health and safety concern; 82% of school safety representatives cite it as a cause for concern in their school (TUC, 2000). Teachers are the most stressed occupational group, with over 40% reporting high stress levels (Health and Safety Executive, 2000). Despite the introduction of an entitlement to guaranteed Planning, Preparation, and Assessment (PPA) time in September 2005, the 2007 School Teachers' Review Body Workload Survey recorded an increase in the working hours of primary head teachers and classroom teachers compared to 2006.

The Academies Program

The newest, perhaps greatest, threat to teachers' securities and those of other staff is the Academies program, formerly called "City Academies." Statutory pay and conditions do not apply in Academies, which are publicly funded independent schools with voluntary or private sponsors. They can set their own pay and service conditions for staff. There are at present 83 academies, the first having opened in September 2002, and by September 2010 there will probably be up to 400. The Government announced as part of its Five Year Plan for education that it aimed to have 200 Academies by the end of the decade and later doubled that figure.

Research on the pay and service conditions for teachers in the operational Academies show that most do not apply the national conditions of employment in full or even in part. Longer contractual working hours are common. The initiative also poses a threat to trade union rights, because some Academies do not recognize unions for negotiating purposes.

Research commissioned by the TUC (Rogers and Migninolo, 2007; see also Hatcher, 2007) suggests that academies have found it difficult to retain staff and that the emphasis on leadership has pushed the salaries of principals beyond those of head teachers in the maintained sector (p.16). A reluctance to transfer to the academy may result from the new ethos, which is often of a Christian nature as the major sponsors are from religious trusts. There are also well publicized concerns that such academies are teaching theories such as creationism or over-emphasising their speciality, which is often business.

The House of Commons Public Accounts Committee (2007) warned the government to stop allowing academies to award contracts to their sponsors without competitive tendering. This followed reports of huge contract awards in violation of public procurement law and employment of relatives on high salaries.

Privatization, Contracting Out, and the Pay, Rights, and Conditions of the Mainly Female Ancillary Schools Workforce[3]

School staff has been affected by significant changes in local government in the last 20 years in England and Wales. As in other parts of the public sector, there has been a drive since the 1980s to decentralize management and funding and to maximize the autonomy of institutions. The local management of schools since 1988 has blurred employer responsibility and led to legal challenges over who employs school staff: the local authority or the school. It has also led to local variations in terms and conditions of school support staff and difficulty in monitoring them. At the same time, statutory and policy measures have been taken to maximize the involvement of the private sector in delivering education services.

Compulsory competitive tendering in local government was introduced in 1980. It first applied to highways and building maintenance and was then extended to all ancillary services, such as catering and cleaning, in the Local Government Act 1988. Within the OECD countries, the United Kingdom was unique in its compulsory model of competitive tendering, and studies, including those commissioned by the U.K. government, found that exposure to tendering led to the often dramatic erosion of terms and conditions of employment (Sachdev, 2001, p. 5). Lewis (2002, p. 11) reports on a report by the Equal Opportunities Commission (1995) that looked at 39 authorities and four companies between 1989 and 1993. It found greater use of temporary workers with fewer employment rights like holidays and sick pay. There was a 22% fall in female and 12% fall in male employment, a decline in hours for female part-timers and an increase in multiple job-holding (Lewis, 2002, p. 11). The figures for the education sector are likely to be higher as women make up 84% of the workforce.

The Thatcher Government paved the way for contracting out in 1983 by denouncing ILO Convention No. 94 and repealing the Fair Wages Resolution, in place since 1891. It was thought that in labor-intensive public services, access to a cut-price workforce would be essential to attracting private bids. A downward spiral of pay and conditions followed for staff, mainly women, who were already the lowest paid in schools (Wing, 2003).

Compulsory competitive tendering forced local authorities to compete on the basis of cost. Contracts were often retained in-house, but with worse pay and conditions. A survey for the Department of the Environment reported that 15% of authorities had withdrawn bonus schemes, 7% had cut wages, 18% had changed sick pay arrangements, and 12% holiday entitlements. Workforce reduction and rearranged hours were the most common response to competition, with manual staff bearing the brunt of changes in working methods, pay, and conditions (Walsh & Davis, 1993).

The Labour Government elected in 1997 adhered to its promise to abolish compulsory competitive tendering but replaced it with a "Best Value" program. This consisted of 12 principles in a performance framework, to apply to a wider range of services, without the necessity of an in-house bid. Unlike local authorities, schools did not have a statutory duty to obtain Best Value, but were required to adhere to its principles. Since January 2000, Ofsted, the inspection body, has included this requirement in its framework for schools.

Research by the UNISON public services trade union indicated that privatization resulted in lower pay and that protection for staff transferring from the public sector contrasted with the inferior pay and conditions for recruits. Wing (2003, p. 4) suggests that gender had re-emerged as an issue, and that there had been no policy appraisal of the gender impact of the various policies that had led to the contracting out of thousands of jobs held by women.

UNISON established a Best Value Intelligence Unit and surveyed 190 private contracts in 2001. Comparisons were difficult as new staff in white-collar jobs were often on personal contracts, but the findings suggest that basic pay in 62% of contracts had worsened, mainly affecting ancillary staff. For school meals contracts, in Nottinghamshire, for example, pay for new staff was £4.60 an hour for 34 weeks as opposed to £4.80 an hour for 38 weeks paid to transferred staff. Conditions of service had also worsened for new starters: 73% had less leave, 58% worse sick pay arrangements, 51% inferior pensions, 44% had lost unsocial hours' payments, and 44% reported less job security (UNISON, 2002, p. 6).

Trade unions have been forced to respond as in the campaign to challenge the two-tier workforce that resulted in the Best Value Code of Practice. Another major initiative is the creation of new national bargaining machinery for school support staff, which should be in place by September 2008. It will cover maintained, voluntary aided, foundation and trust schools, but academies will be outside of the new arrangements.

The E.U., the U.K., and the GATS[4]

GATS incorporate four modes of service supply. Mode 1 (cross-border supply) is the "supply of a service from the territory of one Member to a consumer in the territory of another." Under Mode 2 (consumption abroad), the consumer of the service travels to the service supplier. Under Mode 3 (commercial presence), the service supplier establishes in the foreign market as a legal entity in the form of a subsidiary or a branch. Mode 4 relates to temporary migration of foreign workers to supply a service in another country.

In primary and secondary education, in the first three modes of supply, the E.U. has committed itself not to impose or maintain "restrictions which are inconsistent with GATS rules covering participation in the market by foreign service suppliers" (EU GATS-Infopoint, p. 2; also Yu, 2002).

In the United Kingdom (unlike some other E.U. members), there are no notified "limitations on market access." Thus, U.K. primary and secondary education "markets" seem open to foreign suppliers. WTO members committing themselves to opening up primary and secondary education through GATS (as the E.U. has) must show any limitation on access for foreign suppliers, which may then be open to challenge through the WTO's disputes procedure (Rikowski, 2001, p. 11).

The United Kingdom (via the E.U.) also has no limitations on the national treatment provision of the GATS regarding primary and secondary education. Under this GATS rule, member states must acknowledge any limitation in the treatment of foreign suppliers that puts them in a less favorable position than domestic counterparts. For example, Edison Schools (based in the United States) must be alerted to any differences in the way it is treated compared with U.K. education services suppliers if it enters the U.K. schools market.

Only in Mode 4 supply, the "presence of natural persons" from another country, does some limitation regarding foreign primary and secondary education suppliers possibly apply. Mode 4 is "unbound" for E.U. primary and secondary education, meaning that the E.U. has made no commitment to open its market or keep it as open as it was when the GATS came into force in 1995. If Edison Schools wanted to set up operations in the U.K., the company would have to use U.K. employees, as immigration rules would still apply. It is unlikely that U.S. teachers could just be flown to work in Edison U.K. schools. However, by the same token, no clear barrier to U.S. teachers being jetted into Edison U.K. schools is established on the basis of the E.U.'s GATS commitments.

Public and Private Money and the Deregulatory Framework

From the above account, it might appear that the U.K. (via the E.U.) has a more or less "open door" policy regarding the foreign supply of primary and secondary education services. This is a misleading impression. Section 5 of the E.U.'s Schedule of Commitments for education services under GATS indicates that, in relation to education, the E.U. is referring to "privately funded education services." This suggests that the only education services under threat from the GATS are independent and private schools. They are in the "education market," so must take the consequences and face competing foreign providers.

However, once again, the GATS language is cleverly crafted. The Schedule does not pinpoint private education "institutions," but privately funded "services." It is not the case that a whole education institution has to be a for-profit outfit for the GATS to apply. Any of its constituent services—from frontline ones such as teaching, cleaning, school meals services, and the school library—could fall under the GATS if private capital is involved. Furthermore, private operators in school improvement, equal opportunities and recruitment, and other school services previously supplied by the local education authority, may also fall under the GATS.

One could argue that these services are still "publicly funded" even though education businesses like Nord Anglia and school meals providers like Initial Services are delivering the service. Several points are relevant here.

First, the argument assumes that "public" money remains "public" even when transferred to a for-profit private service provider. However, it could be argued that, once the contract is signed to deliver frontline teaching, school management or improvement services, the "public money" undergoes transformation into private capital.

Second, in the Academies, specialist schools, and in some education action zones, private finance forms an element of start-up capital. The foundational significance of private capital is even clearer in the case of schools built under the Private Finance Initiative (PFI), where money to build a school is raised at commercial rates in the money markets by private companies. The government has fused the replacement and refurbishment of school buildings with education policy. The Building Schools for the Future (BSF) programme is a 15 year, multi-billion pound scheme begun in 2005. It means to involve major private companies and investment firms in consortia with local authorities and other partners like academics and colleges. The Local Education Partnership develops a "vision" for education in its area which can include dealing with underperformance, curriculum development, ICT and worforce reform. It uses PFI which means that some support staff employed as cleaners, caterers, caretakers, or in security become employees of the PFI consortium or its sub-contractors. There are major concerns that the BSF programme lacks transparency and accountability, creates conflicts of interest, provides a group of companies with market advantage, embeds policy inflexibility, invests the private sector with control over public policy, affects staff adversely and is a huge charge on the public purse. (UNISON, 2006). In all these cases, private involvement opens up schools or, at minimum, educational services to the GATS.

Third, under the Education Act 2002, school-governing bodies can set up separate companies, which could trade. They then have the power to invest in other companies. Furthermore, schools can merge to form "federations" to gain economies of scale, thereby increasing profit-making capacity. In September 2002, David Miliband (then Schools Minister) indicated that business leaders running school federations did not need teaching qualifications (Kelly, 2002). Schools can enter into deals with private outfits, and can sell educational services to other schools. (See Rikowski, 2002, 2005, 2006, 2007 for an elaboration of the capitalisation of schools in England and the Business takeover of schools. See Hill, 2006c for an overall critique of New Labour's neoliberal education policy, and Tomlinson, 2005 for a general analytical survey).

Finally, under the 2002 Act, around 1,000 schools are to be given the freedom to vary the curriculum and change teachers' pay and conditions. These powers result from the new "earned autonomy" status that top-performing schools can gain. This gives private sector operators some control over staff costs through manipulating teachers' contracts of employment.

Overall, in Rikowski's view (2002, 2005, 2006, 2007) the 2002 Act provides a regulatory framework for the business takeover of schools. It certainly provides clear opportunities for a much greater role for business in schools, hence also for the application of GATS throughout the school system. Of course, the Government can still argue that the school system is "publicly funded" but, in instances of outsourcing, the Private Finance Initiative and strategic partnerships with companies, public finance is transfigured into private capital. Sponsorship by companies involves injections of corporate cash. Through these mechanisms, schools are exposed to the GATS and school workers to a reduction in their social and economic securities.

CONCLUSION

This chapter has provided evidence to substantiate each of the hypotheses set out at the beginning.

- Neoliberalization of schooling and education services has occurred in many countries around the world.
- Specific identifiable levers are resulting in the neoliberalization of education services.
- Education services are becoming "Americanized" through policies and processes such as privatization, decentralization, deregulation, and the use of "new public management" (business management methods).
- Neoliberalization is making provision of education services more unequal and selective rather than universal. This is intensifying race, gender- and class-based hierarchies, reflected in tiered systems of schooling, with good quality schooling for the rich and the middle classes, and poor quality schooling—or none—for the poor.
- Neoliberalization is eroding workers' pay, rights, and securities.
- Neoliberalization is accompanied by, and attempts to embed, a shift away from universal citizenship rights and identities based on the provision of services to individual consumer rights and identities. In education, this involves treating young people as "human capital" and preparing them for "jobs" rather than providing broad-based learning and critical awareness.

In summary, Neoliberalization of schooling and other education sectors such as further (post-16) vocational education threatens: first, workers' pay, conditions, and securities; second, equity and social justice (with a notable increase in gender- and race-based class inequalities); and, third, critical thought and democratic control.

By contrast, the aim of education policy should be to secure a "race to the top," rather than a "race to the bottom" with ever poorer conditions for workers, students, and general populations. This means it is important to develop schools and education systems with the following characteristics. First, workers' pay, rights, and securities must be levelled up rather than down. Second, access to good education must be widened, by increasing its availability and by broadening access for under-represented and under-achieving groups, to reduce inequalities between groups. Third, local and national democratic control over schooling and education must be enhanced. And fourth, policymakers should recognize and seek to improve education systems that are dedicated to education for wider individual and social purposes than the production of quiescent workers and consumers in a liberalized world. There is more to education than that.

ACKNOWLEDGMENTS

We would like to thank Nick Grant for his comments on this chapter, in particular for writing the sub-section, "power within schools.".

This chapter develops from Hill (2006a). Education services neoliberalization. In E. Rosskam (Ed.), *Winners or losers? Liberalizing public services.* Geneva: ILO, and from Hill (2005a). Globalisation and its educational discontents: Neoliberalisation and its impacts on education workers' rights, pay, and conditions. *International Studies in the Sociology of Education* 15(3) 257–288.

NOTES

1. Naming rights are when a person or company sponsors or funds all or part of a project and is given the right to name the building, or facility in the building, etc.
2. Based on Brown (2004).
3. Based on Lewis (2004b).
4. Based on Rikowski (2005).

REFERENCES

Alexiadou, N. (2001). Management identities in transition: A case study from further education. *Sociological Review, 49*(3), 412–435.

Ball, S. (1999). Performativity and fragmentation in postmodern schooling. In J. Carter (Ed.), *Postmodernity and the fragmentation of welfare* (pp. 187–203). London: Routledge.

Beckmann, A., & Cooper, C. (2004). Globalization, the new managerialism and education: Rethinking the purpose of education. *Journal for Critical Education Policy Studies, 2*(1). Retrieved from http://www.jceps.com/index.php?pageID=articleandarticleID=31.

Borón, A., & Torres, C. (1996). The impact of neoliberal restructuring on education and poverty in Latin America. *Alberta Journal of Educational Research* 62(2), 102–114.

Bottery, M. (2000). *Education, policy and ethics.* New York: Continuum.

Boxley, S. (2003). Performativity and capital in schools. *Journal for Critical Education Policy Studies* 1(1). Retrieved from http://www.jceps.com/index.php?pageID=articleandarticleID=3.

Brown, C. (2004). The Neoliberalization of schools: Impact on teachers' pay and conditions of service in England and Wales. In C. Lewis et al. (Ed.), *Case study* on Neoliberalization of schooling and other educational services in England and Wales. Unpublished manuscript.

Carnoy, M. (2002). Latin America: The new dependency and educational reform. In H. Daun (Ed.), *Educational restructuring in the context of globalization and national policy* (pp. 289–322). New York: RoutledgeFalmer.

Chomsky, N. (2004). *Noam Chomsky speaks out: Education and power.* Retrieved from   http://www.indymedia.ie/newswire.php?story_id=66441andcondense_comments=false#comment88500.

Da Silva Aguiar, M. Â. (2004). A reforma da educação básica e as condições materiais das escolas [The reform of Basic Education and the material conditions of schools]. In A. M. Monteiro Silva & M. Â. Da Silva Aguiar (Eds.), *Retrato da escola no Brasil*. Brasilia: Confederação Nacional dos Trabalhadores em Educação.

Delgado-Ramos, G. C., & Saxe-Fernández, J. (2005). The World Bank and the privatization of public education: A Mexican perspective. *Journal for Critical Education Policy Studies, 3*(1). Retrieved from http://www.jceps.com/index.php?pageID=article&articleID=44.

Delgado-Ramos, G. C., & Saxe-Fernández, J. (2008). World Bank and the Privatization of Public Education: a Mexican Perspective. In D. Hill and E. Rosskam (eds.), *The Developing World and State Education: Neoliberal Depredation and Egalitarian Alternatives*. New York: Routledge.

Devidal, P. (2008). Trading Away Human Rights. The GATS and the Right to Education: a Legal Perspective. In D. Hill and R. Kumar (eds.), *Global Neoliberalism and Education and its Consequences*. New York: Routledge.

EU GATS-Infopoint. (n.d.). *Opening world markets for services: Legal texts and commitments*. Retrieved from http://gats-info.eu.int/gats-info/gatscomm.pl?MENU=hhh.

Gillborn, D., & Youdell, D. (2000). *Rationing education: Policy, practice, reform and equity*. Buckingham, United Kingdom: Open University Press.

Halimi, J. (2004, June). Road map for privatisation: The great leap backwards. *Le Monde Diplomatique*. Retrieved from http://mondediplo.com/2004/06/08privatisationroadmap.

Hall, D. (2003). *Public services work! Information, insights and ideas for the future.* Retrieved from http://www.psiru.org/reports/2003–09-U-PSW.pdf.

Hatcher, R. (2007). TUC report points movement in wrong direction: fighting New Labour's academies. *Socialist Resistance*, 47 (np.) (Sept.) Retrieved from http://www.isg-fi.org.uk/spip.php?article555.

Health and Safety Executive. (2000). *The scale of occupational stress.* Retrieved from http://www.hse.gov.uk/research/crr_pdf/2000/crr00311.pdf.

Hill, D. (2001). State theory and the neo-liberal reconstruction of schooling and teacher education: A structuralist neo-Marxist critique of postmodernist, quasi-postmodernist, and culturalist neo-Marxist theory. *The British Journal of Sociology of Education, 22*(1) 137–157.

Hill, D. (2003). Global neo-liberalism, the deformation of education and resistance. *Journal for Critical Education Policy Studies, 1*(1). Retrieved from http://www.jceps.com/index.php?pageID=article&articleID=7.

Hill, D. (2004a). Books, banks and bullets: Controlling our minds—the global project of imperialistic and militaristic neo-liberalism and its effect on education policy. *Policy Futures in Education, 2, 3–4.* Retrieved from http://www.wwwords.co.uk/pfie/content/pdfs/2/issue2_3.asp.

Hill, D. (2004b). O neoliberalismo global, a resistência e a deformação da educação. [Global neoliberalism, resistance and the deformation of education]. *Curriculo sem Fronteiras, 3*(3). Retrieved from http://www.curriculosemfronteiras.org/.

Hill, D. (2005a). Globalisation and its educational discontents: Neoliberalisation and its impacts on education workers' rights, pay, and conditions. *International Studies in the Sociology of Education,15*(3), 257–288.

Hill, D. (2005b). State theory and the neoliberal reconstruction of schooling and teacher education. In G. Fischman, P. McLaren, H. Sünker, & C. Lankshear, (Eds.), *Critical theories, radical pedagogies and global conflicts* (pp.23–51). Boulder, CO: Rowman and Littlefield.

Hill, D. (2006a). Education services neoliberalization. In E. Rosskam (Ed.), *Winners or losers? Liberalizing public services* (pp. 3–54). Geneva, Switzerland: ILO.

Hill, D. (2006b, April 6). Critical teacher education, new labour in Britain, and the global project of neoliberal capital. *Aula Critica: Revista Educativa de la Fundacion McLaren de Pedagogia Critica*. Retrieved from http://www.fundacionmclaren.org/articulos/hill.pdf.

Hill, D. (2006c). New Labour's Education Policy. In D. Kassem, E. Mufti and J. Robinson (Eds.) *Education Studies: Issues and Critical Perspectives*, (pp. 73–86). Buckingham: Open University Press.

Hill, D. (2007). Critical teacher education, new labour in Britain, and the global project of neoliberal capital. *Policy Futures*, 5(2). Retrieved from http://www.wwwords.co.uk/pfie/content/pdfs/5/issue5_2.asp.

Hill, D. and Kumar, R. (eds.) (2009). *Global neoliberalism and education and its consequences.* New York: Routledge.

Hill, D. and Rosskam, E. (eds.) (2009). *The developing world and state education: Neoliberal depredation and egalitarian alternatives.* New York: Routledge.

Hirtt, N. (2004). Three axes of merchandisation. *European Educational Research Journal*, 3(2), 442–453. Retrieved from http://www.wwwords.co.uk/eerj/.

Hirtt, N. (2008). Markets and Education in the Era of Globalized Capitalism. In D. Hill and R. Kumar (Eds.), *Global neoliberalism and education and its consequences.* New York: Routledge.

House of Commons. (1997, June 27) Further education adjournment debate. *Hansard* (1133). Retrieved from www.the-stationary-office.com/pa/cm199798/cmhansrd/vo970627/debtext/70627-17.htm.

House of Commons Public Accounts Committee. (2007). *Fifty second report: The academies programme. HC 402.* London: Her Majesty's Stationery Office.

House of Commons Public Accounts Committee (1998). *Further education volume 1, select committee on education and employment sixth report. session 1997–1998.* Retrieved from http://www.publications.parliament.uk/pa/cm199798/cmselect/cmeduemp/264/26413.htm.

Hursh, D. (2008). *High stakes testing and the decline of teaching and learning.* Lanham, MD: Rowman and Littlefield.

International Labour Organization (ILO). (2002). *Seven forms of security for decent work.* Retrieved from http://www.ilo.org/public/english/protection/ses/index.htm.

International Labour Organization (ILO). (2004). *Skills insecurity: Why "human capital" will not do, Economic Security for a Better World Fact Sheet No. 13.* Retrieved from http://www.ilo.org/public/english/protection/ses/download/docs/sheet_no13.pdf.

Jeffrey, B., & Woods, R. (1998). *Testing teachers: The effect of school inspections on primary teachers.* London: Falmer Press.

Jones, K. (2003). *Education in Britain, 1944 to the present.* Cambridge: United Kingdom: Polity Press.

Kelly, J. (2002, September 19). Business people may run state school federations. *Financial Times*, p. 4.

Leher, R. (2004). A new lord of education? World Bank policy for peripheral capitalism. *Journal for Critical Education Policy Studies*, 2 (1). Retrieved from http://www.jceps.com/index.php?pageID=articleID=20.

Leher, R. (2008). Brazilian Education, Dependent Capitalism and the World Bank. in D. Hill and R. Kumar (Eds.) *Global neoliberalism and education and its consequences.* New York: Routledge.

Lewis, C. (2002). *Taking the lid off term-time working in education*. London: UNISON.

Lewis, C. (2004a). *Interview with Christine Lewis, National Officer for UNISON*. Unpublished Manuscript.

Lewis, C. (2004b). Some effects of the Neoliberalization of further education colleges in England and Wales. In C. Lewis, D. Hill and B. Fawcett (Eds.), *Case study on Neoliberalization of schooling and other educational services in England and Wales*. Unpublished manuscript.

Mahoney, P., & Hextall, I. (2000). *Reconstructing teaching: Standards, performance and accountability*. London: Routledge Falmer.

Malins, C. (2005). *Comment on "Bolkestein legacy 'too radical' for new Commission."* Retrieved from http://lists.aktivix.org/pipermail/ssf/2005-February/000880.html.

McLauchlin, A. (2005, February 3). The EU Services Directive. *European Voice*, 11(4) (np).

McMurtry, J. (1991). Education and the market model *Journal of the Philosophy of Education*, 25(2), 209–217.

McNeil, L. (2000). *Contradictions of school reform: Educational costs of standardized testing*. New York: Routledge.

Molnar, A. (2001). *Giving kids the business: The commercialization of America's schools* (2nd ed). Boulder, CO: Westview/Harpercollins.

Molnar, A. (2003). *No student left unsold: The Sixth Annual Report on schoolhouse commercialism trends*. Retrieved from Arizona State University Web site: http://www.asu.edu/educ/epsl/CERU/Annual%20reports/EPSL-0309–107-CERU-exec.doc.

Molnar, A. (2005). *School Commercialism: From Democratic Ideal to Market Commodity*. London: Routledge.

Molnar, A., Wilson, G., and Allen, D. (2004). *Profiles of for-profit education management companies: Sixth Annual Report 2003–2004*. Retrieved from Arizona State University, Web site http://www.asu.edu/educ/epsl/CERU/Documents/EPSL-0402–101-CERU.pdf.

Mortimor, P. (2006). *An Education System for the 21st Century*. Retrieved from www.teachers.org.uk.

Mukhtar, A. (2004). *Case study on Neoliberalization of schooling and other educational services in Pakistan*. Unpublished manuscript.

Munín, H. (1998). "Freer" forms of organization and financing and the effects of inequality in Latin American educational systems: Two countries in comparison. *Compare*, 28(3), 229–243.

National Association of Teachers in Further and Higher Education (NATFHE). (2003, April 1). *Better accountability and planning needed for FE colleges, says NATFHE, Press release*. Retrieved from http://www.natfhe.org.uk/says/rels2003/2003pr25.shtml.

Office of the Deputy Prime Minister Circular. (2003, March). *Local Government Act 1999 Part 1. Best Value and Performance Improvement*. London: Author

Puiggrós, A. (2002). World Bank education policy: Market liberalism meets ideological conservatism., In V. Navarro (Ed.), *The political economy of social inequalities: Consequences for health and quality of life* (pp. 181–190). Amityville, NY: Baywood.

Reimers, F. (2000). *Unequal schools, unequal chances: The challenges to equal opportunity in the Americas*. Cambridge, MA: Harvard University Press.

Rikowski, G. (2001). *The battle in Seattle: Its significance for education*. London: Tufnell Press.

Rikowski, G. (2002, January 22). *Globalisation and education prepared for the House of Lords Select Committee on economic affairs inquiry into the global economy*. Retrieved from http://www.ieps.org.uk.cwc.net/rikowski2002d.pdf.

Rikowski, G. (2005). Schools and the GATS enigma. In E. W. Ross & R. Gibson (Eds.), *Neoliberalism and education reform* (pp.).Cresskill, NJ: Hampton Press.

Rikowski, G. (2006). On the capitalisation of schools in England. *The Flow of Ideas.* (1 November), retrieved from http://www.flowofideas.co.uk/?page=articles &sub=On%20the%20capitalisation%20of%20schools%in%20England.

Rikowski, G. (2007) The Confederation of British Industry and the Business Take-over of Schools. The Flow of Ideas. Retrieved from http://www.flowofideas. co.uk/?page=articles&sub=The%20CBI%20and%20and%20the%20Business %20Takeover%20of%Schools.

Rogers, M. and Migniuolo, F. (2007). *A new direction: A review of the school academies programme.* London: Trades Union Congress. Retrieved from http:// www.tuc.org.uk/extras/academies.pdf.

Sachdev, S. (2001). *Contracting culture from CCT to PPPs: The private provision of public services and its impact on employment relations.* London: UNISON.

School Teachers' Review Body. (2002). *Eleventh Report.* Retrieved from http:// www.ome.uk.com/downloads/11%20STRB%20Report.pdf

Tomlinson, S. (2005). Education in a post-welfare society (second edn.). Maidenhead, Berks: Open University Press.

Tooley, J. (1999b). *The global education industry. Lessons from private education in developing countries.* Washington, DC: International Finance Corporation.

Trades Union Congress. (2000). *Safety representatives survey.* London: Author.

UNESCO. (2004). *Raising standards and tackling workload: The use of support staff.* Retrieved from http://www.unesco.org/iiep/eng/research/basic/PDF/ teachers1.pdf.

UNISON. (2002). *Best Value and the two-tier workforce in local government.* Retrieved from http://www.unison.org.uk/acrobat/B318.pdf.

UNISON (2006). *Building Schools for the Future: a branch handbook commissioned from the Association for Public Service Excellence* (APSE). London: UNISON.

Walker, A., & Stott, K. (2000). Performance improvement in schools—a case of overdose. *Educational Management and Administration*, 28(1), 63–76.

Walsh, K., & Davis, H. (1993). *Competition and service: The impact of the Local Government Act 1988.* London: HMSO.

Whitty, G. (1997). "Marketization, the state, and the re-formation of the teaching profession. In A. H. Halsey et al. (Eds.), *Education, culture and economy* (pp. 299–310). Oxford, United Kingdom: Oxford University Press.

Whitty, G. (2000, November 12). *Privatisation and marketisation in education policy.* Speech given to the National Union of Teachers conference on Involving the Private Sector in Education: Value Added or High Risk? London. Retrieved from http://k1.ioe.ac.uk/directorate/NUTPres%20web%20 version%20(2%2001).doc.

Whitty, G., Power, S. and Halpin, D. (1998). *Devolution and choice in education: The school, the state and the market.* Buckingham, United Kingdom: Open University Press.

Wing, M. (2003). *Ending the two-tier workforce: A comprehensive solution?* London: UNISON.

Wolf, M. (1999, December 8). In defence of global capitalism. *Financial Times*, p. 29.

World Trade Organization. (2003). GATS: *Fact and fiction. Misunderstandings and scare stories. Retrieved from* http://www.wto.org/english/tratop_e/serv_e/ gats_factfictionfalse_e.htm.

Yu, V. P. B. (2002). *How to read GATS negotiating requests and offers, Trade Information Project, Centre for International Environmental Law/Institute for Agriculture and Trade Policy/Friends of the Earth International-CIEL-IATP-FOEI.* Geneva, Switzerland: Friends of the Earth International.

6 Changing the Tide of Education Policy in Finland
From Nordic to EU Educational Policy Model

*Joel Kivirauma, Risto Rinne,
and Piia Seppänen*

INTRODUCTION

Numerous authors around the world hold the opinion that we are witnessing the transition to an entirely new historical era, which has been referred to by various names, such as globalization, risk society, neoliberalism, and so on (e.g., Bauman, 1996, 1998; Beilhartz, 2000; Beck, 1992, 1997; Castells, 1997; Castells & Himanen, 2002; Giddens, 1995; Sennett, 1998). In this "global network society," education and social exclusion are also making new connections and searching for new routes and forms. Raising educational standards in the global market offers little insight into how the question of social justice is to be addressed (Brown & Lauder, 2006, p. 334).

Radical changes in educational policy and governance have occurred all around the postindustrialized world in recent years. Mark Olssen (2006, p. 263) has distinguished two interrelated phenomena in globalization: (1) changes in science and technology, and (2) discursive system pursued at the policy level. Our chapter concentrates on the latter of those levels; in other words, we are looking at the impacts of neoliberal policy changes. We are examining the new governance of education and the new mechanisms of educational and social exclusion. Our aim is to examine the changing position of education as a definer, producer, and result of social exclusion by analyzing and comparing Finnish educational policy changes with more general European trends. The effects and consequences of these changes are not yet very clear, but at least in Finland there seem to be astonishingly strong trends of diversification of the whole old honorable Nordic social–democratic comprehensive school.

When comparing educational policy in different European countries, each educational system and type of governance should be contextualised in wider socio-cultural frames. As there are different models of welfare states, are there also "Nordic," "corporated," "neoliberal," and "peripheral" welfare routes or models[1] in the field of educational policies and governance? And if so, are these models now in the process of becoming integrated into a kind of "EU educational policy model"? (Kivirauma, Rinne, & Seppänen, 2003; Rinne & Kivinen, 2003; Rinne, Aro, Kivirauma, & Simola, 2003; Kallo & Rinne, 2006).

Educational exclusion is most often seen as the problem of inequality of educational opportunities and partly as a consequence of this, inequality of social opportunities. Some groups have poorer resources and material opportunities than others on the educational market. This has been the main argument and rationale behind carrying out comprehensive school reforms in many welfare states after World War Two. But on the other hand educational exclusion also deals very deeply with different cultural ways of life, cultural values and languages, power relations and the diversification of knowledge. Discursive rules construct the subjects and subjectivities that differentiate various groups. We need to research the principles of reason and conduct that classify, differentiate, and divide the subjectivities of actors and agents through practices of normalization.

This chapter is connected to a comparative research project funded by the European Union that began in late 1990s, "Educational Governance and Social Inclusion and Exclusion" (EGSIE). The research project is based on the central argument that the recent changes in education systems in Europe will have a great impact on social exclusion and integration. The project tries to clarify relations between educational governance and social integration and exclusion in different national contexts.

The Egsie project compared educational policy in nine countries; Australia, Finland, Germany, Greece, Iceland, Portugal, Spain, Sweden, and the United Kingdom. The selection of countries covers differences in cultures and traditions of educational policies and modern welfare and education strategies. It also covers the four welfare state models mentioned earlier.[2] The educational policies that are practiced in different national contexts, the diversification of the educational system, the segregation, selection, and exclusion and inclusion processes differ from each other due to the different welfare histories and modern models of these countries (Lindblad & Popkewitz, 2001).

In this chapter, first we will have a broad look at governance changes in all E.U. countries. Governance changes are related to different structures of compulsory secondary education and thus to school admission and selection. Second, we concentrate on educational changes and social exclusion in Finland by analysing two sets of data. The first data consists of 18 carefully selected urgent and powerful Finnish educational policy texts and discourses (e.g., committee reports, white papers) over a thirty-year period concerning primary and secondary education (Appendix 1). The second data that we use consists of interviews made with 16 carefully selected important educational politicians, decision-makers, and informants in Finland (Appendix 2). The duration of each interview was from one to two hours and they were carried out at the end of 1998 and the beginning of 1999.

GOVERNANCE CHANGES AND SCHOOL CHOICE POLICIES IN EUROPE

It seems that the most essential trend of education policy changes has been decentralization and deregulation of governance in education in many countries. However, the degree of decentralization varies and takes regional, local, or "market-like" forms in different countries. Green, Wolf, and Leney (1999) identify four models of basic education regulation and governance in the late 1990's EU Member States: first centralised systems with elements of devolution and choice, second regional devolution with some minor devolution and choice, third local control with national "steering" and some school autonomy and fourth institutional autonomy in quasi-market systems of education. (Green et al., 1999, pp. 79–111.)

One central feature of the governance changes in compulsory education has been so called "parental choice" that is used as a policy to allocate children to schools. Choice policies are inevitably connected to admission policies of schools and thus, to student selection. In order to examine education policy changes and structures of exclusion across the countries' school choice policies, focusing on admission policies in different school systems is one of the vital issues. Green et al., (1999, pp. 70–79, 115–121, 144) make a threefold typology of the relationship between admission policies and the structure of lower secondary education, which are called admission models. Admission models are: zoned comprehensive, open enrolment in comprehensive and partially comprehensive systems, and selection by ability. In the zoned comprehensive model specialization into academic or vocational tracks is delayed and students are allocated to schools on the basis of residence according to the principle of mixed ability intake. So called "open enrolment" covers various policies that favor families' choice over school, but sustain some comprehensive features. In the most selective systems, all students are allocated to compulsory secondary schools on the basis of examinations, previous school achievements, and/or advice of primary school teachers.

Green et al. view models of education regulation and governance and models of admission policies separately. In their analysis the Member states of the European Union are allocated to these models in 1975 or 1980, and in 1995 (Green et al., 1999). The models give fruitful tools to view them simultaneously and thus, school choice can be linked more closely to changes in governance. In the following outline, European countries are viewed in relation to both education governance and admission policies of lower secondary schools. In this review there are also used EURYDICE documents, OECD reports, and literature (see Seppänen, 2006, pp. 29–51). Figure 6.1 shows a combination of the models in education governance and models in admission to lower secondary schools in addition to change and stability during 20 years in E.U. countries. In the figure, the policies of countries are seen at the end of 1970s when the name of the country is marked with *italics,* and at the end of 1990s when name of the country is marked in **bold.**

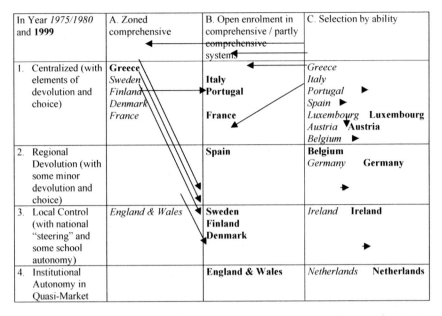

Figure 6.1.   The change in models of education governance in relation to admission models from the end of 1970s to the end of 1990s in Europe (Green et al., 1999; Seppänen, 2006, p. 33).

The arrows in the figure point out the direction of change in relation to education governance and admission to lower secondary schools.

The E.U. Member states can be divided into four groups in relation to education policy changes and school choice policy. A broad outline of education policy changes are viewed from the end of 1970s to the end of 1990s. The Continental European countries and Ireland have been the most stable, both in education governance and in selective admission policies (with the exception of France) during the 20 years period (OECD, 1994; EURYDICE, 1997a; 1997b; Broccolichi & van Zanten, 2000; Duru-Bellat & Kieffer, 2000). In contrast to most continental European countries, Southern European E.U. Member states shifted away from earlier differentiation in compulsory schooling toward more comprehensive school systems by the turn of 2000. Despite some recent pressures Southern European countries have been largely stable in centralized education governance, with the exception of Spain, which is classified as a regional system. (Green et al., 1999; Nóvoa, Alves, & Canário, 1999; Pereyra, Sevilla, & Castillo, 1999; Ossenbach-Sauter, 1996).

Where the Southern European countries, mainly Greece, Spain, and Portugal, have introduced comprehensive school since the end of 1980s, the Scandinavian countries did that at the turn of the 1970s. One of the central ideas in the Scandinavian comprehensive school system has been to allocate students to schools on a basis of residence (catchment area division). Thus, in Figure 6.1, the Scandinavian (E.U.) countries are in the "zoned comprehensive" model of admission at the end of 1970s. At that time, educational provision was planned and exercised under detailed central administration. During the 1990s, several gradual changes in legislation and shifts to local control in governance of basic schooling enabled parents to show a preference for a school of their choice in cities in spite of catchment area divisions. For the first time, the renewed legislation of basic education that came into force in 1999 in Finland stated that students can make a request to go to a school other than the allocated school (Education legislation, 1999, 28§). This doesn't mean that enrolment to comprehensive schools is not entirely "open" in Finland because, according to school law, students have the right to get placed in the nearest school. Also, the ownership and governance of schools for basic education has remained public and free of charge; in other words, the private and independent school sector is modest and does not have a role in school choice in Finland. Only 2% of young people go to private schools (Official Statistics of Finland, 2005, p. 105). Some educational diversity has been introduced. In addition to the National Core Curriculum, schools can offer so called "emphasised classes" that have additional lessons (most typically in music, science, and/or mathematics, languages, sports, and some in arts and technology). This means that students are selected by tests or previous school achievement[3] (see more in Seppänen, 2003; 2006).

It seems that in Scandinavia "open enrolment" to schools is more an additional policy of education whereas, in England and Wales, open enrolment is a key feature of quasi-markets in education governance. In the education reform of England and Wales in 1988, open enrolment meant not only parents' right to express the preference of a public/state school but also it allowed popular schools to attract students up to their physical capacity, instead of imposing limits to popular schools in order that other schools can remain open (Whitty, Power, & Halpin, 1998; Whitty & Edwards, 1998). Also in quasi-markets the institutional diversity among the schools is wide, which is not the case in public comprehensive school systems. The most extreme quasi-markets operate in the Netherlands, which has traditionally had a selective and highly differentiated secondary school system with paramount freedom of school choice (Teelken, 1998).

To conclude, the open enrolment model (Green et al., 1999) as describing education, policy varies considerably nationally and locally. The nature of school choice policies varies whether the policy is accompanied by school funding mechanisms, which are dependant, at least partly, on school enrolments, whether authorities regulate the degree to which schools can expand or contract, whether there is set selection criteria—and what kind—by authorities when schools are oversubscribed, and how wide specialization is allowed at the expense of core curriculum (OECD, 1994; Green et al.,

1999). Thus, policies can encourage diversification between schools, or they can at least try to be more compatible to comprehensive and equivalence principals.

THE TURNING POINT OF FINNISH EDUCATIONAL POLICY

Deregulation, Abolishing Detailed Sector Steering, and Building up the Evaluative State

The heavily centralized planning and steering system in education, which had been under construction in Finland for decades and reached its peak during the rise of the comprehensive school reform, was abandoned by a decision of the government in 1988 to reform the entire management of the state. Behind this new policy there was a politically very influential decentralization committee (CR, 1986). Its task was to plan a strategy for how the various functions and authority were to be shifted from the central government to the municipalities and administrative districts, and to clarify what changes were needed in the functions and status of central administration boards. At that time the prevailing strong planning system was also replaced by a new evaluation system (CR, 1985). The government's proposal in 1988 was to establish one statutory policy system in the field of education. The new plans were now aimed at combining all the school grade levels and types of schools under the same, very general, planning system. The former sector-based planning systems, with their highly detailed and focused steering regulations, were all abandoned. Among the many defects of the former sector planning were its diversity, its unsuitable time-tables, the poor implementation of state planning, the bureaucracy of planning, the waste of time, the futility of detailed and inflexible regulations (CR, 1989a, pp. 1–2, 21; Kivinen, Rinne, Järvinen, Koivisto, & Laakso, 1995; Rinne, Kivirauma, Hirvenoja, & Simola, 2000).

The new "development plan for education" approved by the government viewed the whole education system as an entity, and was more concise than the former detailed sector plans. The aim was to make the planning process lighter and faster, even though the national development plan was still to be drawn up as a multilevel plan. The primary focus of the national development plan was to ensure the implementation of essential goals and lines of action, to improve conditions for the development of the prerequisites for action, and to put far more emphasis on evaluation of the results as well as leading by results. Evaluation was to be made continuous and was to take place at all levels of education (CR, 1989a, pp. 23–25; CR, 1989b, pp. 3, 5–6).

The decentralization of education management was only partially argued for in this development plan, but it mainly followed from the general principles of change seen in the development and goals of the whole Finnish governance policy. The Committee on the Development of Education commented on decentralization in its first report as follows:

> With the help of the education planning system, the general principals of development are being promoted by increasingly the shifting of authority from central management to provincial governments, educational institutions, schools, municipalities and universities. (CR, 1989a, p. 25)

The same kinds of statements were repeated, one after another, at the beginning of the 1990s in the development plans for education (Ministry of Education, 1991, p. 30). The goal was to decentralize the whole of state management and to improve managerialism using quite strong measures; this shift was not limited to the management of education.

The power of local school authorities was increased in 1985 when very strict regulations were replaced by the so-called system of "teaching hours frames."[4] In addition, the steering mechanisms of municipalities were also changed by several development projects of the government that started at the end of the 1980s. The authority of the Ministry and the National Board of Education to steer municipalities was revoked. The law that came in to force in 1999 repealed many of the regulations that had steered municipalities and other organizers of education (CR, 1996, pp. 23–24). The authority of the municipalities as well as schools increased, and the style of management changed due to the reformed allocation of state subsidies after 1993. The central administration no longer regulated the allocation of resources in detail. The purpose of the new "plant-based" budgetary control system was to encourage organizers of education to find solutions that would serve flexible functional and economic purposes. In addition, the allocation of resources became more and more flexible between different administrative areas, so that the allocation of resources after 1993 was more dependent upon local decisions. (CR, 1996, p. 24.)

The former management of municipal education through central steering and regulation was to be replaced by rather massive operations of evaluation. The assessment of goals and essential lines of action, and evaluation and follow-up of outcomes, were chosen as the priorities of national development plans in education (CR, 1989a, p. 24; CR, 1989b, pp. 3–4; Ministry of Education, 1991, pp. 30–31). A plan to develop "evaluation practices and measures of efficiency for both national and local self-evaluation of schools" was drawn up (Ministry of Education, 1991, pp. 12, 31). At the end of the decade the government's resolution was stated more clearly:

> The National Board of Education, together with local and regional experts when needed, will evaluate all the forms of education and their most important sub-sectors by the end of the planning period. (Ministry of Education, 1996, p. 8)

These guidelines were firmly established a little bit later by law. The basic role of evaluation–and, of course, monitoring of results–was one of the main points in the reform of education legislation (Education Legislation, 1999). The statutory evaluation system was seen as necessary when moving from norm steering to steering by outcomes. According to the report of the Committee on the Reform of Education Legislation, "Evaluation is an essential means to guarantee the quality of educational services and their national comparability." The purpose of evaluation is "to support the development of education and improve conditions for learning." On the basis of decisions made in the Ministry of Education, the National Board of Education decides how to execute evaluation. The organizers of education are obligated to evaluate all the education that they organize. This self-evaluation includes both evaluation at the level of schools and at the level of the organizer of education (i.e., most commonly the municipal level; CR, 1996, pp. 55, 82–85, 106–107). The committee several times made use of "soft policy" rhetoric (e.g., stating that the evaluation system was not meant to be a tool for control by the state, but an essential part of developing educational services locally, regionally, and nationally; CR, 1996, p. 84).

Behind this massive decentralization and deregulation there seems to be, among all of those interviewed, the collapse of the earlier almost unquestionable belief in centralized planning and centralized governance (NBE, 1; OAJ; City, 3; RLA; City, 2). The head of National Board of Education explained it as follows:

> Well, I think that the general situation in society was mature for it, that the welfare state had come to the end of its road in the sense that it was noticed that it is not possible to determine every possible thing by planning systems at the national level. In other words, this kind of belief in planning collapsed. . . . and at the same time this devolution got stronger in Finland. It was noticed that the local actors are able to handle their affairs better when they are allowed the freedom of action, and their ability to act is not fettered . . . One version of this devolution is the breakdown of a unified culture. Finland has been an unusually monolithic country . . . it was admitted there is no reason why a comprehensive school in Utsjoki [a town in scarcely populated Finnish Lapland] and one in Kulosaari [a suburb in Helsinki, the capital of Finland] have to function according to the same curriculum. (NBE, 1)

There was an almost surprising unanimity and strong belief in the superiority of local decision-making compared to the older centralized model. Expertise rests in the municipalities and in the schools, and it can only be brought out by giving decision-making power to the local level, it was stated (NBE, 2; MP; ME, 2). The interviewees connected the dissolution of norms and devolution to the economic depression. Without shifting decision making to the local level it would not have been possible to require the municipalities to cut down spending as much as was now (NBE 1; ME 2; City 1). At the same time the central administration was able to transfer difficult decisions to the municipal level.

Several of those interviewed wondered, though, whether the dismantling of national unified standards and increase in local decision-making power had occurred too quickly (ME 1; NBE 2; CH). Some feared that, in the future, we will have to move back toward the old system in which the central government at least partially allocates funds for specific purposes and thus ensures the equal availability of services to its citizens throughout the country (NBE 2; OAJ).

The Discursive Change from Citizenship to Individualism

The "discourse of choice" became a typical part of Finnish education politics in the 1990s. The emphasis of education politics in the 1990s was to increase "choice" at every level of education. In the education development plans in the beginning of the 1990s there were suggestions to increase choice between subjects and also in the number of subjects studied in comprehensive school. This emphasis on individuality may also be seen, for example, in the use of the concept "an individual study plan" in the development plan of education. (Ministry of Education, 1991). Compared to the 1960s and 1970s, the difference is clear. When the old comprehensive school educated citizens, who share some traditional collective values of the modern society, the individualized schooling create opportunities for neoliberal to develop his/her capabilities for himself/herself.

Families' "right to choose" was extended to include the "possibility of choice" between schools in the new reform of education legislation. Municipalities are still obliged to allocate children to schools "on the grounds of as safe and short a distance as possible," but students can make a request to go to a school other than the allocated one (CR, 1996, pp. 62–63; Education legislation, 1999, 28§). Since the introduction of the comprehensive school, there has never before been any mention of choice between schools in the discourse of Finnish state education. The arguments for the school choice policy in Finland in the mid 1990s stated that choice policy "increases learning opportunities of individuals," but choice policy was not mentioned as aiming toward "school improvement" or to "raise standards" (e.g., Chubb & Moe, 1990, pp. 29–35; Whitty & Edwards, 1998) as has been the case in many countries (Seppänen, 2006, pp. 73–78).

One expression of this political change, according to many of the interviewees, is the emphasis on the value of the individual, as opposed to the former idea of collective equality. The value of the individual as a social actor has increased and this can also be seen in educational policy. Highly educated citizens will no longer stand for governance from above, but instead want to make educational decisions themselves, it was felt (NBE 2; City 1; NBE 1).

The rise in the level of general education was also seen as one of the factors that advanced decentralization and promoted the demands for individuality (ME 2, NBE 1, City 3). The head of National Board of Education put it as follows:

> . . . people's education level has risen so that educated people cannot be manipulated that easily, I mean by this that educated people can' t tolerate guardianship as much as maybe uneducated people who may think of it as a security system. And an educated person doesn't accept, just like that, this kind of homogenous system, but requires individuality . . . (NBE 1)

The changes that occurred in educational policy in the 1990s were connected quite strongly with changes in the international environment. Quite a few actors in educational policy thought that increasing international competition called for increased investment in the education of the gifted. A "free the spearheads" mode of speech has become established in the Finnish school administration, according to which, the comprehensive school has done its job, in other words, raised the educational level of the nation, and now it is time to "invest in the best" (ME 1; NBE 2).

According to the interviewees, global competition and the demands for economic success require that education produces better quality learning and top skills. Every nation, to be successful in the global economic competition, has to raise its best forces, even though this may violate the old policy of equity. The Head of the General Education Division of the National Board of Education formulated this as follows:

> . . . maybe then this globalization is another matter, so it was noticed that Finland's economic competitiveness is priority number one and Finland can not manage well with that kind of mass in a world that is becoming more international, but we also have to give opportunities to the most talented to go forwards according to their aptitudes. So, that . . . we also support them. (NBE 2)

Social Segregation and Proceeding Inequality

Along with the increase in choice, there were new kinds of discourse concerning preventive action for youth at risk of exclusion. In the background of the discourse, besides the possible negative effects of educational policy on the equality goals pursued by the comprehensive school, there was also the heavy increase in the number of students requiring special education. The proportion of students in special education was the highest in the OECD countries and, in addition, it was growing continuously[5] (Armstrong, 1999, pp. 76–77). Even though special education was seen as a means of introducing equality during the transition period to the comprehensive school in the 1970s, the growth of segregated special education in particular threatened the goal of equality (Kivirauma, Klemelä, & Rinne, 2006). At the beginning of the 1990s, mention was made of developing "guidance and training methods to prevent exclusion from education and working life" (Ministry of Education, 1991, p. 8). At the end of decade it was stated that, "special attention will be paid to preventive actions geared to students who encounter difficulties in school and those at risk of exclusion" (Ministry of Education, 1996, p. 6).

There was also some mention, for the first time, of the need "to eliminate school harassment" and "to enhance school satisfaction" in state education discourse (Ministry of Education, 1996, p. 6). Connected to this there was a proposal concerning "the pupil's right to a safe learning environment" (CR 1996, 169).

Most interviewees saw the changes as quite positive or at least as neutral or inevitable. They saw almost no alternatives to the educational policy, mainly because they saw it as a part of global, inevitable change. However some of the respondents mentioned social segregation as a frightening part of the unexpected outcomes of changes in education politics. It was thought that the diversification of schools will increase in the future both regionally and socially (SAK; STAKES). The representative of Finnish trade unions predicted that the regional availability of education will suffer, and elite schools will begin to appear (SAK).

> Well, mainly this kind of, you know, er, er, differentiation of schools according to level and district. So, so, well, in this country the city government is going to be, you know, a very significant decision maker in education politics in the future in a very different, different way than previously. The economic circumstances of a municipality are going to be reflected in education and then the decrease of pupils on the register will lead to the fact that, probably you know, regional attainability will suffer. This will lead to profile building, er, er, that has, has of course also a lot of good sides, but if it—one consequence might be that, that it gives rise to this kind of élite school inside the comprehensive school, there are some signs of this. (SAK)

The risk of segregation and exclusion were matters of concern but not seen as reality in the capital city of Helsinki by the representative local education authorities:

> It hasn't been proved till now that, at least not yet in our studies, that selection, exclusion, for example, has occurred, but we have to be fairly careful with it. Thus far it has worked well, but, yes, there are certain risks of course if we think about the future, we have to be, so to say, on the alert here, monitor how the situation develops. (City 1)

However, the famous Finnish free of charge public education in Finland was not considered to be endangered. In a way it was unanimously considered as a civil right that cannot be abandoned. But the higher one goes in the educational system the greater the proportion parents are expected to pay (NBE 2), and business life is also taking a more active part in the educational market (TT), it was stated. With the increasing emphasis placed on individual choices and local color, it was thought that the importance of evaluation would grow significantly (MP).

Toward the Hidden Education Policy

Strengthening the local level and weakening of the central administration were overwhelmingly seen as the greatest changes. There was no disagreement among those interviewed on this point. Whereas earlier there was only one game being played on the field of educational policy, there are now over 400 different games in progress, as stated by the leader of teacher trade union (OAJ). Another point that came out quite strongly was a kind of de-politicalization of educational policy, which showed up as an unshakeable consensus regarding the reforms of the 1990s (SAK; TT). The former director of the National Board of Education called this rather tellingly "hidden education policy," in which, after going through a number of small changes, we are suddenly faced with a completely new educational policy. It is of substantial importance to notice that this change of direction was never made explicitly; it is simply the result of several small reforms concerning funding, the basis of curriculum planning, defining school districts, and so on (Ex-NBE).

The role of the teachers' trade union seems to have changed very radically during the period under discussion. Although it was considered to have a central role in educational policy at the national level in the past (NBE 2), its activities and significance have recently focused more and more on protecting teachers' interests at the local level (NBE 2; City 3).

When the comprehensive school system was being created Finland was influenced by the Swedish system (CH; Ex-NBE). The main influences leading to recent changes in educational policy, on the other hand, were believed to have come from international organizations (e.g., the OECD, the E.U.; ME 2; City 2), as well as from the Thatcherism era in England with the strengthening of market forces (City 1). Those in the central administration stressed the idea that Finland is at present a country that is taken as an example, and that has international clout (ME 1).

The worst dangers of producing inequality are connected with regional inequality, in the opinion of the interviewees. Rural areas will wither away, and migration and school transfers will lead to further inequality in the social map of large urban centers creating good and bad areas (NBE 2; TT; CH). The new educational policy was even referred to by one interviewee as "a triumph for urban Finland" (CH).

Above all, the fact that responsibility has been shifted to an increasing degree to families and students themselves by the new educational policy has made inequality more possible. The risk of creating inequality is, in a way, the price we must pay for this reform. Many think that the price is actually quite small compared to the benefits that the new educational policy will bring (ME 1; City 2). It was stressed that there can never be schools for the rich as long as tuition fees are not charged (ME 2).

Those families who will succeed in school have the skills needed to play the school game and a vision of what they want. When the choice now rests with the family, and later with the students themselves, one informant ironically said that the career plans of a child could now be made starting from day care. The same informant pointed out that families from the upper social classes are the most active users of this right to choose (City 1; NBE 1; City 4). It has been shown that students' applications between schools seems to create tiers of popularity between schools, and that students' "choices" to the differentially popular tiers of schools were social-class related in several cities of Finland. The most popular schools that selected students attracted upper social classes, whereas children from lower classes ended up more often than the average in the most rejected and low-status schools. Due to its hidden and complex class-related mechanisms, school choice policy has segregated schools socially, more than the traditional catchment area system in the Finnish cities (Seppänen, 2006, pp. 181–190, 257–263).

In line with the aforementioned changes, the role of the headteacher has also clearly changed from that of confidant of the teachers to that of an executive representing the employer (NBE 1; NBE 2; City 1). The headteacher was in fact compared to a managing director or orchestra director, who should have the general characteristics of a good leader. We should get rid of the public servant who "pushes papers" and waits for orders from above, and have instead a dynamic, motivating personnel manager. It was not even thought that a teacher education qualification should be required (City 3). Indeed, in line with the managerial model, headteachers were seen as crucial runners-in of the new "hidden" educational policy.

FINNISH DISCOURSES BEFORE AND AFTER THE TURNING OF THE TIDE—CLIMBING UP ON TO THE CLOUD OF RATIONAL CHOICE

The last forty years of Finnish state education discourse can be divided into two narratives. Although we have lived through an almost forty-year period of the comprehensive school and there were similar "comprehensive" features proceeding throughout the whole period, there is quite a clear turning point in the late 1980s. The first narrative represents praise for abolishing inequality of educational opportunity and introducing the comprehensive school in order to strengthen the Finnish welfare state. The second represents the narrative of passing the peak of achievement of the welfare state, the narrative of decentralization, deregulation, marketization, and the rise of evaluation and choice (Rinne, Kivirauma, Hirvenoja, & Simola, 2000; Rinne, Kivirauma, & Simola, 2002).

In the beginning of the comprehensive school period, the great success story included the attempt to raise the level of education of every citizen to that demanded by the structural changes in society in order to contribute to the economy. But an equally important argument was to offer equal educational opportunities to all children, regardless of their place of residence, or the wealth or status of their families, mother tongue, or gender. In the wildest Nordic or "social-democratic" dreams it was almost believed that the whole age cohort, when integrated in the comprehensive school for nine years, would not only be allowed to enter secondary educational as equals, but also to learn the same core-syllabus and the same know-how and end their compulsory comprehensive school equipped with almost the same level of qualifications (Ahonen, 2003). Another myth was that it would be possible to accomplish the goals of comprehensive school through central management and detailed control of education.

At the end of the 1980s and in the 1990s, the omnipotence of central governance came to an end. It was replaced by another myth, the myth of managerialism, individualism, and competitive market orientation: belief in decentralizing authority to local management and schools to ensure better efficiency and the production of services that take into account individual citizens' real needs (CR 1996, p. 23). The aim was to increase not the quantity but the quality of education by "increasing flexibility and choice" (Ministry of Education, 1991, p. 11). The documents of education policy in the 1990s repeated time and again the belief in progress, in the "development of education." Another myth of the last decade of the twentieth century was the myth of evaluation as a tool to develop the quality of education (Ministry of Education, 1996, p. 8; CR 1996, pp. 55, 82–85, 106–107). Although previously it was believed that the goals of education could be achieved by strict norm setting, in the 1990s it was believed that they can be achieved only by setting national core-goals, by evaluating the achievements in the form of the results afterwards, and by forcing educational institutions to compete with one another for the best results. In its rhetoric, the Finnish Planning state had become the Evaluative state, which tries to practice educational policy through governing by results.

During earlier decades, investments made in human capital were aimed at all the members of the nation, so that through equalizing educational opportunities, the national potential of talents could be gathered and liberated on the entire front under the lead of the government and thus, nourish the innovativeness of the nation regardless of social, regional, ethnic, or gender background of the students. Since the end of 1980s, the situation seems to have changed. The leading grip of the government, in some countries even its monopoly in the field of education, is not self-evident anymore. Neither does educational equality nor the idea of the education as long and coherent as possible exist as they used to do in the earlier decades. They have been replaced by a certain "magic of the market" in which education is marketed and made into a product, and in which the demand may direct the supply in liberated markets: The competitive choices of clients and sponsors work up the activities of educational markets without the strong intervention of the paternalistic state (Lauder & Hughes, 1999, pp. 4–20).

The key to understanding the trend in educational policy can be sought in the breakthrough of the so-called theory of rational choice. Individual actors and the individual and parental choice in education are seen as a natural rationality of human activity. People make educational choices that are most reasonable for them in the framework in which the choices must be made. Now children, young people, and their families are seen as rational actors who

> choose among the different educational options available to them on the basis of evaluations of their costs and benefits and of the perceived probabilities of more or less successful outcomes. (Breen & Goldthorpe, 1997, p. 275)

This kind of thinking can naturally be blamed because of the fact that it looks at children and the families as if they were free selectors in free markets, thus completely neglecting examination of the social determination of educational choices. The most probable winners of educational policy practiced on the grounds of the ideas of rational choice will be business life as well as the descendants of middle classes and educated professions; the losers will be the segments of population who have socially, economically, and culturally weaker starting points (Chubb & Moe, 1990; Lauder & Hughes, 1999; Whitty, Power, & Halpin, 1998; Ball, 2003; Brown & Lauder, 2006).

The prizes of the new educational policy in the "Winner-Take-All-Society" that encourages competitiveness between individuals, will most apparently accumulate more than ever to the most socially and economically advantaged socio-economic groups, the middle and upper class strata. Playing the educational game may begin to resemble the sports and entertainment industry, where the most important goal is the success of the top stars and key players. When stepping on this kind of educational field, huge numbers of individuals are fighting for the gleaming prizes but only a few will reach them. The majority gets only to stand outside the winning platform. This results easily in an enormous waste of money, resources, and time, while the mass of people face more and more, higher and higher educational hurdles, and harder and harder competitions in the labor market and in a life in which there is no rainbow's end on the horizon, only risk-prone insecure labor markets and non-stop repetitive competition (Lauder & Hughes, 1999, pp. 24–25; cf. Frank & Cook, 1995; Brown & Lauder, 2006).

APPENDIX 1. EDUCATIONAL POLICY TEXTS: THE COMMITTEE REPORTS (CR), LEGISLATIVE AND ADMINISTRATIVE TEXTS

CR 1966: A 12. The Report of the Committee of School Reform / Koulunuudistustoimikunta

CR 1970: A 4. The Report of the Curriculum Committee of the Comprehensive School part I: / Peruskoulun opetussuunnitelmakomitean mietintö I: Opetussuunnitelman perusteet

CR 1970: A 16. The Report of the Special Education Committee, part I / Erityisopetuksen suunnittelutoimikunnan osamietintö, osa I

CR 1973: 52. The 1971 Report of the Education Committee / Vuoden 1971 koulutuskomitean mietintö

CR 1975: 75. The 1973 Report of the Teacher Education Committee / Vuoden 1973 opettajan koulutuskomitean välimietintö

CR 1975: 109. The Report of the Committee of the Differentiation of Teaching in the Comprehensive School. The Reform of the Secondary Schooling 1 / Peruskoulun opetuksen eriyttämistoimikunnan mietintö. Keskiasteen koulunuudistus 1

CR 1981: 34. The Report of the School Legislation Committee / Koululainsäädännön valmistelutyöryhmän mietintö

CR 1983: 60. The Report of Committee of the Education Planning / Koulutussuunnittelun neuvottelukunnan mietintö

CR 1983: 62. The Report of the Committee of Continuing Education / Jatkuvan koulutuksen toimikunnan mietintö

CR 1985: 41. The Report of the Committee of Evaluation of Education Planning / Suunnittelujärjestelmien arviointityöryhmän mietintö

CR 1986: 12. The Report of the Committee of Decentralisation / Hallinnon hajauttaminen

CR 1989a: 26. The Report of the Committee for Development of Teacher Education: The Developing Teacher Education / Opettajankoulutuksen kehittämistoimikunnan mietintö: Kehittyvä opettajankoulutus

CR 1989b. The Report of the Committee of Development of Education, part I and II / Koulutuksen kehittämissuunnitelmatyöryhmän muistio, osa I ja II

Ministry of Education 1991. Development Plan for Education and University Research for 1991–1996 / Koulutuksen ja korkeakouluissa harjoitettavan tutkimuksen kehittämissuunnitelma vuosille 1991–1996

Curriculum 1994. The Framework Curriculum for the Comprehensive School 1994. The National Board of Education / Peruskoulun opetussuunnitelman perusteet. Opetushallitus

Ministry of Education 1996. Education & Research 2000: Development Plan for Education and University Research for 1995–2000 / Koulutus ja tutkimus: Koulutuksen ja korkeakouluissa harjoitettavan tutkimuksen kehittämissuunnitelma vuosille 1995–2000

CR 1996: 4. Committee Report of the Reform of Education Legislation / Koulutuksen lainsäädännön kokonaisuudistus

Education Legislation 1999. / Lakikokoelma 1999. Koulusäädökset. Edita.

APPENDIX 2. INTERVIEWED INFORMANTS
AND POLITICIANS OF EDUCATION IN
FINLAND AT THE TURN OF 2000

In the central level (7 interviews):

ME 1 = The Head and Chief Secretary of Ministry of Education (representing conservative, The National Coalition Party)

ME 2 = The Head of School Department in Ministry of Education (representing The Left Wing Alliance)

NBE 1 = The Head of National Board of Education (representing agrarian, The Centre Party)

NBE 2 = The Head of the General Education Division of National Board of Education

Ex-NBE = The former Head of National Board of Education (1973–1991) (representing The Social Democratic Party)

MP = Key-actor of education politics in Social Democratic Party, Member of the Parliament, Vice Chairman of the Parliament Board for Education and Culture

STAKES = Director General of National Research and Development Centre for Welfare and Health (STAKES)

In the local level (6 interviews):

RLA = Representative of local authorities (i.e., The Head of the educational office of Finnish Local and Regional authorities)

City 1 = The Head of the Helsinki City Education Department

City 2 = The Head of the Hämeenlinna City Education Department

City 3 = The Head of the Vantaa City Education Department

City 4 = The Head of the Eastern Finnish City Education Department

CH = Chairman of the Association of the Finnish Headmasters for 20 years, Chairman of the Managing Board of National Board of Education, a headmaster of one of the strongest private gymnasiums in Helsinki

Representatives of Finnish labour markets (3 interviews):

OAJ = The Head of the Trade Union of Teachers in Finland (OAJ) and Vice Chairman of the Confederation of Unions for Academic Professionals in Finland

SAK = Secretary of Educational Policy in the Central Organisation of Finnish Trade Unions (SAK)

TT = The Head of the Education Department in the Confederation of Finnish Industries and Employers (TT)

NOTES

1. The criteria of these models are school admission policies and education governance (see Figure 6.1).
2. It should be kept in mind that the welfare state models are ideal-type regimes and all states do not fit very well in any model. Although if we use the relationship between the market, the family, and the state as the

criteria categorizing our data in the late 1990s, it would seem something like this: Australia and United Kingdom represent liberal models, Finland, Iceland, Sweden Nordic, Germany corporative, Portugal, Spain, and Greece, peripheral models (Esping-Andersen, 1990; Rinne, Aro, Kivirauma, & Simola, 2003).

3. This new policy affects principally all schools and students because they must now play in a whole new competitive field. Practically the majority of lower secondary schools in the largest cities of Finland have one or several classes that select their children and offer additional lessons. A half of the age cohort transferring to the 7th grade in the capital Helsinki and on average one third in other Finnish cities made a request to a school other than allocated one (Seppänen, 2006, pp. 148–161; Seppänen, 2003). In smaller towns and countrysides the proportion of applications is smaller, because schools are few and distances long.

4. Law 1985 introduced "teaching hours frame" or "time resource quota system" where the old regulations concerning the division of students into teaching groups were given up. A certain number of hours are now reserved for the teaching of basic teaching groups, and within decreed limits the school itself may choose flexible teaching arrangements. (Nikkanen, 1986, pp. 9–12.)

5. Top countries measured by the number of students in special education in the year 1990: Finland 17.1%; Iceland 15.7%; Denmark 13.0 %; US and Germany 7.0%, Norway 6.0%; Australia 5.2% (Armstrong, 1999; Visilie, 2003; OECD, 2000; Kivirauma & Ruoho, 2007). At least in Finland the growth has continued: over 25% of students got special education in the year 2004 (Official Statistics of Finland, 2005, pp. 58–61).

REFERENCES

Ahonen, S. (2003). Yhteinen koulu: tasa-arvoa vai tasapäisyyttä [A School for all: the history of primary schooling in England] Tampere, Finland: Vastapaino.

Armstrong, F. (1999). Comparative perspectives on difference and difficulty: A cross-cultural approach. In L. Barton & F. Armstrong (Eds.), *Difference and difficulty: Insights, issues and dilemmas* (pp.6–95). Sheffield, United Kingdom: University of Sheffield.

Ball, S. J. (2003). *Class strategies and the education market: The middle class and social advantage.* London: RoutledgeFalmer.

Bauman, Z. (1996). *Postmodernin lumo* [Encantment of Postmodernity]. Tampere, Finland: Vastapaino.

Bauman, Z. (1998). Globalisation: *The human consequenses.* Oxford, United Kingdom: Polity Press.

Beck, U. (1992). *Risk society. Towards a new modernity.* London: Sage.

Beck, U. (1997). *Reinvention of politics rethinking modernity in the global social order.* Cambridge, United Kingdom: Polity Press.

Beilhartz, P. (2000). *Zygmunt Bauman. Dialectic of modernity.* London: Sage.

Breen, R., & Goldthorpe, J. H. (1997). Explaining educational differentials. Towards a formal rational action theory. *Rationality and Society, 9*(3), 275–305.

Broccolichi, S., & van Zanten, A. (2000). School competition and pupil flight in the urban periphery. *Journal of Education Policy, 15*(1), 51–60.

Brown, P., & Lauder, H. (2006). Globalisation, knowledge and the myth of the magnet economy. In H. Lauder, P. Brown, J-A. Dillabough, & A. H. Halsey (Eds.), *Education, globalisation and social change* (pp. 317–340). Oxford, United Kingdom: Oxford University Press.

Castells, M. (1997). *The rise of network society.* Cambridge, MA: Blackwell.
Castells, M., & Himanen, P. (2002). *The information society and the welfare state.* Oxford, United Kingdom: Oxford University Press.
Chubb, J., & Moe, T. (1990). *Politics, markets and America's schools.* Washington, DC: Brookings Institution.
Duru-Bellat, M., & Kieffer, A. (2000). Inequalities in educational opportunities in France: Educational expansion, democratization of shifting barriers? *Journal of Education Policy, 15*(3), 333–352.
Esping-Andersen, G. (1990). *The three worlds of welfare capitalism.* Princeton, NJ: Princeton University Press.
EURYDICE. (1997a). *A decade of reforms at compulsory education level in the European Union (1984–1994).* Brussels, Belgium: European Commission.
EURYDICE. (1997b). Secondary education in the European Union: Structures, organisation and administration. Brussels, Belgium: European Commission.
Frank, R., & Cook, P. (1995). *The winner-take -all society.* New York: Free Press.
Giddens, A. (1995). *Politics, sociology and social theory: Encounters with classical and contemporary social thought.* Cambridge, United Kingdom: Polity Press.
Green, A., Wolf, A., & Leney, T. (1999). *Convergence and divergence in European education and training systems.* London: Institute of Education University of London.
Kallo, J., & Rinne, R. (Eds.). (2006). *Supranational regimes and national educational policies. Publications of Finnish educational research association 24.* Turku, Finland: Suomen Kasvatustieteellinen Seura.
Kivirauma, J., Klemelä, K., & Rinne, R. (2006). Segregation, integration, inclusion—the ideology and reality in Finland. *European Journal of Special Needs Education, 21*(2), 117–133.
Kivinen, O,. Rinne, R., Järvinen, M-R., Koivisto, J., & Laakso, T. (1995). *Koulutuksen säätelyjärjestelmät Euroopassa—kuuden maan lainsäädäntö-, ohjaus- ja säätelyjärjestelmät* [systems of educational steering in six European countries]. Helsinki, Finland: Opetushallitus.
Kivirauma, J., Rinne, R., & Seppänen, P. (2003). Neo-liberal education policy Approaching the Finnish shoreline? *The Journal of Critical Education Policy Studies, 1*(1). Retrieved August 22, 2007, from http://www.jceps.com/?pageID=article&articleID=5.
Kivirauma, J., & Ruoho, K. (2007). Excellence through special education? Lessons from the Finnish school reform. *International Review of Education, 53*(3), 283–302.
Lauder, H., & Hughes, D. (1999). *Trading in futures. Why markets in education don't work.* Buckingham, United Kingdom: Open University Press.
Lindblad, S., & Popkewitz, T. S. (Eds.). (2001). Education governance and social integration and exclusion: Studies in the powers of reason and the reasons of power. *Uppsala Reports on Education, 39.* Uppsala, Sweden: Uppsala University, Department of Education.
Nikkanen, P. (1986). *Tuntikehysjärjestelmän ja tasokurssijärjestelmän tuotoksia koskeva seurantatutkimus* [Follow-up study of streamed and non-streamed teaching in the Finnish comprehensive school]. *Julkaisuja 396.* Jyväskylä, Finland: Jyväskylän yliopisto, Kasvatustieteiden tutkimuslaitos.
Nóvoa, A., Alves, N., & Canário, R. (1999). The Portugal case. In S. Lindblad, & T. S. Popkewitz, (Eds.), *Education governance and social integration and exclusion: National cases of educational systems and recent reforms. Uppsala Reports on Educaiton, 34.* Uppsala, Sweden: Uppsala University, Department of Education.
OECD. (1994). *School: A matter of choice.* Centre for Educational Research and Innovation, Paris: OECD.
OECD. (2000). *Special needs education. Statistics and indicators.* Paris: OECD.

Official Statistics of Finland. (2005). *Education*. Helsinki: Statistics Finland.

Olssen, M. (2006). Neoliberalism, globalization, democracy: Challenges for education. In H. Lauder, P. Brown, J-A. Dillabough, & A. H. Halsey (Eds.), *Education, globalization & social change* (pp. 261–288) Oxford, United Kingdom: Oxford University Press.

Ossenbach-Sauter, G. (1996). Democratisation and Europeanisation. Challenges to the Spanish educational system since 1970. In D. Benner & D. Lenzen (Eds.), *Education for the new Europe* (pp. 93–105). Oxford, United Kingdom: Berghahn Books.

Pereyra, M. A., Sevilla, D., & Castillo, P. J. (1999). The Spanish education system: A report. In S. Lindblad & T. S. Popkewitz (Eds.), *Education governance and social integration and exclusion: National cases of educational systems and recent reforms. Uppsala Reports on Education, 34*, 171–203. Uppsala, Sweden: Uppsala University, Department of Education.

Rinne, R., Aro, M., Kivirauma, J. & Simola, H. (2003). Adolescent Facing the Educational Politics of the 21st Century. Publications of Finnish Educational Research Association 17. Turku: Suomen Kasvatustieteellinen Seura.

Rinne, R., & Kivinen, O. (2003). The Nordic welfare state model and European Union. In P. Rasmussen (Ed.), *Education policy and social global order* (pp. 23–42). Alborg University: Centre for Interdisciplinary Study of Learning. Ahlborg, Denmark: VCL.

Rinne, R., Kivirauma, J., Hirvenoja, P., & Simola, H. (2000). From comprehensive school citizen towards self-selective individual. In S. Lindblad & T. S. Popkewitz (Eds.), *Public discourses on education governance and social integration and exclusion: Analysis of policy texts in European contexts,* (pp. 25–54). *Uppsala Reports on Education 36.* Uppsala, Sweden: Uppsala University, Department of Education.

Rinne, R., Kivirauma, J., & Simola, H. (2002). Shoots of revisionist education policy or just slow readjustment? *Journal of Education Policy, 17*(6), 643–658.

Sennett, R. (1998). *The corrosion of character.* New York: Norton.

Seppänen P. (2003). Patterns of "public-school markets" in the Finnish comprehensive school from a comparative perspective. *Journal of Education Policy, 18*(5), 513–531.

Seppänen P. (2006). Kouluvalintapolitiikka perusopetuksessa—Suomalaiskaupunkien koulumarkkinat kansainvälisessä valossa [School-Choice Policy in Comprehensive Schooling—School markets of Finnish cities in the international perspective]. *Publications of Finnish educational Research association 26.* Turku, Finland: Suomen Kasvatustieteellinen Seura.

Teelken, C. (1998). *Market mechanisms in education. A comparative study of school choice in the Netherlands, England and Scotland.* Amsterdam: Faculty of Educational Science, University of Amsterdam.

Vislie, L. (2003). From integration to inclusion. Focusing global trends and changes in the Western European societies. *European Journal of Special Needs Education, 18*(1), 17–35.

Whitty, G., & Edwards T. (1998). School choice policies in England and United States: An exploration of their origins and significance. *Comparative Education, 34*(2), 211–227.

Whitty, G., Power, S., & Halpin, D. (1998). *Devolution and choice in education. The school, the state and the market.* Buckingham, United Kingdom: Open University Press.

7 The Neoliberal–Neoconservative Reform in Greek Education

Georgios Grollios

THE LIBERAL BOURGEOIS REFORM OF EDUCATION

In 1974, neither Greece nor the developed capitalist countries were dominated by neoliberal and neoconservative doctrines about education and sociopolitical organization. 1974 was an influential year for the Greek social formation because the Greek junta had just collapsed, due to its weakness and failure to overcome the smashing blow of the popular rebellion against it in November, 1973. Toppling from power the lawful Cypriot government (via military coup) so as to control the island politically, the Greek dictatorship originally aspired to project this last tragic act as a "national success" that would contribute to its political legitimization. However, this very act turned out to be a "national disaster" that brought about not only its downfall but also the Turkish invasion of Cyprus.

The political crisis that the military dictatorship was facing, culminating in the Cypriot tragedy, was interrelated with the international capitalist crisis of over-accumulation that broke out in 1973. In Greece, the economic crisis of increased inflation and unemployment was one of the most basic factors that stirred things up and became the underlying cause of the 1973 popular uprising and destabilization of the junta. The fact that Greek governments did not react to this economic crisis by adopting basic neoliberal and neoconservative doctrines (e.g., such as those enforced in Britain and the United States during the 1980s) was due to the special political conditions that resulted from the fall of dictatorship—namely, the phenomenon of social and political radicalism that characterized the seven years (1974–1981) that followed.

The Greek capitalist class attempted to control further developments by supporting New Democracy, the political party founded by Karamanlis who was an old and tested rightist politician and who was in favor of a smooth transition from dictatorship to a type of authoritarian parliamentary democracy. Karamanlis's party succeeded in accomplishing this transition after winning the elections in 1974 and 1977. In the 1974 elections, which were held under conditions of fear because of the increasing probabilities of a Greek–Turkish war, New Democracy was elected by a large majority after polling over 54% of the vote. In the 1977 elections, the percentage of the votes polled by New Democracy decreased by more than 10%.

Karamanlis's government was characterized by the organization of an imperious bourgeois state, the upgrading of the role of the political parties as agents of political representation after a long period of political exclusions and discriminations, the legalization of the Greek Communist Party (it had been illegal from 1946 to 1974), and the abandonment of the protagonist political role of the Greek army and the Palace. From 1974 and on, the political campaigns of the Greek Right did not depend on anticommunism and the political discrimination that was carried out after its winning the civil war in 1949. Instead, its political discourse was to be based on the principles of a fair state and equal opportunities for all the citizens.

The 1976 educational reform promoted by Karamanlis's government was characterized by the logic of the liberal bourgeois reform.[1] The main features of the 1976 reform were: the extension of the compulsory education from six to nine years, the establishment of the Greek demotic language as the official language of Greek education, the abolition of entrance exams for the first cycle of secondary education (junior high school) and their initiation in the second cycle (Lyceum) of secondary education, along with an emphasis on technical–vocational education. The 1976 reform was supported not only by New Democracy but also by the Centre Party whose leading speaker, Papanoutsos, a liberal intellectual, had also attempted to introduce similar educational reforms in 1964. The basic ideological elements of the reform were to approach education as investment in human capital and a motor for economic growth as well as to provide students with equal opportunities. These ideological trends for the sociopolitical role of school, reflected in official education reform documents, were to a large extent the same with those in 1964.

As Sakellaropoulos (2001) contends, there was a remarkable increase in strikes during the seven-year rule by New Democracy. From 1976 until 1980 the percentage of employees participating in strikes more than quadrupled while the loss in hours of work tripled. In the 1953–1962 period, only 57 employees in 1000 went on strike, and during the 1963–1966 period, the number of employees participating in strikes increased to 170. In the 1976–1981 period, however, this number rose to 450 and new types of popular organization and action appeared, such as the factory worker unions' long strikes and sit-ins in factories.

To hinder this type of resistance and social reaction, the government introduced an authoritarian body of laws and also attempted to discourage participation in strikes and sit-ins by arresting and imprisoning unionists, by imposing massive dismissals, and provoking violent clashes with the police. Despite the defeat of factory workers' unions in 1978,[2] their movement generated new forms of social and political radicalism. This movement gave way to strikes organized by several public sector employees' unions (bank clerks, national electricity company, telecommunication, and transport employees) mainly over salary increases. At the same time, during these seven years (1974–1981) the farmers' struggles, although not as intensified as those of the employees, highlighted a different aspect of the phenomenon of social and political radicalism (pp. 58–79).

In addition, university students' restlessness gained momentum. The struggles of the student movement aiming primarily at diminishing the remaining influences of junta and at democratizing university structures, culminated in a massive sit-in movement during the winter of 1979–1980 and resulted in the retreat of the government, which, in turn, caused the withdrawal of the authoritarian law 815[3] that had been voted through a year earlier in Parliament. One of the most intense manifestations of radicalism during the 1974–1981 period was the politicization of students who, in massive numbers, became members of the Panhellenic Socialist Movement (PASOK) and the two communist parties, as well as other left organizations.

Another manifestation of political radicalism in this period was the organization of very successful strikes by the primary and secondary education teacher unions. Even if these strikes were not as dynamic as those of the students, they constituted unequivocal indications of the development of social and political radicalism because they reflected PASOK's and the Communist parties' major influence in the internal processes of the unions.

PASOK owed the victorious 1981 elections (48 % of the votes) and the formation of its own government mainly to the development of the social and political radicalism described previously. Challenging the policy adopted by New Democracy, both in the domain of the Greek foreign policy (Greece's re-accession into the North-Atlantic Alliance, accession into the European Economic Community) and in the domain of internal affairs (incomes and rights of the working classes, democratization and decentralization of state services), PASOK managed to form a powerful coalition of political forces. It gained power by attracting votes from the traditional political domain of the liberal Centre, the political discourse of which had, primarily, after 1974, been adopted by New Democracy. PASOK also attracted votes from the Left by taking advantage of its accumulated mistakes in the post-war period and also its split into two communist parties: (1) the Communist Party of Greece, which was in favor of the transition to a form of government relating to the countries fostering "existing" socialism, and (2) the Communist Party of Greece, Bureau of the Interior, which was in favor of Eurocommunism (the policy of institutional reforms expressed mainly by the Italian and Spanish Communist Parties). Furthermore, PASOK developed a dynamic oppositional political discourse and maintained certain political acts (mainly supporting popular struggles) that kept pace with the development of social and political radicalism.

In 1980, a year before PASOK's rule, the New Democracy government had signed Greece's accession into the European Economic Community (EEC). The participation of Greece into the process of European integration, to which PASOK and one of the two communist parties were opposed, was about to play an important role in the introduction of neoliberalism in the country. Since the mid 1980s, the strategic choices of the EEC economic policy have, almost exclusively, been determined by neoliberal views. The state intervention provided for in the framework of European integration concerns primarily the formation of proper infrastructure for the enforcement of economic competitiveness and the cutting down of the so-called inflexibilities so that private investments are attracted in order to develop both national economies and the overall EEC economy.

At the beginning of the 1980s, the introduction of radical changes in the Greek economy and the Greek political system was hindered by the rise of neoliberal–neoconservative forces on the international political scene (in particular in the United States and in Britain) and also because of Greece's accession into EEC. Moreover, it proved to be quite difficult for PASOK to implement its program because it came into power during a period of economic recession. In fact, PASOK had to choose between two alternatives: (a) to activate the oppressed and disadvantaged social classes toward radical changes of the socioeconomic and political structures, and (b) to implement marginal reforms that would entail a social–democratic conduct of affairs. What was important was that the possibilities for a social–democratic conduct of affairs were reduced because of (a) the international situation that prevailed at that particular juncture, and (b) the commitments undertaken by Greece while participating in the process of European integration.

According to Argitis (2002), PASOK's economic policy combined short-term stabilization measures and medium-term measures for the productive reform and modernization of the Greek economy. It did not only limit its policy to a macroeconomic management of demand but it also aimed at structural changes in the process of accumulation in order to increase the volume and to improve the quality of domestic supply. The most important issue for the economic policy of the new government was to harmonize these elements so that the aims of self-reliant development and more equitable distribution of wealth could be accomplished. The government, according to statements of its top members, would pursue the productive reform of economy and institutional modernization of Greek society by means of a five-year program of economic and social development. Very important roles this five-year program would play were: (a) the formation of a new framework for the cooperation of the public and private sectors of economy, (b) the modernization of public administration via a plan for the decentralization of decision-making mechanisms, and (c) the democratic participation of citizens, co-operatives, and local authorities in economic, social, and political processes[4] (pp. 75–82).

Given this economic policy, it became evident that PASOK was gradually distancing itself from its socialist proclamations and, at the same time, setting the scope of the lower social classes' radicalism well away from reforms that would challenge the existing social power relations and relations for production. To make matters worse, the popular social classes were disappointed by: (a) the continuous concessions to the dominant social classes and the pressures exercised on foreign policy matters within the frameworks of the North Atlantic Alliance and the European Economic Community, (b) the undertaking of managing and paying the debts of many private enterprises prejudicial to the government's interests, and (c) the fact that many members of the party were assigned with managerial posts in state institutions. As a result of these issues, passivity and adjustment to the existing social and political framework were cultivated to a large extent, leading to a shrinking of social and political radicalism.

PASOK's educational policy during its first four years of rule (1981–1985) may be seen as an expansion of the 1976 reform (i.e., a completion of the liberal bourgeois educational reform). PASOK, as part of its educational policy, promoted the democratization of the educational structures and functions through the following:

- Law 1268/1982 made provision for substantial student participation in many forms of University life and also restricted the authority of University professors,
- the institutionalization of the Comprehensive/multi-branched Lyceum as a new type of senior high school (added to the already existing types of General and Technical Lyceums),
- the abolition of Lyceum entrance examinations and the increase in the number of students to be accepted by Greek universities,
- the abolition of the institution of school inspectors and the introduction of school counselors, instead
- the institutionalization of parents' and other social forces' participation in school administration,
- the abolition of the two-year teacher Colleges and the establishment of University Education Departments, and
- the insertion of democratic ideological elements in the curricula and the school course books.

Democratization, of course, did not mean a total change of orientation and radical restructure of education. The educational reforms of the 1981–1985 period continued to move within the boundaries set by PASOK's general policy (i.e., a policy of liberal–democratic reforms of the state functions with technocratic characteristics, which would not undermine the interests of dominant social classes and would not challenge their sociopolitical power).

As Kiridis (1997) mentions, although it was claimed that the new University entrance system would reduce the inequalities of opportunities in accessing University education, during the 1981–1985 period there was no increase in the number of university students coming from lower social classes (pp. 239–242). Also, as Noutsos (1986) points out, the Greek

Christian Orthodox ideals were legitimized and fostered by the dominant state ideology about education via the enforcement of the Educational Act 1566/1985, which was supported by the majority of PASOK MPs. Moreover, there was an attempt to obscure the contribution of education to the reproduction of the distinction between manual and intellectual work by setting a special educational aim according to which the students had to become conscious of the social value and equivalence between intellectual and manual work, which, of course, does not possibly apply in real life and, as a result, students cannot become conscious of it. The law provided for committees participating in school administration; however, these committees could not decide on the orientation and content of education. No steps were made to change or transform the ways by which the content of school knowledge was selected, organized, and imposed; nor were any steps made to reduce student selection in secondary education through the institutional maintenance of many types of Lyceums, the Comprehensive/ multi-branched Lyceum included. Besides, the latter was in danger of having some of its branches either atrophied or being popular with students coming from certain social classes, which would eventually lead to the phenomenon of nonequitable secondary schools and the implementation of different curricula (pp. 75–85, 95–105).

THE IMPOSITION OF NEOLIBERAL AND NEOCONSERVATIVE POLICIES

Despite the fact that PASOK won the 1985 elections, its economic policy changed because of stagnating production and the economic recession. At a crucial juncture during which the international rise of neoliberalism and neoconservatism was more than evident, there was no longer a dilemma in deciding which way to follow: Activate the oppressed and disadvantaged social classes, thus aiming at radical changes in socioeconomic and political structures, or initiate marginal reforms that would lead to a kind of social–democratic consensus. PASOK had followed this second, social–democratic path between 1981 until 1985. Then it reached a deadlock after the failure of its economic policy and the exhaustion of democratic reforms in the state services. To go back and follow the first socialist way was exceptionally difficult, taking into consideration the fact that power interrelations in the party itself had changed and the leftist groups had lost much of their power. The new way that PASOK chose to follow was to adjust to the EEC orientation set by the European Commission under the guidance of Jacques Delors.

European integration, after the shock undergone due to protective–interventionist policies implemented by the governments of the member-states during the first oil crisis (1973–1974), had already gone into a new phase. The logic for the prevalence of supranationality had its origins in the recession that followed the second oil-crisis (1977–1978). The bourgeois classes of the European countries contended that the promotion of the plan for the formation of a market of three hundred million consumers would be the only possible solution to ensure that the European countries would not be lacking in international competitiveness. This plan, known as "Europe 1992," was included in the White Paper by the European Commission in 1985 and provided for the abolition of duties on trading goods, services, and capitals. The unified market, as the foundation of a new form of alliance between the bourgeois classes of the twelve European member-states,[5] would keep pace with the decrease in state interventions in economy,[6] the imposition of fiscal discipline, austerity policies, and retrenchments in social welfare benefits, the promotion of strategic coalitions and business mergers in Europe, and the encouragement of the European Commission to intervene in sectors like education, so as to accomplish the strategic aim of strengthening the economic and political role of Europe internationally.

After PASOK's new government applied for and received a loan from the EEC, it implemented a two-year program of economic stabilization that became a turning point for its ideological and political image. The program was based on rigid austerity on the part of the employees so that macroeconomic stability was accomplished. The leading role of the private sector toward development was clearly recognized, following a four-year rhetoric on the importance of the state and co-operatives. The public sector was considered to be antiproductive, an obstacle to the smooth running of the market. The two-year stabilizing program was not overthrown despite the rising tide of public discontent and strikes against it. PASOK was considered to be the pivot of promoting the neoliberal–neoconservative reform of Greek society by adopting authoritarian practices[7] (legal action against the Greek Workers' Union, prohibitions of strikes that contested the government's economic policy) so as to weaken the strike movement. These actions and laws radically changed PASOK's image and reduced its influence on the trade unions. From that moment, PASOK adjusted much more flexibly to the dominant policy already implemented by the conservative and social–democratic governments in the powerful EEC countries.

In the field of education, democratic reforms did not expand and, more importantly, they were not systematically backed up. It is not accidental that Gerou (1988), an educator who supported the ideas of PASOK and contributed to the formation of the governmental policy during the period 1981–1985, expressed his discontent about these reforms. He claimed that, three years after the 1981–1985 educational reform, even those who started it could no longer recognize it, because it was not awarded the prestige that it should originally have had: "A small tragedy in the field of ideas, when they become orphans" (p. 7).

According to Noutsos (1990), the 1982 Educational Act on universities had changed the existing power correlations, resulting in reactions by a group of conservative professors. However, at the end of the 1980s, there was still no answer to the question of if the new correlations and the new forms of hierarchy had promoted the drafting of new curricula and teaching methodologies. The institution of the Comprehensive/multi-branched Lyceum was only partly implemented. At the end, many right-wing journals and periodicals were presenting a body of fabricated arguments about education. The institutional framework of Universities was held responsible for absence of meritocracy, disorienting professors from their research and teaching, and also for undermining research. University students were accused of intimidating professors and their degrees were called "useless papers." Universities had been brought to the brink of becoming a huge provider of prospective unemployed people. A solution, suggested by a diverse group of people not only coming from the area of conservative Rightists but also from the Left, was to introduce up-to-date managerial practices to the University administrative services. They even suggested establishing private Universities; a proposal that is against the Greek Constitution. As for primary and secondary education, the starting point for the neoliberal–neoconservative laments about the low level of studies was nothing more than proposing to include ancient Greek texts in their curricula, to enforce the authority of the teacher, and to execute the teacher's orders as solutions for the organization of school life. Concepts like sociology, Marxism and socialism, the democratization of education, criticism on the content of studies, the historical character of schooling, students' rights, organization of school life, and school communities had to be abandoned as products of decay. This elitist approach, interspersed with ideas of putting a high premium on the individual and the individual value or talent, was promoted by a group of neoliberals (pp. 13–16, 50–59, 96–101).

The movement of university students, which, as it has already been mentioned, had played an important role in the rise of social and political radicalism in the 1970s, had lost its strength and fighting spirit, and its sociopolitical influence was reduced. The conservative forces strengthened their power in Tertiary Education by taking advantage of PASOK's weakening due to its policy and the marginalization of the Left that did not prove to be able to offer an alternative proposal. However, things were different in the primary and secondary teacher unions where both PASOK and the Left continued to be quite influential. As a result, the proposal for a strike during the University entrance examinations in 1988, made by the Left, enjoyed vast acceptance in the secondary teacher unions. The PASOK government was forced to retreat, giving in to part of the teacher unions' demands for higher salaries. Most importantly, the teachers, by going on strike massively, sent a clear message to the government as to what their reactions would be like against neoliberal–neoconservative policies and the ideology thereby effected in the domain of education. The 1988 strike became the turning point for the formation of new radical left pockets of resistance in education whose role was decisive against the domination of neoliberalism and neoconservatism. For example, it is not at all accidental that the journal *Antitetradia tis Ekpaidefsis* (Counter-Notebooks of Education), whose publication started during the 1988 teacher strike, formed and presented a radical criticism against dominant policies, thus mobilizing around it a significant number of people with a fighting spirit against neoliberal–neoconservative ideas.

According to one of my earlier studies (Grollios, 1999), the 1990s bear the stamp of the fall of the "existing" socialist regimes in Eastern Europe, the end of the cold war, and the reunification of Germany. These events, accompanied by the rhetoric about the end of the social class system, the end of social struggles, and of history, contributed to the development of a new optimism about the future of European integration. The Maastricht Treaty was seen as a tangible proof of the power of globalization and as a model for the vision of a unified world where the role of national States would be diminished. However, the consequences of the implementation of monetarist economic policies could no longer be ignored and the optimism began to fade: decrease in industrial production in Europe, economic recession, increase in the number of the unemployed, the poor and the homeless, problems with monetary reform, massive immigration, racist incidents, rise in many forms of nationalism, blue and white collar workers' demonstrations, large percentage of the negative vote in referendums on the Maastricht Treaty in Denmark and France. The victories of the Labour Party in Britain, the Socialists in France, the "Olive-Tree" coalition in Italy, and PASOK in Greece, were attributed to the fact that the Right wing parties, which voiced originally and authentically these neoliberal–neoconservative policies, could not keep their promises. As for European integration, the aforementioned issues led to a theoretical and practical re-evaluation of the neoliberal–neoconservative policies, which, of course, were not substituted but rather they were corrected, in a way that the reform that was due would succeed. The core of the neoliberal reform remained immutable (i.e. restrictions on state investment interventions and on national social policies, changes in the forms of productive and social relations, re-orientation of the organization of production toward labor flexibility). The aforementioned correction, in the context of the social–democratic parties fully acceding to neoliberalism,[8] consisted principally in forming an amalgam of policies characterized by the domination of neoliberal and neoconservative trends, whereas the maintenance of social cohesion was of secondary importance. This amalgam was reflected in the White Paper on development, competitiveness, and economic growth, as well as in the White Paper on education and training, both published by the European Commission in mid 1990s (pp. 30–71).

Ten years later, the process of European integration continued to be dominated by the neoliberal logic as has been made clear by the recent proposal for the Constitutional Treaty of the European Union where the most important key phrases were *market economy* and *free competition*. In Greece, in the beginning of the 1990s, the economic policy implemented by the government of New Democracy was based on approaching the huge expansion of the public sector and the national budget deficits as the major culprits for causing unpropitious economic prospects in the 1980s. The Greek government, aiming to become a full member of the EU and take part in the processes of economic and monetary European integration, adopted an internationally accepted neoliberal economic policy based on strict macroeconomic stability and the denationalization of certain enterprises. In 1992, after the drastic cuts in fixed prices in salaries (no rise in the salaries of public sector employees and an increase in a rate lower than that of inflation in the salaries of those working in the private sector), the New Democracy government presented the main aims of its convergence program, which were fully adjusted to the demands of the Maastricht Treaty: (a) reduce inflation to the percentages of the EU member states, and (b) reduce the national budget deficit so that monetary stability and rapid economic growth are accomplished. In the years to come, Greek economic policy continued to be dependent on the aforementioned convergence program so that Greece would succeed in participating in the economic and monetary integration of the European Union. The 1993 and 1996 PASOK governments implemented exactly the same economic policy enriched, however, with some measures for the maintenance of social cohesion. The decrease in salaries and the increase in unemployment was the price that the lower social classes had to pay.[9]

As for the teachers, according to official data, the fluctuation of their average salary in fixed prices represented the gradual transition to the domination of neoliberalism. If, for example, the price of the average salary was €100 in 1975, it increased by 22.34% in 1980, while in 1985 (the first year of the implementation of the stabilizing program) it declined from €122.34 to €102.54, and in 1993 it was dramatically reduced to €74.79. However, the per capita Gross National Product increased from €100 to €112.98. The fact that 42% of the teachers participating in research carried out in 1996 claimed that, during the past five years, they had a second job (mostly as waiters, taxi drivers, sales persons, builders etc.) is a further indication of the serious economic problems they faced due to their low salaries (cited in Katsikas, 1999, pp. 129–134).

The dramatic decline in teachers' salaries from 1985 forward went hand in hand with that of expenditure on public education. In 1985, the expenditure on education was 10% of the national budget. In 1993 it went down to 7.1%, and in the 1994–1999 period it ranged from 6.7% to 7.9%. On the contrary, the average percentage of expenditure on education of family budgets increased from 6.9% of the total family expenditure in 1987–1988 to 7.2% in 1993–94 (cited in Katsikas & Kavvadias, 2000, pp. 66–67, 80).

As claimed in the earlier discussion, the undertaking of New Democracy to implement its neoliberal–neoconservative program in education (which included privatizations in tertiary education and rigid state control over the students' and teachers' work in primary and secondary education) encountered a strong reaction of a massive movement that resulted in public demonstrations and sit-ins in many schools by both teachers and students. In the 1993 election, PASOK returned to government and proceeded immediately to "freezing" the legislative regulations endorsed by the Right-wing during New Democracy Party's three years of rule. Nevertheless, the term *freezing* actually meant nothing more than an unstable equilibrium due to two reasons. First, PASOK could not immediately bring forward a neoliberal–neoconservative policy that would be identified directly with New Democracy, especially when it had participated, to a certain degree, in the students' and teachers' movement in 1990–1991. Second, the newly formed political group, within PASOK, with clear preference to uphold and employ a neoliberal–neoconservative policy (under the central slogan of *Modernization,* which definitely replaced *Change*) occupied a hegemonic role within PASOK after the resignation and death of its longstanding President, A. Papandreou, and the election of the technocrat, K. Simitis, in his place in 1996. The pressure to bring to the surface the ideological postulations about the dissociation between education and the labor market, coupled with the intensification of the rhetoric associating teachers and students with an ethos of laziness made it clear that the neoliberal–neoconservative attack on education had not been entirely withdrawn from the frontline of the political agenda. On the contrary, both criticisms composed one pillar of a "logical necessity" to which the Greek nation "had to" conform, in order to anticipate competitiveness and international antagonism, in an epoch where the "end of history" had already been declared and the "new values of the age" had become uncompromising and beyond any critique. The epoch of homo-economicus, individualism, and social cynicism accompanied with "inevitable" political apathy was on its way. The repertoire of the new age proved to accommodate ideally an amalgam consisting of the old but recently revived Greek-Orthodox triptych: "nation–religion–family" and postmodern verbosity.

Thus, the neoliberal–neoconservative rearrangements of education were not defeated but postponed till the general ideological–political relations of power between work and labor would allow. In the area of social struggles in education, the 1993–1997 period terminated with teachers of both secondary and primary education often going on strike; the former, demanding salary increases, would go on long-lasting strikes, while the latter for shorter periods of time. The new PASOK government, shortly after winning the elections in 1996, did not satisfy teachers' aiming to diminish the power of teacher unions, thus obliging them to retreat in a climate of bitter disappointment. These tactics are to be understood in the framework of a general governmental decision espoused to put an end to any social and labor demands because they would render the country's economic development inefficient and inadequate and hence endanger the "national objective" to participate in the Economic and Monetary Unification of Europe. The aforementioned defeat of the teacher unions, in the spring of 1997, initiated the advancement of the neoliberal–neoconservative rearrangements in primary and secondary education. In the summer of 1997, the Parliament voted in favour of the PASOK Education Act 2525/1997. This Act replaced the three types of Lyceum (General, Technical, Comprehensive/multi-branched) with one type, the General Lyceum (having only a theoretical perspective) and the Technical and Vocational Institutions (which are not equated with the General Lyceum). Another crucial element included in Act 2525/1997 was the intensification of the Panhellenic examination system by increasing the subjects examined for entry to tertiary education. These elements reveal the neoliberal character of the Act attempting to adjust education to the labor market. According to a published research (July, 2002) by the Secondary Teachers' Union, just four years after the implementation of the new Education Act, the percentage of students who graduated from the Lyceum decreased by 33%. The percentage of students who followed the degraded Technical and Vocational Institutions rose from 25.5% to 37.2% (the great majority of them were students from the lower social classes). It is obvious that the reform deepened the existing social inequalities in educational achievement. Moreover, the new Education Act introduced an authoritative frame of control (over teachers' work exercised by the school headmasters and the body of the so-called counsellors whose role in actual fact was that of inspectors) whereby the restriction of pedagogic freedom in the educational praxis became prescribed and the neoconservative character of the Act was revealed.

The neoliberal–neoconservative hard nucleus of the Education Act was embellished with elements that sprang from PASOK's social–democratic tradition, such as the introduction of the "All Day Schools" for working parents and the provision of the "Second Chance Schools" for those who have not completed the obligatory education. To put it differently, Act 2525/1997 shapes the overall institutional school framework toward an autocratic route from the moment certain democratic characteristics were minimized because they are considered to have a negative influence over the effectiveness of schooling mechanisms. The consequences are more than evident in that filtering out of the lower social classes had increased and pedagogic freedom tended to become ever narrower and more compressed. The democratic characteristics distinguishable in the bourgeois modernization (orchestrated in the mid-1980s educational reform by PASOK) have been shrunk and PASOK, in the late 1990s, supported by groups of intellectuals in education, had already adopted its "Third Way" political agenda. Nevertheless, the legal statute for the system of teachers' assessment and rigid state control had not yet been materialized. This delay, along with the modifications suggested and already adopted for University entrance examinations (in 2001) were the results of social discontent and of a large movement against governmental educational policy conducted by the reaction of unions in education. More precisely, the movement was expressed in teacher demonstrations (and the consequent clashes with state police forces in June of 1998) and in the long-lasting sit-ins of the schools by the students during the two school years, 1998 and 2000 (Grollios & Kaskaris, 2003).

The results of the aforementioned research were confirmed by evidence shown three years later by Psacharopoulos (2005), one of the most fervent supporters of neoliberalism in Greek education. Upon enforcing the Educational Act 2525/ 1998, the number of University candidates was 174,511, while, only four years later, this number fell to 98,400. Also, the number of students failing to graduate from the Lyceum quadrupled (pp. 211, 224).

The neoliberal–neoconservative reform in Greek education resulted in restricted access to Tertiary Education. It also resulted in dividing education into two major areas: the area of compulsory education and that of apprenticeship and re-training. However, the latter included a range of levels and types of education, which do not provide any accredited right to work. Of critical importance to this second area of education is the concept of flexibility, which, as Bouzakis (2002) points out, is repeatedly used in the 1997 reform Educational Acts, especially in Law 2640/1998 concerning technical and vocational education. In this framework, the main aim of education is to promote employment flexibility that the conservative and social–democratic governments put forward on the one hand, and as a means of strengthening the competitiveness of European enterprises and economies, and reducing unemployment, on the other (p. 64).

The high failure rate in graduating from the Lyceum was related to the increasing number of students who failed to even successfully complete their first year in the Lyceum. According to data presented by the Greek Ministry of Education, the number of students in their first year of the Lyceum who failed in 1999 were twice as many as in 1998 (13.4%), while the percentage of second-year Lyceum students who failed was 30%. Moreover, the majority of the 672 second-year Lyceum students who participated in a research conducted in 1998 in several regions across the country expressed their opposition to the neoliberal–neoconservative changes brought about in their school environment. Specifically, more than half of the students (59%) believed that the new evaluation system would foster unnecessary competition among them, while almost two thirds (71%) stated that it would negatively influence teacher–student relationships (Katsikas & Kavvadias, 2002, pp. 51–52, 107–108).

In the 1990s, a decade during which the ideological doctrines of neoliberalism and neoconservatism gained ground in Greek society despite reactions against them, there were specific indications of other consequences, as well. Assessment in schools confined itself, almost exclusively, to assessing memorization ability thus diminishing the possibility of the students developing critical thought. Knowledge became instrumentalized, a fact that discourages students from abstraction and also confines them to partial thinking. One of the findings of a research carried out in 1996 was that 81.2% of the 446 students, coming from diverse areas, already studying at university, responded that the organization of teaching and learning at

Lyceum level promotes, to a great extent, the reproduction of sterile and unproductive knowledge (Konstantinou, 1999, pp. 159–163).

Other research, conducted in only one region in 1999, showed that Lyceum students focused more on the lessons (fully adjusted to the demands for a successful performance in the University entrance examinations) they were attending at frontistiria[10] than those offered at their state schools, undermining the rhetoric of law 2525/1997 on abolishing these institutes. During the school year 1998–1999, there had been 2,713 frontistiria, while in the beginning of the 1980s there were no more than 1,000 (Katsikas & Kavvadias, 2002, pp. 172–173, 192). Eventually, "good schools" came to be considered those that imitated the frontistiria most successfully, which resulted in influencing the content of school subjects in a formalist and scholastic way.

At the end of the 1990s, as Sakellaropoulos & Sotiris (2004) point out, teachers' and students' demonstrations, as well as anti-war marches against NATO bombardment in the then Yugoslavia, demonstrations of farmers, hospital doctors' strikes, and so on took place in a political setting that was becoming increasingly conservative. Social movements no longer organized co-ordinated action against social injustice; instead, they were spontaneous reactions of social groups. In the 2000 elections there was a decrease in the percentage of votes for the Left parties when compared with the 1999 European elections. This fact reflects the lack of a left strategy that would take those involved in social struggles to victory; it also failed to offer a persuasive anti-hegemonic political plan (i.e., a clear process of making the social contradictions more acute and proposing an alternative social organization, in a tangible and recognizable way so that masses of people could be socially activated, pp. 251–255).

These findings are correct and valid since they were confirmed by the 2004 elections, when the spontaneous reaction of the employees against being deprived of their social security rights (which resulted in PASOK's retreat) and the massive antiwar movement against the U.S. invasion in Iraq did not continue and the influence of the Left did not significantly increase. In the domain of education there were a few and sporadic demonstrations organized by teachers and students. These demonstrations were not as massive or as vigorous as the ones in the 1990s. A fact that does not leave the lower social classes unaffected is that the public dialogue on education was conducted, to a great extent, on the basis of ideological and political terms of the dominant bourgeois power block. This dialogue usually centered on competitiveness, productivity, effectiveness, and employability concepts that reduced education to a market of products.

In light of the aforementioned, the reasons why certain Bills that promote the subordination of the universities to business enterprises were voted through by the new right-wing government in 2005, are more than evident. As Zambeta (2000) points out, during the 1990s, despite the fact that no general reform took place in tertiary education, certain changes of a limited nature and some fragmentary regulations were adopted so that a particularly diverse university system was formed. The expansion of tertiary education was not accompanied accordingly by an increase in public expenditure and universities were accused of ineffective economic management, irrational waste of public money, inadequate profit, and failure to meet the contemporary economic and social needs, as well as lacking in accountability. In a competitive environment and in the context of poverty and public demerit, universities turned to research programs for funding from the European Support Framework. At the end of the decade, the institutions that received additional funding were only the ones that proved to be successful enterprises. The principles of "New Public Management" started to apply despite the lack of an institutional framework. The new terminology included concepts such as effectiveness, competitiveness, quality control, and performance indicators. This situation is illustrated in the eighty-five University and Higher Technological Education Departments undergoing evaluation processes with their own consent.

Voting in a number of Bills that aim at the hierarchical categorization of university departments, the most important of which refer to quality control, not only reverses the connection between being awarded a Degree and the automatic granting of employment but it eventually leads to a wider subordination of tertiary education to the needs of capitalist enterprises. The imposition of laws of a neoliberal character has kept pace with the adoption of neoconservative measures. Among the most recent laws voted through by the majority of the New Democracy Party is the Educational Act enforcing the conversion of post-secondary Ecclesiastic Schools into University departments. The contradiction between elements of neoliberalism and neoconservatism in the reform of Greek education is exemplified by a special provision for the submission of a document issued exclusively by the Greek Church authorities, whereby Ecclesiastic School candidates need to confirm their Christian Orthodox Faith.

Of course, the resistance against neoliberalism–neoconservatism as components of the struggles between the dominant and dominated social classes will not diminish in the future. According to Vergopoulos (2005), in the eight-year period, 1997 through 2004, the "ambitious" Greek modernization has been marked by the "unbelievable adventure at the Greek Stock Market" that left economic polarization in its wake. In Greece, economic and social inequalities have deepened and crystallized into social despair more than in any other European country, perhaps with the exception of Portugal. The proportion of salaries in the national income, already low during the 1990s (66% in Greece compared with 69% in the European Union) became even lower in 2004 (63.8%) due to an increase in the profits and revenues of large enterprises in Greece (pp. 59–61, 84–86, 91–96).

This fact, combined with the intense oppression entailed in the neoliberal reform both within and outside of education, means that the material factors of developing new kinds of resistance have been strengthened.[11]

However, this fact does not lead, automatically, to new forms of widespread organization and struggle of the lower social classes. The crucial question is: Are the forces that resist neoliberalism–neoconservatism able to plan social and educational transformations with a radical content and a socialist orientation?

NOTES

1. The reasons why it was not enforced by the Greek governments before the military coup will not be discussed in the present chapter.
2. The reasons for this defeat were the governmental attacks that destroyed the political vanguard, as well as other political and organizational weaknesses of the movement. For a detailed analysis about the factory worker unions' demands see *Simvoulia (Councils)*, July 1982, second edition, Centre of Mediterranean Studies.
3. Law 815 of 1978 provided for the minimization of examination periods and the expulsion of students who delayed to finish their studies, aiming to reduce students' social and political activities.
4. It is important to note that the economic policy adopted by PASOK was not influenced by Keynes theory and that the latter did not constitute a matter of dispute among those who planned Greek economic policy in the 1980s (Psalidopoulos, 1999, pp. 257–259).
5. Alliance does not necessarily involve the participation of the bourgeois classes of all the European countries on equal terms; nor does it involve the abolition of competition among them. Inequality and competition are evident in many meetings and other decision-making processes.
6. The decrease in investment interventions does not mean that the government will cease to intervene systematically in economic relations. In actual fact, the state is a necessary precondition for the existence of markets as they depend on the state as far as the protection of property rights and currencies are concerned (Hyman, 2004, pp. 34–35).
7. PASOK's government undertook legal action against the Greek Workers' Union, establishing prohibitions of strikes that contested the government's economic policy.
8. Chalaris (2005, p. 43) provides an explanation for the failure of social democrats to put forward an alternative model of economic development in the new international context: the diminishing of the unions' power, the strengthening of the bourgeois classes, the absence of an effective European political system, and the conservative character of European Union.
9. The lowest incomes and the average income of employees were cut in the 1990s, a fact that influenced favorably the increase of the enterprises' net profits. This fact shows clearly that the burden of the stabilizing policies was suffered by the low-income social classes (Stasinopoulos, 2005, p. 143).
10. The plural form of the word frontistirio; a Greek term used to describe private tuition institutes where students attend classes so as to master the subjects already taught in state schools.
11. This chapter was written in March 2006. Thus, it does not refer to the primary education teachers' great strike and the two massive waves of University students' sit-ins and demonstrations during 2006–2007. These forms of resistance against the dominant neoliberal–neoconservative policy in education need further analysis.

Argitis, G. (2002). *Pangosmiopiisi, ONE ke oikonomiki prosarmogi. I periptosi tis Elladas* [Globalization, economic and financial integration and economic adjustment. The case of Greece]. Athens, Greece: Tipothito.
Bouzakis, S. (2002). *Ekpedeftikes metarithmisis stin Ellada, Vol. II* [Educational reforms in Greece]. Athens, Greece: Gutenberg.
Chalaris, G. (2005). I Ellada sto plaisio tis pangosmiopiisis [Greece in the context of globalization]. In G. Argitis (Ed.), *Oikonomikes ke koinonikes antitheseis stin Ellada. Oi prokliseis stis arches tou 21ou aiona.* Athens, Greece: Tipothito.
Gerou, T. (1988). *Kritiki Pedagogiki* [Critical Pedagogy]. Thessaloniki, Greece: Kiriakidis.
Grollios, G. (1999). *Ideologia, pedagogiki ke ekpedeftiki politiki. Logos ke praxi ton Evropaikon programaton gia tin ekpedefsi* [Ideology, pedagogy and education policy. Discourse and praxis of the European programs for education]. Athens, Greece: Gutenberg.
Grollios, G., & Kaskaris, I. (2003). From socialist-democratic to Third Way politics and rhetoric in Greek education (1997–2002). *Journal for Critical Education Policy Studies, 1*(1). Retrieved January 16, 2006 from http://www.jceps.com/?pageID=article&articleID=4.
Hyman, R. (2004). Exevropaismos i diabrosi ton ergasiakon scheseon? [Europeanization or erosion of the labor relations?]. In A. Moschonas & S. Koniordos (Eds.), *Evropaiiki oloklirosi ke ergasiakes scheseis.* Athens, Greece: Gutenberg.
Katsikas, C. (1999). *Scholio, taxi ke ideologia* [School, class and ideology]. Athens, Greece: Ellinika Grammata.
Katsikas, C., & Kavvadias, G. (2000). *I Anisotita stin Elliniki Ekpedefsi* [Inequality in Greek education]. Athens, Greece: Gutenberg.
Katsikas, C., & Kavvadias, G. (2002). *To egcheiridio tou kalou ekpedeftikou* [The handbook of the good teacher]. Athens, Greece: Ellinika Grammata.
Kiridis, A. (1997). *H anisotita stin Elliniki ekpedefsi ke I prosvasi sto panepistimio 1955–1985* [Inequality in Greek education and the access to university 1955–1985]. Athens, Greece: Gutenberg.
Konstantinou, C. (1999). Organosi tis pedagogikis epikinonias ke perithoriopiisi tou mathiti [Organization of pedagogical communication and marginalization of the student]. In C. Konstantinou & G. Pleios (Eds.), *Scholiki apotichia ke kinonikos apoklismos.* Athens, Greece: Ellinika Grammata.
Noutsos, C. (1986). *Ideologia ke ekpedeftiki politiki* [Ideology and educational policy]. Athens, Greece: Themelio.
Noutsos, C. (1990). *Singiria ke ekpedefsi* [Conjuncture and education]. Athens, Greece: Politis.
Psacharopoulos, G. (2005). To kinoniko kostos enos aparchaiomenou nomou [The social cost of an antiquated law]. In D. Gravaris & N. Papadakis (Eds.), *Ekpedefsi ke ekpedeftiki politiki. Metaxi kratous ke agoras.* Athens, Greece: Savvalas.
Psalidopoulos, M. (1999). *Politiki oikonomia & Ellines dianooumenoi. Meletes gia tin istoria tis oikonomikis skepsis sti sigchroni Ellada (Political economy & Greek intellectuals. Studies on the history of economic thought in contemporary Greece).* Athens, Greece: Tipothito.
Sakellaropoulos, S. (2001). *I Ellada sti metapolitefsi. politikes ke kinonikes exelixeis 1974–1988 (Greece at political changeover. Political and social developments 1974–1988).* Athens, Greece: Livanis.
Sakellaropoulos, S., & Sotiris, P. (2004). *Anadiarthrosi ke eksichronismos. Koinonikoi ke politikoi metaschimatismoi stin Ellada tis dekaetias tou 1990* [Restructuring and modernization. social and political transformations in Greece in the 1990s]. Athens, Greece: Papazisis.

Stasinopoulos, G. (2005). Epichirimatikotita: I ellimmatiki anaptixiaki parametros tis Ellinikis oikonomias [Enterprising: The deficit parameter of Greek economy). In G. Argitis (Ed.), *Oikonomikes ke koinonikes antitheseis stin Ellada. Oi prokliseis stis arches tou 21ou aiona.* . Athens, Greece: Tipothito.

Vergopoulos, K. (2005). *I Arpagi tou ploutou. Chrima–exousia–diaploki stin Ellada* [The snap of wealth. money–power–interwoven interests in Greece]. Athens, Greece: Livanis.

Zambeta, E. (2000). *Modernization and the would be Entrepreneurial Culture in Greek Education.* Retrieved January 18, 2006, from http://www.ioe.ac.uk/ccs/conference2000/papers/pc/papers/zambeta.html.

8 The Third Way and Beyond

Global Neoliberalism, Education, and Resistance in Taiwan

Hui-Lan Wang and Michael Loncar

The hegemonic conception of our age is that of linear-time (the idea of progress) that presents itself as a post-linear time-space (the idea of globalization). Whatever is currently dominant in social and political terms is infinitely expansive, thereby encompassing all future possibilities. The total control over the current state of affairs is deemed to be possible by means of extremely efficient power and knowledge. Herein lies the radical denial of alternatives to present-day reality. This is the context underlying the utopian dimension of the WSF, which consists of asserting the existence of alternatives to neo-liberal globalization. (Whitaker, Sousa Santos, & Cassen, 2006, p. 73)

INTRODUCTION

For much of the world, the 1980s marked the beginning of the era of neo-liberalism, a period dominated by New Right ideology in which governments connect economic development with political liberty and focus on promoting efficiency in the public sphere. These developments have been associated with the introduction of "New Public Management" (NPM) as a new mode of governance, one that advocates the contracting out of social services, limiting government responsibility, advocating consumerism, and streamlining and re-engineering service structures through downsizing and merging (Walsh, 1995). NPM has been very influential in many countries, including the United States, United Kingdom, Canada, Australia, New Zealand, and Asian NICs (New Industrial Countries). It has also been used both as a legitimizing basis and instrumental means for reforming state educational bureaucracies, educational institutions, and the processes that shape public policy (Fitzsimons, 1999).

In discussing contemporary issues of public policy and educational change under the impact of global capitalism and particularly of neoliberal ideology, this chapter analyzes social developments in Taiwan during the last three decades. The discussions in this chapter are divided into four sections. The first explores the shift of educational control in Taiwan since the

1980s, from an emphasis on political to economic ideology, one that parallels the transformation of the government itself. The second offers a brief review of the impact of neoliberalism and globalization on education in Taiwan. The third illustrates how education in Taiwan, particularly higher education, has been recognized by the government as an important mechanism for the development of human capital and international competition based on the idea of a knowledge-based economy and New Managerialism. The final section explores the reaction to neoliberalism, including the anti-globalization movements in Taiwan.

THE SHIFT OF EDUCATIONAL CONTROL IN TAIWAN: FROM POLITICAL TO ECONOMIC IDEOLOGY

From the perspective of critical pedagogy, Paulo Freire (1985) claimed that "education is politics." Indeed, there can be little doubt that education has characteristics in correspondence with the goals of those who control it. Change occurs because those who have the power to modify education's previous structural form as well as the power to define "instruction" and its relationship to society have new agendas and thus pursue new goals. In Taiwan and the rest of the world, political and economic powers are still the major factors influencing education.

During the last three decades, education in Taiwan has experienced an asymmetrical development, one that could be characterized as reacting to political and economic ideologies and moving "from de-regulation to re-regulation."

The history and issues that are present, due to Taiwan's unique social–historical–geographic position, the complexity of its regional and internal politics, its military relationships, economic activities, and labor conditions, have all made it rather difficult to evade the influence of global capitalism and globalization. The nation as an arena is an interweaving of economic and political strands; as a result, the nation's power to control, its legitimacy, its policies for its future survival, and its government's public policy proposals must be understood in terms of the many complex conditions and variables present.

Following the loss of the Chinese Civil War after World War II, the Kuomintang (KMT) government in China transplanted itself to Taiwan in 1948. In doing so, they established an official "reading" of the history of the island and the ethnicity of its people as provincially Chinese. They also instituted an authoritarian framework for the government in general, including an official national education policy. Under an authoritarian state, political and economic dominance made conditions ripe for stable social order and rapid economic growth; at the same time, however, it deepened the contradictions and tensions submerged within society (Hu, 1994).

In the late 1970s and 1980s, turbulent social movements originating from long-repressed grass-roots forces, including political dissidents and the democracy movements, teachers and students under campus control, victims of pollution, farmers who suffered from the government's price-fixing policy for rice, slowly but methodically forced the KMT government to pursue a reform agenda (Tang, 2004). A discourse of social reform, reconstruction, and democracy was formulated through numerous conflicts, struggles, and controversies between the state and civil society. As the KMT dictatorship attempted to defend their legitimacy, the people increasingly demanded more freedom and social justice, as well as a more open discourse on issues of national and ethnic identity. Educators at different levels of the system shared significant parts in the formation of reform discourse.

Deregulation From Political Ideology and Power

During the late 1970s and 1980s, Taiwanese citizens pushed for a more democratic society and for more open-mindedness from the ruling KMT regime, including the lifting of Martial Law and a measure of tolerance for political opposition.[1] In particular, "the Kaohsiung Incident" of December 1979,[2] which claimed democracy, human rights, and the independence of Taiwan as its core values, turned into a series of political protests, arrests, and public trials and convictions, and is considered a critical turning point for prodemocracy groups' struggle against KMT political oppression. These movements eventually became the basis for the formation of the Democratic Progressive Party (DPP), which was established on September 28, 1986. Its founding members included defense lawyers and political activists and their families who had been imprisoned for their involvement in "the Kaohsiung Incident."

In 1987, President Lee Teng-hui of the KMT ended the almost 40-year period of Martial Law. This defining moment for the political democratization of Taiwan was followed by sustained economic, political, and social change,[3] thus transforming the power structure and state's mode of operation in which education had been situated. Most importantly, after its defeat in the 2000 presidential election in Taiwan, the long-entrenched KMT assumed the mantle of "opposition party," and for the first time, political power was peacefully transferred to another party: the DPP. Chen Shui-bian, a lawyer from a family of poor farmers and former counsel for the Kaohsiung incident defendants, became the second president elected, after Lee Teng-hui, and the first non-KMT president. The DPP is a member of the Liberal International and a founding member of the Council of Asian Liberals and Democrats, two international organizations advocating liberal and progressive values. Although the KMT still remains powerful, this "cohabitation" with a new president from the DPP implies a greater surface openness for the KMT in domestic politics and a definitive chance to move beyond the policies of the past.

Regarding the long, intense cross-strait situation between Taiwan and China, a situation in which the United States also plays a critical role,

President Chen declared in his May 2000 inaugural speech a series of concessions: "The Four No's and One Without."[4] He stressed that he would not formally declare Taiwan's de-facto independence, change the nation's name, nor change the "state-to-state" description in Taiwan's constitution, and finally, not promote a referendum on independence or unification. Furthermore, there was to be no question of abolishing the controversial guidelines for national unification. These promises received overwhelming approval by the public in Taiwan because they negated China's conditions for attacking Taiwan. These promises were obviously aimed at easing cross-straits tensions, in which the United States has played an important mediating role since the end of the Chinese Civil War. However, President Chen's aforementioned statements revealed that the great political challenges the DPP government faced were not solely internal, but also regional, international, and economic.

Democratization is a process of prolonged institutional adjustments that ensures that some basic democratic values and practices will be legally maintained. Before the DPP won the presidency, there was evidence of their reform platform. As their strength grew in the legislature, they turned their efforts to the passage of a number of new education laws. *The New University Law* (passed in 1994) highlighted the self-governance of universities to ensure greater academic freedom and campus democracy (Wang, 1999). *The Basic Education Law* (passed in 1999) lessened the state's power and authority and increased students' and their parents' rights, increasing equity among all students, regardless of race, class, or gender.

Since 2000, the DPP government has attempted, under the process of political democratization, to make policy more accountable and responsive to the public. For example, a series of laws were created or revised by the DPP government to regulate the acts of government and to protect the rights of the public.[5] During the amendment process, many ideas and appeals from social movements or interest groups were included, which widened space for the further development of civil society in Taiwan.

The many problems for late capitalist states have already been highlighted by scholars from the perspective of social system crises (Offe, 1984; Habermas, 1973). Ball (1994) points out that there are the problems of capital accumulation and economic efficiency, problems of social order, authority, and stability, and the technical and managerial problems of the state itself—of governance and control (legal and administrative procedures), costs (public spending), and planning. These meta-problems are "both structural and played out in micro-political struggles inside the state itself" (p. 5) in which education policies and reform are embedded. Nevertheless, the deregulation from decades of KMT political ideology is just one side story in Taiwan; since the transfer of power, problems of capital accumulation and economic efficiency have become formidable challenges for the DPP government.

Re-regulation by Economic Ideology and Power

McMichael (2004) argued that within the Third World, export-oriented industrialization fueled rapid economic growth and legitimized a new development model characterized as the "free market" model; in the 1980s, it was presented as *the solution* to the debt crisis. Development, which had previously been defined as nationally managed economic growth, was redefined in the World Bank's *World Development Report* 1980 as "participation in world markets."(p.116). Japanese economist, Kenichi Ohmae, described the global economy as a "borderless world," rendering states "powerless." He suggested that in a borderless world, economic zones (e.g., the San Diego/Tijuana zone; the growth triangle of Singapore, Johore of southern Malaysia, and the South China region, linking Taiwan, Hong Kong, and the Chinese province of Guandong) exist as natural "regional states." Because of the unique production and trade situation of these economic zones, regional states are economic rather than political units. These regional states are such powerful engines of development because their primary orientation is toward–and their primary linkage is with–the global economy (p.190).

Throughout President Chen's campaign for presidency and into his first term, he characterized his administration's philosophy as "the New Middle Way." This phrase is an obvious reference to "the Third Way" claimed by Tony Blair in Britain as well as Bill Clinton in the United States, and Chen further emphasized its importance by including it in the government's official documents. According to Lee (2005), based on a research approach of discourse analysis of the DPP's political rhetoric, including Chen's speeches, interviews, official documents, and publications, the major themes raised by the DPP between March 2000 and September 2001 include "New Middle Way" (34 times), "globalization" (181 times), "knowledge-based economy and green silicon island" (79 times), "Taiwan first" (62 times), and "social justice" (112 times; p. 635). President Chen has emphasized both "globalization" and "social justice," as the government's intended routes to reach a balance between the development of the global economy as well as greater social equity.

President Chen's idea of "the New Middle Way" originated from the idea of "the Third Way" raised by Anthony Giddens, the British sociologist considered a guru to Tony Blair, as an instrument to challenge the orthodoxies of political extremes as well as the sterile ideological debate between left and right. Giddens (1998) stressed that "the Third Way" politics stands in between the traditions of European social democrats and American liberals and transcends both old-style social democracy, with its reliance on Keynesian economics, as well as the New Right, with its reliance on market fundamentalism. "The Third Way" calls for decentralized forms of government based on transparency and accountability, efficient administration, more opportunity for direct democracy, social inclusion, and an environmentally friendly economy. In brief, "the Third Way" is a new socio-democratic path for post-welfare states to adopt a reflexive response to the complex and dynamic situations of social change and global development. Giddens (2000) pointed out that the development of civil society, or so called "third sector," is the core component of Third Way politics (p. 64). However, many have criticized the New Third Way's tendency to favor capitalism and globalization rather than critique or resist them (p.11).

The transfer of political ideas from one country to another is evidence of ideological diffusion and clearly suggests that politicians' ideas are linked. However, with the process of policy borrowing, much critical thinking and consideration, including a thorough understanding of the differing social contexts, must be carefully considered; otherwise, the original ideal or impulse might appear weakened, displaced, or even counterproductive once transplanted to a new social context.

With regard to the economic development of Taiwan, the real annual growth in GDP has averaged about 8% over the past three decades. Since World War II, exports have grown considerably and provided the primary impetus for industrialization. During the last decade, Taiwan has been moving from a production based economy toward a more high-tech and service-based economy. Currently, unemployment is comparatively low (4.1% in 2005, 3.9% in 2006), and the sectors of agriculture, industry, and service contribution to the GDP is 1.70%, 43%, and 55%, respectively. Traditional labor-intensive industries have been steadily moved off-shore and replaced with more technology-intensive industries. Particularly the semiconductor manufacturing and microelectronics industries together occupy a significant role in the word's foundry production.[6] Taiwan now produces more semiconductors than the United States.[7]

In the aftermath of the 1997 East Asian economic crisis, unemployment, poverty, homelessness, and other social problems increased. In response, East Asian governments have reviewed several normative approaches, including neoliberalism along with new managerialism. In a comprehensive review, Tang (2005) concluded that a neoliberal approach is not suitable to the East Asian situation, suggesting that the social development approach, with its emphasis on the harmonization of economic and social policy, extensive social investments, and managed pluralism, offered a better alternative.

Taiwan emerged relatively unscathed from the Asian financial crisis of 1997. Under the impact of global capitalism, however, particularly the rapid rise of China's economic and political power during last decade, huge numbers of middle and small enterprises have transferred production and investment to China; as a result, economic development in Taiwan faces severe challenges. Under the trend of Neoliberalism, most large government-owned banks and industrial firms have been privatized in Taiwan, and the BOT (Build, Operation, and Transfer) model has been adopted for many large public transportation projects (Jan, 2006).[8]

One important question to consider is what would happen if a country were to go through both democratization and NPM simultaneously. Tang (2004) argued that although the conflicts between the two movements are widely acknowledged in the existing literature, the facts of Taiwan's case indicate that the contradictions have been overemphasized. His main argument is that there is in fact a synergy between the reforms during their initial phase. Because NPM reforms actually advocate certain core values also shared by liberal democracies, and because NPM measures helped fulfill certain political functions for regime transition in Taiwan, the two reforms actually reinforced each other early on in the process. Nevertheless, as democratization matures, it tends to pursue more complex goals, such as improving the quality of civil society and promoting grass-roots participation in a collective future; conversely, the later stages of NPM impose challenges to further democratization.

NEOLIBERALISM, GLOBAL CAPITALISM, AND EDUCATION

Neoliberalism, Capital, Marketization, and Commodification

Neoliberals led by Friedrich Hayek use "economic efficiency" and "freedom" as cornerstones for their arguments against "inappropriate" controls and market intervention by governments. They are criticized, however, because markets do not always function as forecast, and the public nature and external outcomes of education make it difficult to operate exclusively in terms of market-oriented thought.

Since the 1980s, New Right political ideology, including neoconservatism and neoliberalism, has impacted education in many countries, including America, Britain, Canada, Germany, and even the Labour governments of Australia and New Zealand (Ball, 1990; Kenway, 1994; Apple, 2001). All of these countries, to different extents, set out to change their education systems in general and higher education in particular in the direction of free market economic principles. The language of education has been widely replaced by the language of the market. The concepts of *management* and *accountability* as related to outsourcing of social services have attracted new attention in public administration. Contracting out social services gives rise to a more sophisticated administrative process and a less stringent mechanism in ensuring accountability. However, as Amin argued, people in different social positions will support different values and perspectives. For the people in the Third World, critical appraisal of the global capitalism is imperative:

> On the one hand, there are those Galbraith calls the "haves." From their viewpoint all our society needs is managers . . . Anything beyond that frame presents, according to these "haves," a public danger. On the other hand there are those who say our society's overriding need

is for critical thinking leading to a better understanding of the mechanisms of change, and therefore able to influence such change in ways that will free society from capitalism alienation and its tragic consequences. As far as the overwhelming majority of humanity—the people of Asia, Africa and Latin America—are concerned, this need is vital, since they experience actually existing capitalism as nothing short of savagery. (Amin, 1997, pp. 141–142)

Hill (2003) argued that neoliberal policies, both in the United Kingdom and globally, have resulted in the loss of equity, economic and social justice, democracy and democratic accountability, and perhaps most importantly, critical thought within a culture of performativity. The marketization of education has altered a number of important aspects of education, such as goals, motivations, methods, measurement of excellence, and standards of freedom in education. Indeed, the process of the marketization of education is very much connected with performance, outcome, and competition; the discursive formation and rhetorical strategies of education policy-making played an important role for shifting people values, concerns and actions in daily life (Mulderrig 2003).

Commodification and consumerism should be understood as fundamental principles of capitalism itself. Many educational left scholars have highlighted the increasing subordination of education to the demands of Capital, including university education, and its commodification (Burbules and Torres, 2000; Stromquist, 2002). Karl Marx successfully exposed the "alienation" engendered by capitalist society, in which "economic laws" are supposed to operate as "natural laws." Based on Marx's critique on capital, Rikowski points out three modes of critique: (1) the difference between the *Ideal* according to government policy, or a mission statement, or various aims and objectives and how they actually *are*. These are differences between theory and practice; (2) questions of individual fairness and justice, and social justice (fairness in terms of relative equality between social groups); and most fundamental (3) how the core processes and phenomena of capitalist society (value, capital, labor, labor-power, value-creation, capital accumulation, and so on) generate contradictions and tensions in everyday life—for individuals, groups, classes, societies, and on an international scale (cited from Hill 2003).

Global neoliberalism as the Expanding Logic of Capitalism

Globalization is not a new socio-economic phenomenon intrinsic to capitalism's expansionary tendencies and growth. With regard to competitiveness, Amin (1997) argued that capitalism is more than just an economic system. Capitalism has a close relationship with space; therefore, we have entered a new era characterized by a separation between the globalized space of capitalism's economic management and the national spaces of its political and social management (p. 32). Capitalism is a complex product of economic, political, and social factors; in the accumulation of capital, five monopolies must be analyzed: control of technology, financial control, access to the planet's natural resources, media and communication, and weapons of mass destruction (pp. 4–5).

Seen in terms of cultural diversity or geography, the idea of global–local dialectics does not really refer to a whole divided into opposing halves or an absolute division between parts, but rather the true basis and possible context that appears as globalization actually happens, what Roland Robertson (1995) calls *glocality,* which is what results when the process of globalization is observed from a local spatial context. Different cultural systems arise from social context with different interactions between the elements, both visible and invisible, that take part in informing and structuring the principles that reflect these systems.

It is worth noting that globalization does not necessarily cause nation-states to disintegrate or lose their cohesion, and partial loss of autonomy is not tantamount to loss of control, since the power of nation-states actually continues to operate by being visibly or invisibly transformed into influence over international or local organizations, because, after all, the nation-state is the foundation upon which international power rests (Green, 1997, p.165).

Globalization has altered the objective characteristics of time and space; global capitalism has caused a certain convergence in transnational media and technology, and also the politics, economies, habits of consumption, and cultures of the world. Eventually, global capitalism leads to the uneven development of space (Harvey, 2006); however, as globalization progresses, a greater number of local characteristics, divergent voices, and cultural differences are stimulated and become visible.

Critical Pedagogy versus Global Capitalism

With the goals of impeding further globalization, realizing humanist alternative strategies for resisting globalization, and renewing the perspective of global socialism, Amin (1997) pointed out four basic questions on the ideological cultural front: (1) the dialectic between the universal and the particular; (2) the relationship between political democracy and social progress; (3) the dialectic of so-called economic efficiency (and the way it is expressed, "the market") and values of equality and fraternity; and (4) the definition of a global socialist objective in the light of all of the above (p.11).

Allman (2001) stresses that the primary task of critical pedagogy is to subject capitalism to dialectical readings while applying critical revolutionary pedagogy to it and unwaveringly subjecting it to class analysis. Because capitalism is an unfeeling and monolithic process that molds our daily lives in every way possible, in order to best resist it, we must understand capitalism's logic of operation. Furthermore, in *Capitalist and Conquerors,* McLaren (2005) argued that

> critical revolutionary pedagogy serves the important purpose of generating new ways of thinking about the state and its relationship to the production of and possibilities for human agency both now and in the crucial years ahead of us. (p. 9)

Humans are conditioned by structures and social relations but also can create and transform them. In his view, the critical point to consider is "the over-determining effects of capital as a social relation." (ibid)

Based on a number of current discussions concerning globalization and education, Jennifer Chan-Tiberghien (2004) has drawn up a summary of different research orientations to globalization in education. (see Table 8.1) Her four research orientations include: (1) educational restructuring; (2) educational institutionalism; (3) educational multilateralism; and (4) global educational justice. Educational restructuring and educational institutionalism are obviously evidenced by discussions such as education reform based on neoliberal ideology and international comparative education, as both are responses to "global" and "globalization." Global educational justice advocates critiquing the research orientations mentioned previously and proposes appropriate strategies.

Chan-Tiberghien synthesizes critical pedagogy, cognitive justice, and decolonizing methodology to create a fourth approach for studying globalization and education with which she attempts to overturn the exclusive dominance of Neoliberal market-oriented ideology. Basically, it is a strategic alliance designed to resist imperialistic pressure, one that embodies both Marxist critiques of capitalism and the social movements organized against it, as well as post-structuralist feminism and post-colonialism's emphasis on recognition and representation. This also involves justice in distribution and justice in recognition.

Table 8.1. Different research orientation to globalization in education

Orientations	Focus	Approaches
Educational restructuring	Economy	There is no alternative (TINA)
Educational institutionalism	Culture	Isomorphism
Educational multilateralism	Politics	Cooperation
Global educational justice	Counter-hegemony	Diverse people for diversity

Source: Chan-Tiberghien (2004, p. 194)

From the viewpoint of social justice, globalism is a new kind of impe-rialism, especially with regards to the way America has taken the lead in military and commercial expansionism, adopted an egocentric world view, exploitated third-world resources, and embraced and profited from cultural imperialism. Global capitalism can be seen as more than just "standard-ization of products" or "global sales" when, for example, transnational corporations such as McDonalds, Nike, Coca Cola, and Sony appear ubiq-uitous throughout the world and spur endless consumption. Particularly when they invade the realm of education to serve their commercial inter-ests, one sees clearly the global spread of capitalism's logic of production and the division of labor in society, as well as the global diffusion of the "commercialized" or extremely "materialistic" style of thinking (McLaren & Farahmandpur, 2005).

HIGHER EDUCATION IN TAIWAN UNDER
NEOLIBERALISM AND NEW MANAGERIALISM

Many of the problems widely discussed about privatization and the mar-ketization of education in the West (Apple, Kenway and Singh, 2005) do not correlate to all education levels in Taiwan. The compulsory primary and secondary school levels (Grades 1–9), are still mainly supported by the government (Table 8.2). However, in higher education, particularly univer-sities, there is increasing evidence of privatization and the marketization.

With regards to preschool education, the Taiwanese government has implemented an education voucher policy since 2000. Based on a detailed analysis of the formatting process of vouchers policy, Ho (2006) pointed

Table 8.2. Number of Public/Private schools in Taiwan, 2007

School level	Total	Public schools	Private schools
Kindergarten	3283	1528	1755
Elementary school	2651	2613	38
Junior high school	740	723	17
Senior high school	320	179	141
Senior vocational school	156	92	64
University	100	42	58
Five-year junior college	15	3	12
Two-year or four-year senior college	49	10	39
Special Education	24	23	1
Open university	2	2	—

(Source: Taiwan Ministry of Education Statistics, 2007)[9]

out that the preschool voucher policy in Taiwan did not originate from neoliberalism, as we generally see in the top-down policy in western countries, but occurred rather as the result of a social movement. This movement was promoted by an alliance: the *National Union of Preschool Education*, UNPE, formed in 1997. This alliance was organized by the owners of private kindergartens, through the bargaining and the employment of lobbying strategies, to alleviate a crisis for private kindergartens. In addition, the preschool voucher policy was also supported by the DPP government's policy for promoting equal opportunity for women by providing more and higher quality preschool care in order to help women working full-time jobs.

Most Asian countries have been deeply influenced by Confucianism, especially with regard to socio-cultural and educational values. Indeed, the impact of Confucianism's core values of "humanity" and the development of "social harmony" are not to be underestimated. When employed as a mechanism of political rule, one detects an emphasis on the hierarchy of human relationships, such as the strict regulations between ruler and ruled, parent and child, elder and youth, husband and wife, teacher and student, and so on. In education, Confucianism has historically manifested itself as authoritative and teacher-dominated transmission models of learning (Lee & Van Patten, 2003). Thus, these deeply rooted cultural mental mechanisms have restricted critical thinking as well as the general cultural value of autonomy, and as a result, political and educational participation.

During the KMT's authoritarian rule, there was a high commitment toward a new industrial society; accordingly, higher education was strongly controlled by the KMT government and financed both through tax-supported and private financial sources to meet the overriding goals of labor industrialization and economic development. Concurrently, education also functioned as a vital ideological state apparatus, one located in an effective and highly connected political and administrative network headed by the KMT and the MOE respectively.

As the higher education system in Taiwan was greatly influenced by western university models,[9] liberal and critical philosophy provided a vital foundation for Taiwanese universities in seeking their modern identity. This was evidenced by the great effort invested in the whole process of the amendment of *the University Law* by university teachers and students as a search for self-identity and freedom from political control. Currently, to some degree, higher education in Taiwan is still actually controlled and managed by the government in ways both visible and invisible, especially in the case of the public universities, where the MOE has strict regulations concerning recruiting, the adding or merging of academic schools or departments, evaluation, personnel hiring and human resources, and the use and granting of supplements for expenditures (Wang, 1999).

In brief, the transformation in the quantity and quality of higher education in Taiwan can be seen as one aspect of the country's macroeconomic adjustment, one that is also related to socio-political change. It includes the rapid expansion of higher education, an emphasis on students as human capital, civic rights to higher education as manifested by the establishment of additional private schools, the reduction of public expenditures and the increase in tuition fees for higher education based on the idea of payment by the users, and the redistribution of higher education resources based on the outcomes of academic evaluation (Tai, Mok, & Shieh, 2002).

The Academic Evaluation Index, Ranking, and Issuing of Competitive Grants

With the influences of the global spread of neoliberalism, and its tendency to demand that academic production contribute to international competitiveness and performance, the government has attempted to establish more transparent evaluation criteria in distributing public expenditures and reforming academic promotion. In aiming to gain more subsidies from the government and to establish a dominant position both in academic reputation and "market-share," most higher education institutions are zealous in gaining advantages (Bok, 2003). For example, in Taiwan, in the field of humanities and social sciences, aside from peer review, currently volume criteria and SSCI (Social Science Citation Index) criteria are increasingly being adopted. The "instrumental reason" of science and English as a powerful academic capital has become one kind of academic hegemony. Thus, the criterion of academic evaluation of higher education in Taiwan has been an important apparatus reshaping the direction of knowledge production, and as a result, university teachers' academic research and teaching.

"To promote one of our excellent universities among the world's top 100 within ten years" was a claim made forcibly by the DPP government in 2005, following a policy called *The Five-year NT$50 billion* competitive grants plan.[10] As the DPP government increasingly vocalized their concern for the excellence of higher education, the distribution of funding in higher education has ironically become a zero-sum game. The official classification and ranking of higher education institutions in Taiwan has impacted the aims, organizational culture and operation, curriculum and instructions in higher education institutions. With slogans such as "knowledge-based economy" and "international competition," it must be asked, what kind of ideology is hidden beneath the distribution of resources of higher education in Taiwan, and who has really benefited from it?

In 2003, the MOE published a highly criticized evaluation report, which polarized many scholars in the humanities and social sciences in Taiwan. They made an urgent appeal to the MOE against blindly imposing academic standards that were developed in the West, particularly America. Late in 2003, the scholars joined together to hold a symposium, which resulted in humanists and social scientists making heated accusations about the inappropriateness of the MOE and the National Science Council using SCI, SSCI, and

TSSCI [*Science Citation Index, Social Sciences Citation Index, and Taiwan Sciences Citation Index*] as standards for academic evaluation in Taiwan.

The most important criticism consisted of the following three points: (1) Use of the guidelines mentioned previously showed that those powerful intellectual elite in charge had a very narrow mindset that equated "Americanization" with "internationalization," in turn equating both with "globalization"; (2) Use of SSCI and TSSCI for evaluation of academic quality in universities was unfair and did not constitute internationalization, but rather only served to expose the power held in academia by the field of econometrics; (3) Taiwan's international competitive strength should not be confused with conversion of the academic system to using English as the medium of scholarly debate or with complete identification with America (The Task Group of Reflexivity Conference, 2006, pp. viii–ix).

Criticism by scholars, grounded in higher education's obligation for social responsibility, holds that if education in Taiwan consists of nothing more than blindly following recommended guidelines from America, this will be a distortion of Taiwan's academic autonomy, one which shows a lack of independent reflection and ignores the importance of the Chinese language in academic expression and social communication, while at the same time neglecting the Asian identity of the Taiwanese. If Taiwan scholars are coerced into solely seeking participation and publication in well-known foreign journals without applying to their fields a Taiwan-centric focus, it is doubtful that they will be able to provide the people of Taiwan with analyses and solutions for important local social problems; in addition, there is a real danger that academics will abandon their social responsibility as public intellectuals, and in doing so, will lose the unique niche Taiwan scholarship could occupy in the international arena.

The preceding is actually closely tied in with the academic colonization of Taiwan and has its historical linkages. After World War II, the closeness in Taiwan–American relations and the numbers of Taiwan students studying in America stayed at very high levels; thus, Taiwan academia was influenced again by America. More than ten years ago, the underlying causes and factors involved in this were analyzed by Yeh (1991) as consisting of "the diffusion of cultural superiority" and an antithetical relationship formed between "the center and the periphery." Technological domination evolves in combination with a product-oriented model of market economy. How it evolves is closely related to the characteristics of capitalist society (p. 176). Embracing the central country's (also called superior country) cultural symbols occurs because they are symbolic of the market for highly profitable products whose value derives not only from actual profit, but also comes in the form of social position, as embodied in the criteria currently used by the government and the various colleges for incentives, hiring, transfer, and promotion.

When subjected to the standards just described, one fears a conspiracy between political power and professional ideology that might herald the diminishing of the humanities; a sphere increasingly looked upon with pessimism in modern society and subject to scorn and neglect within higher education in general. The definition of "performance" should not be proscribed by external standards set by the government and technical experts, but should also include negotiation that evolves from the bottom upward among members of an organization, or "internal performance"(Carnoy, Elmore, & Siskin, 2003).

Education, whether in theory or practice, has always been imagined as a training base for national productivity, particularly in the age of globalization. "Academic capitalism," according to Slaughter and Leslie (1997), can be seen as one kind of compulsory response that universities have made in response to the rush of globalization.

With regard to the meaning of labor, Marxism offers a definition of social labor as the exchange between personal body and wage, and it is also connected with the production and reproduction of social relations. Labor is usually drawn into this, becoming part of capital and functioning for capital's benefits. From a critical perspective, Stanley Aronowitz (2001) argues that there is scarce evidence of "higher learning"—as opposed to "training" or "education"—really taking place in American post-secondary educational institutions. Even in today's best universities, students are rewarded for uncritically packaged knowledge, rather than for participating in or challenging "established intellectual authority." Universities have actually become "factories of knowledge." Key areas to observe include how university teachers envision their jobs and rewards, how they usually invest their time and energy, how their self and professional identities and social relationships are formulated, and how they maintain subjectivity.

The Anti-high Tuition Fee Movement

According to MOE statistics, from 1996 to 2006, the number of universities and colleges in Taiwan more than doubled. The number of students in both undergraduate as well as postgraduate levels increased rapidly, and consequently, the distribution of available resources among different higher education institutions became a contentious issue.

In Taiwan, as well as other East Asian countries such as Japan, Korea, China, and Singapore, higher degrees have always been an important cultural and economic symbol, one connected with an image of higher income, social status, and quality of life. Moreover, to obtain a higher degree is not only considered an honor for the student; it is also considered a reflection upon the efforts of the parents. On the one hand, the demand for higher education has accelerated over the years in Taiwan; on the other, the government's public expenditures have gradually decreased. Eventually, the "user-pay" policy was launched, which, in consequence, was followed by a rise in tuition (Tai, Mok, & Shieh, 2002).

In early 2006, according to MOE statistics, 57 colleges and universities, both private and public, submitted official documents requesting permission to increase tuition because they did not show budget surpluses in the prior three years. Some presidents of universities claimed that in an age of shrinking government subsidies for universities, raising tuition was the last option for them to ensure the quality of higher education. On July 2, 2006, the *Coalition against High Tuition*[11] demanded that the government create more sources of education funding and asked the ministry to promise not to raise the tuition for the upcoming academic year.

In response to the appeal from students, the ministry proposed tuition-aid programs to ease college students' financial burden and announced that it would allocate a NT$17.4 billion (US$550.5 million) scholarship fund for college and graduate students. However, even with rising tuition, the cost of higher education in Taiwan is still much lower than that in Singapore, Japan, and South Korea, and the higher education cost per student in Taiwan is only 1/3 to 2/3 that of developed countries. Under the pressure of public expenditure, as well as NPM's idea of efficiency, which had been employed widely in the merger of enterprises and banks, the DPP government has strongly pressed for universities and colleges in close proximity to merge together in order to increase efficiency.[12]

In fact, government inefficiency, particularly the inertia of entrenched bureaucracy, has received considerable critique, especially as regards the lack of flexibility of government personnel and accounting systems applied to all public universities. Government regulations on accounting also apply to all university revenue, such as private gifts and contracts, tuitions and fees, and endowment income. Faculty salary scale is designated by government regulations and based mainly on seniority. To some degree, all of these obstruct university autonomy and administrative flexibility.

Furthermore, "inefficiency" is not only a problem in higher education. Since 2000, the MOE has strongly urged that public elementary or secondary schools numbering less than one hundred students per school and financially supported by the Local Education Authority (LEA), merge together or become branch schools in order to avoid closure. These schools are mostly located in remote rural and mountainous areas of Taiwan with poor transportation infrastructure.

EDUCATION, SOCIAL JUSTICE, AND CIVIL SOCIETY IN TAIWAN

Teachers' Resistance and Self-empowerment
Teacher Unions and Organizations

Widely seen as the most important education reform in Taiwan since 1990, Grades 1–9 Curriculum Reform in Taiwan during the last decade was based on the educational philosophy of constructionalism. Learner-centered, it placed students as the subject of instruction. With the aim to reduce boundaries between different subjects and enhance the connections of knowledge and practice, "integrated" and "school-based" curricula were adopted for learning local cultural experience. In addition, action research as well as an emphasis on teachers' professional portfolios has been highlighted in order to enhance the self-empowerment of schoolteachers. Under these ongoing social and educational changes, the idea of "school as a learning organization" has been claimed by schools to adjust their organization culture as well as revise in-service teacher training programs.[13]

Obviously, Grades 1–9 Curriculum Reform has set a high standard for education in Taiwan, in which teachers are highly valued as the core of the vision and take responsibility to fulfill their mission. However, in reality Grades 1–9 Curriculum Reform, combined with deregulation in multiple levels—textbooks, organization and school management, curriculum and instruction, and finally the relationship of learners and knowledge—is a mammoth task. As a total shift of education philosophy, it has taken a long time for administrators and teachers to respond. Sadly, most schools and teachers have received inadequate financial or social supports to make real improvement possible.

Since the formation of the KMT government, teachers in Taiwan have been designated as "civil servants" or "office holders"; as a result, teachers must obey the government's order, be it the central or local government. This classification, and the relative regulations as well as hierarchical culture of school organizations in general, have severely restricted their professionalism, as well as their subjectivity and autonomy.

In 1995, Dr. Hsia Lin-Ching, a female scholar with a background in psychology and counseling who has been very active in social movements for empowering labor workers and disadvantaged women, organized the *Grassroots' Teachers Association* (GTA) in Taipei, although the history of the GTA can be traced back to 1985. Because the majority of primary and secondary school teachers in Taiwan are female, the majority of GTA members are also female. Based on critical and liberal ideas from the educational left, with regard to education reform, the GTA highlights the importance of the search for "real education" as opposed to "deceitful education." The core of real education must be the teachers and students, and real situations and problems occurring on campus must be taken seriously and improved through real and equal dialogue. With the aims of promoting teachers' collective professional autonomy and helping disadvantaged students to have equal educational opportunity, the GTA has become a collaborative teachers' group in which action research had been adopted as a key approach for teachers' self-reflection and action. Since 2000, Dr. Hsia has stressed that teachers must have a deeper understanding of those students who come from working-class poor families and urges teachers to honestly review, explore, and clarify their own life histories, particularly those negative experiences related to schools and families. Through multiple methods of critical reflection and action, such as workshops for teacher dialogue and self-empowerment, the discussions of documentaries, and the formation of an embodied plan for education reform action, the GTA has raised critical consciousness by urging teachers to rethink both education and themselves.

Moreover, based on the growth of local teacher's associations and the announcement of the Teacher's Law in 1995, the *National Teacher's Association* (NTA)[14] was established in February, 1999, in Taipei. A self-initiated, self-governed, and grassroots organization, the NTA is also the single government-sanctioned professional organization for full-time teachers in all sectors of education. Currently, the NTA has 25 branch teacher associations located in 25 counties and cities, 1,960 branches in schools, and more than one hundred thousand teacher-members. The NTA claims that it is a professional teacher and labor organization that represents all teachers across Taiwan, as well as a social movement organization interested in promoting social justice and public well-being.

The aim of NTA is to uphold the professional dignity and autonomy of teachers and to protect the working rights of teachers as well as the learning rights of students. The main activities that the NTA promotes include the creation and revision of education-related laws, the supervision of educational policies and administration, and negotiation with the government in terms of national educational policies, particularly those involving educational budgets, as well as teachers' and students' rights. For example, the NTA negotiated the guiding principles of the National Teachers' Contract, held hearings on class-size reduction in public schools, and organized conferences and workshops for discussing the organization and management of teachers' associations and school organization, as well as curriculum and teaching materials reform.

Following the development and expanding influence of the GTA, in 2007, the *Indigenous Grassroots' Teachers Association* (IGTA) was established in Pingtung, located in the south of Taiwan. The aims of the IGTA are rather similar to the GTA in general, but are more focused in drawing attention to and solving aboriginal teachers' problems, in particular, those related to issues of race, language, tribal culture, geographical location, and resource distribution.

In *The Battle in Seattle*, Glenn Rikowski (2001) argues that teachers are the most dangerous of workers because they have a special role in shaping, developing and imposing the single commodity on which the whole capitalist system rests: labor-power. Teachers are intimately connected with the social production of labor-power, equipping students with skills, competences, abilities, knowledge, attitudes, and personal qualities that are essential in the capitalist labor process. Without a doubt, teachers in Taiwan, in all levels of the education apparatus, are the workers involved in the construction of symbolic or academic labor. From the perspective of critical pedagogy, as well as the ideals of social justice, teachers must be cultural workers as well as organic intellectuals. On the one hand, teachers must understand, particularly in the age of globalization, what kind of role they are supposed to play, based on national, economic, and political ideologies. On the other hand, teachers must also understand what routes are available, in order to escape the logic of capitalism and to reach the reality of humanity.

Indeed, the development and mobility of teachers' organizations during the last two decades in Taiwan signifies teachers' self-awareness and self-empowerment, not just in defending teacher benefits, but rather toward a wider role in social development. In palpable ways, critical perspectives from the educational left or social sciences inspired these organizations. The most critical task for these teachers' organizations to undertake is to counterbalance the government's power and voice in education and globalization, and become a collective civil force to advance real education and social justice.

Critical Discourses and De-colonization in Education

During the last ten years in Taiwan, there has been an increase in publications related to critical education discourse and critical pedagogy advancing explorations of power, ideology, cultural politics, and empowerment of education (Lee & Wang, 2006). Among critical educational discourses, Marxism, neo-Marxism, post-materialism, and post-structuralism, with different theoretical basis and conceptual tools, have been used by scholars to reframe and explore different issues, from the macro to the micro level.

However, because of Taiwan's specific historical context, including the Chinese Civil War and Cold War, Marxism is not so popular in Taiwan, particularly in the field of educational research. Under the governance of the KMT, with its strong anti-Communist agenda, the theory of Marxism was labeled as the doctrine of the Communist and therefore entirely excluded from textbooks and censored from public discourse. However, during the last two decades, under the rapid development of the global economy, Marx's idea of political economy, with its power in analyzing the logic of capitalism, labor processes, labor movement, class hierarchy, and social injustice within one country or cross countries, has stimulated many insights in both academic and practical fields in Taiwan.

Beyond post-colonialism, the writings of Edward Said, Gayatri Spivak, and Homi Bhabha, have become pertinent. Their ideas, such as "representation," "the Subaltern and marginality," and "hybrids" have been employed to explore and rethink the complex cultural–political experiences surrounding Taiwanese self-identity. For example, from the perspective of de-colonialization, Kuan-Hsing Chen (2006), in his book *De-imperialism: Asia as Method,* attempts to draw counter-discourses against the dominance of imperialism in Taiwan. Reflexive thinking about the cultural studies and political practices of radical trade unions, gay–lesbian groups, and media activists are all mentioned. Chen argues that the history of the Cold War made for a close and ultimately dependent relationship between the United States and Taiwan, because the Cold War was a period of conflict, tension, and competition between the United States and the Soviet Union and their respective allies from the mid-1940s until the early 1990s.

Actually, there are multiple dimensions in Taiwan's post-coloniality, in which Taiwanese seek to take their role as historical subjects, not only in opposition with Japan and China, but also America. The appeal of "United Nations for Taiwan" currently pushed by the DPP government, is a Taiwanese-centric effort to free itself from a colonized historical context, by redefining itself in the international arena. Currently, China's objection and direct pressuring of other countries, including the United States, to silence any debate on the issue is the main stumbling block for Taiwan's entrance to the United Nations, in spite of the fact that UN experts and academics have argued Taiwan's exclusion from the world body is the single biggest scandal in UN history.[15] In order to fully understand this issue, more study needs to be done on how globalization, by directing unrestricted economic flows into authoritarian regimes such as China, helps to empower the shackling of freedom of expression, debate, and participation on a global scale.[16]

The Force of the Third Sector: Community Universities and NGO/NPOs in Taiwan

The third sector is one of the most significant parts of civil society. Briefly, the development of the third sector, or NGOs (nongovernment organizations) could be seen from different points of view: (1) as part of new public management and mixed economies of welfare; (2) as central to "civil-society-social capital" approaches; (3) as an instrument for achieving greater transparency, heightened accountability, and improved governance of public institutions; and (4) as a counter-hegemony and contestation (Glasius, Kaldor. & Anheier, 2006, pp. 23–24). There are always technocratic overlaps between new public management and decentralization; but they differed in terms of civil engagement and empowerment. The Third Way foresaw a re-organization of the state that required an activation of civil society and social participation, the encouragement of social entrepreneurship, and new approaches to public–private partnerships in the provision of public goods and services (ibid).

As Hsiao (2000) has pointed out, since the 1980s, the development of non-profit organizations (NPOs) in Taiwan witnessed a new and unprecedented phase in which economic growth and political liberalization gave strong support to the resurrected civil society. Briefly, Taiwan's NPOs can be classified into social movement sectors (SMS) and non-social-movement sectors (NSMS) in terms of the broad objectives claimed and strategies employed by individual NPOs. The majority of the NPOs in Taiwan belong to the latter, and SMS organizations have been new forces that have played a crucial role in promoting democracy in Taiwan since the 1980s. In recent years, many of the NSMS institutions and organizations in Taiwan have moved beyond traditional philanthropic activities to focus on more emerging social concerns.[17]

For example, with the intent to promote the liberation of knowledge, self-empowerment of people, the development of public opinion and a real civil society in Taiwan, in 1998, the first community university (or so-called community college, with no degree but credits for adult learners) was established in Taipei; as of 2007, there are 74 community universities in Taiwan.[18] In 1999, the National Association for the Promotion of Community University (NAPCU)[19] was established in order to enhance communication and organizational mobility for all community universities in Taiwan, formulate the working issues of community universities, and negotiate with the government about policies concerning admissions, degrees, and credits. Furthermore, 12 indigenous universities have been opened since 2003. Some community universities and indigenous universities in counties with specific geographic issues, such as Pingtung, Hualien and Taitung in the southern and eastern part of Taiwan, have built many learning-settings in local communities and remote areas to provide more easily accessible learning opportunities.

Compared with general universities, community universities in Taiwan provide an alternative approach for liberal adult learning, one that is more informal and more open to a wide range of knowledge and learners. Their teachers come from both academic and practical backgrounds. In designing curriculum, instead of focusing solely on skill-mastering or vocation-training, they focus on local cultural, historical, industry, business, and ecological problems as well as civil rights issues. Currently, "the study of the place or community" based on theoretical perspectives from human geography, and the employment of *Geographical Information System* (GIS) in local areas has been emphasized.

In addition to the development of community universities, civil groups organized by parents have also played a critical role in Taiwan. The *National Alliance for Parents Organization*" (NAPO)[20] was established in 2005, although it actually developed from long-term social movements begun in the 1990s that highlighted the protection of children's right to learn and parents' rights to be involved in school affairs. Briefly, the aims of NAPO include five key points: (1) to clarify the roles and subjectivity of parents' participation in education affairs; (2) to build legal regulations concerning parent's participation in education from the local to central government level; (3) to empower parental participation in education affairs and develop active organizations; (4) to enhance parents' self-learning; and (5) to develop a constructive multiple negotiation link between parents, teachers, and the government. Most NAPO members are middle-class professionals, and their educational philosophies tend to be more liberal-oriented and child-centered. They strongly oppose test-based and over-disciplined schooling in Taiwan and have also expanded their concerns into wider public affairs, such as the protection of the environment. With powerful claims and actions, NAPO plays a significant role as mediator between government, schools, teachers, and parents.

As of 2007, there are more than one thousand NPOs in Taiwan, including religious, charity, and social welfare organizations, many of which overlap. A remarkable example is the Tzu Chi Foundation,[21] which states four main missions: religion, medicine, education, and humanism. Aiding the sick and impoverished is emphasized, as is the importance of recycling and organic agriculture in promoting environmental protection. Members, supporters, and volunteers come from a wide cross-section of the public and include successful entrepreneurs as well as the working-class. Tzu Chi has developed a network of hospitals and health care, a publication sector, an independent TV Channel, and even a unique school system–from kindergarten, primary and secondary school, to university; in addition, many volunteers have been involved in supporting the practice of life education on campuses.

In summary, organizations such as the Tzu Chi Foundation, as well as many NPOs in Taiwan, with clear core values, well-organized and active action agenda, stable donations as well as tremendous volunteers, have actually compensated for a shortage of social welfare and played a significant role in promoting new cultural movements in society. Under the competitive thinking logic of global capitalism, these NPOs have raised the civil consciousness about caring for other people and demonstrate a will to share personal earnings as payback to global society. They can be seen as one kind of tender reaction to aliened social relations.

Anti-globalization Action and Immigrants Issues

Under the last three decades of Taiwan's economic transformation, from agricultural, to industrial, and then service economy, many farmers in Taiwan have suffered. As a result, there have been many pro-farmer voices and movements, especially against Taiwan's entrance to the WTO; in particular, the case of Yang Ju-men, a former chicken vendor given the name "The Rice Bomber" by the Taiwan press, is a remarkable example.[22] Yang's illegal acts won widespread public sympathy when he claimed that he took the actions to draw attention to the government's ignorance of the plight of Taiwan farmers caused by the island's accession to the WTO and the opening of the domestic market to foreign-grown rice. The case of Yang in some ways exposed the common sorrow and sadness of Taiwanese farmers under the impact of global capitalism as well as the WTO, and Yang was credited for helping Taiwan negotiators resist U.S. pressure to raise the rice import limit and lower the import tariff rate (The China Post, June 20, 2007).

With the aims of facing the challenges of globalization, promoting environmental protection, and developing the local economy, some intellectual activists and farming communities during the last decade in Taiwan have tried to revive rural communities by developing green agriculture, creative cultural industries, and ecologically sustainable villages. The above local movements can be recognized as the reconstruction of rural communities in which the uneven development of space between the urban and rural areas within the process of capitalism's development has been evidenced. Local inhabitants have searched for possible solutions through collective reflection, re-learning, empowerment, and action. These remarkable examples include the *Daai Cultural Life Circle Promotion* in Pei-pu, a Hakka village in Hsin-chu County, led by Shu-Shih Wei and established in 1997, as well as the *Meinung People's Association* in Kaohsiung County, which originated from a local 1992 anti-dam social movement that has since become a very active organization in community building.

Since the 1990s, there has also been another important national dynamic directly related to the development of global capitalism: an influx of migrant workers from Southeast Asia, mainly Vietnam, the Philippines, and Indonesia. Many of these immigrant workers, who will accept lower salaries than local Taiwanese workers, come to Taiwan to fill a labor shortage, particularly in traditional manufacturing, construction, and domestic care. In addition, many women from Southeast Asia as well as China have entered Taiwanese society through marriages.[23] As of 2007, immigrant workers in Taiwan number around 350,000, foreign mothers number around 390,000, and 200,000 children as the new Taiwanese. As most of these immigrant workers do "3-D jobs" (dirty, difficult, and dangerous), they obviously are burdened by problems of labor rights and security. Immigrant wives experience unique problems surrounding citizenship, cultural identity, social status, and gender-related issues, while education and cultural identity remain problems for the children of these mixed marriages. Furthermore, the existence of these immigrant issues heightens the need for debate regarding social justice and how to improve multicultural education in Taiwan.

With regard to these immigrant workers, some organizations have been established by the NGOs recently to disseminate information, address their concerns, and protect their rights. These include the *Taiwan International Workers Association* (TIWA), a public internet space for discussing immigrant issues, *Taiwan Migrant's Forum,* and a space for criticizing globalization and injustice in the government's immigration policies. These organizations have all been established to facilitate communication between migrant workers and the local Taiwan community, in order to improve migrant workers' labor conditions and social status, and to advocate all laborers' rights and welfare.[24]

CONCLUSION

The legitimacy problem that neoliberals must face, as Stiglitz identified, is underlined by a growing dissatisfaction with neoliberalism. Each January, synchronized with the WEF meeting, hundreds of global civil society organizations meet at the WSF. The WSF slogan is "another world is possible," and it celebrates difference, viewing itself as a process, not an organization (McMichael, 2004, p 302).

Amin (1997) argued that it is the duty of the intelligentsia, especially those of the Third World and Africa, to deconstruct the new justificatory rhetoric, thus laying bare its functional connections with the tactical and strategic objectives of crisis management (p.149). The Intelligentsia needs to respond with a positive contribution to the crystallization of alternative proposals offering real solutions to the crises. As McLaren (2005) argues, the real struggle of critical pedagogy, particularly in a world increasingly filled with the powerful discourses of neoliberalism and machinations of global capitalism, is to reflect upon the critical questions waiting to be asked in order to adopt the necessary actions in time:

> How can we liberate the use value of human beings from their subordination to exchange value? . . . How can we make critical self-reflexivity a demarcating principle of who we are and critical global citizenship the substance of what we want to become? How can we make the cultivating of a political of hope and possibility a radical end in itself? How can we de-commodify our subjectivities? How can we materialize our self-activity as a revolutionary force and struggle for the self-determination of free and equal citizens in a just system of appropriation and distribution of social wealth? (McLaren, 2005, p 10)

One thing is certain: a wide political–economic critique of global capitalism is revealing and necessary. In an effort to identify the core problems of global neoliberalism, a spokesperson for the *Living Democracy Movement*, Vandana Shiva argued the following:

> The philosophical and ethical bankruptcy of globalization was based on reducing every aspect of our lives to commodities and reducing our identities to that of mere consumers in the global marketplace. Our capacities as producers, our identity as members of communities, our role as custodians of our natural and cultural heritage were all to disappear or be destroyed. Markets and consumerism expanded. Our capacity to give and share was to shrink. But the human spirit refused to be subjugated by a world-view based on the dispensability of our humanity. (cited from McMichael, 2004, p 303)

The impacts of globalization, particularly the ideology of neoliberalism and its resistance, reaction, and alternative possibilities raised during the last three decades in Taiwan have been briefly illustrated in this article. Under the simultaneous impacts of rapid social–political change and the rise of global neoliberalism, education reform has become a significant and heavily debated issue. As a small East Asian island with a complicated past struggling for it's economic and political future in the international world, Taiwan has a wealth of untold stories waiting for further documentation, exploration, and decoding.

Surely as the process of globalization intensifies, many impacts and reactions will follow. While education reform is usually a process of internal social reconstruction, in Taiwan in particular, it is connected with complex global contexts and external power struggles; as a result, much can be learned by exposing, identifying, and detangling the multiple frameworks of power at play in Taiwan. These issues surely require more national and international dialogue, debate, and ultimately, resistance.

NOTES

1. In the aftermath of the 228 Incident of 1947, martial law was declared in 1948, and the perceived need to suppress Communist and pro-democracy activities on the island meant that the martial law was not lifted until 1987. This gives Taiwan the distinction of having the longest period of martial law in modern history. http://en.wikipedia.org/wiki/Martial_law
2. "The Kaohsiung Incident" also known as "the Formosa Incident" was the result of pro-democracy demonstrations that occurred in Kaohsiung, Taiwan on December 10, 1979. The incident is also referred to as "the Formosa Magazine incident" or "the Meilidao (beautiful island) Incident."
3. Hsiao, S. T. Hsiao, M. C. Economic Liberalization and Development: the Case of Lifting Martial Law in Taiwan. http://www.colorado.edu/Economics/mcguire/workingpapers/9aMLawPpr.pdf
4. President Chen Shui-bian's inaugural address http://www.president.gov.tw/en/
5. The Laws or Acts created or amended under the DPP government since 1990s mainly include the Act of Asset Disclosure by Public Functionaries, the Government Procurement Act, the Administrative Procedures Act, the Environmental Impact Assessment Act, the Public Nuisances Prevention Act, the Human Rights Basic Act, the Gender Equality in Employment Act, the Sexual Harassment Prevention Act, the Children and Youth Welfare Act, the Protection Act for the Handicapped and Disabled, the Indigenous Peoples Basic Act, the Labor Standards Act, the Labor Safety and Health Act, the Volunteer Service Act.
6. Statistic of Economy, Ministry of Economic Affairs, R.O.C. http://www.moea.gov.tw/
7. Taiwan will overtake the United States to become the world's second biggest microchip supplier this year, the Central News Agency (CNA) reported Oct 29, 2007, citing a report by Industrial Technology Research Institute (ITRI). Taiwan will account for 18% of global semiconductors, behind Japan with 24%, the report said. http://www.taipeitimes.com/News/front/archives/200 7/10/29/2003385241

8. Since 1990, the BOT cases in Taiwan including the High-Speed Rail connecting Taipei in the north and Kaohsiung in the south, in Taipei City and east coast of Taiwan. Other examples include Song Shan train station, Taipei arena on Donghua, and Kaohsiung MRT.

9. Ministry of Education, R.O.C. http://www.edu.tw/EDU_WEB/EDU_MGT/STATISTICS/EDU7220001/data/serial/b.xls?open

10. Higher education in Taiwan originated from the late Ching Dynasty (as called Shu-yuan, an academy of classical learning), and then under Japanese occupation, the model of Germany university was introduced. After 1949, under the KMT government, the American university became the dominant model.

11. The "New Ten Major Construction Projects" in Taiwan was passed by the DPP government in November 2003, and included multiple public projects, including transportation, cultural, and digital development. The top priority is to support and promote the excellence of universities and research centers within five years. Ministry of Education, R.O.C. http://www.moe.gov.tw/

12. The Coalition Against High Tuition in Taiwan, organized mainly by students from colleges and universities and consisting of more than one hundred college students and their supporters, protested outside the building of the MOE against the ministry's policy of tuition hikes, decrying the hikes as the commercialization of education as well as an unfair taxation system. Students argued that the government should not place the burden of increased education costs directly onto students and their families. http://blog.elixus.org/highfight/archives/week_2004_07_04.html and http://youth.ngo.org.tw/antihightuition-index.htm (in Chinese)

13. The Statement for the Higher Education Tuition Fee, Ministry of Education, ROC http://www.moe.gov.tw/ (in Chinese)

14. Ministry of Education, R.O.C. http://www.moe.gov.tw/

15. National Teachers Association. http://www.nta.org.tw/

16. See the following :
http://timesofindia.indiatimes.com/Raw_deal_to_Taiwan/rssarticleshow/2374887.cms
http://www.taipeitimes.com/News/taiwan/archives/2007/09/18/2003379297
http://www.taipeitimes.com/News/taiwan/archives/2007/09/19/2003379432
http://online.wsj.com/public/article/SB118997983548228983.html

17. Indeed, much could be uncovered by increased focus, study, and debate on the exact reasons why the 23 million people of Taiwan continue to be denied the rights afforded the rest of the world according to the UN Charter, and the influence of globalism. The recent case of the internet giant Yahoo's decision to supply information to Chinese authorities, which was then used to sentence the Chinese dissident journalist Shi Tao to ten years in prison, is another example of how globalism is not quite the democratizing force it claims to be. http://abcnews.go.com/Politics/International/story?id=3827564&page=1

18. http://mpa.ngo.org.tw/english/e-index.html

19. In Taiwan, community universities are partly funded by the government, but run by local "legal groups," particularly non-profit organizations such as the Associations of Social Development in local areas. The key members of the establishment of community universities in Taiwan were earlier involved in the social movements of the 1980s and 1990s. Afterwards, promoting community university education became their focus to continue their progressive ideas and initiate longer social reconstruction.

20. http://www.napcu.org.tw/napcu/Default.aspx

21. http://www.napo.org.tw/ (in Chinese)

22. The Tzu Chi Foundation is a Buddhist organization founded in 1966 by a young Buddhist nun named Cheng Yen in a remote area of Hualien in east Taiwan. Under Master Cheng Yen's guidance, the Tzu Chi Foundation has gradually become an influential international organization with over 5 million supporters and over 30,000 certified commissioners around the globe. http://www.tzuchi.org.tw/global

23. In 2005, Yang Ju-men was sentenced by a district court to seven and a half years for "planting" bombs that were sprinkled with rice and attached with notes such as "oppose rice imports" in public places throughout Taipei. Eventually, six of the bombs went off; thankfully, no one was hurt. During the appeals process, the Taiwan High Court in 2006 reduced the jail term to five years and 10 months, plus a fine of NT$100,000. President Chen Shui-bian later gave a special pardon to Yang.

24. The Ministry of Interior's data shows that the number of Taiwanese choosing foreign spouses had increased annually since 1987 until peaking in 2003 at 31.85% of all marriages. By the end of last year, the number of foreign spouses in Taiwan had increased to 365,000 individuals, while the percentage of unmarried Taiwanese men fell from 39.04% to 37.55%. The percentage of single women, however, increased from 29.80 to 31.18%. http://www.taipeitimes.com/News/taiwan/archives/2007/11/06/2003386433.

25. http://www.formosa319.org/migrants/ (in Chinese)
http://www.tiwa.org.tw/ (in Chinese)
http://www.coolloud.org.tw/node/166 (in Chinese)

REFERENCES

Allman, P. (2001). *Critical education against global capitalism: Karl Marx and revolutionary critical education.* Bergin & Garvey.

Amin, S. (1997). *Capitalism in the age of globalization: The management of contemporary society.* London and New York: Zed.

Apple, M. (2001). *Educating the "right" way Markets, standards, God and inequality.* New York and London: RoutledgeFalmer.

Apple, M. W., Kenway, J., & Singh, M. (Eds.). (2005). *Globalizing education: Policies, pedagogies, & politics.* New York: Peter Lang.

Aronowitz, S. (2001). *The knowledge factory: Dismantling the corporate university and creating true higher learning.* : Boston, MA: Beacon Press.

Ball, S. J. (1990). *Politics and policy making in education: Explorations in policy sociology.* London: Routledge.

Ball, S. J. (1994). *Education reform: A critical and post-structural approach.* Buckingham, United Kingdom: Open University Press.

Bok, D. (2003). *Universities in the marketplace: The commercialization of higher education.* Princeton and Oxford: Princeton University Press.

Burbules, N., & Torres, C. A. (Eds.). (2000). *Globalization and education: Critical perspectives.* New York and London: Routledge.

Carnoy, M., Elmore, R., & Siskin, L. S. (Eds.). (2003). *The new accountability.* New York: RoutledgeFalmer.

Chan-Tiberghien, J. (2004). Toward a global educational justice research paradigm: cognitive justice, decolonizing methodologies and critical pedagogy. *Globalization, Societies and Education, 2*(2), 191–213.

Chen, K. H. (2006). *De-imperialism: Asia as method.* Taipei: Flaneur. (in Chinese)

Fitzsimons, P. (1999). Managerialism and education. *Encyclopedia of Philosophy of Education.* Retrieved from http://www.ffst.hr/ENCYCLOPEDIA/managerialism.htm.

Freire, P. (1985). *The politics of education: Culture, power and liberation* (D. Macedo, Trans.). South Hadley, MA: Bergin and Garvey.

Giddens, A. (1998). *The third way: The renewal of social democracy.* Cambridge, United Kingdom: Polity.

Giddens, A. (2000). *The third way and its critics.* Cambridge, United Kingdom: Polity.

Glasius, M., Kaldor, M., & Anheier, H. (Eds.). (2006). *Global civil society 2005/6.* London: Sage.

Green, A. (1997). *Education, globalization and the national state.* London: Macmillan Press Ltd.

Habermas, J. (1973). *Legitimization crisis.* (T. McCarthy, Trans.). Cambridge, United Kingdom: Polity.

Harvey, D. (2006). *Spaces of global capitalism.* New York: Verso.

Hill, D. (2003). Global neo-liberalism, the deformation of education and resistance. *Journal for Critical Education Policy Studies, 1*(1). Retrieved from http://www.iceps.com/print.php?articlesID=7

Ho, M. S. (2006). The politics of preschool education vouchers in Taiwan. *Comparative Education Review, 50*(1), 66–89.

Hsiao, H. H. (ed.) (2000) Non-profit Sector: Organisation and Operations. Taipei: Chu Liu. (in Chinese)

Hu, J. C. (Ed.). (1994). *Quiet revolutions: On Taiwan, Republic of China.* Taipei: Kwang Hwa.

Jan, C. Y. (2006). *The challenge of public policy in Taiwan; The governance of the new right.* Retrieved from http://www.npf.org.tw/

Kenway, J. (1994). *Economizing education: The post-Fordist directions.* Geelong, Victoria: Deakin University Press.

Lee, J. F., & VanPatten, B. (2003). *Making communicative language teaching happen* (2nd ed.). New York: McGraw-Hill.

Lee, S. J. S., & Wang, H. L. (2006). *Critical pedagogy: The explorations in Taiwan.* Taipei: Psychology. (in Chinese)

Lee, Y. K. (2005). New government, new language? The third way discourse in Taiwan. *Modern Asian Studies, 39*(3), 631–660.

McLaren, P. (2005). *Capitalists and conquerors: A critical pedagogy against empire.* Lanham, Maryland: Rowman and Littlefield.

McLaren, P., & Farahmandpur, R. (2005). *Teaching against global capitalism and the new imperialism.* Lanham, Maryland: Rowman & Littlefield.

McMichael, P. (2004). *Development and social change: A global perspective* (3rd ed.). Thousand Oaks, CA: Sage.

Mulderrig, J. (2003). Consuming education: A critical discourse analysis of social actors in New Labour's education policy. *Journal for Critical Education Policy Studies, 1*(1). Retrieved from http://www.iceps.com/pageID=article&articleID=2.

Offe, C. (1984). *Contradictions of the welfare state.* London: Hutchinson.

Rikowski, G. (2001). *The battle in Seattle.* London: Tufnell Press.

Robertson, R. (1995). Glocalization: Time–space and homogeneity–heterogeneity. In M Featherstone, S. Lash, & R. Robertson (Eds.), *Global modernities* (pp. 25–44). London: Sage.

Slaughter, S., & Leslie, L. L. (1997). *Academic capitalism: Politics, policies, and the entrepreneurial university.* Baltimore, MD: Johns Hopkins University Press.

Stromquist, N. P. (2002). *Education in a globalized world: The connectivity of economic power, technology and knowledge.* Lanham, MD: Rowman & Littlefield.

Suarez-Orozco, M. M., & Qin-Hilliard, D. B. (Eds.). (2004). *Globalization: Culture and education in the new millennium.* CA: University of California Press.

Tai, H. H., Mok, K. H., & Shieh, A. B. (Eds.). (2002). *The marketization of higher education: Comparison study of Taiwan, Hong Kong and China.* Taipei: Higher Education Press. (in Chinese).

Tang, C. P. (2004). When new public management runs into democratization: Taiwan public administration in transition. *Issues and Studies, 40*(3/4), 59–100.

Tang, K. L. (2005, June). *Post-crisis East Asian social policy: In search for a new foundation for welfare.* Paper presented in the Conference of Cross-strait Social Welfare Institutions, Wuhan, China.

The Task Group of Reflexivity Conference. (2006). *Globalization and knowledge production: Critical reflexivity on the practices of academic evaluation in Taiwan.* Taipei: Taiwan Sociological Forum. (in Chinese).

Walsh, K. (1995). *Public services and market mechanisms: Competition, contracting and the new public management.* New York: St. Martin's Press.

Wang, H. L. (1999). *Higher education reform and 1994 new university law in Taiwan—A sociological exploration of education policy.* Unpublished doctoral dissertation, University of Wales, Cardiff, United Kingdom.

Wang, H. L. (2007). Education and the discussions on globalization: Between "winning the competition" and "social justice." *Chinese Education and Society, 40*(1), 22–35.

Whitaker, C., Sousa Santos, B., & Cassen, B. (2006). The world social forum: Where do we stand and where are we going? In M. Glasius, M., Kaldor, & H. Anheier (Eds.), *Global civil society 2005/6* (pp. 64–86). London: Sage.

Yeh, C. J. (1991). *The social logic of institutions.* Taipei: Tung-Da. (in Chinese).

9   Israel: Neoliberal and Nationalist Education
Toward a Political Pedagogy

Aura Mor-Sommerfeld, Ehud Adiv, and Arnon Dunetz

All (by and large, happiness) is not theirs it seems:
One fatal tree there stands of knowledge called,
Forbidden them to taste: knowledge forbidden?
Suspicious, reasonless. Why should their Lord
Envy them that? Can it be sin to know,
Can it be death? And do they only stand
By ignorance, is that their happy state,
The proof of their obedience and their faith?
O fair foundation laid whereon to build
Their ruin! Hence I will excite their minds
With more desire to know.
   (John Milton, *Paradise Lost*, IV, 1667, pp.513–524)

INTRODUCTION

It seems that the current consensus among most critical researchers and scholars in Israel is that critical pedagogy is the ultimate answer to the positivist, one-dimensional perspective and teaching of capitalism. However, very little attention has been paid to the political perspective and to political pedagogy in particular, within educational systems. The new Age of Neoliberalization and Globalization makes this discussion both relevant and crucial. The aim of this chapter is to present the educational system in Israel and to suggest a political perspective to analyze it.

Henry Giroux (1991) defines what he calls "critical pedagogy" as a synthesis of the best ideas of modernism and post-modernism (i.e., of rational positivist modernism and critical relativistic post-modernism). In other words, according to Giroux, critical pedagogy should restrain the global pace of modernity by highlighting alternative ways of learning that are specific, historical, and social. We, on the contrary, suggest a new perspective of political pedagogy as an alternative for achieving a truly universal society as the realization of the common capacity of people as political beings.

Generally speaking, we believe that conscious political praxis *by and for* the people, as the unified object and subject of history, is an emancipated alternative to the economic pace of modernity. Our criticism is directed against both the global materialism and the cultural particularism of post-modernism and post-colonialism, the two extremes of hegemonic world order. In other words, it is directed against the material objectives (*Dingheit*) of economic activity and the subjective aspects of cultural identity.

Historically, it was by means of traditional culture and religious belief that people raised themselves to higher levels. People were able to transcend their individuality and find some self-satisfaction vis-à-vis the totalitarian political world. However, in the ancient world people were still only "in themselves" precisely because individuals were not spiritually free and consequently did not recognize themselves as such. The modern nation-state, or, as Gellner (1983, 1992) called it, "the marriage of politics and culture," is simultaneously, philosophically speaking, the historical unity of subject and object. To rephrase Hegel, politics is the real incorporation of being with thought, the finite with the infinite (Millar, 1969).

Thus, in opposition to the power of American globalization and the cultural particularism of post-modernism, we consider what can make people transcend their unmediated "self love" by "exciting their minds with more desire to know" and to act (Ake, 1997; Adiv, 2005). Education, as we see it, can be the medium by which this can and should happen; and for Israel, this transformation is most urgent and crucial.

This chapter presents the Israeli education system as a case study for examining and suggesting political perspectives of education in the age of Neoliberalization and globalization. The first part shows how the educational system has adopted the ideologies and cultural subjectivism of national patriotism to establish ideology of segregation and links it to the competitive approach of Neoliberalism. The second part considers the general implications of left-radical political approach, discussing how it can challenge mainstream educational systems today. By that, we hope to elaborate on the basic assumption of Marxism regarding education in general and the Israeli education system in particular.

THE EDUCATIONAL SYSTEM IN ISRAEL: REFLECTING THE REALITY

In the following sections, we discuss a variety of aspects that we find crucial to understanding and analyzing the situation in Israel. We begin with a general background—information about economic procedures related to schools, and depiction of the educational system focusing on language and curricula. Relying on historiography, we analyze the connection between language, education, and the national ideology that controls the educational system, and examine the economic agenda of Israel's governments before referring to critical approaches to education in Israel. Then we discuss bilingual education as a possible alternative (i.e., a political alternative to the current segregated system in Israel, that is, segregation of Jews and Arabs, as well as to American Globalization).

BACKGROUND

Israel was established in 1948, after 28 years of British Mandate government, and became essentially a multilingual country with a multicultural society. Eras of colonization and imperialist rule plunged the area into conflicts and bloodshed, affecting the whole society in general and the educational system in particular.

Historical developments have created a unique and complicated situation in the country. Two populations with two different languages live in the same state. These are the Israeli-Jews, who speak Hebrew, though this language is not necessarily their mother tongue, and the Arab-Palestinian population, whose mother tongue is Arabic, though most of them also speak Hebrew. The foundation of the Israeli State has thus created a paradoxical situation in regard to language. Hebrew is the language of the Israeli majority, but it is a minority language in the Middle East. Arabic, the language of Israel's minority population, is a majority language in the Middle East, and is accepted as a world language to some extent.

In the course of time, various populations with different mother tongues and backgrounds have joined the Israeli-Jewish Hebrew speakers. Thus, a set of complicated relationships exists between the two main populations in Israel—the Hebrew speakers and the Arabic speakers: These two populations live separately and together at the same time. There are separate cities, small towns, and villages for each community. Only a few cities have both populations, and even those generally inhabit separate neighborhoods; and community life also includes separate schools. Nevertheless, although the two populations interface in some areas—at work, in public institutions (hospitals, government offices, football stadiums, universities, etc.), through cultural events or, in some cases, in political activities—the basic general status is one of segregation.

The ongoing conflict between Israelis and Palestinians affects not just everyday life but, and mainly, the educational system. The most dramatic events, the expulsion of 700,000 Palestinians during the 1948 War[1] and the demolishing of more than 400 of their villages, have given rise to hostile relationships between the two nations (Svirsky et al., 2007). This is the core majority–minority relationship, which obviously comes into play in education.

The educational system in Israel is basically public, and schools are controlled by the Ministry of Education.[2] Under this control and supervision there are two separate systems—one for Arabic speakers and one for Hebrew speakers. There are very few private schools for Hebrew speakers. Those for

Arabic speakers are usually established by the churches and attached to them. This means that Palestinian citizens of Israel and Jews are educated in separate schools, each with its own particular culture, religion, and linguistic heritage. A few Arabic-speaking families choose to send their children to Hebrew schools (this appears to be on the increase), but the reverse is unheard of. However, there is no official record of numbers in respect of this phenomenon (Mor-Sommerfeld et al., 2007).

There is also a variety of streams and divisions within each main sector. The Jewish-Israeli (Hebrew) sector's main division is of secular (state) and religious streams, while the religious schools are also divided into orthodox and state-religious. As concerns the Arabic-Palestinian schools—their situation is one of *divide et impera*: Druze and Bedouin are separated from the general Arab sector. Additionally, for many years Arab teachers and educators were questioned by the security services in Israel about their political attitudes and activities before receiving permission to teach in the state system. Obviously, the separation also applies to teachers, parents, and regular staff in schools, and impinges on the courses in teacher-training colleges.

A small framework of bilingual—Arabic-Hebrew—schools has been developing over the last few years. There is no doubt that these are radical streams, not only in the educational system, but probably also in Israeli society, which we discuss in a later section.

Education in Israel cannot be defined only by its degree of adherence to purely Jewish nationalism. There is, for example, a network of "democratic schools" across the country. To date, there are about thirty schools of this kind, two of which are Arabic L1 (first language). Although these schools claim their educational innovativeness from a democratic point of view and as respecting people on the basis of the universal Declaration of Human Rights, they work and act within the current system that separates Hebrew and Arabic speakers. The concept of segregation according to identities dominates education. Borders are, however, sometimes crossed, so that this division is not absolutely rigid.

The aforementioned then explores pluralism within Israel's diverse society, together with control and hegemony, and its socio-political reality.

NEOLIBERALISM

The economic agenda of Israeli governments is not detached from political–economical–educational changes that occurred worldwide in the last few decades. This is reflected best by a fundamental change in policy from a situation in which the state defines itself as the sole provider of its children's education to one in which the state seeks to shift this responsibility to private agencies or local authorities. This is mainly related to promoting big businesses and privatization, while diminishing social responsibility and avoiding implementing programs to promote equality.

According to leading neoliberal guidelines, such as that of the Reagan and Thatcher administrations in the United States and United Kingdom respectively, "the Adam Smith assumption" of the optimal market guided by an "invisible hand," which produces the right amounts and variety of products, is the cornerstone of the "liberalized" attitude, aspiring for a government to reduce its involvement to a minimum. Depending on the government to create full employment will bring about high inflation and price stability causing unemployment; and "market forces" are the natural and most effective means for lowering prices and for higher employment, through competition and the desire of each individual organization for self-excellence. Unemployment mainly benefits those who make their profit at the expense of their employees. Employees in a market characterized by high unemployment are fearful of asking for better work conditions and are expected to be grateful for just having a job. The free market of today is easily dictated by one of the most prudent manifestations of the neoliberal world.

SCHOOL BUDGETS

During the first three decades of the state's existence, the education budget generally increased, as a result of massive growth in the school population and the reforms of 1968, making secondary school education practically universal and prompting the massive construction of schools. In the 1970s, the education budget increased at a rate of 10% a year in the first half of the decade and 7% a year in the second. In 1980, this trend was reversed, and a reduction period had begun. The education budget was provisionally increased, with the immigration waves from the former Soviet Union and Ethiopia, but as the immigration eased, in 1996, the education budget was once again reduced. During the second Intifada (2001–2006), when the state budget underwent unprecedented slashing, the education budget was also affected: Teaching hours were cut by 19% per student in this period.

The consequences of these budget cutbacks are increased expenditure on education by households, shifting responsibilities from the authorities onto private households. Between 1986–1987 and 2001, the proportion spent on education by the average household increased from 3.8% to 6.1% of the total family consumption. This increase reflected the large burden on the household, now required to finance more and more activities that, in the past, had been funded by the state. The extent of the school system's reliance on the "private pocket" is expressed by the increase in household spending on education, in comparison with the general increase in household spending: between 1986–1987 and 2001, average consumer spending increased in real terms by 11% per household, while spending on education increased 78% per household. No doubt, the greater reliance on private funding leads to deepening gaps in education. In wealthy towns, students enjoy private funding, which compensates for diminishing public funds. In contrast to this, in low-income neighborhoods and towns, parents cannot afford supplementary education, and schools rely solely on the state budget.

NEOLIBERALISM IN THE ISRAELI EDUCATION SYSTEM

The percentage of children per capita in Israel is the highest in the western world (38% of the population is 18 and under). Since 1997, the number of students in Israel has grown by 33% percent. Following the failure of the Oslo Peace Accord in 1999–2000, a steady process of abolishing the social and democratic nature of the country has begun, eroding its welfare nature. Until 2000, all citizens of Israel were entitled to free public education, ensured and protected by law, including empowerment programs for poor and marginalized populations.

As part of the new reform, Israeli municipalities started implementing a new system called The Self Management of Schools. This somewhat sterile expression actually meant that school principals were now to function as company directors, having to raise funds for their school on their own and take care of a balanced budget, as if school is to function as a business. This self-management process was followed by an additional policy, during which the distribution of resources to schools was made solely according to equal distribution of resources to schools according to the number of students each school had, neglecting other parameters altogether, instead of a more sophisticated and socially conscious distribution based on each school's particular needs and unique parameters. Despite the fact that basic education was still free, this reform actually meant that in wealthy areas, mainly in the prosperous center of the country, when a school ran out of funds, parents were asked to pay for their children's education. In other places, where parents could not afford to pay, the students received considerably fewer class hours, no field trips, and lower standard of education, although they were funded equally. Having the standard of education lowered meant that more students dropped out, and schools now received even lower funding in areas where more investment in education was most needed.

COMMERCIALIZATION OF EDUCATION

In accordance with the new neoliberal trend, and as part of the self-management and self fund-raising policy, schools in Israel were encouraged to rent their facilities (classrooms, gymnasiums, etc.) for after-school hours and during school vacations. As the center of Israel is characterized by high cost and well-off populations, the business of renting out school classrooms and workshops went very well. Many workshops and night courses for adults and adolescents rent the empty classrooms and halls at very high rates. The situation is quite different in the periphery, where poverty is a fact of life, and it is much more difficult for the schools to rent their rooms to different private companies, and when they do succeed, the money they receive is considerably lower. In addition, children in these neighborhoods often do not have many playgrounds and playfields, and usually use the schoolyards in the afternoons instead, which is denied them each time the schools are rented, often meaning their only playgrounds are the streets. This has a chain effect, as children in need of supervision means that women, especially single mothers, have to stay at home very often at after school hours, to look after their children, compromising their opportunity to make a decent living.

The neoliberal climate in the country does not miss a chance, and private companies have discovered the lucrative opportunities in schools by donating to schools, and in exchange, having their commercial products and services promoted at schools, even inside the classes. Most companies prefer, of course, to promote their products at the wealthy and more rewarding schools, located in the center. Less rich schools have to agree to have companies' representatives teach in their schools, including reference to their companies' products, convincing boys and especially girls that they must consume certain products, in order to feel like competent, significant, and worthy individuals. Since successful results were shown in achieving self-management goals, at least where it did, this process of commercialization of education, with the commodification of schools grounds and curriculum and the apparent gender bias, was not questioned and was accepted as legitimate and adequate by teachers, school principals, and the Education Ministry experts who advised and assisted them. The embrace by the Israeli government of this management program has actually created a "grey" education system that allowed parents who can afford it to buy quality education for their children, while parents with fewer economic means have to compromise on schools and a standard of education that will not allow their children the option of entering the higher educational system if they choose to.

LANGUAGE EDUCATION AND CURRICULA IN ISRAEL

Educational policies and curricula derive from a socio-political reality. In Israel, this means that both Hebrew L1 (first language) and Arabic L1 schools derive from the Zionist origins of the State and its logic of separation.

The school curriculum is always in Hebrew for Hebrew schools and Arabic for Arab schools. In some subjects they differ in content (e.g., literature, religion, tradition), while in others the programs are similar (e.g., sciences, citizenship). The marked difference is in the cultural and historical approaches (Benavot & Resh, 2003; Al-Haj, 2002, 2005). Hebrew-speaking students receive extensive courses in Judaism and Jewish and Israeli history. Palestinian history and culture are not taught in Arab schools in Israel. Asymmetry is also "reflected in the allocation of teaching hours in the two streams for world history, Arab history and Jewish history" (Al-Haj, 2002, p. 175). While Arabic speakers receive extensive schooling in Hebrew, and regard Hebrew literature and tradition as part of their curricula, Hebrew students have no programs concerning Arabic literature or tradition in theirs. Hebrew students read Arabic literature only in translation (some books, edited for Hebrew L1 lessons, contain short stories written by Arab authors). Very few schools do so privately, and serious exposure to Arab-Palestinian culture can be found only at occasional events or by the enterprise of local school principals or supervisors (Bar-Tal, 2004).

All L1 (first language) Arabic children study Hebrew as a second language as part of their general curriculum and formal education. This is not the case with Arabic for Hebrew L1 students. Naturally, the results of such a policy have a great deal of influence on children's attitudes from both communities, not just concerning each other's language, but also about each other's beliefs, rights, and emotions (Spolsky & Shohamy, 1999; Amara & Mari, 2002).

Hebrew as a Second Language

In Arab schools, students begin studying Hebrew as a second language in 3rd grade (at first 3 to 4 times a week, later 4 to 5 times a week). Some schools start teaching oral Hebrew in 2nd grade. Since knowledge of Hebrew is vital for acquiring higher education and social or economic status in the Israeli community, the Palestinian-citizen-of-Israel student's attitude toward Hebrew is generally positive, though it is impossible to generalize in this regard. Considering the various factors influencing acquisition of a second language, most Arab students do much better in Hebrew than in other languages (Brosh, 1996; Mor-Sommerfeld et al., 2007).

Arabic as a Second Language

The status of Arabic as a second language for Hebrew students is a little vague, and there is a discrepancy between the official or desired policy and the field, arising among other things, from upheavals connected with the status of Arabic and attitudes toward it. For many years, Arabic was regarded as the language of the enemy, and learning it, for Hebrew speakers, was connected to the need "to know the enemy." Very few believed in needing "to know their neighbour's language" (Mor-Sommerfeld, 2005), though from time to time, the idea reemerges. Indeed, official documents recommend studying Arabic, and the beginning of the peace process between Israel and the Palestinians emphasizes the importance of studying this language. In the schools, however, nothing much has changed. In general, Hebrew students do not study Arabic. If they do, it is usually for no more than 1 to 3 hours a week. Some schools offer Arabic as a second language in study groups but, as stated earlier, studying Arabic as a second language is still largely due to the enterprise of principals or supervisors. The fact that there are so few L2 Arabic students may be why only 6% of Hebrew students are examined in the Israeli matriculation test (Brosh, 1996).

THE SCHOOL CURRICULA: THE IDEOLOGY OF NATIONALISM

Educational policies and curricula in Israel derive from the Zionist origins of the State of Israel, and this is true for all sectors. This was obviously also true for Jewish and Israeli studies that interpreted the Zionist ideology. The categorical falsity lies here, in trying to explain Israeli history in terms of Jewish ethnic identity, or what Hans Kohn (1967) calls Jewish "organic nationalism." To paraphrase E. H Carr (1961), the question is not what Israeli history really was, but how this history has been reconstructed not just by the Israeli school curricula but by the completely educational system.

The historiographic argument is the foundation of our discussion. Israeli school curricula identify Zionism and the State of Israel as the "telos" of Jewish history. That is to say, Israeli history is "teleological" (i.e., read in a linear process, instead of reading it from the bottom up, as an historical process that could be interpreted differently). The relevance and importance of this issue lies mainly in the context of mainstream Israeli education, according to which it was the Jewish people who single-mindedly determined Israeli history and consequently established the State of Israel. Historically, it was the Zionist hardliner militaristic leadership that prevailed in the unique historical circumstances of the Second World War, the power struggle against the other more enlightened and moderate Zionist currents, as well as against the forces of the Palestinian national movement. Israeli history should thus be read *politically* (i.e., in the context of what Gramsci [1991] called "the unity of the historical process," rather than *ideologically*, in terms of the dominant Jewish national discourse).

A short survey of the Israeli historiographical and educational books reveals that they claimed for Zionism what Hobsbawm (1989) calls "the status of a nation a priori," or what Smith (1991) defines as "a community of common descent." The State of Israel was thus classified as a spontaneous revival of an ancient people, by itself and for itself, independently of the social and political conditions of the first half of the 20th Century. Consequently, Israel is represented as a national revival deriving from Eastern European Jewish conditions at the turn of the century. To use Max Weber's typology, the establishment of the State of Israel is mainly defined there as a value-rationale action, i.e., is motivated by conviction of an absolute end regardless of possible cost (Gerth and Mills, 1974). Accordingly, the Israeli settlers were portrayed as *Halutzim* (pioneers) precisely because they acted on their Jewish national convictions regardless of possible cost to themselves and, what is worse, to others.

One of the earliest textbooks to put forward the Zionist ideological perspective was *Toldot Hatzionut: Tnuat Hatekhiya Vehageula Beisrael* (History of Zionism—the Movement of Revival and Redemption in Israel) published in 1940. The author, Baruch Ben-Yehuda, was a prominent figure in the Zionist educational system. In 1947–1948, he headed the educational department of the *Va'ad Leumi* (the National Council) and later became the first director of the Ministry of Education and Culture. In fact, Ben-Yehuda, both as a scholar and as a political activist, played a major role in what Hobsbawm (1989) and Gellner (1983) called "the invention" of Jewish nationalism (i.e., the Jewish nationalist doctrine of the State). He was among those who created the nationalist ideology as a writer, and practiced and disseminated this ideological invention as a pedagogue, headmaster, and director of the Zionist-Israeli education system. As such, his study represents the nationalist-ideological orientation of the Israeli education system, shaping the Jewish nationalist viewpoint of further generations of Israeli scholars.

Other examples are David Vital's *The Origins of Zionism* (1975), and *Zionism, The Formative Years* (1982). Vital's studies epitomize the "value-rationale" paradigm of Israeli historiographical textbooks according to which Zionism is the fulfillment of the Jewish past. His first chapter is "Exile, Return and Redemption." Zionism is perceived by Vital in terms of Jewish Messianism, the return of the Jews after years of exile, and their consequent redemption. He traces the origin of Zionism in Jewish history rather in the historical context of the Zionist movement itself. In his preface he argues that the history of the Jewish People is long and complex and does not lend itself to discussion in the terms in which the histories of other nations, however ancient, are, by conviction, conceived. Vital obviously considers only the Jewish past, and consequently overlooks the autonomous involvement of the Zionist movement itself. In other words, Israeli history is glorified in the Israeli education system as the national revival of Eastern European Jewry. Thus, its subject matter is the Jewish origins of Israel, rather than Israel–Palestine as a modern political society.

Yet the difficulty with the presentation of these books is the modern invention of Israel as a metaphysical teleology of Jewish history. Zionism's concern was to reconstruct the semi-feudal decentralized Ottoman province of Palestine, and transform it into a modern centralized nation-state. The historical past, inasmuch as it determines the present, is simultaneously determined by it. Hence, as a political phenomenon, Israel is inevitably the Jewish historical past articulated and re-articulated in terms of the historical context of Ottoman and Mandate Palestine in the first half of the 20th century. *Post factum* it is evident that, in reality, the Zionist settlers' attitude could be better defined in terms of "rational expedient" (i.e., a type of action that corresponds rather more to a modern capitalist society than to the old-new Jewish community).

Indeed, the founders of Zionism were inspired by the notion of a Jewish national identity. But, Jewish national identity, "like everything which is historical" is inevitably interpreted and reinterpreted in the political terms of its time and place. In other words, Zionist-Israeli history is glorified in the Israeli education system as the national revival of Eastern European Jewry. Thus, their subject matter is the Jewish origins of Zionism, rather than Zionism as a modern political phenomenon or entity in what Gramsci (1991) called "the Historical Block" of Ottoman and Mandate Palestine. Following the 1967 War, there has been an on going attempt by the mainstream writers to revive and reconstruct the old Zionist ethos, and simultaneously, an attempt by the critical writers to undermine that ethos. That is to say, a critical attempt to redefine the Israeli identity as it really became after 1967 vis-à-vis the Palestinians, rather than as it was before 1967, as a Jewish entity, in and of itself. Thus, the 1967 War aroused an internal dispute that has since divided the Israeli intelligentsia. Mainstream still defines the State of Israel in the spiritual terms of "a Jewish defensive ethos," while the critics see it the other way round (i.e., they explain Israeli identity in the light of the new circumstances created by the 1967 War).

In the 1980s, new critical studies, such as Benny Morris's *The Birth of the Palestinian Refugees Problem* (1987) and Ilan Pappe's *The Making of the Arab-Israeli Conflict* (1992), represent a qualitative shift in Israeli historiography and, consequently, in the Israeli ideological discourse. Works of the "New Historians" appeared alongside the works of the "Post-Zionist" sociologists and political scientists who suggested a critical analysis and/or deconstruction of the old ideological discourse. Accordingly, they proposed what Uri Ram (1995) called a "critical sociology" (i.e., sociopolitically oriented analysis of Zionist-Israeli subject matter). Our work should thus be viewed mainly in the context of the works of these writers who criticize Israeli schools for their failure to discuss the significance of the Israeli–Arab conflict. The more recent approach has integrated Jewish Israelis and the Palestinians, citizens of Israel, into a single analytical framework, a major category of Israeli–Palestinian subject matter.

In light of the above, the curriculum for Arabic schools has been even more problematic. In general, the national discourse has played a unified and progressive role. In Europe, national languages developed from bottom up after the invention of the printing press, and later on the popular literature and the press (Gellner, 1983; Anderson, 1991; Hobsbawm, 1989). In the case of Israel, Hebrew pushed the popular Arabic language aside, symbolic of the Zionist hegemonic ideology. Moreover, within the political circumstances of the conflict with the Palestinian people, the new Jewish national entity was in complete contrast to the Palestinians, who were represented in the Israeli textbooks as stereotypically oriental, backward, and violent. Thus, from the very beginning of the state, the Palestinians in Israel were excluded from the nation-building process precisely because they were represented as a part of the Arab world, the ultimate "other" (El Kudsy, 1970).

Following Marx and Weber, Horkheimer (1947) distinguished between conservative and radical doctrines. A conservative doctrine, Horkheimer explained, argues for compliance and conformity with reality as we know it. Radical doctrines are motivated by imaginative and/or teleological perspectives, and their task is to criticize the world for the purpose of improving it. Moreover, the former is forced upon the society from above as an integral form of a natural\moral\divine or scientific "given," whereas the latter comes from below as an articulation of society's "general will." From this, we can deduce that the Israeli educational discourse fits into the frame of reference of the conservative doctrines. Following the Jewish national ideology, it is an attempt to reconstruct and/or to redefine Israeli history and society in ethnic\cultural terms, which aims at replacing the pluralistic Israeli–Palestinian society with an exclusively Jewish nation.

Stuart Hall (1988) argues that identity is not something that already exists, transcending place, time, history, and culture. Cultural identities comes from somewhere and have histories. But, like everything that is historical, they undergo constant transformation (Eriksen, 1993; Hobsbawn, 1996). Israeli educators and writers were indeed inspired by the Jewish identity. And yet, Jewish identity "like everything which is historical" was inevitably interpreted and reinterpreted by them in the political terms of their time and place. Subsequently, it was rather Jewish identity as it was for them, as agents of the hegemonic ideology.

The hegemonic ideology should be understood in the context of domination and power struggles in Israeli society, especially vis-à-vis the Palestinians. In this situation, the educational system is recruited in aid of militarism and domination. The paradox, in the case of Israel, derives from the fact that the Government of Israel is a dichotomy of globalization and militarist nationalism. Thus, 40 years after the 1967 War and the occupation of all Palestinian lands, the time has come to set aside the "Jewish defensive ethos" and to make the Israeli–Palestinian conflict the real starting point and focus of Israeli political and historiographical discourse.

CRITICAL APPROACHES TO THE ISRAELI EDUCATIONAL SYSTEM

Since the early 1980s, critical approaches—*humanist pedagogy, critical* or *resistant pedagogy,* and *multiculturalism*—to education in Israel have been discussed by researchers and educators, all of them Jewish Israelis, Hebrew first-language speakers (e.g., Aloni, 1997; Gur-Ze'ev, 1999; Yona, 1998, 2005, and others). These scholars, although criticizing not just the educational system but Israeli society in general, still use the Jewish national curriculum, constructed by mainstream scholars. Accordingly, the discourse of these studies remains within the dominant context, viewing Israeli society in what Kimmerling (1995) called "a sociological vacuum" (i.e., as an historical and cultural Jewish *Volk* existing independently of the *realpolitik* of the conflict with the Palestinians, the indigenous people of the country). Let us examine these approaches.

The *humanist pedagogy* approach (Aloni, 1997) captures the individual perfection as the means to educate Israeli society as a whole. As rational, enlightened scholars, its agents are aware of the oppressive character of Israeli society. In light of Kant's purely subjective reasoning, they believe that by means of education they can rationalize the Israelis as individuals.

However, the main problem has remained—after more than half a century—Israel is still in a constant state of war and conflict; so that the question is, as Marx asked, who would educate the educators? Certainly, one cannot humanize and enlighten Israeli society single handedly. It seems that instead of describing in idealistic terms the humanistic perspective as the "must" and "ought" of the Israeli education or its telos, the best thing would be to analyze and to explain the "is" of the Israeli political circumstances; the circumstances that determine the education and prevent it from achieving the humanist ideal (Marx and Engels, 1968).

The "resistant pedagogy" or *critical pedagogy* is advanced as a kind of radical critique of the current state of the educational affairs. Following Horkheimer and Adorno (1970), Gur-Ze'ev (1999) criticizes Israel's political practice from a philosophical standpoint. He views education as the manifestation of the primacy of theory over politics, and consequently as a negation of the existing socio-economic circumstances. However, we have to remember that Adorno's *Negative Dialectics* (1990), which propose criticism for the sake of critics, an end in itself, leads nowhere precisely because practice, especially political practice, does matter.

Multiculturalism is proposed as an alternative to Israel's global economic pace of modernity that challenges occidental hegemony with the cultural identity of the Orient (Yona, 1998). Marx argued for the destruction of capitalism by means of internal political struggle, but multiculturalist writers in Israel are not so much engaged in opposing American globalization as in redefining its hybrid offspring (Marx and Engels, 1968; Adiv, 2005).

These new boundaries between opposing cultural identities derive from what Homi K. Bhabha (1996) called the "Third Space." In one of her major works, Gayatri Chakravarty Spivak (1988) asks, "Can the subaltern speak?" Similarly, in his *Orientalis*, Edward Said (1978) criticizes Marx for disregarding the "subalterns'" ability to represent themselves. He insists that globalization is basically a European invention, a post-modern version of the attitude that, during the colonial period, aimed to universalize Eurocentricity. In his own words:

Without examining *Orientalism* as discourse one can not possibly understand the enormously systematic discipline by which the European
culture was able to manage—and even to produce—the Orient. (Said,
1978, p. 3)

What matters for Said is the "Orientalist discourse," what Foucault (1972)
called a "governing statement." Globalization, he said, is merely how the
American and European cultural apparatus[3] has been covering Islam.
Accordingly, it is only the Orientalist discourse that produced the Orient,
the ultimate "other" of the Occident, passive and devoid of historicity. It
seems that Said, and agents of the multicultural approach in Israel (Yona
1998, 2005), viewed globalization as arbitrary, wrong, and immoral, as
glorifying western rationalism and modernity by ignoring their dark and
oppressive aspects.

In political terms, the difficulty with this approach lies in its pseudo-
libertarianism. In spite of some radical tones, multicultural education is
a kind of "libertarian" argument in favor of civil society (i.e., a simplistic
dichotomy between the arbitrariness of the state apparatus from above,
and the authentic Jewish oriental identity from below[4]). It is, then, the lack
of challenging the Jewish-nationalist hegemony among the critical pedagogic leaders in Israel that leads us to the understanding of the necessity of
a political–pedagogical approach to education.

Said (1978) and Spivak (1988) certainly present the new states of the
third world and the Orient vis-à-vis the dominant cultural apparatus of
the Occident. However, they fail to see that "we" (rather than "they") are
already living in a global world, and that we simply cannot speak in terms
of what **we were**. Instead, they insist that "**they**" (rather than "**we**") can
stop the clock, or even, as Fanon (1968) argued, turn it back in order to be
and be seen by virtue of what we **were** (Callinicos, 1999).

In this regard, one could ask what is the role of Palestinian citizens of
Israel, in criticism of Israeli policies in particular, and globalization in general?
Sadly, their critical response is rarely heard. When it is, it is usually a variant
of the Arab-nationalist discourse. This lack of any real Palestinian contribu-
tion deepens and reinforces the Zionist-national discourse, but a new, shared
Hebrew–Arabic voice is now being heard in Israel's bilingual schools.

BILINGUAL EDUCATION IN ISRAEL:
CHALLENGING THE REALITY

It seems that the most critical, and the only critical-political, approach to
the educational system in Israel is to be found within bilingual education.
To date, there are only four successful bilingual schools in Israel, all of
which define themselves as bilingual and binational. The first was set up in
1984 at Neve Shalom / Wahat al-Salaam (*Oasis of Peace*), a village founded

jointly by Israeli Jews and Palestinian citizens of Israel, to prove that the two peoples can live together peacefully. In 1998, another school was opened in the Galilee, and one year later a third school was opened in Jerusalem, both of them by "Hand in Hand" (NGO). In 2004, the most recent school opened in Wadi Ara, in cooperation with "The Bridge across the Wadi Fellowship" (NGO) and "Hand in Hand." These schools are integrated in the Israeli educational system even though they are the result of private and limited enterprise and have their own curricula and syllabus.

The schools have approximately equal numbers of Arabic and Hebrew L1 children and teachers *of* and *in* both languages, cultures, and narratives. In two of the schools, pedagogy was originally based on a cultural–cognitive model for bilingual education (Mor-Sommerfeld, 2005). According to this model, most lessons are initially run by two teachers, one Arabic L1 and the other Hebrew L1, each speaking and teaching in her or his first language. Bilingual education in these schools is not just about languages, but also about other people's history and culture (Amara, 2005).

The socio-historical narrative of both populations is crucial to the school curriculum. In fact, these are the only schools in Israel where both narratives are taught and learned to the same extent. This is not just a matter of bridging between people and cultures or societies and languages, but of sharing and building a community based on common interests and mutual concerns.

The bilingual pedagogy in these schools derives from critical pedagogy (Freire, 1970) and critical literacy approaches (Mor-Sommerfeld, 2004). Offering alternative modes of thought and behavior, both are at the core of bilingual education, inherent to it, and crucial for its development. Universal values of equality and mutual respect become not just slogans to hang on walls, but a way of life.

Bilingual education in Israel is thus about society and politics, people and narratives, needs and rights, dreams and visions, reality and challenge. It is about language and culture—Arabic and Hebrew—and about teaching, learning, and criticism, the means and the goal, not just for the Israeli educational system, but also for the Israeli society in general.

Several studies have been conducted in these schools in recent years (Amara, 2005; Bekerman, 2005; Bekerman & Shhadi, 2003; Bekerman & Horenczyk, 2004; Feuerverger, 2001; Mor-Sommerfeld, 2005). These studies indicate that there is a great deal of willingness to deal with the conflict and to talk, listen, and study the "past"—Palestinian and Israeli narratives alike. At the same time, these schools present an alternative, shared way of living and studying. However, so far, these schools do not seem to challenge the communities around them, so they remain within their own boundaries and discourse. It is thus to society's own benefit to change matters, and it is the role and duty of the educational system to motivate and effect such a change. Even so, a bilingual society can never be fully democratic if it separates communities and their languages. Wherever two languages exist concomitantly, progress toward bilingual education is inevitable. When these languages are used by both populations of the same area, this should be their modus vivendi, their hope for the future.

FROM CRITICAL PEDAGOGY TO POLITICAL PEDAGOGY—TOWARD A POLITICAL APPROACH IN EDUCATION IN ISRAEL

Politics is a realm that encompasses such "positive freedom," and people transcend themselves to become what Marx called "species-beings." In this section, we refer to some relevant theories and perspectives before addressing the political approach in education (Fleischer, 1973).

A person is a political animal, and the Polis, the modern state, is the realm in which she or he can express her or his potential as a rational being. The full actualization of globalization would be tantamount to an absolute and irrevocable bill of divorce from substantiate political freedom. Indeed, historically and conceptually, it is only the social states in the second half of the 20th century that succeed in controlling the capitalist system and set it in harmony with a moral-political perspective. As Habermas (1984/1987) put it, against the "instrumental" and "strategic" action that characterized the capitalist globalization, these states represent a communicative rationality underlying action that is aimed at mutual understanding, conceived as a process of reaching agreement between speaking subjects to harmonize their interpretations of the world.[5]

Evidently, as concerns education in Israel, the Jewish-versus-Arab approach leads nowhere. Global economy and Jewish national identity seem to be two aspects of the same reality within Israel. Thus, Giroux's "border pedagogy" is not a synthesis, but consists rather of thesis and antithesis that negate and oppose each other as "either but not both." As such, this is not a critical, but a conservative theory, precisely because of the absence of any emancipatory political perspective (Barber, 1995; Korten, 1996; Cohen and Rai, 2000).

What is lacking in Israeli education as suggested first by Plato and Aristotle, and later by Rousseau, and in the world at large is such a perspective. In Israel, capitalism undermines political emancipation by encouraging American globalization, consumerism, utilitarianism, and individualism. The Jewish–Arab dichotomy as the dominant discourse in Israeli education is indeed specific and divisive as compared to MacDonald's and Toyota (Poulantzas, 1968; Miliband, 1983; Freidman, 1998). However, only an Israeli–Palestinian republic could be a unifying and a progressive force against the antagonisms of Jewish and Arab patriotism on the one hand, and the hegemonic power of American globalization on the other. Thus, political education means constant efforts to rear our children in the rational critical spirit, manifesting itself in a political action.

In today's world, political education, as suggested first by Plato and Aristotle, and later by Rousseau, is highly significant. In Israel, the task is to create a Jewish–Arab patriotism for which the state embodies "communicative action," a realization of the "idea of good," a patriotism that replaces both American globalization and the particularism of Jew versus Arab. A "no" to segregation in education could be a first step toward this goal.

NOTES

1. For Israeli Jews: the War of Independence. For Arab-Palestinians: the *Nakbeh* (the disaster).
2. There are some Jewish religious streams that are not under the Educational Ministry's control, but are financially supported by the government.
3. Said borrowed this term from C. Wright Mills. However, for Wright Mills, the American "cultural apparatus"is mainly a representation and/or interpretation of the global hegemony of the "American Power Elite," whereas for Said the "cultural apparatus" is presented as the historical subject and as such, it is the point of departure.
4. One must say that this is, in fact, not liberal–conservative. It is "natural," "immediate" freedom; Rousseau's "State of Nature," as defined in terms of "immediacy"; except that here "culture" replaces primordial "nature." To be free is to be "culturally authentic" (i.e., to be authentic in the eyes of what Heidegger calls *Das Mann*). The way out of this estrangement is to be consciously at home in what is a protected and impregnable existence. The freedom of the culturist is to be consciously chained to his given cultural milieu.

REFERENCES

Adiv, U. (2005). The challenge of globalization for the left: Marxism, postcolonialism or republican nationalism. *Discourse of Sociological Practice, 7*, 1/2, 61–74.

Adorno, T. W. (1990). *Negative dialectics*. London: Routledge.

Ake, C. (1997). Dangerous liaisons: The interface of globalization and democracy (pp. 282–296). In A. Hadenius (Ed.), *Democracy's victory and crisis*. Cambridge, United Kingdom: Cambridge University Press.

Al-Haj, M. (2002). Multiculturalism in deeply divided societies: The Israeli case. *International Journal of Intercultural Relations, 26*, 169–183.

Al-Haj, M. (2005). National ethos, multicultural education, and the new history textbook in Israel. *Curriculum inquiry, 35*(1), 47–71.

Aloni, N. (1997). Aliyato unefilato shel hachinuch hahumanisti: mehaclassi la'postmoderni [The Rise and Fall of Humanistic Education: from Classicism to Post-Modernism]. In I. Gur-ze'ev (Ed.), *Chinuch be'idan ha'siach hapostmodernisti* (pp. 13–42). Jerusalem: Magnes.

Amara, M. (2005). *The bilingual education model of Hand-in-Hand*. Jerusalem: Hand in Hand, Centre for Jewish-Arab Education in Israel.

Amara, M., & Mari, A. (2002). *Language education policy: The Arab minority in Israel*. Dordrecht, Netherlands: Kluwer.

Anderson, B. (1991). *Imagined communities*. London: Verso.

Aristotle. (1959) *Politics*. London: Heron Books.

220 *Aura Mor-Sommerfeld, Ehud Adiv and Arnon Dunetz*

Barber, B. (1995). *Jihad vs. macworld: How globalism and tribalism are shaping the world*. New York: Times Books.

Bar-Tal, D. (2004). Nature, rationale: An effectiveness of education for coexistence. *Journal of Social Issues, 60*(2), 253–271.

Bauman, Z. (1998). *Globalization. The human consequences*. Cambridge, United Kingdom: Polity Press.

Bekerman, Z., & Horenczyk, G. (2004). Arab–Jewish bilingual coeducation in Israel: A long-term approach to intergroup conflict resolution. *Journal of Social Issues, 60*(2), 389–404.

Bekerman, Z., & Shhadi, N. (2003) Palestinian–Jewish bilingual education in Israel: Its influence on cultural identities and its impact on inter-group conflict. *Journal of Multilingual and Multicultural Development, 24*(6), 473–484.

Benavot, A., & Resh, N. (2003). Education governance, school autonomy, and curriculum implementation: A comparative study of Arab and Jewish schools in Israel. *Curriculum Studies, 35*(2), 171–196.

Ben-Yehuda, B. (1940). *Ttoldot hatzionut: Tnuat hatechiya ve'hageula be'israel*. [The History of Zionism—The movement of Revival and Redemption in Israel] Tel Aviv: Masada.

Bhabha, K. H. (1996). *Location of culture: Discussing post-colonial culture*. London: Routledge.

Brosh, H. (1996). Arabic to Hebrew speakers in Israel—"Second language" or "foreign language." *Helket Lashon, 23*, 111–131.

Callinicos, A. (1999). *Social theory*. Cambridge, United Kingdom: Polity Press.

Carr, H. E. (1961) *What is history?* New York: Vintage Books.

Cohen, R., & Rai, S. (Eds.). (2000). *Global social movements*. London: Athlon Press.

El Kudsy, A. (1970). *Nationalism and class struggles in the Arab world*. New York: MR.

Eriksen, T. H. (1993). *Ethnicity andnationalism*. London: Pluto Press.

Fanon, F. (1968). Wretched of the earth. New York: Grove Press.

Feuerverger, G. (2001). Oasis of dreams: Teaching and learning peace in a Jewish–Palestinian village in Israel. New York: Routledge.

Fleischer, H. (1973). *Marxism and history*. London: Penguin.

Foucault, M. (1972). *The archeology of knowledge*. New York: Pantheon Books.

Freidman, T. (1998). *The lexus and the olive tree*. Port Moody, Canada: Anchor.

Freire, P. (1970/1990). *Pedagogy of the oppressed*. New York: Seabury Press.

Gellner, E. (1983). *Nation and nationalism*. Oxford, United Kingdom: Blackwell.

Gellner, E. (1992). *Post-modernism, reason and religion*. London: Routledge.

Gerth, H. H., & Mills, C. W. (Eds.). (1974). *From Max Weber*. London: Routledge & Kegan Paul.

Giroux, H. A. (1991). *Border crossing: Culture workers and the politics of education*. London: Routledge.

Gramsci, A. (1991). *Selections from the prison notebooks*. London: Lawrence and Wishart.

Gur-Ze'ev, I. (1999). Philosophiya, politika ve'chinuch be'israel [Philosophy, Politics and Education in Israel]. Haifa, Israel: Haifa University Press.

Hall, S. (1988). *The hard road to renewal*. London: Verso.

Habermas, J. (1984/1987). *The theory of communicative action* (Vols. 1–2). Cambridge, United Kingdom: Polity Press.

Hobsbawm, E. (1989). *Nation and nationalism since 1789*. Cambridge, United Kigdom: Cambridge University Press.
Hobsbawm, E. (1996). Identity politics and the left. *New Left Review,* 39–50.
Horkheimer, M. (1947). *Eclipse of reason.* New York: Continuum.
Horkheimer, M., & Adorno, T. W. (1970). *Dialectic of enlightenment.* London: Allen Lane.
Kant, I. (1974). Toward perpetual peace. In C. M. Sherover (Ed.), *The development of the democratic idea* (pp. 272–292). New York: New American Library.
Kimmerling, B. (1995). Academic history caught in the crossfire: The case of the Israeli-Jewish historiography. *History and Memory, 7* (1) pp. 44–66. CO: Westview Press.
Kohn, H. (1967). *Prelude to nation-states: The French and German experience, 1789–1815.* Princeton: Van Ostrand.
Korten, D. C. (1996). *When corporations rule the world.* San Francisco, California: Berret-Koehler.
Marx, K., & Engels, F. (1968). *Selected writing.* New York: International.
Miliband, R. (1983). Debates on the state. *New Left Review, 138,* 57–68.
Millar, A. V. (1969). *Hegel's science of logic.* London: Allen and Unwin.
Morris, B. (1987). *The birth of the Palestinian refugees problem, 1947–1949.* Cambridge, United Kingdom: Cambridge University Press.
Mor-Sommerfeld, A. (2004). Into the future: towards a universal approach to cultural bilingualism. In J. Conteh, E. Gregory, C. Kearney and A. Mor-Sommerfeld, *On Writing Educational Ethnographies: The Art of Collusion* (pp. 167–172). Stoke-on-Trent, England: Trentham Books Limited.
Mor-Sommerfeld, A. (2005). Bilingual education in areas of conflict—bridging and sharing. *Race Equality Teaching, 24*(1), 31–42.
Mor-Sommerfeld, A., Azaiza, F,, & Hertz-Lazarowitz, R. (2007). Into the future—towards bilingual education in Israel—manifesto. *Education, Citizenship, Society Journal, 2*(1), 5–22.
Pappe, I. (1992). *The making of the Arab–Israeli conflict, 1947–1951.* London: I.B. Tauros.
Plato. (2000). *The republic.* New York: Dover.
Poulantzas, N. (1968). *Political power and social classes.* London: Verso.
Ram, U. (1995). *The changing agenda of Israeli society.* New York: State University of New York Press.
Rousseau, J. J. (1998). *The social contract.* Hertfordshire: Wordsworth Editions.
Said, E. (1978). *Orientalism.* London: Routledge & Kegan Paul.
Smith, A. D. (1991). *National identity.* London: Penguin.
Spivak, C. G. (1988). Can the Subaltern speak? In C. Nelson, & L. Grossberg (Eds.), *Marxism and the interpretation of culture* (pp. 271–313). Chicago: University of Illinois Press.
Spolsky, B., & Shohamy, E. (1999). *The languages of Israel: Policy, ideology and practice.* Clevedon, Avon, U. K.: Multilingual Matters.
Svirsky, M., Mor-Sommerfeld, A., Azaiza, F., & Hertz-Lazarowitz, R. (2007). Bilingual education and practical interculturalism in Israel. *The Discourse of Sociological Practice, 8*(1), 55–79.
Vital, D. (1975). *The origins of Zionism.* Oxford, United Kingdom: Clarendon.
Vital, D. (1982). *Zionism, the formative years.* Oxford, United Kingdom: Clarendon.
Weber, M. (1995). *The Protestant ethic and the spirit of capitalism.* London: Routledge.

Yona, Y. (1998). medinat kol ezracheha, medinat leom o demokratia rav-tarbutit: Israel ugvulot va'demokratia ha'liberalit [A state of its citizens, a nation state or a multicultural democracy: Israel and the liberal-democratic boundaries]. *Alpa'yim, 2000* (16), 238–263.

Yona, Y. (2005). *Be'zkhut hahevdel* [In Virtue of Difference]. Jerusalem: Van Leer.

10 Education in a One-Party "Democracy"
Singapore

Steve McKenna and Julia Richardson

INTRODUCTION

This chapter investigates developments in education in Singapore. Singapore is ostensibly a multi-party democracy but effectively functions as a one-party state, dominated since 1959 by the People's Action Party (PAP). This political background is important in positioning the role of education in Singapore and how it has been influenced by neoliberalism. This chapter evaluates the impact of neoliberalism on the Singaporean education system using a range of critical insights. In particular we suggest neoliberalism, not only as an ideology, but also a set of techniques and practices reflecting educational governance. The aim is to offer a critical appreciation of these developments in Singaporean education rather than to describe developments in detail.

First, after a general introduction to the impact of neoliberalism on education, we consider changes to do with the commercialization, commodification, and marketization that have occurred in education in Singapore in recent years, placing them in a broader socio-political context. Next, we consider the implications of neoliberal initiatives in Singapore including the development of education as an industry. The impacts on people of neoliberal developments in Singapore are then considered, and we give some space to the issue of resistance to these initiatives. Finally, we summarize and review the management of education in a tightly controlled one-party "democracy."

NEOLIBERALISM AND EDUCATION

There has been considerable debate in recent years over the impact of neoliberalism on education (Altbach, 2001; Apple, 2001, 2004; Olssen, 1996) and on higher education in particular (Adams, 1995; Bessant, 1995; Currie & Newson, 1998; Deem, 2001; Enders, 2004; Giroux, 2002; Yang, 2003). Some of the more critical work on the global impact of neoliberalism on education, views neoliberalism as "a theory, an ideology, a juridical philosophy of individual freedom" (Burchell, 1996, p. 21) that seeks to change the way education is offered and funded. Stromquist (2002) has suggested that local education systems have become vassals in which the values of transnational corporations (TNCs) can be embedded in order to promote globalization, "free-trade," and meet global labor market requirements.

This implies that changes in education, as a consequence of neoliberal thinking and discourse, serve two purposes. First, education is redefined as an industry, not a public good. It is something from which money and profits can be made. Second, education serves to provide global capitalism with suitable "workers." This is not a new argument within the sociology of education, but globalization gives such purposes a new impetus as education is increasingly geared toward aiding the ability of nation-states to compete and prosper in the globalized economy. The discourse of education has, therefore, altered in recent years as the forces of neoliberalism have sought to occupy the space left vacant by the desire of governments, in both developed and developing parts of the world, to reduce financial commitments to education as a public good. As Stromquist (2002, p. 37) notes, the "educational systems across nations are changing, becoming less a public good and more the manifestation of an economic sector that happens to be concerned with knowledge."

In a broad sense, the discourse and practices that support neoliberalism in education are well established globally, if not universally. For example, there has been a move toward the application of economic rationalism, academic capitalism, and corporate managerialism in the way education is administered (Apple, 2004). Such concepts are reflected in the use of certain techniques for their achievement, for example, deregulation, privatization, marketization, educational entrepreneurship, commercialization, competition, and commodification (Bessant, 1995). These techniques collectively promote, through agents, the centrality of the "market" and "marketplace" as the organizer of the educational system. It is considered by proponents of this approach that "competition is necessary to increase educational standards, improve efficiency, and reduce costs" (Stromquist, 2002, p. 38).

For the ideology/discourse of neoliberalism to become embedded in education, not only are discursive techniques necessary, but actual practices that reflect these techniques are required. Stromquist (2002) has identified some of these practices as the development of business norms in education. Such practices include: increasing accountability at the school level for the performance outcomes of schools; an emphasis on performance outcomes (performativity) and constant assessment and measurement; offering more parental choice in education; enhancing school "quality" through competition; managing costs through efficiency of the market; identifying students as "consumers"; encouraging educational entrepreneurship, and the production of enterprising students. In addition, competition between schools requires the marketing of schools and their educational programs. Furthermore, once educational systems are exposed to the market, privatization and educational entrepreneurship develops.

> With neo-liberal economics, in which the market is seen as a key path to efficiency, quality, and innovation, a large number of enterprises are entering the educational arena. For them, while the question of efficiency is important, the main objective in setting up educational institutions is the procurement of profit. (Stromquist, 2002, p. 48)

Education, globally, is a two trillion dollar industry (Ministry of Trade and Industry, n/d). The discourse that is increasingly at the centre of educational debate is also the very discourse that supports and sustains the neoliberal system and ideology. Education is no longer a "public good" but is rather a source of private profit and vocational training.

EDUCATION AND THE ECONOMY IN SINGAPORE

After defence, education is the largest area of government expenditure. Since gaining independence in 1965, the primary objectives of Singapore education policy, as articulated by the People's Action Party (PAP), who have held power since 1959, has been to maintain racial harmony and to meet its economic needs through the production of an appropriate workforce (Kong, 2004). In this sense, education policy has always been driven by its utility and functionality. Kong (2004) has identified three phases of education strategy since 1965. Between 1965 and 1984, educational strategy in Singapore focused on building a standardized basic and technical education system aimed at supporting the desire of the government to attract foreign investment. Singapore's survival required foreign investment and, in order for corporations to find Singapore appealing, a relatively well educated workforce was required. At the secondary education level five types of schools were established; academic, vocational schools, technical schools, commercial schools, and vocational institutes (Kong, 2004). The emphasis was on hard technical skills development to facilitate the attraction of foreign investment.

The relationship between educational strategy and policy and the economic needs/survival of Singapore are very clear from the beginnings of Singapore as an independent city-state. Education has had a central role in supporting the survival of the nation and in nation-building. The PAP were also committed to using education as a mechanism to prevent too much "westernization" and to develop a set of values that would support "harmony" and "stability," against a backdrop of intense coercion if willing commitment failed (Mok, 2003; Tan, 1998). Stability was also critical for the attraction of foreign investment, which required an educated and compliant workforce that was inexpensive and able to be highly productive in an increasingly competitive global manufacturing environment.

The early focus on labor-intensive industry led to substantial economic growth in the late 1960s and 1970s. However, as other Asian countries were able to offer cheaper labor, corporations relocated, leaving the Singapore government to re-evaluate its educational strategy and policies. This led to the second phase of educational strategy development (Kong, 2004); promoting the expansion of science and technology education in order to assist the economic drive toward higher value-added products. Precision engineering, financial services, and information technology became important sources of revenue for Singapore and the education system needed to support their development and continued success.

The third phase in education strategy and policy development runs from 1995 to the present (Kong, 2004). Discoveries in microelectronics, computers, telecommunications, material science, robotics, and biotechnology have stimulated attempts by the Singapore government to equip people with the ability to be innovative, flexible, creative, and to engage in lifelong learning and to be entrepreneurial. Kong (2004) notes:

> The role of science and technology remains important but increasing attention has come to be given to broad-based multi-disciplinary efforts in curricula, including some expectations that scientists and engineers learn humanistic modes of inquiry. (p. 5)

With this background in mind we pick up the story of change in education in Singapore more recently. The system of education in Singapore has, since independence, always been designed to support economic development and growth. Kong (2004) views recent changes as attempts to ensure that education continues to support economic needs and drivers; suggesting that the "education landscape is being quite fundamentally overhauled to provide a broader based intellectual foundation, critical thinking skills and creativity that the economy demands." She further suggests that this has led to an "ability-driven approach towards education, allowing students' aspirations and interests to be better met" and an education system that "values innovation, nurtures diversity, and encourages individuals with irregular strengths" (Kong, 2004, p. 6). We offer an alternative perspective on these developments.

NEOLIBERALISM AND EDUCATION IN SINGAPORE

Neoliberal initiatives in education are identifiable through techniques and practices designed to embed this way of thinking. Privatization, marketization, commodification, commercialization, and competition reflect such techniques, while practices such as accountability, quality initiatives, performativity (focus on performance and ranking), and a focus on efficiency and "excellence" support the development of a neoliberal discourse in education. In this section we identify how such practices have become a central feature of educational discourse in Singapore as it seeks to maintain its attractiveness to foreign investors and maintain its economic position as a competitive state. We will also consider how certain practices act to create new norms of action that serve to maintain and perpetuate a particular discourse.

The desire of the Singapore government to maintain its economic competitiveness has required that educational strategy and policies are driven by economic demands. The rise of industries such as microelectronics, computers, telecommunications, material science, robotics, and biotechnology has led to the development of a new vision for education in Singapore—Thinking Schools, Learning Nation (TSLN) in 1997 (Mok, 2003). This vision has required implementation practices, and one such practice is the School Excellence Model (SEM).

In essence, the SEM is a form of quality self-assessment and was intended to replace external inspection with internal self-monitoring of school outcomes. SEM derives from Total Quality Management (TQM; Badri, Selim, Alshare, Grandon, Younis, Abdulla, 2006) and is an application of corporate managerialism to a school environment. In short, the relevant government Ministry of Education establishes a set of guidelines against which individual schools assess themselves and their outcomes. Instead of being inspected, schools are "validated" against external criteria. Such an approach is underpinned not only by "quality," but also performativity, another important practice in new managerialist thought (Mok, 2003). Mok (2003) notes that, "to make its schools and citizens more competitive and competent," the Singapore government has adopted principles and strategies from the "business and commercial sectors" (Mok, 2003 p. 360).

The Singapore government has attempted to replace direct control of schools through inspection with indirect control through validated self-assessment. It hopes that by doing so, individual schools will operate more creatively and innovatively in the development of curricula, teaching, and resource management. However, as Mok (2003, p. 361) notes, this is ultimately a little disingenuous, particularly in Singapore's one-party "democracy," where control is never willingly surrendered by the government, and "such developments could be conceptualized by the notion of 'centralized decentralization' in educational governance."

A second example of the impact of neoliberalism on education in Singapore relates to the confluence of marketization, competition, commodification, and enterprise in the delivery of education and how education is conceived. Here the idea is that by enabling the forces of the market to prevail, the quality of education is likely to increase as schools will need to compete for students and, in doing so, their standards will need to improve.

> Education is described as a consumer product, with parents being encouraged to shop around for the best schools. Policy-makers argue that such measures will eventually lead to improved standards in all schools, increased choice for parents and students, greater accountability on the

part of school authorities, and a greater diversity of school programmes. (Tan, 1998, p. 49)

Marketization of education also facilitates the involvement of the private sector in the provision and delivery of education, and the increasing use of corporate management practices in the promotion and marketing of education.

In Singapore since the late 1980s, the government has allowed the controlled development of private (independent) schools and enabled some schools to become autonomous (Tan, 1998). This has not been stimulated by a desire of the Singapore government to remove itself from education for financial reasons, as in some other countries, but has been driven by the belief that competition will enhance quality, standards, creativity, and innovation. As Mok (2003, p. 362) notes: "what really characterizes the marketization project in Singapore is the adherence to 'economic instrumentalism,' whereby market principles and practices are adopted to improve government and management of the education sector."

A key aspect of this "marketization project" is the stimulation of competition among students and between schools. Quality of education is partly measured against its capacity to produce competitive individuals and thus, a competitive Singapore. Competition has been encouraged through the establishment of independent and autonomous schools, and through the development of a ranking system for schools. In the Singapore context, the use of "autonomous" to describe a degree of freedom in planning courses and curriculum is something of a misnomer. Ultimately, the Singapore government retains absolute control over these matters. Such Schools can charge additional fees and can take in a percentage of "elite" primary school students. Performance outcomes are measured against success in examinations compared to other schools; the increase in student performance within the school over time; and school performance against the national physical fitness as well as in percentage of overweight students in the school (Tan, 1998).

The neoliberal developments in education in Singapore are apparent, yet they do not represent a break with the past provision of education in the city-state that such initiatives may imply in other countries. For example, while the government has encouraged competition through independent and autonomous schools, it is heavily regulated. There were 6 independent secondary schools in 2001 and 5 in 2005; in 2001 there were 17 autonomous secondary schools and 21 in 2005. The Singapore government maintains, directly or indirectly, and despite the rhetoric of autonomy and independence, strict control over what schools do and how many are doing it (Mok, 2003). This has been the situation since 1965 and the philosophy, strategy, and policy with respect to education has always been to standardize and organize its provision in the interests of Singapore's economic development (Wong & Apple, 2002). Current neoliberal initiatives in Singapore simply fit the changing discourse that dominates this relationship between economy and education in the post-industrial environment.

IMPLICATIONS OF NEOLIBERAL INITIATIVES

The system of education in Singapore has always been based on "high-stakes examinations" (Gopinathan & Deng, 2006) and a commitment to the idea of "meritocracy." This is clearly reflected in the values of the Ministry of Education: "Every child must be encouraged to progress through the education system as far as his ability allows. Advancement must always depend on performance and merit to ensure equal opportunity for all" (Ministry of Education, Singapore). Recent neoliberal initiatives, however, have undermined the rhetoric of equal opportunity. The Singapore government has always been of the view that it is innate ability that determines educational outcomes and performance, and that other sociological factors play an insignificant role; such as the confluence of race and class. Malays, for example, consistently perform worse in high-stakes examinations than Chinese students. In 2004, 59.3% of Malay students scored 5 Ordinary Level examination passes compared with 86.5% of Chinese students; and while 86.3% of the 2004 Chinese cohort went to post-secondary education, only 75% of Malays did so (Ministry of Education, Singapore, 2006). Here class and race come together.

While Singapore has tended to ignore inequality of outcomes in education as a function of ability alone, neoliberal initiatives potentially exacerbate and institutionalize such inequalities further. For example, the marketization of education, and particularly practices aimed at stimulating competition and performance are likely to enhance selectivity in schools (Mok, 2003). This may lead to the ghettoization of schools based on performance and ranking. While the Singapore government has supported elitism in education, neoliberal initiatives will entrench elitism and make it even more difficult for those students who under-perform to enjoy whatever benefits may exist in a system that is based on regular assessment.

Neoliberal initiatives in education have enhanced aspects of the selective, elitist philosophy that has always underpinned educational policy and practice in Singapore, and has enabled the "best" schools, whether government, independent, or autonomous to benefit in terms of selection of the "best" students and enhancement of their teaching complement (Tan, 1998). It is to be remembered that Singapore is an exam-driven education system, and decisions concerning "best" are exam driven. More recently the Ministry of Education has moved away from the discourse of ranking to a softer discourse of achievement and awards (Figure 10.1).

MOE MASTERPLAN OF AWARDS FOR SCHOOLS

Such initiatives are not, however, loosening the control of government over education. On the contrary, the government directs the nature and extent of competition and is obsessively involved in the management of schools in the interests of the growth and survival of Singapore as a nation. As the criteria

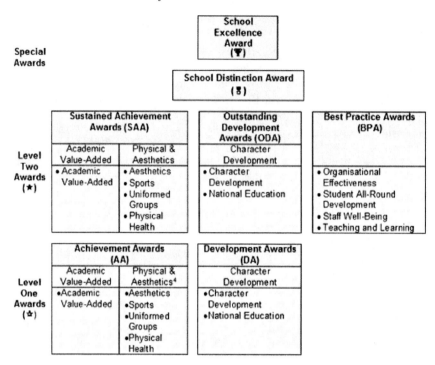

Figure 10.1   Masterplan of awards (http://app.sis.moe.gov.sg/schinfo/index.asp).

for school awards shows there is an attempt to use a more holistic framework for the classification of schools, yet the principles of selection and elitism persist, as does a clear stratification of schools. Indeed, they are fundamental to the limitation on educational and social mobility that the Singapore government feels is necessary in a socially engineered and hierarchicalized society.

EDUCATION AS INDUSTRY

Neoliberalism has impacted on Singapore's approach to education in other ways. While the discourse has influenced thinking about the provision of education in Singapore, it has also influenced thinking about how Singapore can increase its share of the market for education globally. In other words, Singapore has put much effort into articulating itself as a hub for education in the Asia-Pacific, and as a centre for the provision of education as a commodity. This is best reflected in the report of the Education Workgroup set up to consider "Developing Singapore's Education Industry" (Ministry of Trade and Industry, n.d.). In this report education is treated as purely a commodity:

Singapore can capture a larger share of the global education market (estimated at US$2.2 trillion), and increase educational services' contribution to GDP from the existing 1.9% of the GDP to a projected 3 to 5% in 10 years. The growth in the education sector would come from the increases in institutional and student spending, particularly from full-fee paying international students. The efforts to build education as a business through attracting full-fee paying international students should be over and above the existing MoE talent attraction schemes. (Ministry of Trade and Industry, n.d.)

The emphasis in the above quote is significant as it indicates that not only is education a potentially important generator of revenue for Singapore, it may also be a means of attracting and retaining overseas talent. Furthermore the report indicates that, as early as 1985, the idea of nurturing and promoting education as a business was recognized but "socio-political concerns limited efforts to promote this sector and develop education as a business" (Ministry of Trade and Industry, n.d.). In the 20 years since 1985, the discourse has changed enough for education to have become "mercantilized," the idea that education is an industry and can operate through the market mechanisms of economic exchange. The report emphasizes that developing an "education ecosystem" has the two major benefits of revenue generation and the enhancement of Singapore's capability and talent pool.

Development of the education industry will clearly require the full range of business management techniques and practices to support this: marketing, promotion; enterprise, and entrepreneurship; employee capability; quality control mechanisms, as well as government funding initiatives and incentives. The report concludes:

The proposed changes are meant to create a pro-enterprise greenhouse, such that existing and new schools are able to anchor and grow their Singapore-based operations as well as expand into the region. The proposed changes need to be implemented quickly. Otherwise, the industry could face hollowing out in terms of international students heading to other countries. (Ministry of Trade and Industry, n.d.)

In addition, it is private sector enterprise and entrepreneurship that will facilitate the growth of the education industry in Singapore and commodify it for the regional market.

THE PEOPLE IMPACT OF NEOLIBERAL
DEVELOPMENTS IN SINGAPORE

There are, then, two ways in which neoliberalism is affecting education in Singapore. The first way is through changes that are related to the way the

Singapore government has sought to introduce corporate managerialism and economic rationalism into the public education system, and to stimulate competition through independent and autonomous schools. Second, neoliberalism is perpetuated through the explicit development of Singapore as a hub for the education industry in Asia and a source of increased revenue for the Singaporean economy.

The desire to produce more innovative and creative individuals has, in recent years, led to significant changes in school-based curriculum in Singapore. This has been enhanced somewhat by the processes of decentralization that have taken place in Singapore. Gopinathan and Deng (2006, p. 97) imply that these changes will lead to work intensification for teachers, "adopting the role of curriculum developers creates tremendous demands on classroom teachers; many teachers are not adequately prepared nor do they have the experience necessary to undertake curriculum design tasks."

In particular, teachers have a lack of time; lack of expertise; lack of resources; too many external pressures and restrictions, and sometimes a managerially threatening environment. This may be especially a problem in Singapore where teachers have been traditionally "doers" rather than "thinkers." Their role has been to deliver, not develop, curricula (Gopinathan & Deng, 2006, p. 101).

> Taken together, school-based curriculum enactment creates significant demands on classroom teachers. It entails the need to develop new beliefs about the curriculum, curriculum materials, and the role of teachers. It requires teachers to work across the five intersecting domains, making informed decisions on what to teach and how to teach it.

Work intensification of this kind has increased the "pressure to perform" on teachers (Chan, Lai, Ko, & Boey, 2000). The "innovation and enterprise" drive introduced in 2004 and the inappropriately named "Teach Less, Learn More" (TLLM) initiative of 2005 placed emphasis on teachers as the drivers of this change (Gopinathan & Deng, 2006). For example, teachers were to act as role models for active and continuous learning and were also expected to gain experience of working environments outside of their schools through the Teachers' Work Attachment. Teachers were also expected to introduce innovative pedagogies, indeed, the TLLM initiative "was started to encourage frontline educators to re-examine the fundamental questions of the teaching and learning process, and innovate in their curriculum design, pedagogy and assessment" (Gopinathan & Deng, 2006, pp. 100–101). Teachers were also encouraged to develop learner-centred pedagogies, and be curriculum designers and innovators. They were expected to "reflect" on their practice and carry out "action-research and attend preferred courses of study" (Gopinathan & Deng, 2006, p. 101). This was not in the interests of creating the self-reflexive, critical teacher, but to focus on technical reflection.

It is not, therefore, surprising that performance pressure has been found to have a strong relationship with job satisfaction and mental health among Singapore teachers (Chan et al., 2000). The increasing emphasis on competitiveness, performativity, and surveillance, in the context of developments in global capitalism, have largely negative outcomes in working conditions and health for Singapore teachers (Chan et al., 2000). To gain compliance with this work intensification, the Ministry of Education has put in place a number of policies/incentives to build commitment to change. These include regular reviews of salary; incentives to upgrade qualifications and skills, and to build loyalty. In addition, a range of professional development opportunities have been introduced, more teachers have been recruited, and administrative workload has been reduced. Most importantly, the Ministry of Education (MoE) has introduced distinctive career tracks within the education service and performance-based pay (Singapore Ministry of Education, n.d.).

The introduction of performance-based pay for teachers is a clear example of managerialism in education. While pay scales have traditionally been and continue to be related to seniority, there are different pay scales related to a teacher's competencies and potential for advancement. Annual performance-related bonus systems enable outstanding teachers to get "up to two or more months' bonus" (Ministry of Education, Singapore, n.d.); there are awards, annually, for outstanding individual and team contributions and "substantial monetary incentives" (Ministry of Education, Singapore, n.d.). In addition, more salary grades have been established as well as responsibility allowances. In short, the intensification of work has been traded off against material gain. Some teachers may gain financially as a result of these changes, but to benefit in this way teachers are required to comply to certain new ways of "being" in the Singapore educational context. They have to self-monitor in relation to new competencies and performance standards in order to be perceived as performing.

It is difficult to get information on the reactions of teachers to working conditions, at least formally. For example, a search for published papers on this topic returns a very meagre response. Trade unions in Singapore have been appropriated by the governing elite and consequently, overt resistance is neither encouraged nor possible. Striking among teachers is outlawed. There is, as we have reported, some work on stress and workload issues of teachers in Singapore (Chan et al., 2000), however, a more interesting source of information regarding the lives of teachers in Singapore can be found on internet blogs rather than in published work. One blogging teacher writes the following:

> Now, what's the rationale behind the stressful education system on both students and teachers.

> Basically, the school wants to give parents like yourself a very good impression. What would you, as a parent, think of the school, if the school

234 Steve McKenna and Julia Richardson

shows very little interest in sending its students for robotics competitions, public music performances? You would probably think that the school isn't doing a good job. Chances are you may mot want to send your kid there. You might even think of writing into the Straits Times, asking the school to shape up by enrolling the kids in more activities.

So, this is the price your kids have to pay. You should be able to figure out by now that teaching is only one of my many responsibilities. In the entire education system, the only educators who do real teaching full-time are private tutors.

Do you really think we teachers take pleasure in spending so much time in the office each day? Most of us are easily spending more time with your kids than you are.

Obviously we need to be sensitive to the confessional nature of internet blogs, yet in societal circumstances where freedom of speech is a very limited right, such as Singapore, they offer opportunities for oppressed voices to be heard. Furthermore, they offer a counterweight to those who advocate increasing use of "high-performance work systems" in teaching that reflect the impact of corporate managerialism in education (Tan, 2000).

Despite a dearth of research, we might speculate that recent changes in education in Singapore have led to an intensification of an already intense working environment for teachers. According to one study (Tan & Quek, 2001) teachers in Singapore were oriented, in this order, to lifestyle, service, and security as the most important anchors in their career. It is likely, therefore, that increased workload and stress will negatively influence teacher intentions to stay in the profession as they become unable to manage work–life balance (Chan et al., 2000).

RESISTANCE?

How will they/do they resist? In Singapore, the mere idea of "resistance" is a dangerous topic to raise if one wants to remain employed and employable. Hodson (1995, p. 90) defines worker resistance as "any individual or small group act intended to mitigate claims by management on workers or to advance workers' claims against management." In doing this, employees are seeking to retain or regain dignity, and to exercise some control and autonomy over their working lives. Hodson suggests that debates concerning worker resistance are too "structuralist" and resistance should be understood more broadly, particularly its subtleties and the "micro-level events of day-to-day resistance." It should be noted, however, that when more "structural" forms of resistance are constrained, individual employees will have the only option of resisting individually. This, of course, suits the purposes of those controlling the labor process.

This, we believe, to be the case among Singapore teachers. The importance of "economic instrumentalism" as the value system in Singapore has been cultivated meticulously by the PAP over the last 50 years. There is little room for political opposition and pluralism in Singapore and even "internet weblogs came in for thematic scrutiny by authorities" (Rodan, 2006, p. 181), implying that any teacher engaging in venting via a blog is taking a considerable risk. Resistance among teachers in Singapore then, is likely to be muted, possibly of the type Hodson (1995) describes; influencing the effort bargain; restricting output; playing dumb; venting; absenteeism, and quitting and so on. It is likely to be "subtle, frequently secretive, and sometimes carried out on an individual basis, though at least tacit group consent is almost always required" (Hodson, 1995, p. 102).

CONCLUSION

The education system in Singapore has, since independence, always been managed in the interests of the economy. The Singapore government argues that the very survival of the city-state depends on this connection. Every development in education is designed to continue and enhance this connection. Neoliberalism, being the most recent manifestation of late 20th century, attempts to manage global capitalism, and has had a predictable impact in Singapore. The government of Singapore has sought to exploit neoliberal opportunities in two ways; first, to introduce more choice and more autonomy in schooling, ostensibly to enhance competition and quality; second, to develop education as an industry and increasing its contribution to GDP.

The fundamental principle on which education in Singapore is based however, remains the same. Elitism and a commitment to equality of opportunity, based on measurements of "natural" ability, remain in place, thus disadvantaging groups in society who are economically weakest. This, inevitably in Singapore, has a racial dimension. Also, despite the rhetoric of autonomy, the educational system in Singapore remains highly centralized; it is far too important as a mechanism for control for the PAP to accept school-level control of anything but the most mundane of matters.

From a critical perspective, neoliberal techniques have attempted to alter what teachers have to "be"; more innovative, creative, and so on. More importantly, teachers have to accept this new identity as "normal" and accept the intensification of work that accompanies such change. Teachers in Singapore continue to be under close control and surveillance: If nothing else, Singapore is the Panoptican par excellence (Foucault, 1995). The opportunities to resist overtly are nonexistent, and the philosophy of economic instrumentalism is perpetually used as a way of "buying" compliance.

In the developing private sector of education, the prospects for work intensification, poor pay and benefits, and exploitation of teachers is greater.

Neoliberal initiatives in education in Singapore are merely extensions of previous policies to align education with the needs of the economy. This has not led to any tectonic shifts in the philosophy or structure of education in Singapore. This sector remains a pressure-cooker of stress for students and teachers driven by the rhetoric of "economic survival" on one side and, in the case of teachers, coerced by the employer on the other. Whatever economic fashion arrives next, the Singapore government will be sure to follow and "change" its education system accordingly.

REFERENCES

Adams, T. (1995). Internationalising the University: An Australian case study. *Higher Education Policy, 8*(2), 40–43.

Altbach, P. G. (2001). Academic freedom: International challenges and realities. *Higher Education, 41,* 205–219.

Apple, M. (2001). Comparing neo-liberal projects and inequality in education. *Comparative Education, 37*(4), 409–423.

Apple, M. W. (2004). Creating difference: Neo-liberalism, neo-conservatism and the politics of educational reform. *Educational Policy, 18*(1), 12–44.

Badri, M. A., Selim, H., Alshare, K., Grandon, E., E., Younis, H., & Abdulla, M. (2006). The Baldridge education criteria for performance excellence framework: Empirical test and validation. *International Journal of Quality and Reliability Management, 23*(9), 1118–1157.

Bessant, B. (1995). Corporate management and its penetration of university administration and government. *Australian Universities Review, 38*(1), 59–62.

Burchell, G. (1996). Liberal government and techniques of the self. In A. Barry, T. Osborne, & N. Rose (Eds.), *Foucault and political reason* (pp. 19–36). Chicago: University of Chicago.

Chan, K. B., Lai, G., Ko, Y. C., & Boey, K. W. (2000). Work stress among six professional groups: The Singapore experience. *Social Science and Medicine, 50,* 1415–1432.

Currie, J., & Newson, J. (1998). *Universities and globalization: Critical perspective.* Thousand Oaks, CA: Sage.

Deem, R. (2001). Globalisation, new managerialism, academic capitalism and entrepreneurialism in universities: Is the local dimension still important? *Comparative Education, 37*(1), 7–20.

Enders, J. (2004). Higher education, internationalisation, and the nation-state: Recent developments and challenges to governance theory. *Higher Education, 47,* 361–382.

Foucault, M. (1995). *Discipline and punish.* New York: Vintage Books.

Giroux, H.A. (2002). Neoliberalism, corporate culture, and the promise of higher education: The university as a democratic public sphere. *Harvard Educational Review, 72*(4), 425–463.

Gopinathan, S., & Deng, Z. (2006). Fostering school-based curriculum development in the context of new educational initiatives in Singapore. *Planning and Changing, 37*(1/2), 93–110.

Hodson, R. (1995). Worker resistance: an underdeveloped concept in the sociology of work. *Economic and Industrial Democracy, 16,* 79–110.

Kong, L. (2004). *Science and education in an Asian tiger,* 2007. Retrieved from www.brightminds.uq.edu.au/TRC/presentations.htm

Ministry of Education, Singapore (n.d.). Retrieved from http://www.moe.gov.sg/corporate/aboutus.htm.

Ministry of Education, Singapore. (2006). *2006 Education Statistics Digest.* Singapore.

Ministry of Education, Singapore. (n.d.). *Singapore Country Summary.* Retrieved May 16, 2007, from http://64.233.167.104/search?q=cache:nNMNKsy-5-OEJ:www.aspeninstitute.org/atf/cf/%257BDEB6F227–659B-4EC8–8F84–8DF23CA704F5%257D/ED_SingaporeProfile.pdf+singapore+country+summary,+education&hl=en&ct=clnk&cd=1&gl=ca.

Ministry of Trade and Industry, Singapore. Education Workgroup. (n.d.). *Executive Summary—Developing Singapore's education industry.* Retrieved 2007, from http://app.mti.gov.sg/default.asp?id=507#3.

Mok, K.-h. (2003). Decentralization and marketization of education in Singapore. *Journal of Educational Administration, 41*(4), 348–366.

Olssen, M. (1996). In defense of the welfare state and of publicly provided education. *Journal of Education Policy, 11,* 337–362.

Rodan, G. (2006). Singapore in 2005. *Asian Survey, XLVI*(1), 180–186.

Stromquist, N. P. (2002). *Education in a globalized world.* Lanham, Maryland: Rowman and Littlefield.

Tan, C. Y. (2000). High-performance human resource strategies in learning schools. *The Learning Organization, 7*(1), 32–39.

Tan, H.-H., & Quek, B.-C. (2001). An exploratory study on the career anchors of educators in Singapore. *The Journal of Psychology, 135*(5), 527–545.

Tan, J. (1998). The marketisation of education in Singapore: Policies and implications. *International Review of Education, 44*(1), 47–63.

Wong, T.-H., & Apple, M. (2002). Rethinking the education/stet formation connection: Pedagogic reform in Singapore, 1945–1965. *Comparative Education Review, 46*(2), 182–210.

Yang, R. (2003). Globalisation and higher education development: A critical analysis. *International Review of Education, 49*(3–4), 269–291.

11 Education Reforms in Japan
Neoliberal, Neoconservative, and "Progressive Education" Directions

Kaori H. Okano

INTRODUCTION

If an outsider had followed Japanese media coverage over the last three decades, he or she could not help thinking that the country has been undergoing a continuous series of "major educational reforms" over that period. Various "problems" were revealed, possible causes for these problems were speculated on, and solutions were presented. Journalists, academics of diverse disciplines, and educational practitioners contributed to these debates, as seen in a large number of publications on the topic. The public was repeatedly told that their schools had problems, and that the nation needed a large-scale "education reform" by all political parties at every election.

Indeed, the government has produced a large number of reports on education. Over the period of 1984 to 1999 seven policy deliberation councils within the Ministry of Education were asked to produce 39 reports with recommendations. On top of all of these, the Ad-Hoc Council of Education (directly under the auspices of then prime minister), issued four reports between 1984 and 1987. Several major changes were subsequently introduced since the late 1990s. Debates continue as to the effectiveness (or otherwise) of these and other changes, as well as further changes. The former prime minister Shinzo Abe[2] (who took office in September, 2006) vowed that he would undertake major reforms and established yet another committee to explore possibilities. The public is starting to wonder how long these "reforms" will continue and if any positive consequences will result from them. Academic debates over Japan's recent education reforms have resulted in wide range of conclusions, as represented by the contributors to Goodman's edited collection (2003).

This chapter tries to understand this series of educational reforms during the last three decades. What changes have been implemented? Who are pushing them, and with what agenda? In what ways were proposed changes resisted, with what consequence? How have the changes impacted on the practice of schooling, equity, and teachers at the level of the individual school? I explore how the changes compare with so-called global trends observed in Anglophone countries, and how specific local circumstances might have guided the development of change in Japan.

Despite the media hype, the educational reforms implemented in Japan over this period have not been as drastic and as far reaching as in many Anglophone societies (Cave, 2001). For example, the Japanese education system did not undergo the radical devolution of power and simultaneous strengthening of evaluative control by central government as seen in charter schools in the United States, and grant-maintained schools in England and schools in Victoria, Australia (Whitty Power, & Halpin, 1998; Gillborn & Youndell, 2000; Davies & Gumpy, 1997). Concrete changes have been: (1) "the slimming of schooling" whereby Saturday schooling was phased out, and roles once performed by schools are transferred to the community and families; (2) curriculum reform (introduction of compulsory interdisciplinary studies, reduction of content covered, and more teacher autonomy in curriculum design); (3) diversification of upper secondary schooling; (4) greater choice for parents (although still considerably limited); (5) recruitment of principals and vice-principals from non-teachers; and (6) official promotion of the national anthem, the national flag, and patriotism at school (although its implementation varies across the country).

The most significant impact of these changes is a widening gap in children's educational experiences and opportunities, based on family background. This derives, on one hand, from the "slimming of schooling," which has provided children with a greater amount of time to explore their interests outside schools, and on the other from greater parental choice in selecting schools, in certain local areas. The introduction of horizontal diversity, as seen in a flexible curriculum and new types of high schools, affected changes in learning practice at the school level and benefited some students (e.g., newcomer ethnic minorities); but vertical diversity in the form of the existing school hierarchy still remains unchallenged. Little has changed in terms of what occurs at elite academic schools, and of the privileges that they confer to their graduates. Teachers' workloads became greater, and private education industries more active. Regarding the "patriotism" to be nurtured at school, schools and teachers remain unsure as to what exactly it means.

I suggest that these reforms constituted a pragmatic package in response to demands from neoliberals, neoconservatives, and progressive educationalists. They reflect the on-going struggles amongst major players, namely, big business (seeking a global standard in a competitive global market), political parties, the Ministry of Education, Culture, Sports, Science and Technology (MEXT in short), which has resisted relinquishing its power, other ministries in the central bureaucracy, local governments, and those on the left (i.e., mainly academics and teachers). The changes have been slow and gradual, formulated and implemented cautiously by the Ministry of Education. The incremental process of reforms is underpinned by the Ministry's deliberate reluctance to exercise the executive power that it possesses, and its willingness to leave substantial scope for interpretation and implementation to lower levels of the education system. The result is great divergence across localities.

I start with a briefing on the context and the drivers of change. I will then examine the content of changes that were implemented, and the impact of these changes in terms of social inequality and teachers. This chapter is a result of research based on primary and secondary sources, as well as my regular fieldwork on schools in Japan, the most recent being a year long sabbatical in 2006. As with any similar research, my interpretation is influenced by the comparative perspective that I bring from my prior experience. This includes a series of education reforms that I experienced as a secondary school teacher in Australia and New Zealand in the late 1980s.

THE CONTEXT AND THE DRIVERS OF REFORMS

The modern system of education, since its establishment in the late 19th century, has always played a transformative role in Japan. A centralised system of mass schooling was established by the imperial state in the mid-19th century to act as an engine for transforming a feudal society into a modern and industrialised state that could resist Western colonization. School attendance and literacy/numeracy levels improved steadily in the early 20th century, and contributed to the industrialization and modernization of the society (Amano, 1995). Following World War II, the allied occupation authorities established a new system of schooling with the aim of affecting another social transformation, from an ultranationalist state to a democratic society, and to underpin economic growth. Because Japan needed to catch up quickly with the West, a centralized system was considered most effective. Subsequently, by the late 1970s, Japan became a successful liberal democracy and the world's second largest economy, characterized by a relatively even wealth distribution. In the 1980s, the system of education remained centralized nationally in terms of school registration, teacher certification, and a national curriculum.

By the mid-1980s the public felt that Japan had "caught up" with the West (in terms of, for example, per-capita income and income distribution). Both the government and the public started exploring new directions. This exploration was influenced by various theses on the "uniqueness of Japan" (*nihonjinron*; Mouer & Sugimoto, 1986; Befu, 2001), which tried to explain supposedly unique features of Japanese society (e.g., Japan Inc., trade practices, corporate human resource practices, high academic achievement with low standard deviation). There were also external pressures to conform to a "global standard," and a marked slowing of economic growth in the 1990s after the bursting of the economic bubble. We saw a general climate of uncertainty, with the public no longer sharing a consensus regarding social goals (i.e., of economic progress, democratic governance, and rising living standards).

It was in this context, during the 1980s, that seemingly endless debates on educational reforms started—debates that have continued to this day. Seen from outside (where more drastic reforms were implemented, as in many Anglophone societies), educational reforms in Japan over this period have been neither radical nor substantial. They have been gradual and slow, implemented very cautiously by the MEXT and local governments, a point that I shall return to later.

Changes in the last three decades have been a combination of neoliberal, neo-conservative, and "progressive" education directions. There are varying understandings of the configuration of these three strands.

Until the mid-1980s, the configuration was straightforward. There were two camps. On one hand, the ruling Liberal Democratic Party sought "reforms" in order to make the system of schooling more efficient and relevant to a changing society and advocated schooling for economic growth but this was accompanied by a sense of nostalgia for what they saw as "traditions." On the other hand, the Japan Teachers' Union (JTU, which had played a leading role in the national federation of unions; Duke, 1973; Aspinall, 2001) and academics opposed any moves to change pre-existing practices based on the 1947 Fundamental Education Law, and stressed human rights, democratic process, and social justice (Okano & Tsuchiya, 1999). During the post-war period, the JTU effectively refused to implement a number of top-down changes. For example, schools in union-strong prefectures refused to implement a national academic achievement test in 1961 and 1964, rendering the whole initiative meaningless to the extent that the Ministry was eventually forced to abandon it. They resisted the introduction of medium level positions of responsibility (between vice-principal and ordinary teachers) by pooling the extra allowance given to holders of such positions for scholarships for disadvantaged students. While facing antagonism from teachers' unions, the government also had to deal with a central bureaucracy that was reluctant to initiate and implement changes. These struggles in the field of education policy-making and implementation made it extremely difficult for the central government to implement significant changes. The term *immobilist politics* (Schoppa, 1991) is an apt word to describe the situation of this period. The configuration of the power struggle, however, underwent changes when the national union federation was restructured in 1989 (Okano & Tsuchiya, 1999, pp. 167–172). The struggle widened beyond the JTU and the MEXT.

Examining the reforms of the late 1990s and early 2000s, Motani (2005) sees the picture in terms of progressive educators (who support child-centred, problem solving learning) versus traditionalists (who advocate "back to basics"), and interprets recent curriculum reforms as a victory for progressive educators. She considered that the neoliberal and neoconservative camps are unified, and attributes curriculum reform to a convergence of neoliberal/neoconservative and progressive education agendas. The neoliberal/neoconservatives wanted to grant individual teachers and schools more room for discretion so that schools would become more diverse, in turn offering parents and students greater choice, and simultaneously making individual schools more accountable. Progressive education proponents, on the other hand, welcomed the opportunity that individual schools and teachers were given to design and deliver teaching suited to local contexts and individual student needs.

I would suggest that the configuration of the three camps is more complex than Motani suggests. There are considerable differences between the views held by the neoliberals and those of the neoconservatives (Komigawa, 2000). There are also other significant players. First, neoliberal advocates represent the interests of big business, which is eager to see Japan follow "global norms." Concerns of the neoliberal camp are most clearly represented in a report prepared by a think tank, *Shakai Seisanbu*. The report called on schools to produce human resources for a competitive international market, and for individual families to be more accountable for their children's education. It proposed radical reforms, such as abolishing school zones, greater powers for principals in the management of their schools, the establishment of school councils as self-managing bodies, abolition of entrance examinations, and the introduction of strict requirements to graduate from senior high school and university (Tsutsumi & Hashizume, 1999).

Second, neoconservative advocates, including rural farmers and urban small business operators, are on the political right. They had been the dominant source of votes for the conservative Liberal Democratic Party that governed post-war Japan until 1993. They can be seen as so-called traditionalists who view the past with a kind of nostalgia, and lament the present state of young people, which they blame on an education system (which, they contend, is staffed with unionised and idealistic leftist teachers). The neoconservative nostalgia for the past has not been shared by neoliberals in wanting to pursue a competitive edge in the global market and advocating global norms. The neoliberal business establishment, for instance, opposes the prime minister's visits to the Yasukuni Shrine (where leading Japanese war criminals are enshrined) and his controversial comments on historical events of the World War II, which they see as constraining Japan's relationships with Asian neighbors.

Third, the left in the political spectrum, consisting of intellectuals, teachers, unions, human rights organizations, and political parties (e.g., the Japan Communist Party, the Social Democratic Party) are variously concerned with social justice and social inequalities that persist in Japanese society. Among them are self-categorised "progressive educators" who pursue student-centered and problem-solving educational practices that nurture creativity and exploration, as opposed to what they see as rigid, structured teaching and learning (geared to senior high school and university entrance examinations), which they claim stifles students. However, those on the left who are more concerned with structural inequality do not feel comfortable with the progressive educators' focus on micro-classroom level practice, without due reference to factors external to schools (Kariya, 2002; Fujita, 2000).

In addition, there are the bureaucrats in the central MEXT. They have been reluctant, at least in comparison to their counterparts in Anglophone countries, to initiate and implement changes that would weaken their power, and where there was not some assurance of unopposed implementation at the local level. The MEXT wants to avoid confrontations with, and open defiance from, teachers and civil movement groups (as seen in the 1960s and 1970s in relation to national policies, and in recent years in relation to the Tokyo metropolitan government's reforms), which, they consider, undermine the Ministry's reputation and authority. In between these interest camps remain the vast majority of people, including employees, some teachers, and parents, who are undecided and prepared to listen to different views.

Against this backdrop, the government found itself needing to accommodate these distinctive interest groups, and to persuade reluctant bureaucrats, and still be seen as responding to the public's general dissatisfaction with schooling. Toning down particular lines of argument was one strategy. Indeed, the government discourse on education reforms has "toned down" considerably since the mid-1980s when the series of inquiries and discussions started with Prime Minister Nakasone's ad hoc Committee report. The Liberal Democratic Party politicians still needed to please their traditional base of voters, rural farmers (who hold a disproportionate influence in voting compared with urban voters), as well as big business. The Liberal Democratic Party's original supporter base was rural farmers and urban small business owners, but the party transformed itself into a "catch all" party in the 1970s in order to survive politically in a changing society; and did not wish to alienate any voters.

The result is a series of changes framed in language that has appeal to different groups and to the general public. Vague language concerning major initiatives included: diversification of learning, internationalization, meeting individual needs, giving more autonomy to teachers and more choice to parents and students, reducing the role played by institutionalized schooling so that students can be engaged in more creative activities, and making schools more socially relevant. The neoliberal camp would endorse the moves to enhance diversity, parental choice, individual decision making power, accountability to stake holders, and competition amongst education providers. It would also support student-centered and problem-solving learning so that schools produce innovative elites for the knowledge-based economy. The neoconservative camp would be happy with a focus on the promotion of national anthem and flag, and an emphasis on instilling "love of Japan," and an introduction of nationwide achievement tests (in 2007). Progressive educators are pleased to see the introduction of interdisciplinary studies at compulsory school levels that individual teachers are encouraged to innovate according to the needs of their students, and the addition of new types of senior secondary schools that offer a large number of elective subjects. These initiatives, they would believe, promote student-centered learning based on individual needs.

CONTENT OF REFORMS AND THEIR IMPLEMENTATION

Impetus for changes lay in dissatisfaction with the existing system and practices of schooling. Various concerns have been raised since the mid-1980s: for example, inflexibility of the curriculum that failed to encourage student creativity, a perceived lowering of academic standards, inadequate provision for gifted children, lack of accountability amongst education providers, school refusal, overtly competitive entrance examinations to senior high schools and universities, young people's delinquent behaviors outside school, a perceived decline in teacher quality and a claim that children are "too busy." Claiming to address them, various educational reforms were proposed and implemented. The public and the government have two assumptions here: that schooling has somehow contributed to causing these "problems" (when outside-school factors might be more significant), and that schooling can somehow alleviate them (when this may be impossible without structural reforms outside schooling). Sociologists like Kariya (2002) question these assumptions. For example, the claim that academic achievement has declined over the last few decades is not supported by any empirical evidence; and attribution of this to perceived reduction in teacher quality is similarly unsupported.

Publicly announced slogans for educational reforms centered on individualization and diversification of learning, more choice, and creativity. They were typically vague so that no one had grounds to object to them, such as catering for and encouraging individuality, more relaxed learning, and child-centered and problem-solving learning to nurture creativity.

Concrete changes that we have witnessed are: (1) a reduction in the hours of schooling (i.e., abolition of Saturday classes), and in the roles of schools (e.g., shift from school-based to community-based sports activities); (2) curriculum reform (introduction of compulsory interdisciplinary studies, reduction of covered content, more teacher autonomy for design); (3) introduction of new types of upper secondary schools where students can structure their courses by selecting electives; (4) greater choice for parents (including relaxation of school zoning); (5) recruitment of principals and vice-principals from non-teachers; and (6) official promotion of the national anthem, the national flag, and a "love of Japan" at school. Let me discuss each of them in turn.

Slimming of School Functions

The moves to reduce the roles played by schools in educating children have been popularly described by the term *the slimming of schooling*. School days were gradually reduced from 6 to 5 over the ten-year period. In 1992, one Saturday per month became a school-free day. This was followed by two school-free Saturdays per month in 1995, and in 2002 all Saturdays became holidays. The curriculum coverage went down by 30%. It was claimed that this would provide children with a more relaxed environment for learning, including experiential and exploratory processes. Children, it was said, would have more free time to themselves to develop their own interests over a longer weekend. Another measure has been to gradually shift sport and cultural club activities (*bukatsudô*)[3] away from the school and into the community. There had been criticism that after-school sport club activities at secondary schools were too rigid and intensive, involving training at school every morning and afternoon in addition to weekend inter-school matches, leaving little time for teenagers to develop other interests. Teachers (often male teachers) were said to be working long hours to supervise these activities. Thus, the initiatives to reduce the amount and intensity of institutional schooling in children's lives were based on the assumption that such a reduction would grant children more time and room for relaxations and personal exploration and development in areas outside school.

The consequences of these moves were threefold. At school level, teachers became increasingly under pressure to cover the curriculum over a shortened length of time. At middle and senior high school levels, this is more serious because the schools are expected by parents to prepare students for the upcoming entrance examinations to senior high schools and universities respectively. Many academic high schools conduct "voluntary" Saturday teaching. Second, outside schools, more parents, concerned with "lowered" school expectations of students' achievement, started sending their children to commercially operated cram schools. Without structural reforms to the system whereby students are admitted to senior high schools and universities through examinations, these initiatives failed to achieve their aims (i.e., more relaxed and exploratory learning). The third, and most important impact, is the cumulative consequences of what children do during free time outside school. Children's school performance, motivation to study, and future aspirations are increasingly affected by their family resources. Some children may go to cram schools or be involved in sports activities on Saturdays (when they used to go to school), while others may be absorbed in watching television at home all day. I shall return to this point later.

Curriculum Reform

The direction of recent curriculum reform in Japan has been opposite to that in Anglophone countries, where the emphasis has been on national curriculum and standardization (Shimahara, 1997; Rohlen, 2002; DeCoker, 2002). Japan has maintained a national curriculum since the beginning of modern schooling. The central Ministry of Education issues and revises the course of study for the respective subjects, and schools are expected to follow the curriculum guidelines. Textbooks are prepared by teams of academics and school teachers based on the prescribed course of study, and are published by private publishers. A council within the Ministry checks titles for conformity to the course of study and approves them. Local education boards then select textbooks from those approved.

Recent reform has introduced more interdisciplinary and student-centered learning, and granted more freedom to individual teachers to design their classes. At primary Grades 1 and 2, the former science and social studies subjects became one interdisciplinary subject called "living" (*seikatsu*). Another interdisciplinary subject called "integrated study" (*sogo gakushu*) was introduced as a required component throughout schooling. This new subject was a major break from the past in that individual teachers had almost complete freedom to design its content, free from the Ministry's guidelines. In most cases, teachers in individual schools collectively adopt a main theme for integrated study for a three-year period, and then teachers in each grade collectively design curriculum and methods to suit the interests and knowledge of the age group. A large number of professional books and journals discuss the ways in which integrated study is designed and implemented, as well as report what is considered good practice. Frequent topics are international understanding, world cultures, and environmental issues. A program can involve excursions to relevant places, projects, library research, and presentation of student work to parents and community members. This initiative was particularly well received by progressive educators.

The introduction of compulsory interdisciplinary study was welcomed and implemented more successfully at primary schools, compared with middle schools. At middle schools and senior high schools, which are requested by parents to prepare their children for entrance examinations, teachers understand the new approach and the merits of interdisciplinary study but have found its implementation difficult. Teachers at middle schools thus faced a gap between what was expected from education authorities and what parents wanted, while at the same time facing a greater amount of paper work for the local education boards (Morota et al., 2006).

Introduction of New Types of Senior High Schools

Japanese secondary schooling has been predominantly offered at two separate institutions, in the compulsory education years (ages 13–15) at uniform middle schools, and in the post-compulsory years (ages 16–18) at senior high schools. Admission to senior high school is based on the result of an entrance examination (Okano & Tsuchiya, 1999). Senior high schools exist in various forms (namely, academic, vocational, night, and correspondence senior high schools); three quarters of the age group are enrolled in academic high schools. New reforms have introduced new types of senior high schools in order to diversify secondary schooling, which was seen as not keeping up with changing needs of the age group and the society. Since the 1970s, almost all 16- to 18-year-olds have attended senior high schools, and the existing types of schools were no longer considered sufficiently diverse to accommodate the diversity of students.

The new types of high schools allow individual students to choose subjects and create their own courses to suit their interests and needs (Okada, 1999). The new types of schools include integrated comprehensive high schools (*sogosei*; created by merging existing vocational high schools and medium-ranked academic high schools), and "unit-based" high schools (*tan'isei*), and "integrated course" (*sogogakka*) high schools.[4] The governments also allowed the establishment of "super science high schools" and "super language high schools," as well as 6-year government secondary schools. In 2005, 286 integrated courses, 684 unit-based courses, 99 super science schools, and 100 super English language high schools were operating (Monbukagaku-shô, 2007).

Detailed studies give us an insight into how newly established schools cope with the assigned missions (e.g., Okabe, 2005). Being able to decide on and design subject offerings made these schools more colorful than the pre-existing types of senior high schools. In particular, they are able to provide unique subjects not required for entrance examinations that are not offered elsewhere. I saw great benefits in this flexibility for newcomer ethnic minority students. In response to the needs of their student populations, schools are able to offer Chinese and Korean languages and studies, and Japanese as a second language. These schools often administer special entry systems for those whose first language is not Japanese. Minority students are able to construct a course to suit their specific needs more effectively in one of these schools than at a conventional school. On the other hand, such schools are not able to fully accommodate involuntary students who have been alienated in a conventional school environment, as originally hoped; and this might have contributed to an increase in enrolment in correspondence high schools in recent years (Oba & Minamimoto, 2006). Some of these schools have attracted students with academic aspirations who have been able to construct a course to better prepare them for their chosen university's entrance examination. This pushed these schools above the middle level in the school hierarchy, which made it difficult for those with poor academic achievement to gain admission.

Greater Parental Choice and Relaxed Zoning

The Tokyo metropolitan government, under a conservative governor, spearheaded initiatives to relax school zoning for primary and middle schools in 2002, and to abolish zones for senior high schools in 2003. This, along with other educational reforms, is popularly referred to as "the Tokyo experiment." Nineteen of 23 Tokyo urban wards have now implemented zoning changes in some form either at primary or middle school levels.

Some Tokyo wards started to display the results of a metropolis-wide primary and middle school achievement test on the internet in 2004. Parents used the result as one criterion when choosing their children's schools. For example, the intake at one middle school was 26 in 2003, 0 in 2004, 21 in 2005, and 18 in 2006 (Yomiuri Shinbun, January 16, 2007). The parents' association of this school was so alarmed at the zero intake in 2004 that it worked hard to market the school in the subsequent year.

In the case of senior high schools, the Tokyo metropolitan government abolished zones all together in 2003, after gradually merging schools and introducing new types of senior high schools. The move, it was claimed, aimed to make government schools more competitive with private schools; and four schools were designated as "elite academic high schools with focus on preparation for university." The impact was seen in an increase in the number of applicants (the first in 8 years) and in the number of cross-zone applications. Schools became increasingly bipolarised. On one hand, the number of schools with applicant numbers more than double the available places went up from 33 to 37; while the number of schools where places were not filled also rose from 29 to 39 (Murakami, 2004, p. 30). Middle school teachers found it difficult to be well informed about the much larger number of senior high schools to which their students could now apply, and started to depend more on commercially operated specialist companies providing detailed information about requirements for entry into each senior high school (Murakami, 2004, p. 45).

The nature of choice that parents can exercise varies greatly. Tokyo's case is one of the most radical. Other cities and regions have offered parental choice only in relation to a few "designated special schools" with distinctive features, which accept children from all zones (e.g., Yokohama metropolitan, some rural communities). Just under 9% of local government areas with more than two schools (234 areas) have implemented a system allowing some form of "parental choice" regarding government compulsory schools in 2006. Out of those, in only about 160 of them can parents exercise genuine choice amongst all schools in a zone (Yomiuri Shinbun, January 19, 2007). Of the 15 metropolitan cities (those with populations over 1 million), nine refused to introduce any system of parental choice of any form, and three cities adopted only a "designated special schools" system (Yomiuri Shinbun January 19, 2007). It is fair to say that the vast majority of Japanese parents continue to send their children to local government schools according to zoning.

Recruitment of Principals from the Non-Teaching Force

By 2006, 107 people without teaching experience were recruited for principals' and vice-principals' positions in government schools. They came from both the public sector and private corporations (Yomiuri Shinbun, May 2, 2006). Recruitment from nontraditional sources was an attempt to counter the criticism that schools are not effectively and efficiently managed (e.g., regular long staff meetings seeking consensus). It was also claimed that schools had been too insulated from the "real world" and would benefit from somebody with prior experiences other than teaching. The outcome has been mixed. Some schools claimed that having leaders from a non-teaching background has had positive consequences to the teaching profession, while at other schools the principal's unfamiliarity and maladjustment to "school culture" resulted in conflict within the school (Yomiuri Shinbun, May 11, 2006).

Studies suggest that the impact of these principals on schooling processes has been limited because of their lack of "professional knowledge and skills" to share with teachers (Ushito, 2004), and of differences in basic assumptions of work (such as collaboration versus competition, manual-based versus indefinite range of work, and a sense of fulfilment independent of monetary reward; Sakano, 2006). Many local education boards remain very cautious in recruiting principals from non-teaching staff, following failed cases of such appointments.

Promotion of "Love of Japan"

The national flag and anthem were not recognised as such in legal terms until 1999. Neoconservatives welcomed the move and hoped that schools would regularly use them on ceremonial occasions. Some local education boards have promoted the national flag and anthem more enthusiastically than others—the Tokyo metropolitan education board is perhaps the most vigorous in enforcing their use in school entrance and graduation ceremonies. Resistance from teachers, students, and parents has been reported in the media, prompting the public to question the education boards' high-handed approach (Murakami, 2004).

The 1947 Fundamental Education Law, which set the foundation for post-war schooling, was revised in December, 2006. In response to demands from neoconservatives, it now stipulates that schools are to nurture a "love of Japan" and a national identity in a globalized world. The public remains concerned over the nature of patriotism and national identity; and teachers remain unsure of how to foster them.

THE IMPACTS OF REFORMS

While it is still premature to assess the long-term impacts of reforms, we see a few signs of where they may be leading.

The most significant is a widening gap in children's educational experiences and opportunities based on their family background. This derives, on the one hand, from the "slimming of schooling," which has provided children with a greater amount of time to explore their interests outside schools. On the other hand, greater parental choice in selecting schools has also contributed to this gap, but only in local areas where de-zoning was introduced. This is consistent with the consequences of more radical neoliberal education reforms elsewhere (e.g., Apple, 2006; Whitty et al., 1998).

We know that how children spend their outside-school hours and develop interests in varying pursuits are influenced by place of residence and their family resources (Bourdieu, 1984). This trend has been reinforced as schools have gradually transferred their tasks to parents, in terms of both children's academic activities and their sports and cultural pursuits. Kariya (2001, p. 155) compared the results of surveys on the number of hours high school students spend studying outside schools in 1979 and 1997 and found that the average hours of study decreased considerably over this period, that for both years the hours were shorter for those from families with low socioeconomic status (as measured by father's occupation and parents' educational qualifications); and that, most importantly, the rate of decrease was sharper for this group of students. Another study suggests that the proportion of 8th graders who do not study at home increased sharply after 1992 (when Saturday schooling was reduced) and that the hours that they spend watching television or playing computer games increased during the same period (Kariya, 2002).

The gap in participation in after-school sports and cultural activities also widened. Prior to 2002, middle and senior high schools provided compulsory weekly club activities and voluntary after-school club activities. Often schools considered the latter to be a replacement of the former. Under this system of school-based clubs, all students were required to participate in sport or cultural activities; and because it was part of schooling and used school facilities, everyone, regardless of place of residence and family resources, was able to participate (Nishijima, Nakazawa, Fujita, Yano, & Miyamoto, 2006). Under the new system, school-based club activities are no longer compulsory; and although some school-based after-school clubs have remained, community-based sports and cultural clubs are promoted. The move to shift roles previously played by schools to the community was promoted partly because teachers were often seen as over-burdened with supervising extra-curricular activities outside school hours (including weekends). During the period from 2001 to 2004 (when the change occurred), many students quit school-based clubs. Some of them subsequently joined community-based clubs. Those with families who were active in recreation pursuits and possessed economic resources were much more likely to join community-based clubs. That is, whether one joined community-based clubs was strongly influenced by family background (such as the family's prior participation in sport and cultural activities, and their economic resources; Nishijima et al., 2006). Compulsory participation in school-based clubs provided an opportunity for students (who otherwise might not have developed an interest) to try out new activities.

The impact of greater parental choice varied across the country. The effect of the relaxation of zoning for compulsory schools, for example, has been felt only in a limited number of local areas, such as in the Tokyo metropolitan area, where the most radical changes were implemented. In contrast, the Osaka metropolitan area remains a stronghold of resistance (Shimizu, 2005). Cities in the western part of Japan (including five metropolitan cities) have continued the existing zoning practice whereby parents were required to send their child to a neighborhood government school designated by the local education board and remain highly critical of the Tokyo experiment. Also critical were academic commentators (e.g., Fujita, 2000) who argued that less involvement by schools and public institutions, together with deregulation of schooling (e.g., de-zoning), led individual families to exercise more power in decision making about their children's education; and that this would result in a situation where one's family background and resources determine educational opportunities. Local education boards that had long worked with children of *buraku* communities (descendants of the former outcaste population)[5] are least sympathetic to the idea of relaxed zoning. Instead, parental choice given by most local education boards has been in the form of parents being able to send their children to a non-zoned school with unique features.

Curriculum reform has brought flexibility and diversity to schools to a degree; and this direction in many ways contrasts with the moves toward a national curriculum seen elsewhere. The mainstream call for curriculum reform has been to address what was seen as a rigid curriculum and unidirectional teaching methods. Programs of interdisciplinary study, designed by individual teachers, have resulted in more group projects, fieldwork and/or library-based classes, and interaction with local communities, which has encouraged student-centered and exploratory learning. "Integrated study" has been more enthusiastically received at some schools and students than others. Teachers have found that students who were interested in learning or "finding out themselves" and who possess higher levels of literacy and numeracy skills, like such an approach, and benefit the most. In contrast, students who are less interested in learning, as well as those with limited skills in literacy, research, and presentation became further disengaged and could not participate effectively in such exploratory studies (Nagayama, 2002, p. 67). Teachers in disadvantaged schools often find it more difficult to design and conduct such studies (Togawa, 2002). This is consistent with the dominant view that child-centered, problem-solving learning assumes student interest in learning (Kariya, 2002, pp. 143–147); and that children from middle class families tend to possess an interest in learning and basic literacy and numeracy, upon which such child-centered learning can most effectively occur. Primary teachers generally accepted the benefits of such studies in principle, but suitable conditions at school (e.g., infra-structure, resources) were lacking (Nagayama, 2002, p. 67).

There is a consensus that teachers' workload substantially increased. After curriculum content was reduced by 30% in order to provide learning in a more "relaxed" environment, teachers faced parental demand for adequate preparation of their children for entrance examinations. Teachers were also expected to design and implement a newly introduced integrated study subject to suit the needs of their students. While welcoming the opportunity, and despite a large number of published manuals, teachers felt that they were not equipped with sufficient time to prepare for these subjects. Furthermore, the emphasis on school accountability led some local education boards and governments to require individual schools to prepare an increasingly large volume of documents (e.g., surveys and reports). The amount of paperwork required of individual schools is particularly large in localities that decided to monitor schools more closely.

Another consequence has been that the private education industry became more active. Parents resorted to the private sector to fulfil roles that schools had once performed, for example, sending children to cram schools on Saturdays. Providers of private correspondence education courses to supplement formal schooling, and publishers of a wide range of manuals for parents and drill and reference books also benefited from "the slimming of schooling."

The distinctive features of education reforms in Japan are four-fold, when compared with reforms in Anglophone countries as summarised in Davies and Gumpy (1997) and Whitty et al. (1998). First, curriculum reform was directed toward progressive education, rather than national standardization. Second, decision making power was not moved from the local government level to the national government or individual schools. For example, in the United Kingdom, power over the curriculum has been centralized, while that of budgets, staffing, and admissions has been decentralized. Third, the reforms did not promote multiculturalism to address internal diversity in a society. It has been individual local governments that have taken initiatives in developing multicultural education policies in the face of an increasing number of immigrants (Okano, 2006). And last, educational reforms have been moderate and implemented slowly, despite all the hype in the media. Let me elaborate on the last point.

In recent years, the central MEXT has not exercised its power to unilaterally formulate and implement education policies, contrary to the views held by some (Horio, 1988; Cutts, 1997). Local governments, local education boards, and individual schools retain a considerable say in policy formulation, and at the time of policy implementation. Ethnographic studies (e.g., Shimahara and Sakai on teacher education reform, 1995; McConnell on the introduction of native speaker English teaching assistants, 2000) reveal how local education boards, individual schools, and individual teachers have exercised autonomy in interpreting and implementing national reform policies to suit their immediate environment. This is not unique to Japan. Whenever a policy is implemented, it is recontexualized and mediated at lower levels of implementation (Ranson, 1995; Power, Halpin, & Fitz 1994). But the potential scope for recontextualization varies, influenced by specific political and institutional circumstances, as Hill (2001, 2004, 2005) argues when referring to the limited scope for recontexualization in England and Wales. Within Japan, the Kansai metropolitan region seems to possess the greater opportunity for recontexualization than the Tokyo metropolitan region.

What is interesting is the Ministry's deliberate reluctance to exercise the executive power that it possesses, and its willingness to leave substantial room for discretion in implementation to lower levels of the education system. The Ministry is not willing to implement a policy when it sees a lack of support at the lower levels of implementation and has therefore tried to consult with these levels through local committees and workshops. When the Ministry subsequently decides to adopt a policy, it deliberately leaves room for a wide range of interpretations and further negotiation among the different lower level parties by, for example, framing the policies in vague language open for diverse interpretation. This whole process slows down reforms. Perhaps the Ministry has learned, from its past experience of publicized confrontations with teachers and practitioners in the 1960s and 1970s, that coercive use of directive power without due support at lower levels of implementation is not only ineffective (since they were sabotaged by, and further alienated, participants in the implementation), but also undermines the Ministry's authority and reputation within the wider public.

On the one hand, some (e.g., Sanuki, 1996, 2003) argue that because of the incremental nature of education reforms in Japan (without radical changes to the system as a whole) the hierarchical nature of schools does not seem to have been affected significantly at senior high school level. Introduction of diversity (i.e., new types of senior high schools) has had a benefit for individual students with specific needs (e.g., newcomer minority students) at the school level, but has not changed the hierarchical structure in which the status of elite academic high schools remains unchallenged. Strengthening horizontal diversity did not challenge vertical diversity. This is because recent reforms have not touched the basic structure of entrance examinations; and they remain a driving force in guiding schooling and parental choice, at least beyond middle school level. On the other hand, others (e.g., LeTendre, 2002; Rohlen, 2002) argue that these changes may have significant long-term consequences although they look unsubstantial in a short term. Indeed, as McConnell (2002) argues, it may be more appropriate to assess the impact of the reforms in terms of decades rather than years in Japan. The judgement of success or otherwise will also depend on what kind of society the public wants in the future, which continues to be a source of debate.

CONCLUSION

Japan's educational reforms in the last three decades have been moderate and incremental, in comparison with Anglophone countries, which witnessed more drastic changes underpinned by a globally dominant neoliberal agenda. Japan's reforms represented a pragmatic package to accommodate demands from three directions: neoliberals, who pursue deregulation of schooling, greater individual choice and accountability; neoconservatives, seeking to reinstate what they regard as "traditions"; and progressive educationalists, who want what they regard as rigid structured teaching to be replaced with student-centered and problem-solving learning. Thinking that student-centered learning would produce innovative elites, neoliberals supported a flexible curriculum. The left have criticized emerging national reform policies, but their views have been largely ignored at the national level. However, local governments have, to varying degrees, incorporated their views; and this has resulted in diversity in the implementation of the national reform policies at the local level.

Deregulation and greater choice were introduced in the form of a more flexible curriculum, new types of upper secondary schooling, and relaxation of school zoning in some localities. The private education industry now plays a greater role in the form of cram schools, publishers, and consultancy and examination companies, as well as in sending senior staff members to schools as principals and vice-principals. While student-centered exploratory learning through curriculum reforms and new types of senior high schools have required greater teacher involvement in innovative design, teachers have also continued to face middle class parents' expectations to prepare their children through conventional teaching for entrance examinations to higher levels of education. This has resulted in a greater workload. The most significant impact of the reforms is a widening gap in children's engagement with learning, increasingly determined by their family background; and this has come mainly from "the slimming of schooling," whereby Saturday schooling was phased out and roles once performed by schools have been delegated to communities and families. "The slimming of schooling" was justified on the grounds that children needed more time to develop outside school. However, outside activities are more dependent on family resources (including home study and sport and cultural activities) than are many school-based activities. If sufficient family resources are lacking, the expected development outside school is unlikely to eventuate. How the left would challenge this widening gap remains to be seen; and I suspect that this challenge, if mounted, would lead to negotiation of some kind at local government implementation levels (e.g., Yamamoto, 2005). I also suspect that the Ministry of Education has been aware that such a challenge and negotiation would occur at local government levels in due course.

Japan's educational reforms diverge considerably from those witnessed in Anglophone countries in recent years. By saying this I do not intend to challenge convergence theorists since whether or not, or to what extent, Japan's trajectory of education reforms as a whole conforms to global trends seems to be a subjective judgement (e.g., Green, 2000). (We could say perhaps that "the Tokyo experiment" resembles the English model; but Tokyo does not represent the whole of Japan.) The direction of curriculum reform has been toward progressive education rather than national standardization; a shift of decision-making power from the local government level to the national government and to individual schools did not occur; and national reform did not address an increasingly multicultural population. Most of all, the reforms have been moderate and cautiously implemented—we have indeed seen only slight "moves" since Schoppa (1991) argued for "immobilist politics" in his analysis of Japanese education reforms in the 1980s. While, at the time, Schoppa's thesis contained a sense of pessimism, we now ironically find a positive element in it, since radical reforms elsewhere, guided by globally dominant neoliberalism, have benefited the socially advantaged.

NOTES

1. I would like to acknowledge the Japan Foundation for providing a research fellowship, and Kobe University for housing me, when I conducted fieldwork from January to December 2006.
2. Since September 2007, Prime Minister Yasuo Fukuda has been heading the ruling conservative Liberal Democratic Party (LDP), which dominates both upper and lower houses. As of June 2008, the LDP held 305 of 480 lower house seats and 84 of 242 Upper House seats. Japan has never enjoyed the kind of two-party system whereby the government regularly shifts between two major parties. Instead, the LDP was continuously in power from 1955 to 1993 (with the Japan Socialist Party as the main opposition), and then since 1998. The LDP consists of competing factions with diverse views, but as a whole represents the center-right in the political spectrum. (See Curtis, 1999.)
3. See Cave (1997) for a detailed study of after-school club activities in Japanese schools.
4. Unit-based high schools (*tani'sei kôtôgakkô*) were introduced first for evening courses and correspondence courses in 1988, in order to enable employed people to undertake studies at their own pace to accumulate the required number of units. In 1993, the unit-based system was implemented in some high schools. An integrated studies course (*sôgô-gakka*) was introduced as a new alternative to the existing two courses (academic and vocational) at senior high schools in 1994. Unlike the existing academic and vocational courses where students are required to complete a set of subjects, the integrated studies course allows students to create their own curriculum by selecting from a wide range of subjects (both academic and vocational).
5. *Buraku* people are descendants of a feudal outcaste population, estimated to currently number about 3 million. Although the institutional class system was abolished by the modern state in mid-19th century, *buraku* marginalization and discrimination have continued in terms of employment and marriage. In the 1970s, active civil movements challenged this situation through

radical strategies of denunciation in the field of education, with some positive consequences (Hawkins, 1983; Okano & Tsuchiya, 1999, pp. 110–140).

REFERENCES

Amano, I. (1995). *Kyôiku kaikaku no yukue: Jiyûka to koseika o motomete* [The future of education reforms: In search of liberalisation and individualisation]. Tokyo: Tokyo Daigaku Shppan.

Apple, M. W. (2006). Producing inequalities: Neo-liberalism, neo-conservatism, and the politics of educational reform. In H. Lauder, P. Brown, J.-A. Dillabough, & A. H. Halsey (Eds.), *Education, globalization and social change* (pp. 468–489). Oxford, United Kingdom: Oxford University Press.

Aspinall, R. W. (2001). *Teachers' unions and the politics of education in Japan.* New York: State University of New York Press.

Befu, H. (2001). *Hegemony of homogeneity: An anthropological analysis of Nihonjinron.* Melbourne, Australia: Trans Pacific Press.

Bourdieu, P. (1984). *Distinction.* Cambridge, MA: Harvard University Press.

Cave, P. (2001). Educational reform in Japan in the 1990s: "Individuality" and other uncertainties. *Comparative Education, 37*(2), 173–191.

Cave, P. (2004). Bukatsudo: The educational role of Japanese school clubs. *Journal of Japanese Studies, 30*(2), 383–415.

Curtis, G. L. (1999). *The logic of Japanese politics: Leaders, institutions, and the limits of change.* New York: Columbia University.

Cutts, R. (1997). *An empire of schools.* Armonk, NY: M.E. Sharp.

Davies, S., & Guppy, N. (1997). Globalization and educational reforms in Anglo-American democracies. *Comparative Education Review, 41*(4), 435–460.

DeCoker, G. (Ed.). (2002). *National standards and school reform in Japan and the United States.* New York: Teachers College, Columbia University.

Duke, B. (1973). *Japan's militant teachers.* Honolulu: University of Hawaii Press.

Fujita, H. (2000). *Shimin shakai to kyôiku: Shinjidai no kyôiku kaikaku shian* [Civil society and education: An education reform proposal for the new era]. Yokohama: Seo Shobô.

Gillborn, D., & Youdell, D. (2000). *Rationing education: Policy, practice, reform and equity.* Buckingham, United Kingdom: Open University Press.

Goodman, R., & Phillips, D. (Eds.). (2003). *Can the Japanese change their education system?* Oxford, United Kingdom: Symposium Books.

Green, A. (2000). Converging paths or ships passing in the night? An "English" critique of Japanese school reform. *Comparative Education, 36*(4), 417–435.

Hawkins, J. N. (1983). Educational demands and institutional response: Dowa education in Japan. *Comparative Education Review, 27*(2), 204–226.

Hill, D. (2001). State theory and the neo-liberal reconstruction of schooling and teacher education: A structuralist neo-Marxist critique of postmodernist, quasi-postmodernist, and culturalist neo-Marxist theory. *The British Journal of Sociology of Education, 22*(1), 137–157.

Hill, D. (2004) Books, Banks and Bullets: Controlling our minds- the global project of Imperialistic and militaristic neo-liberalism and its effect on education policy. *Policy Futures in Education,* 2, 3–4 (Theme: Marxist Futures in Education). http://www.wwwords.co.uk/pfie/content/pdfs/2/issue2_3.asp.

Hill, D. (2005) State theory and the neoliberal reconstruction of schooling and teacher education. In G. Fischman, P. McLaren, H. Sünker and C. Lankshear, (eds.) *Critical theories, radical pedagogies and global conflicts.* Boulder, CO, Rowman and Littlefield.

Horio, T. (1988). *Educational thought and ideology in modern Japan*. Tokyo: Tokyo University Press.

Kariya, T. (2001). *Kaisôka nihon to kyôiku kiki: fubyôdô saiseisan kara iyoku kakusa shakai e* [Education in crisis and stratified Japan: From reproduction of inequality to incentive divide]. Tokyo: Yushindo.

Kariya, T. (2002). *Kyôiku kaikaku no gensô* [The myth of education reforms]. Tokyo: Chikuma Shinsho.

Komigawa, K. (2000). *Shinjiyûshugi to kyôiku kaikaku* [Neo-liberalism and education reforms]. Tokyo: Fukinotou Shobou.

LeTendre, G. K. (2002). Setting national standards: Educational reform, social change, and political conflict. In G. DeCoker (Ed.), *National standards and school reform in Japan and the United States* (pp. 19–32). New York: Teachers College Press.

McConnell, D. (2000). *Importing diversity: Inside Japan's JEP program*. Berkeley: University of California Press.

McConnell, D. (2002). "It's glacial": Incrementalism and Japan's reform of foreign language education. In G. DeCoker (Ed.), *National standards and school reform in Japan and the United States* (pp.123–140). New York: Teachers College Press.

Monbukagaku-shô. (2007). *Kôtôgakkô kyôiku no kaikaku no suishin* [Reforms for upper secondary education]. Retrieved March 3, 2007, from http://www.mext.go.jp/a_menu/shotou/kaikaku/main8_a2.htm.

Morota, Y., & Kaneko, M. (2006). *Kyôiku kaikaku no shakaigaku: Chihôbunkenka jidai no kyôiku katei to kyôshi* [The sociology of education reforms: Curriculum and teachers in the era of decentralization]. Paper presented at The Annual Meeting of the Japan Society of Sociology of Education.

Motani, Y. (2005). Hopes and challenges for progressive educators in Japan: Assessment of the "progressive turn" in the 2002 educational reform. *Comparative Education, 41*(3), 309–327.

Mouer, R., & Sugimoto, Y. (1986). *Images of Japanese society*. London: Kegan Paul International.

Murakami, Y. (2004). *Tokyo to no "kyôiku kaikaku": Ishihara tosei de ima naniga okotte iruka [Education reforms in Tokyo: What is occuring under the Ishihara governor]*. Tokyo: Iwanamii Shoten.

Nagayama, H. (2002). *Genba kara mita kyôiku kaikaku* [Education reforms as seen from the classroom]. Tokyo: Chikuma Shobô.

Nihon-kyôshokuin-kumiai [Japan Teachers' Union](Ed.). (2006). *Nihon no kyôiku dai 55-shu* [Education in Japan volume 55]. Tokyo: Adobanteiji Sâbâ.

Nishijima, O., Nakazawa, A., Fujita, T., Yano, H., & Miyamoto, S. (2006). *Shizuokaken no koukoubukatsudou no henka to gakkouseikatsu* [Changes in school-based after school club activities, and school lives in Shizuoka prefecture]. Paper presented at the Annual Meeting of the Japan Society of Sociology of Education.

Oba, T., & Minamimoto, N. (2006). *Kôkô kaikakuki ni okeru tsûshinsei kôkô no jittai* [The realities of upper secondary cooorespondence schooling in the era of education reforms]. Paper presented at The Annual Meeting of the Japan Society of Sociology of Education.

Okabe, Z. (2005). *Kôkôsei no sentakusei karikyuramu eno tekiô katei: Sôgôgakka no esunogurafi*. [High schoolers' adaptation to the newly introduced elective curriculum: An ethnography of an integrated study course].Tokyo: Kazawa Shobô.

Okada, A. (1999). Secondary education reform and the concept of equality of opportunity in Japan. *Compare, 29*(2), 171–189.

Okano, K. (2006). The global–local interface in multicultural education policies in Japan. *Comparative Education, 42*(2), 473–491.

258   *Kaori H. Okano*

Okano, K., & Tsuchiya, M. (1999). *Education in contemporary Japan: Inequality and diversity.* Cambridge, United Kingdom: Cambridge University Press.
Power, S., Halpin, D., & Fitz, J. (1994). Underpinning choice and diversity. In S. Tomlinson (Ed.), *Educational reform and its consequences.* London: IPPR/Rivers Oram Press.
Ranson, S. (1995). Theorizing educational policy. *Journal of Education Policy, 10*(4), 427–448.
Rohlen, T. P. (2002). Epilogue. Concluding observations: Wider contexts and future issues. In G. DeCoker (Ed.), *National standards and school reform in Japan and the United States* (pp. 177–205). New York: Teachers College Press.
Sakano, M. (2006). *Minkanjin kôchô no kenkyû* [A study of principals recruited from non-teaching backgrounds]. Paper presented at The Annual Meeting of the Japan Society of Sociology of Education.
Sanuki, H. (1999). *"Jiyûshugi shikan" hihan to heiwa kyôiku no hôhô* [Critique of neo-liberalism, and approaches to peace education]. Tokyo: Shin Nihon Shuppansha.
Sanuki, H. (2003). *Shin-jiyûshugi to kyôiku kaikaku* [Neo-liberalism and education reforms]. Tokyo: Junposha.
Schoppa, L. J. (1991). *Education reform in Japan: A case of immobilist politics.* London: Routledge.
Shimahara, N., & Sakai, A. (1995). *Learning to teach in two cultures.* New York: Garland.
Shimahara, N. K. (1997). Japanese lessons for educational reform. In A. Hargreaves & R. Evans (Eds.), *Beyond educational reform: Bringing teachers back* (pp. 94–104). Buckingham, United Kingdom: Open University Press.
Shimizu, K. (2005). *Gakuryoku o sodateru* [Nurturing the capacity to learn]. Tokyo: Iwanami Shinsho.
Togawa, M. (2002). *Kyôiku fubyôdô: Dôwa kyôiku kara tou "kyôiku kaikaku"* [Inequality in education: Dôwa education questions "educational reforms"]. Osaka, Japan: Kanho Shuppan.
Tsutsumi, S., & Hashizume, D. (1999). *Sentaku Sekinin no rentai no kyôiku kaikaku (kanzenban)* [Education reforms for choice, responsibility and solidarity]. Tokyo: Keiso Shobo.
Ushito, J. (2004). Minkanjin kochô dônyû no igi to kadai [The significance and issues surrounding recruitment of principals from non-teaching backgrounds]. In H. Kojima (Ed.), *Kôchô no shikaku yôsei to daigakuin no yakuwari.* [Qualifications and training of principals, and the role of universities]. Tokyo: Toshindo.
Whitty, G., Power, S., & Halpin, D. (1998). *Devolution and choice in education: The school, the state and the market.* Buckingham, United Kingdom: Open University Press.
Yamamoto, Y. (2005, September). Shinjiyûshugi kyôiku kaikaku no gendankai to chiisana gakkô o mamoru torikumi [Neo-liberal education reforms, and the protection of small-sized schools]. *Kyôiku, 716,* 14–21.
Yomiuri Shinbun. (Yomiuri Newspaper) May 2 2006; May 11 2006; January 16 2007; January 19th 2007.

Contributors

Ehud Adiv was born and brought up in a Marxist Kibbutz in Israel. He studied philosophy and economics at Haifa University before being arrested and sent to jail for 12 years as a political prisoner because of his political activity. Then he returned to the academy and studied Middle East Studies at Tel Aviv University, Israel, and later at the Department of Sociology and Politics, Birkbeck College, London. Since 1998, he has taught politics at the Open University in Israel and writes on various aspects of the Israeli society and politics with relevance to the Israeli–Palestinian conflict. Correspondence: eadiv1@ bezeqint.net

Karen Anijar is Associate Professor of Curriculum and Cultural Studies at Arizona State University. She is the co-editor of the *Journal of Public Resistance* (with David Gabbard). Her most recent books include *Culture and the Condom* (edited by Thuy Dao Jensen, NY: Peter Lang, 2005), *Science Fiction Curriculum, CyborgTeachers, and Youth Culture(s)* (edited by John Weaver and Toby Daspit, NY: Peter Lang, 2003), and *Teaching Towards the 24th Century:The Social Curriculum of Star Trek* (NY: Taylor and Francis, 2001. Correspondence: anijar@asu.edu

Adam Davidson-Harden is Assistant Professor in Global Studies at Wilfrid Laurier University, Waterloo, Ontario, Canada. His research interests focus on neoliberalism in contemporary conflict dynamics, education restructuring, and other critical public services, as well as peace pedagogy and praxis. Correspondence: adavids6@uwo.ca

Arnon Dunetz is a teacher and educator at an inner-city public high school in South Tel Aviv Israel. Arnon was born in the United States. He obtained his BA (1990) at the University of Haifa, Israel, in English Literature, his MA (2007) at the University of Northampton, England, in the field of Critical Education Studies and Marxist Critique of Education Policy, and is currently working on his Phd at the University of Northampton, England. Correspondence: arnond@netvision.net.il

Barry Fawcett is Assistant Secretary, Salaries, Superannuation, Conditions of Service and Health and Safety Department for the National Union of Teachers in England and Wales. He has been responsible for all teachers' pay negotiations since 1972. He has extensive involvement and experience in all national negotiations for teachers in primary and secondary schools, Sixth Form Colleges, Soulbury Staff, Youth and Community Workers and Residential Teachers. He is Senior Consultant to the European Trade Union Committee for Education (ETUCE) Electronic Network on Teachers' Working Conditions and assists the ETUCE in its work with the European Commission and on other European Federations on Public Services. Correspondence: b.fawcett@nut.org.uk

David Gabbard teaches at East Carolina University, North Carolina, United States. He has published six books and more than fifty articles and book chapters. The first edition of his *Knowledge and Power in Global Economy: Politics and the Rhetoric of School Reform* (2000) received the Critic's Choice Award from the American Educational Studies Association in 2001. The second edition of that book (2007) takes a new focus: *The Effects of School Reform in a Neoliberal / Neoconservative Age.* Correspondence: GABBARDD@ecu.edu

Georgios Grollios was born in Thessaloniki, Greece (1960). He studied pedagogy at the Department of Primary Education in Aristotle University of Thessaloniki, he finished his PhD (1995) and, now, he teaches as an assistant professor at the same deparment. Before (1985–1999), he had been a teacher in Greek State Education for 14 years. He is author and co-author of four books about a) the European programs for education b) the scientific activity of Greek teachers, c) an adult literacy program based on Paulo Freire's pedagogy at the "Ulysses School for Immigrants" in Thessaloniki and d) the Paulo Freire's view on the curriculum. Also, he is author and co-author of about 40 articles published in Greek and international journals and edited volumes, mainly on Pedagogy and Curriculum.

Dave Hill is Professor of Education Policy at the University of Northampton, England, and Chief Editor of the *Journal for Critical Education Policy Studies,* online at www.jceps.com. He is Routledge Series Editor for *Education and Neoliberalism* and for the *Education and Marxism* series. He is a Socialist political activist, former Labour Parliamentary candidate, Labour Council Group Leader, and trade union regional leader. He co-founded the Hillcole Group of Radical Left-Educators (in England) in 1989, and chief edits the *Journal for Critical Education Policy Studies* (www.jceps.com). Correspondence: dave.hill@northampton.ac.uk and dave.hill35@btopenworld.com

David Hursh is an Associate Professor at the Warner Graduate School of Education at the University of Rochester, New York State, United States. His recent research examines the rise of high-stakes testing and accountability within the context of neoliberal ideologies and changing forms of governmentality. Some of his recent publications have appeared in the *American Educational Research Journal, Policy Futures in Education, and Race, Ethnicity, and Education*. His book, *High Stakes Testing and the Decline of Education*, was recently published by Rowman-Littlefield. Correspondence: dhursh@its.rochester.edu

Joel Kivirauma has been Professor in Special Education in the University of Turku, Finland, since 2000. He received his PhD in Educational Science from the University of Turku, Finland, in 1989. He has also been Professor in Special Education in the University of Jyväskylä, Finland (1995–2000). His main research interests are the sociology and history of (special) education. Among his articles are those in *Behavioral Disorders, Disability and Society, Paedagogica Historica, European Journal of Special Needs Education, International Journal of Contemporary Sociology, Journal of Education and Teaching,* and *Scandinavian Journal of Educational Research*. Correspondence: joel.kivirauma@utu.fi

Larry Kuehn is Director of Research and Technology at the British Columbia Teachers Federation in Canada. He is Associate Editor of *Our Schools, Our Selves,* a Canadian progressive periodical on education, and co-author of *Pandora's Box: Corporate Power, Free Trade and Canadian Education*. Correspondence: lkuehn@bctf.ca

Christine Lewis is a National Officer for UNISON, the trade union in Britain that represents local government workers including school administrative, support staff, and teaching assistants. Correspondence: c.lewis@unison.co.uk

Michael Loncar is a Lecturer in the Department of English, National Pingtung University of Education, Taiwan. He has taught previously at the University of Michigan, and has published a book of poetry (*66 galaxie*, University Press of New England. 1998). His research interests include 20th century literature, film, and art, cognitive linguistics, as well as EFL and autonomy in education. He is currently working on a study of Taiwan political discourse according to the framework of George Lakoff. Correspondence: violaptw@yahoo.com

Gregory Martin is a Lecturer in the School of Education and Professional Studies at Griffith University, Gold Coast Campus, Queensland, Australia. His research interests include Marxist theory, revolutionary critical pedagogy, and socially critical action research. He is currently a member of Australia's National Tertiary Education Union and the Gold Coast branch of Socialist Alliance. Correspondence: gregory.martin@griffith.edu.au

Steve McKenna teaches at York University, Toronto, Ontario, Canada. He has published in the area of Management, Organizations, and HRM, and undertaken many consulting projects over the years with a range of small, medium, and large organizations including, British Aerospace, Kodak, Xerox, London Transport, and ICI. In the Far East he has worked with government bodies and departments in Singapore, Indonesia, and Vietnam. Correspondence: smckenna@yorku.ca

Aura Mor-Sommerfeld is an expert in bilingual education; cooperates with Jewish-Israeli-Hebrew and Arab-Palestinian organizations and activities to develop mutual relationships between the two populations in a variety of disciplines, especially in education. Over the last years, she has trained teachers for bilingual (Hebrew-Arabic) schools in Israel and has developed their curricula; and has been researching them. Currently, she is the head of the Programme for Bilingual Education at the Jewish-Arab Centre, University of Haifa. Correspondence: email: aura.mor.s@gmail.com

Kaori H. Okano is a Reader/Associate Professor in the School of Social Sciences, La Trobe University, Melbourne, Australia. Her publications include *Education in contemporary Japan: Diversity and Inequality* (1999, Cambridge University Press, with M. Tsuchiya), *School to work transition in Japan: An Ethnographic Study* (1993, Multilingual Matters), and *Language and Education in Asia: Globalization and Local Forces* (Ed. 2006, Multilingual Matters). Correspondence: K.Okano@latrobe.edu.au

Julia Richardson teaches at York University, Toronto, Ontario, Canada. She has broad-based expertise and interest in career theory, with a specific interest in career self-management both at an international and national level. With the putative move away from organizationally managed careers she is currently researching the "boundaryless career" where career decisions are managed by the individual rather than being managed "from above." Her work also explores the organizational implications of this trend. Correspondence: jrichard@yorku.ca

Risto Rinne is Professor of Education and Head in the Department of Education and CELE (Center for Research on Lifelong Learning and Education) at the University of Turku, Finland. He is also the director of Finnish National Graduate School on Educational Research. Rinne is the member of the Finnish Academy of Science and Letters and has published over 300 scientific publications. His main interests and publications include sociology of education, international comparative education, educational policy, history of education, higher education, and adult education. Correspondence: rinne@utu.fi

Piia Seppänen is currently a coordinator of The Finnish Graduate School in Education and Learning (FiGSEL). Her doctorate is from the Centre for Research on Lifelong Learning and Education (CELE), at the University of Turku, Finland. Her dissertation (2006) is the first comprehensive study on school choice policy in compulsory education in Finland. Her research interests are on educational systems, educational politics and policies, sociology of education, and comparative perspectives on general. Correspondence: piia.seppanen@utu.fi

Daniel Schugurensky is Associate Professor at the Ontario Institute for Studies in Education of the University of Toronto (OISE/UT), Canada, and Acting Director of the Center for Urban and Community Studies at the University of Toronto. His current areas of teaching and research focus on the political economy of education, popular education, and university–community relationships. Correspondence: dschugurensky@oise.utoronto.ca. For more information please visit his website at http://fcis.oise.utoronto.ca/~daniel_schugurensky/

Harry Smaller teaches at the University of York, Toronto, Ontario, Canada. Among his recent publications and projects is *Informal Learning Among Teachers: Canadian Teacher Learning Survey*. He teaches and researches in the area of teachers' work and teachers' unions, in both historically and contemporary contexts. Prior to York, he taught for many years in regular and alternative schools located in inner-city Toronto. Correspondence: hsmaller@EDU.YorkU.CA

Hui-Lan Wang is Associate Professor in the Department of Education, National Pingtung University of Education, Taiwan. Her research interests include critical pedagogy, sociology of education, politics of education, globalization, and education. She is the co-editor of "*Critical Pedagogy: Explorations in Taiwan*." with Samuel Lee (in Chinese, 2006). She is currently working on the theory of space and critical place pedagogy in Taiwan. Correspondence: hlwang@mail.npue.edu.tw

Index

Canadian Teachers' Federation (CTF) 55
Capital, 4–5, 11, 13, 15, 17, 77, 79, 80,
    82, 87, 89–93, 95, 128–9, 130,
    149, 177, 181–2, 183, 186, 188
capitalism 74–5; decay of 75, 77, 92;
    expanding logic of 181–2; modes
    of critique 181; *see also* global-
    ization; Marxist perspectives
capitalist class, 5, 77, 92, 157
Carnevale, A. 42
casualization of employment 109,
    110–11, 114, 124
catchment areas *see* zoning
Chan, K.B. *et al.* 232, 233
Chan-Tiberghien, J. 183
Charter of Rights and Freedoms,
    Canada 52–3
charter schools, US 28–31
Chen, K.-H. 192–3
Chen Shui-bian, President of Taiwan
    176–7, 178–9
cherry-picking 120–1
China xi–xiii, 82; Taiwan relations
    175, 176–7, 179, 193
choice: Australia 85, 86, 87, 88, 91;
    England and Wales 120; Finland
    144, 148, 149, 150; and
    governance changes in Europe
    138–41; Japan 247–8, 250; US
    42
Chomsky, N. 21, 22, 34, 123
Christianity 22–3, 44, 87–8, 125;
    Greece 160–1, 166, 170
citizenship 35, 87, 130; discursive
    change to individualism 144–5
civil society: NGOs/NPOs, Tai-
    wan 193–5; *see also* social
    movement(s)
class: "boundary blurring" 74, 76–7,
    88, 89–90, 92; and child-centred
    learning 251–2; and choice 148,
    150; and educational achieve-
    ment 86; elites/specialized 33–8,
    46; and race 229; relations,
    Greece 159–60, 161, 167, 169;
    struggle 77, 89, 90, 94, 95;
    see also inequalities; Marxist
    perspectives
Cleveland Scholarship and Tutoring
    Program, US 25–6
Coase, R. 78
collective bargaining, abolition of
    123–4
collectivism, opposition to 36, 40

Combet, G. 83
commercialization *see* marketization/
    commercialization
community universities, Taiwan 194
competitive grants plan, Taiwan 186
compulsory competitive tendering *see*
    contracting out
Confucianism 185
Connell, R. 94
consumerism, 181, 197
consumption, 54, 182
contracting out 55, 107, 114, 126
contractual issues, teachers' 110–12,
    114, 124
Conway, J. 76
Costello, P. 77–8
Council of Ministers of Education
    (CMEC), Canada 51–2
counter-hegemonic struggle 6–8
"country of origin" principle 118–19
critical cultural workers' role 2–11
critical discourses/approaches 192–3,
    214–16, 215, 217
critical pedagogy 2–4, 203; vs global-
    ization 182–4, 197; vs neutrality
    8–9
critical thinking 3, 122
curricula 5; England and Wales 113,
    120, 121–2, 129; Finland 140;
    Israel 209–14;   Japan
    245–6, 251–2; Singapore 232;
    Taiwan 189–90

D

Davis, M. and Monk, D.B. ix
decentralization/deregulation: England
    and Wales 108, 114, 115, 123,
    125–6, 128–9;   Finland
    138, 141–4, 145, 146, 149;
    Taiwan 176–7
delegation of staffing powers 124
Democratic Progressive Party (DPP),
    Taiwan 176–7, 186, 193
democratization, Taiwan 177, 180
Department of Education, US xi
deprofessionalization 113, 121; *see also*
    autonomy
deregulation *see* decentralization/dereg-
    ulation; privatization
DeVry Institute of Technology, Canada
    58–9
dialectic(s), 77, 182
Donelly, K. 87
Dowd, D. 78